BUREAU FOR PARANORMAL RESEARCH AND DEFENSE

# The Black Flame

*Created by* Mike Mignola

# CAPTAIN BENJAMIN DAIMIO

A United States Marine whose distinguished thirteen-year career ended in June of 2001 when he and the platoon he was leading were all killed during a mission. The details of his death remain classified. Exactly how it was that he came back to life is an outright mystery.

# ROGER

A homunculus made from human blood and herbs. Discovered in Romania, Roger was first brought to life by Liz's pyrokinetic touch. Whether or not he is actually alive may be up for debate, but his child-like love of that life is not.

# LIZ SHERMAN

A fire-starter since the age of eleven, when she accidentally burned her entire family to death. She has been a ward of the B.P.R.D. since then, learning to control her pyrokinetic abilities and cope with the trauma those abilities have wrought.

# ABE SAPIEN

An amphibious man discovered in a long-forgotten subbasement beneath a Washington, D.C. hospital sealed inside a primitive stasis chamber. All indications suggest a previous life, dating back to the Civil War, as scientist and occult investigator Langdon Everett Caul.

# JOHANN KRAUS

A medium whose physical form was destroyed while his ectoplasmic projection was out-of-body. That essence now resides in a containment suit. A psychic empath, Johann can create temporary forms for the dead to speak to the living.

# DR. KATE CORRIGAN

A former professor at New York University, an authority on folklore and occult history. Dr. Corrigan has been a B.P.R.D. consultant for over ten years, now serving as special liaison to the enhanced-talents task force.

# MIKE MIGNOLA'S
# B.P.R.D.™
## THE BLACK FLAME

*Story by*
MIKE MIGNOLA and JOHN ARCUDI

*Art by*
GUY DAVIS

*Colors by*
DAVE STEWART

*Letters by*
CLEM ROBINS

*Editor*
SCOTT ALLIE

*Assistant Editors*
MATT DRYER and DAVE MARSHALL

*Collection Designer*
AMY ARENDTS

*Publisher*
MIKE RICHARDSON

DARK HORSE BOOKS™

*Special thanks to Jason Hvam and John Nortz*

www.hellboy.com

Published by Dark Horse Books
A division of Dark Horse Comics, Inc.
10956 SE Main Street
Milwaukie, OR 97222

First edition July 2006
ISBN 10: 1-59307-550-2
ISBN 13: 978-1-59307-550-7

1 3 5 7 9 10 8 6 4 2

Printed in China

B.P.R.D.: The Black Flame.
July 2006. Published by Dark Horse Comics, Inc., 10956 SE Main Street, Milwaukie, Oregon 97222.


This book collects the *B.P.R.D. The Black Flame* comic-book series, issues 1-6, published by Dark Horse Comics.

# CHAPTER ONE

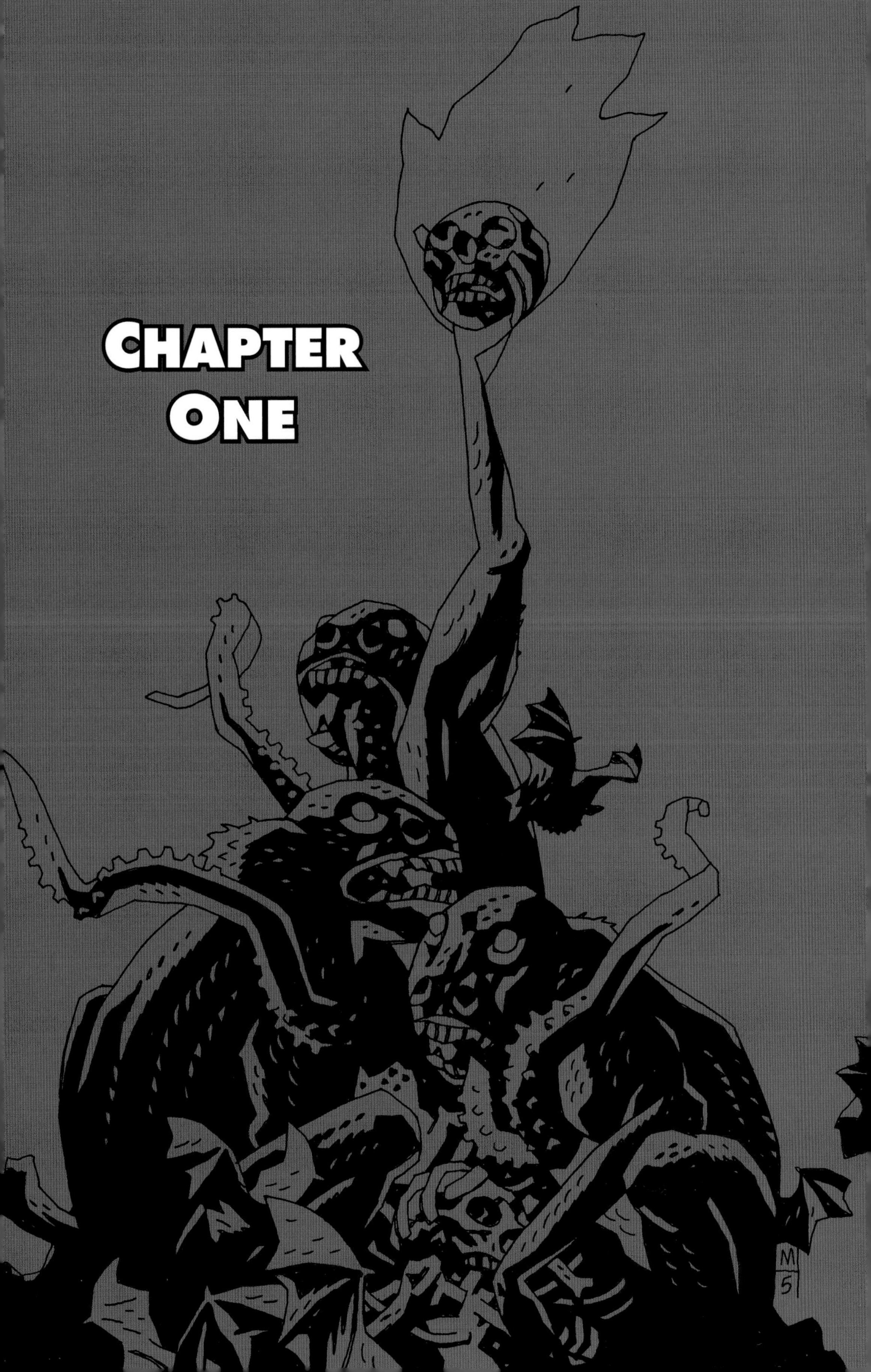

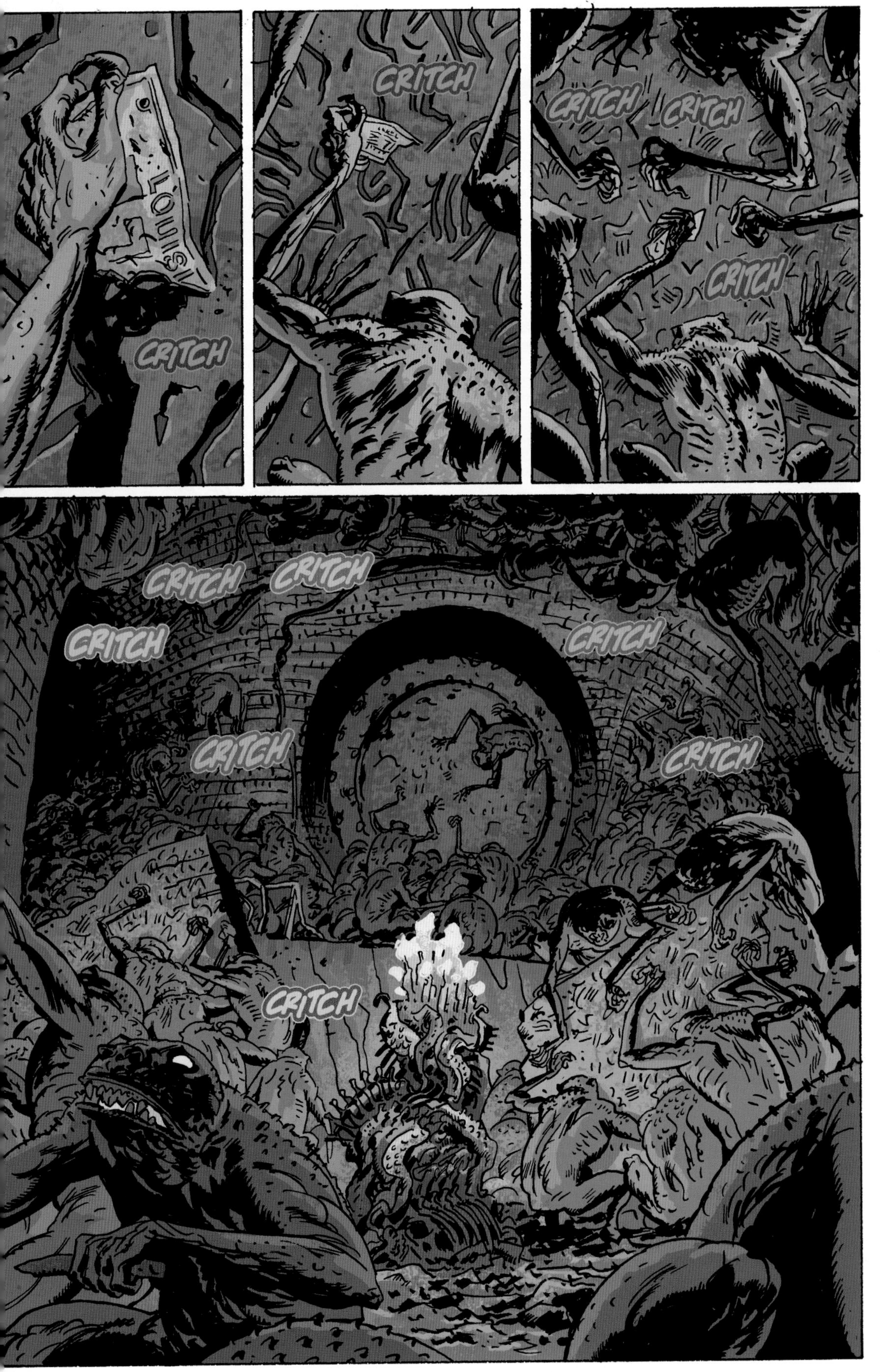
LOUIS
CRITCH
CRITCH
CRITCH
CRITCH
CRITCH
CRITCH
CRITCH
CRITCH
CRITCH
CRITCH
CRITCH
CRITCH

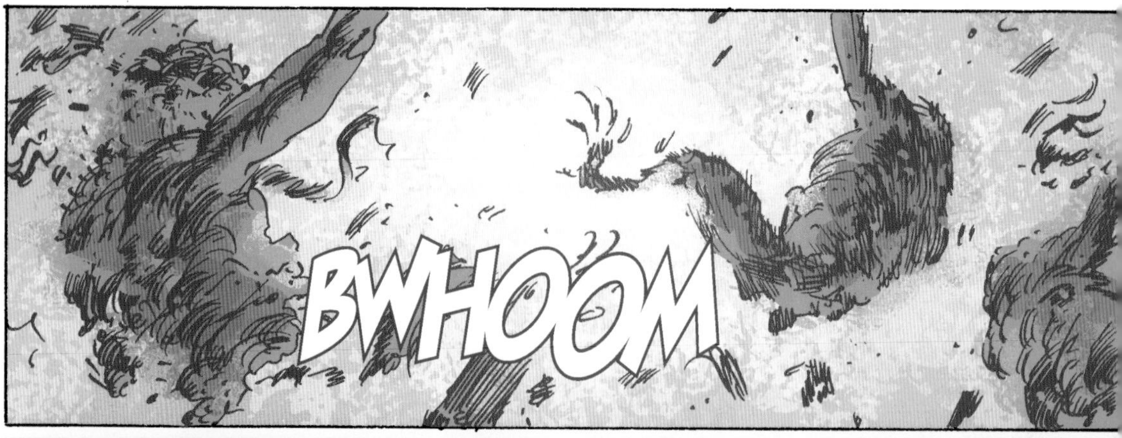
BWHOOM

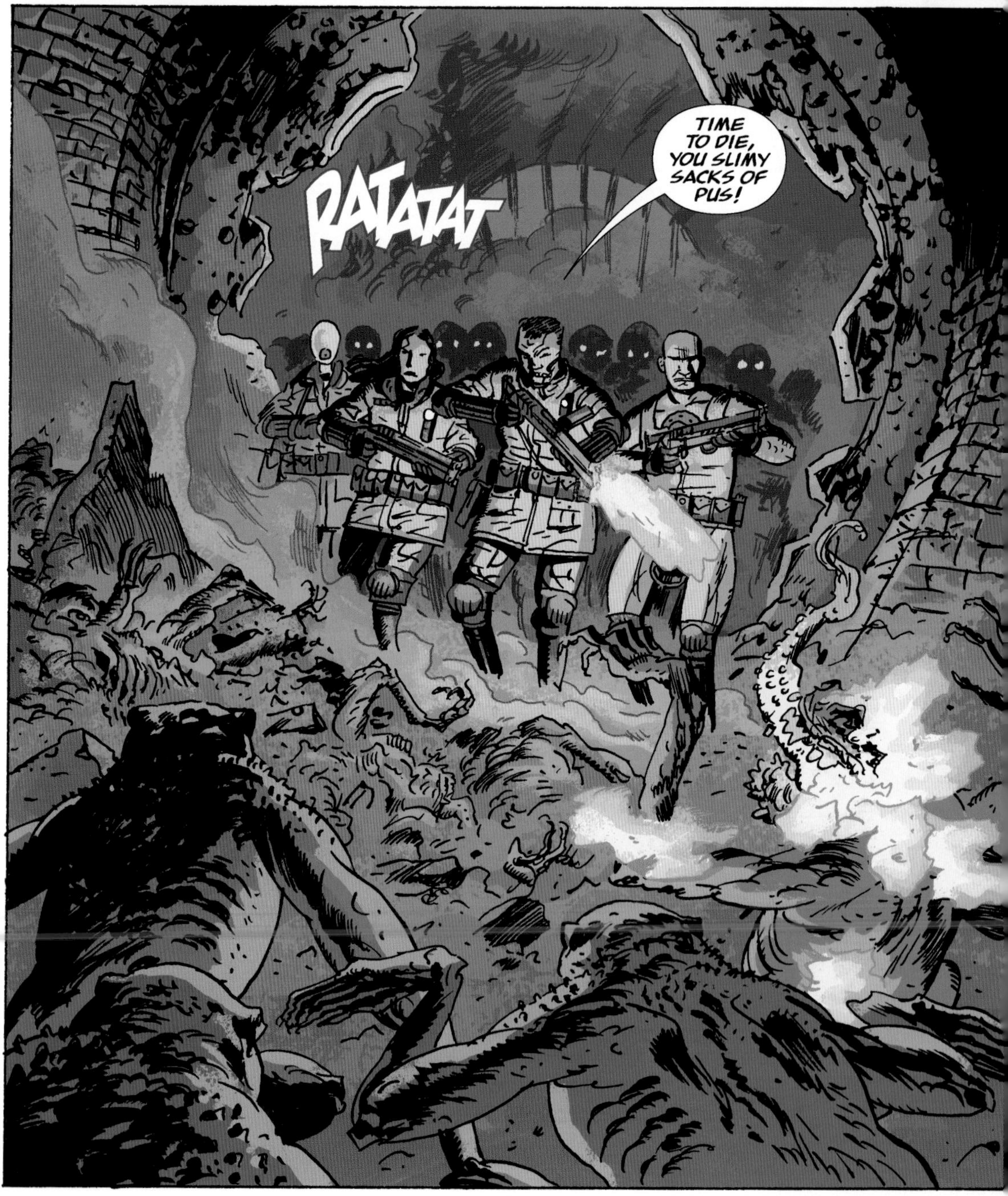
RATATAT
TIME TO DIE, YOU SLIMY SACKS OF PUS!

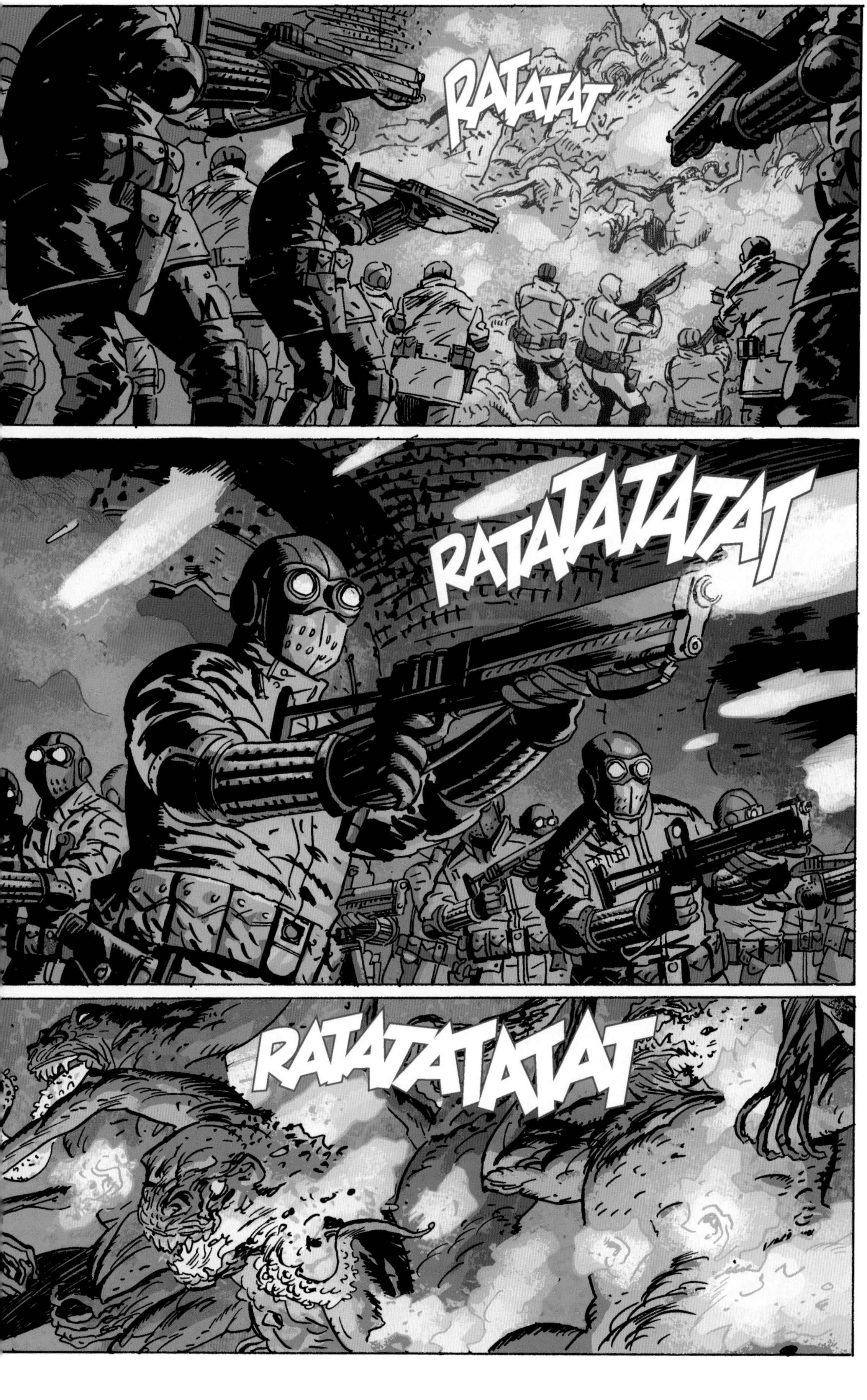
RATATAT
RATATATATATAT
RATATATATAT

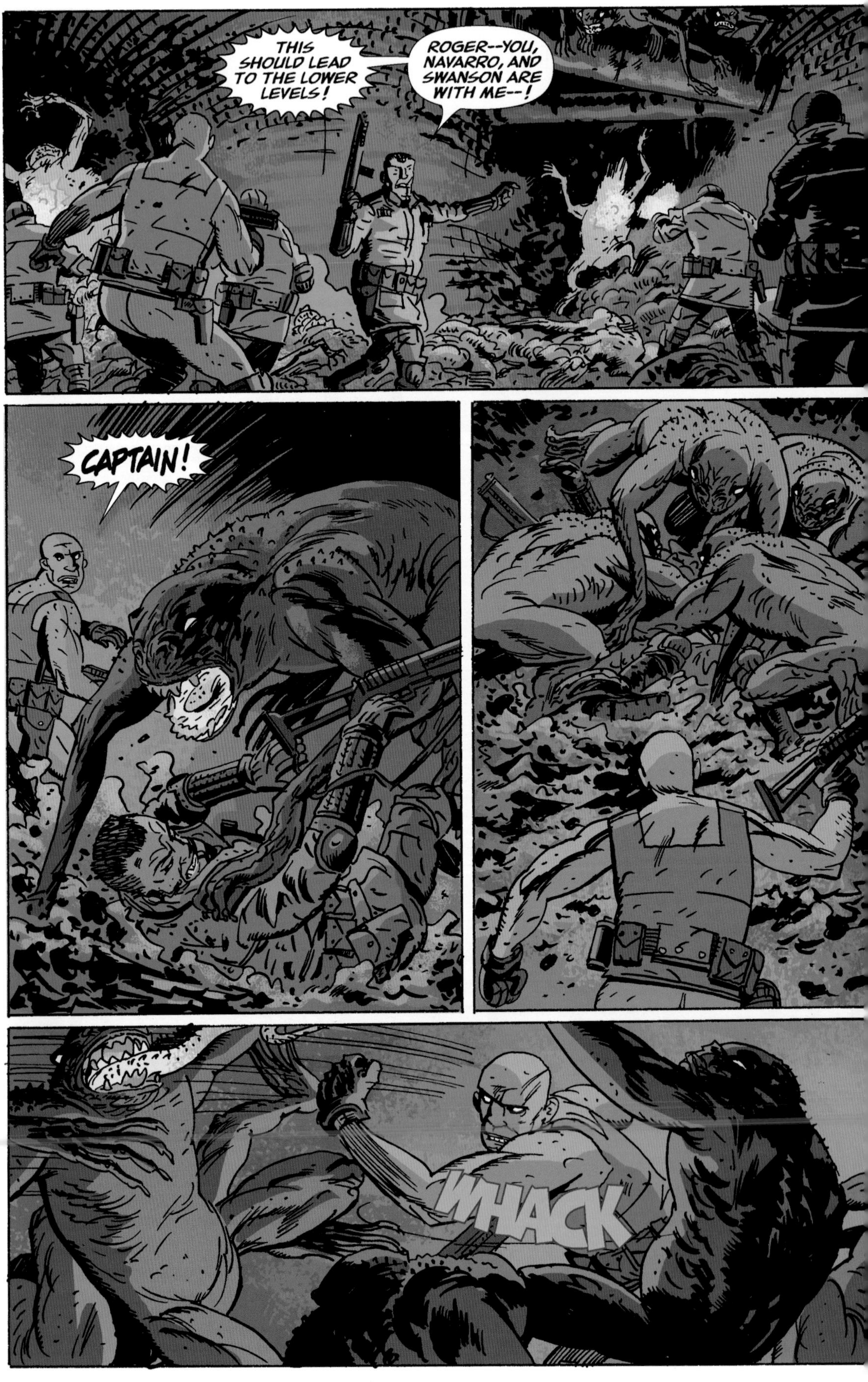
THIS SHOULD LEAD TO THE LOWER LEVELS!
ROGER--YOU, NAVARRO, AND SWANSON ARE WITH ME--!
CAPTAIN!
WHACK

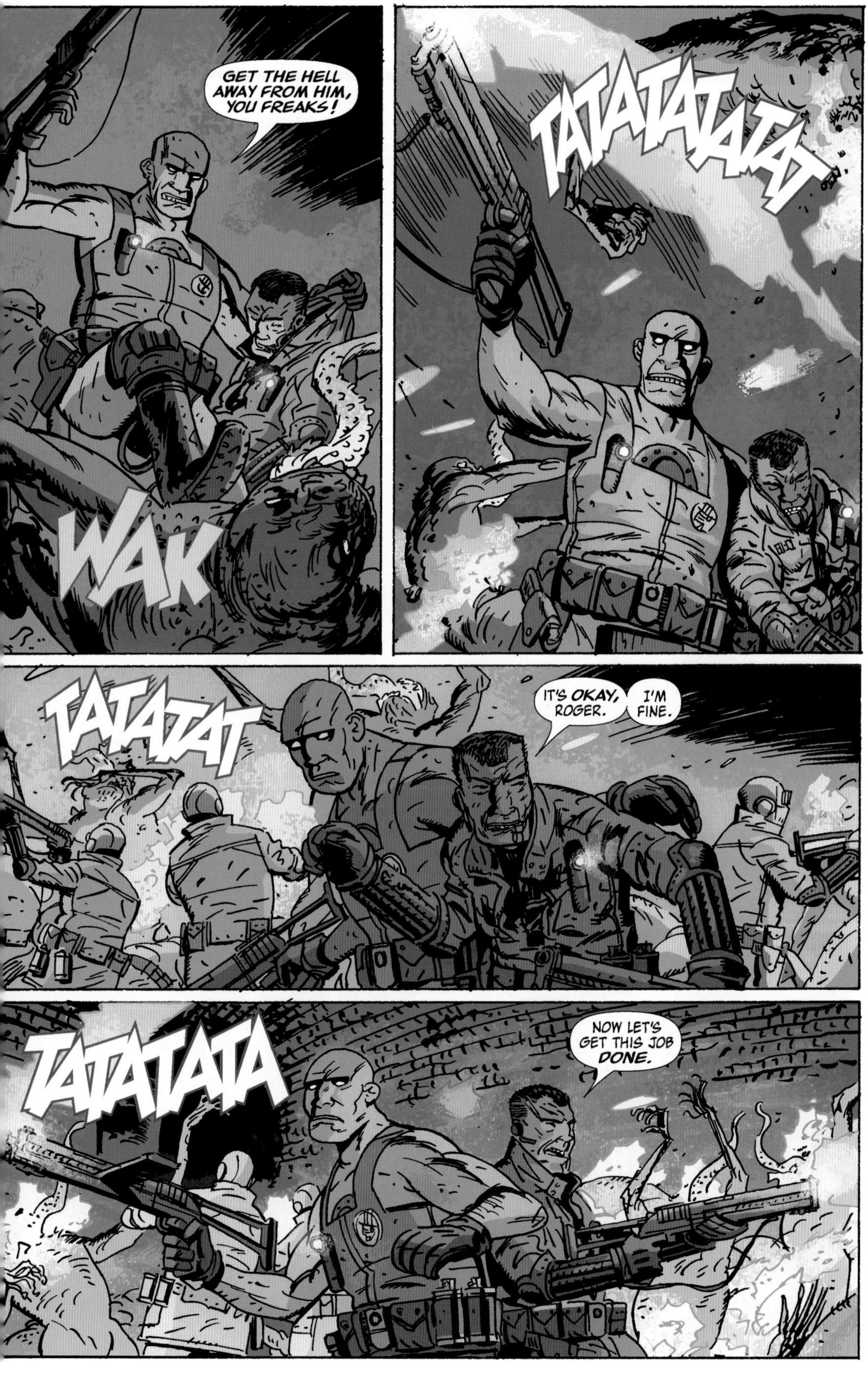
GET THE HELL AWAY FROM HIM, YOU FREAKS!
WAK
TATATATATATAT
TATATAT
IT'S OKAY, ROGER.
I'M FINE.
TATATATA
NOW LET'S GET THIS JOB DONE.

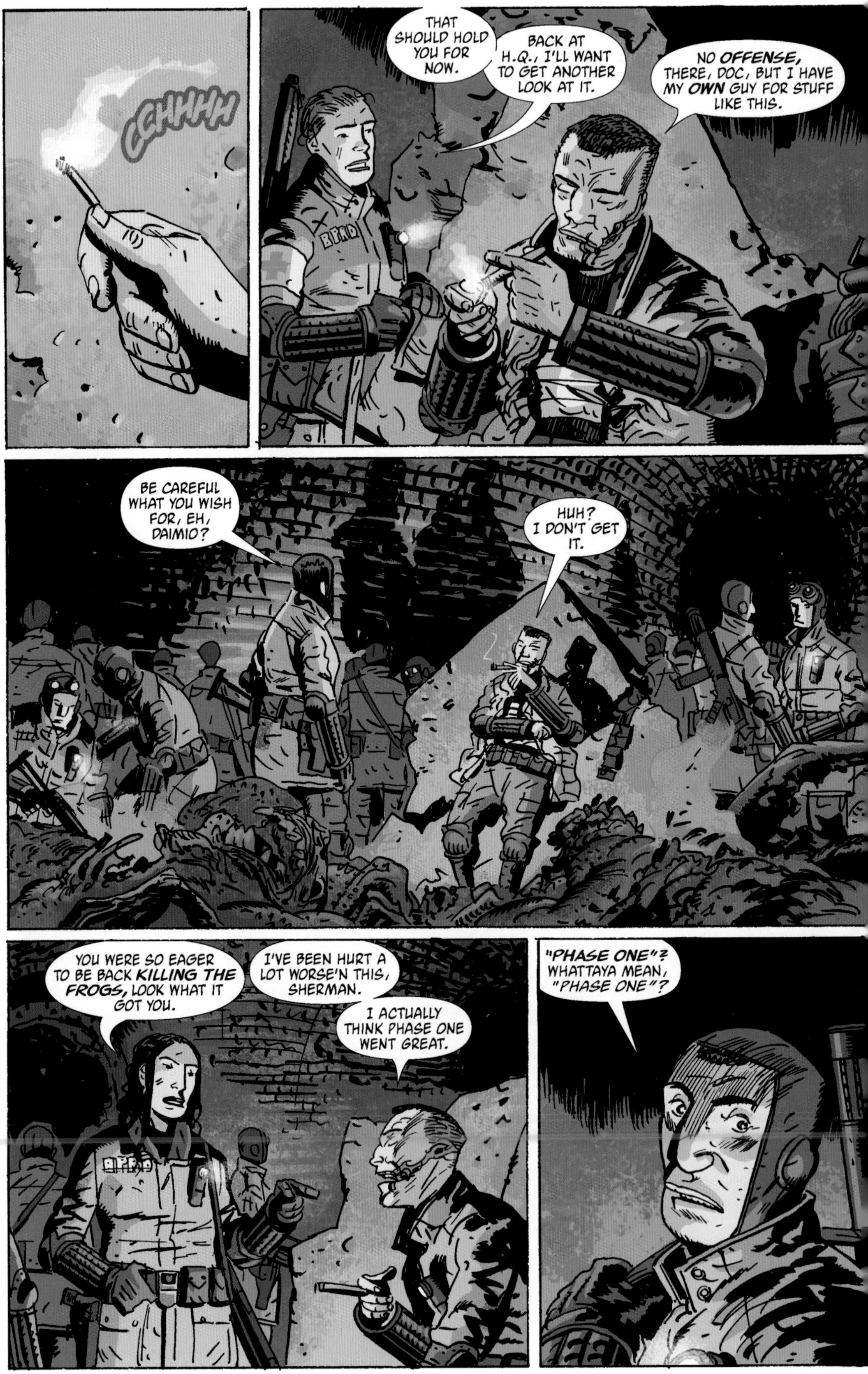
CCHHHH
THAT SHOULD HOLD YOU FOR NOW.
BACK AT H.Q., I'LL WANT TO GET ANOTHER LOOK AT IT.
NO *OFFENSE,* THERE, DOC, BUT I HAVE MY *OWN* GUY FOR STUFF LIKE THIS.
BE CAREFUL WHAT YOU WISH FOR, EH, DAIMIO?
HUH? I DON'T GET IT.
YOU WERE SO EAGER TO BE BACK *KILLING THE FROGS,* LOOK WHAT IT GOT YOU.
I'VE BEEN HURT A LOT WORSE'N THIS, SHERMAN.
I ACTUALLY THINK PHASE ONE WENT GREAT.
*"PHASE ONE"?* WHATTAYA MEAN, *"PHASE ONE"?*

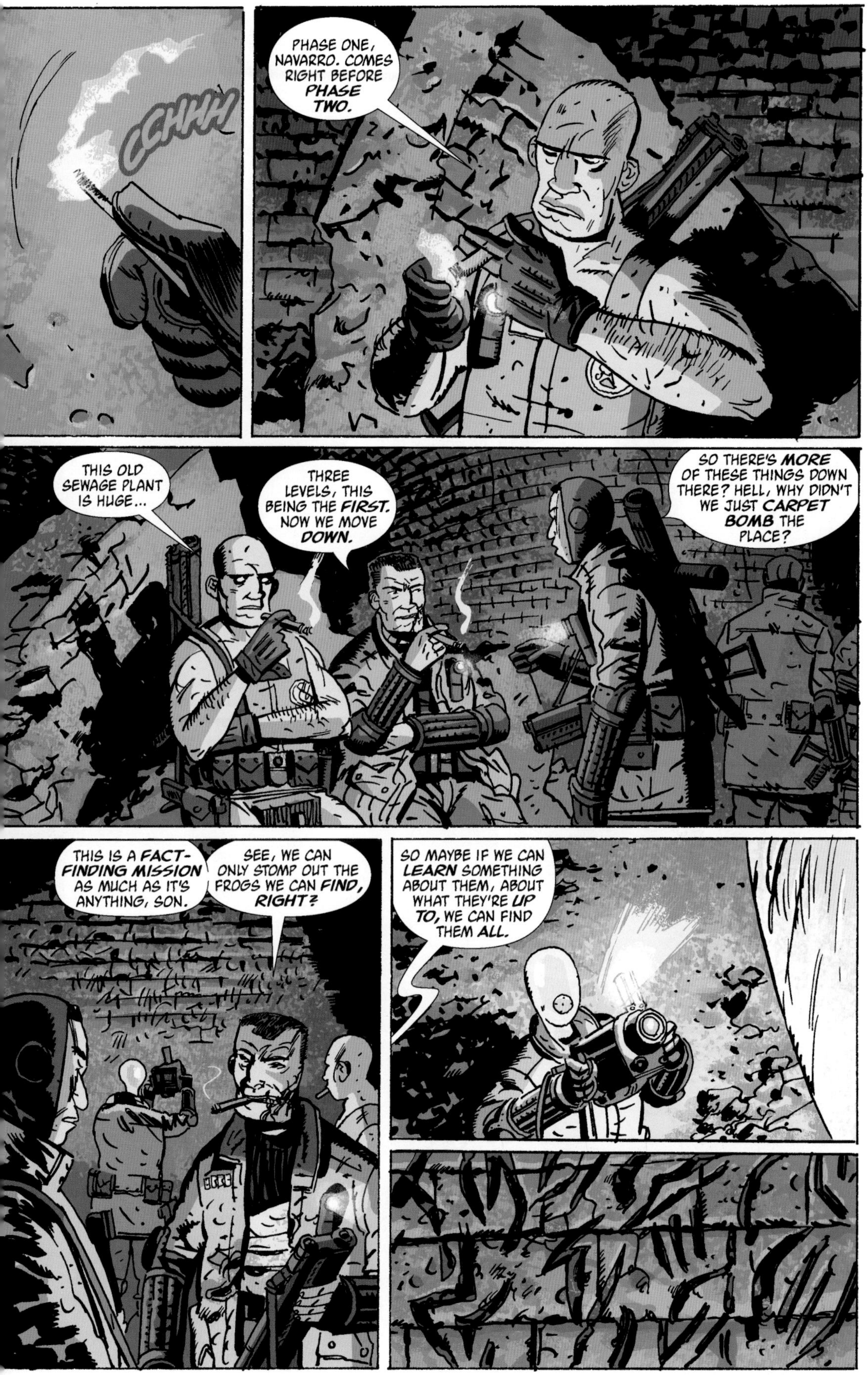
CCHHH
PHASE ONE, NAVARRO. COMES RIGHT BEFORE PHASE TWO.
THIS OLD SEWAGE PLANT IS HUGE...
THREE LEVELS, THIS BEING THE FIRST. NOW WE MOVE DOWN.
SO THERE'S MORE OF THESE THINGS DOWN THERE? HELL, WHY DIDN'T WE JUST CARPET BOMB THE PLACE?
THIS IS A FACT-FINDING MISSION AS MUCH AS IT'S ANYTHING, SON.
SEE, WE CAN ONLY STOMP OUT THE FROGS WE CAN FIND, RIGHT?
SO MAYBE IF WE CAN LEARN SOMETHING ABOUT THEM, ABOUT WHAT THEY'RE UP TO, WE CAN FIND THEM ALL.

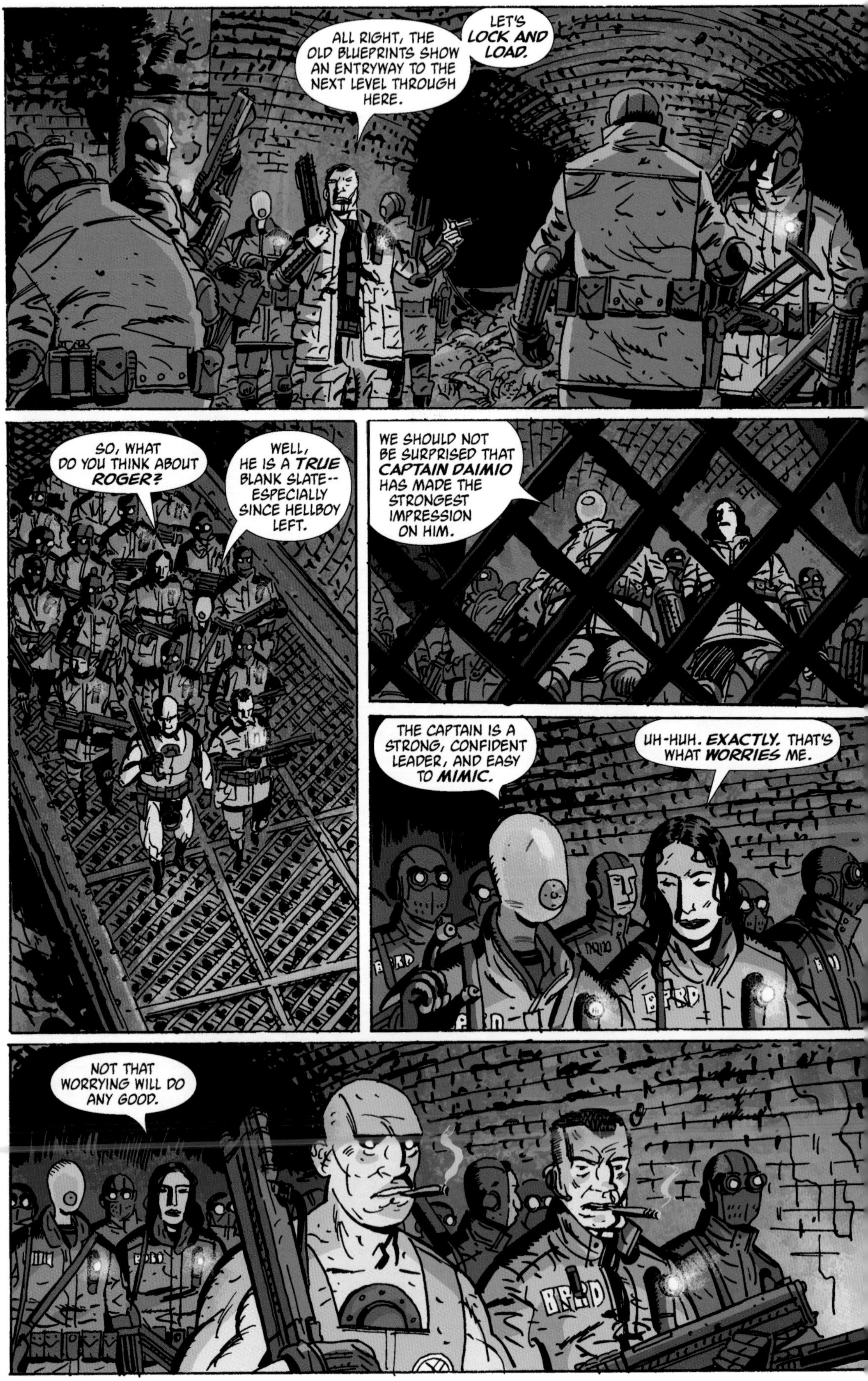
ALL RIGHT, THE OLD BLUEPRINTS SHOW AN ENTRYWAY TO THE NEXT LEVEL THROUGH HERE.
LET'S LOCK AND LOAD.
SO, WHAT DO YOU THINK ABOUT ROGER?
WELL, HE IS A TRUE BLANK SLATE-- ESPECIALLY SINCE HELLBOY LEFT.
WE SHOULD NOT BE SURPRISED THAT CAPTAIN DAIMIO HAS MADE THE STRONGEST IMPRESSION ON HIM.
THE CAPTAIN IS A STRONG, CONFIDENT LEADER, AND EASY TO MIMIC.
UH-HUH. EXACTLY. THAT'S WHAT WORRIES ME.
NOT THAT WORRYING WILL DO ANY GOOD.

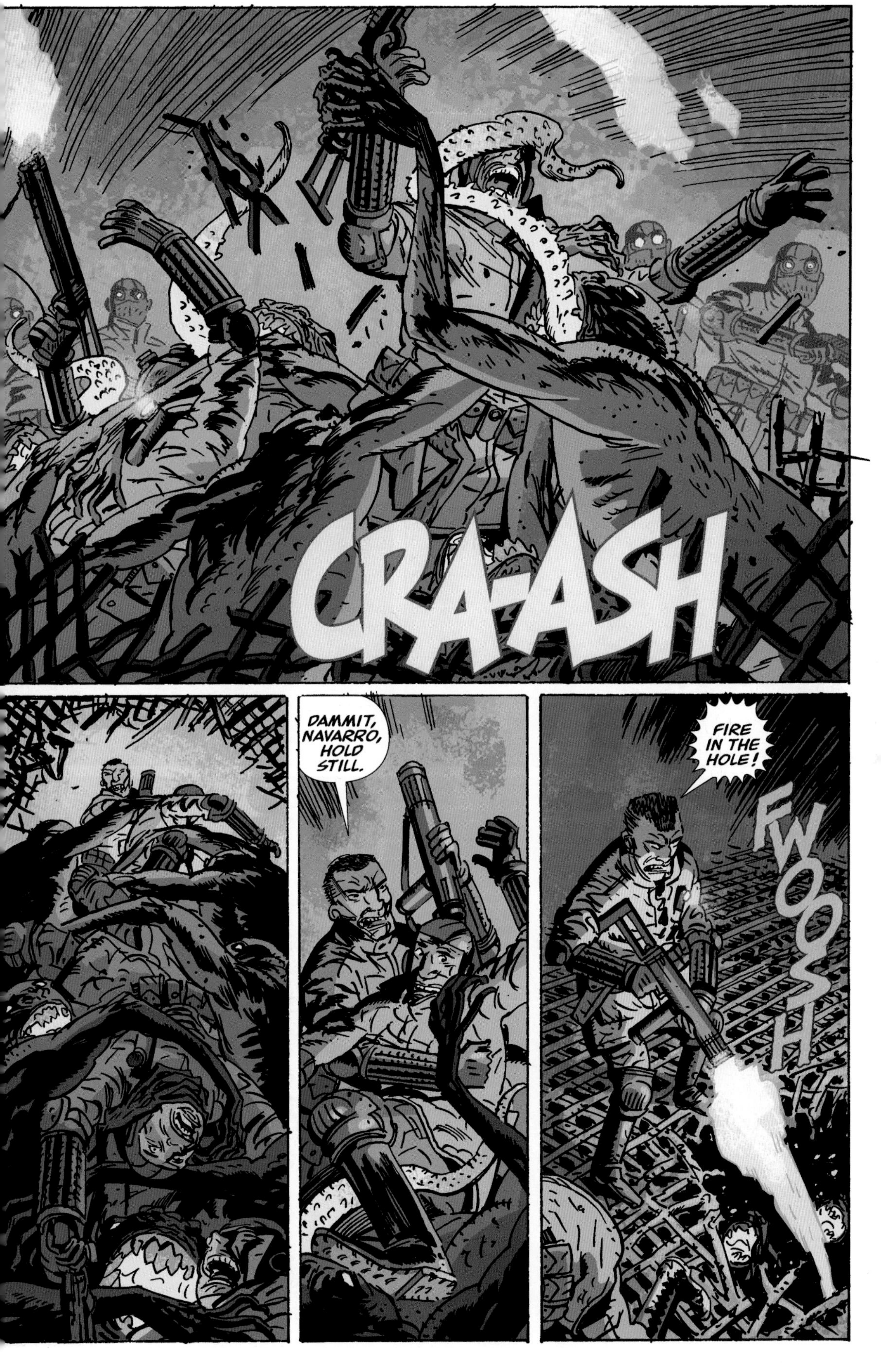
CRA-ASH
DAMMIT, NAVARRO, HOLD STILL.
FIRE IN THE HOLE!
FWOOSH

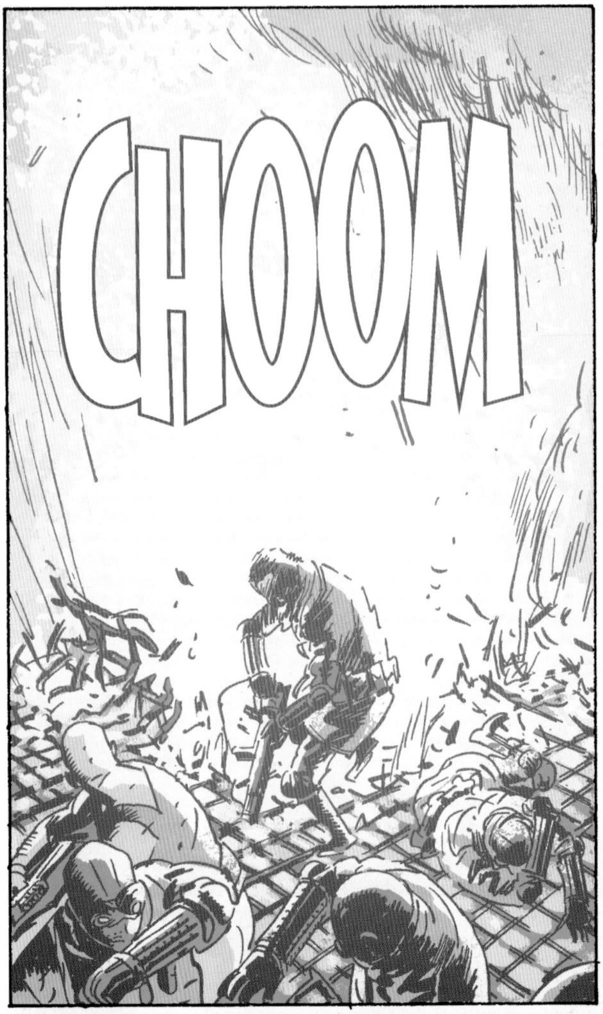
CHOOM

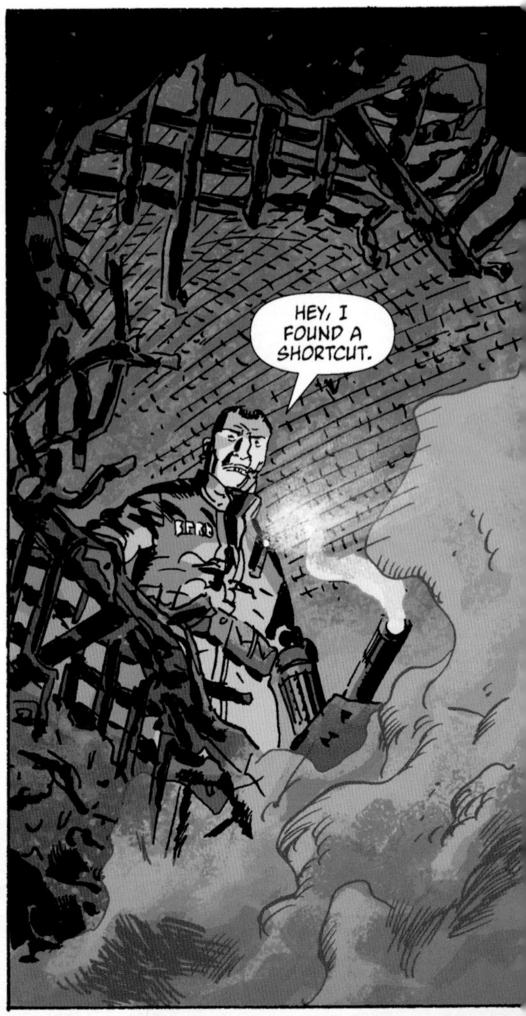
HEY, I FOUND A SHORTCUT.

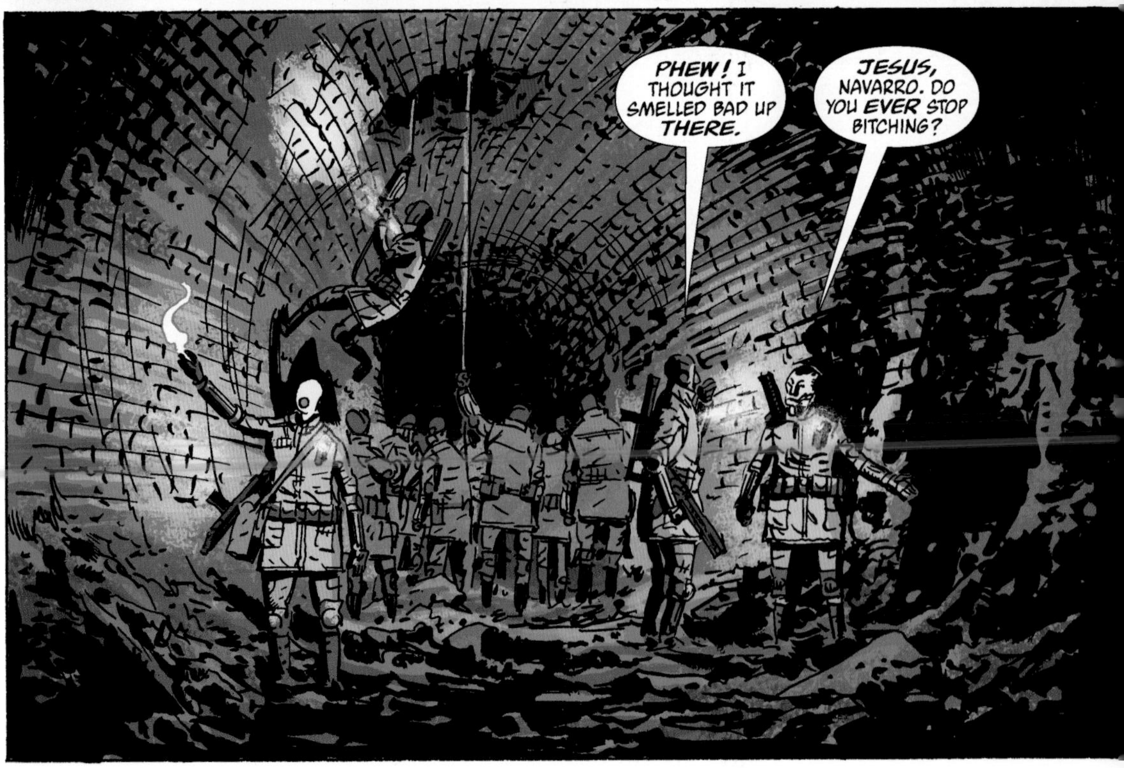
PHEW! I THOUGHT IT SMELLED BAD UP THERE.
JESUS, NAVARRO. DO YOU EVER STOP BITCHING?

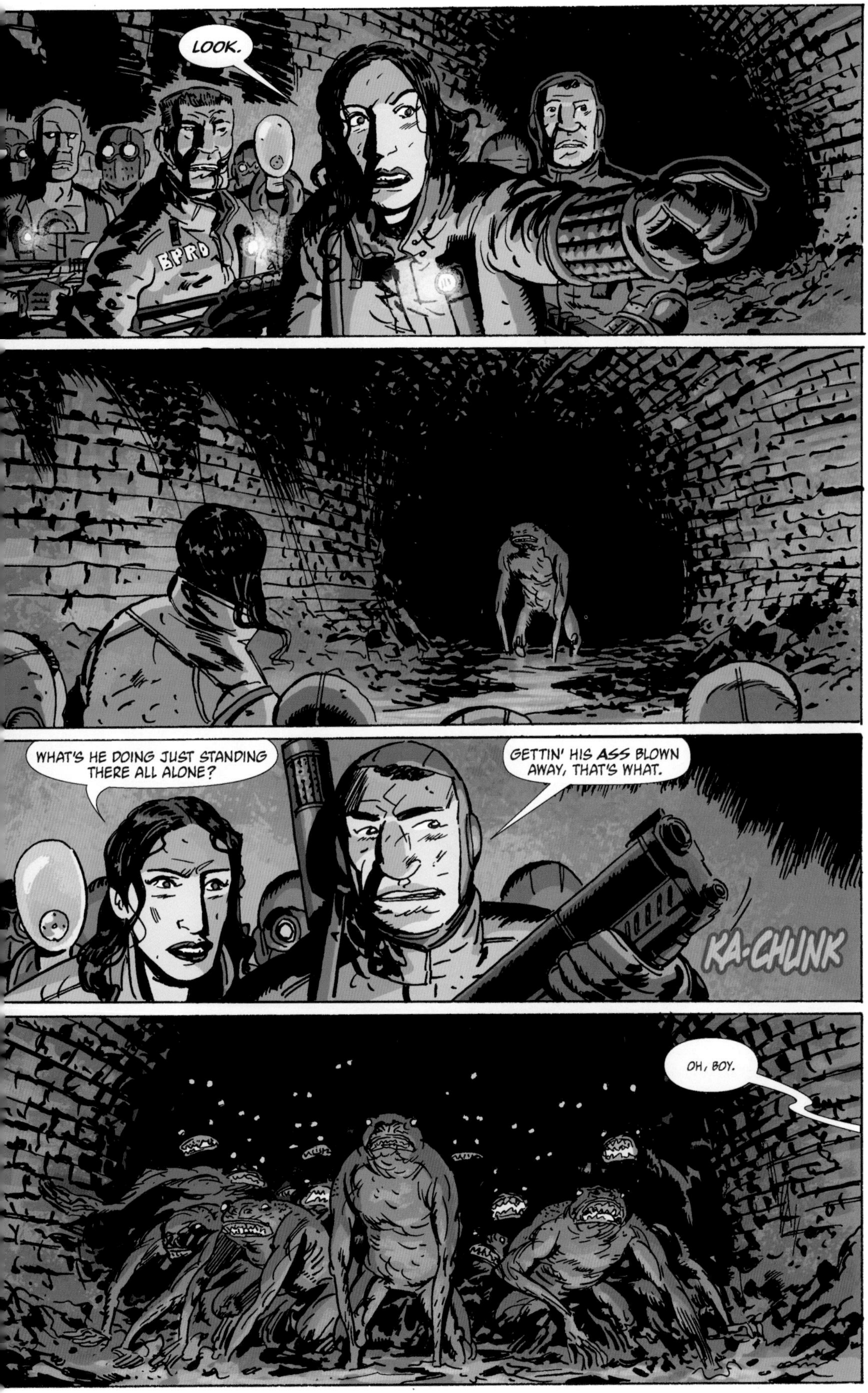
LOOK.
WHAT'S HE DOING JUST STANDING THERE ALL ALONE?
GETTIN' HIS ASS BLOWN AWAY, THAT'S WHAT.
KA-CHUNK
OH, BOY.

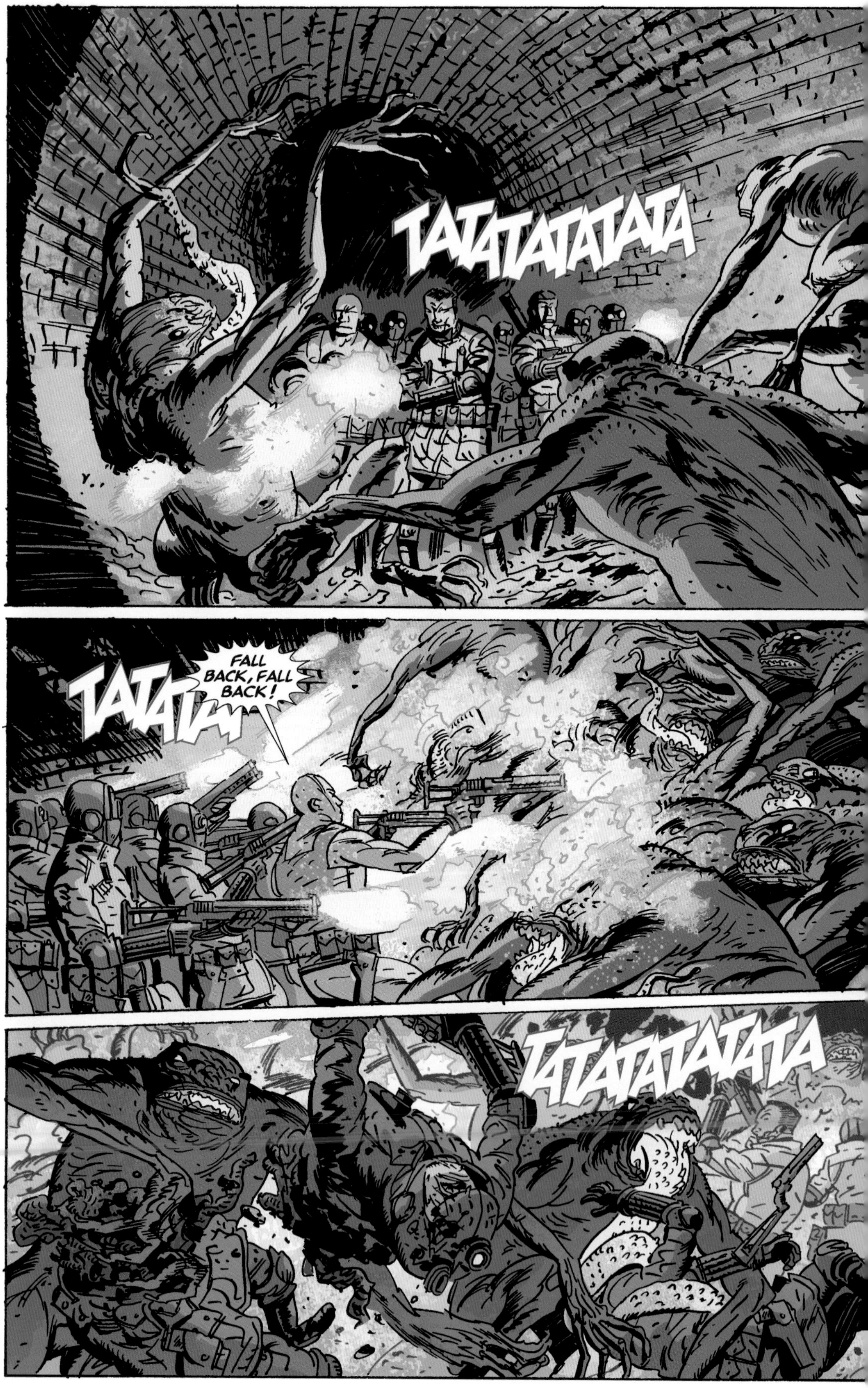
TATATATATATA
TATATA
FALL BACK, FALL BACK!
TATATATATATA

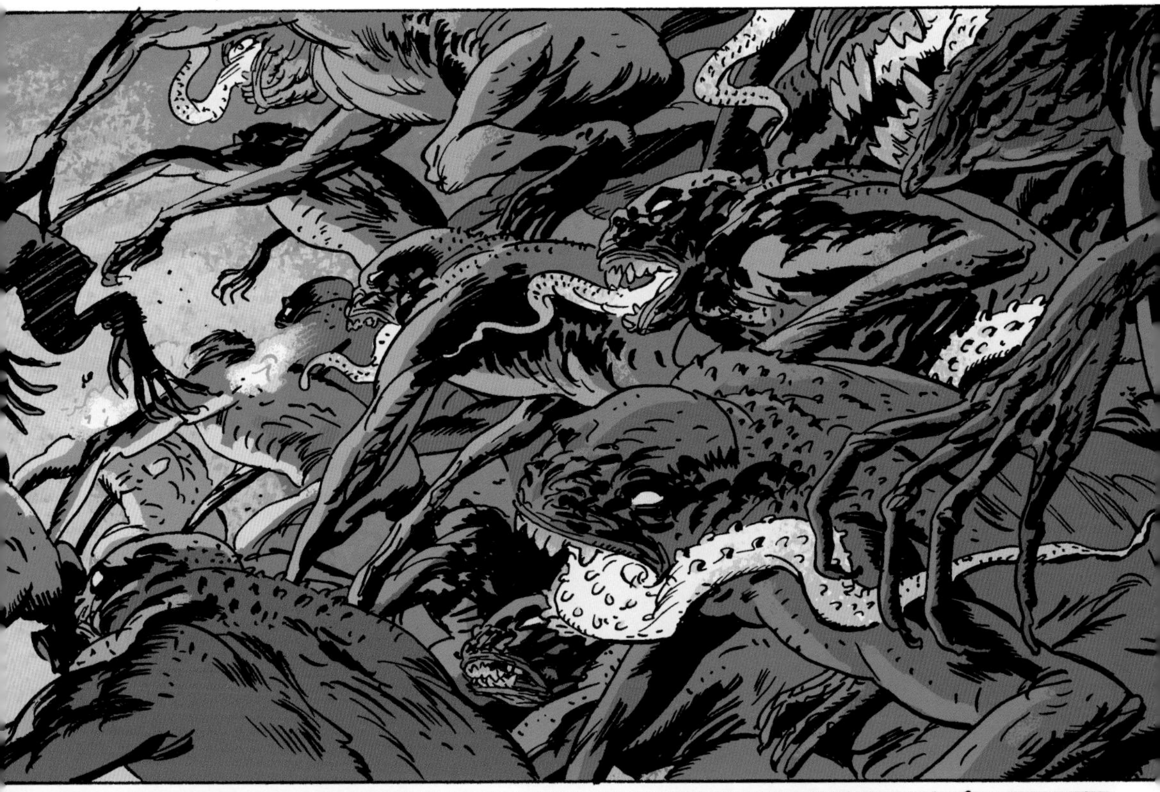
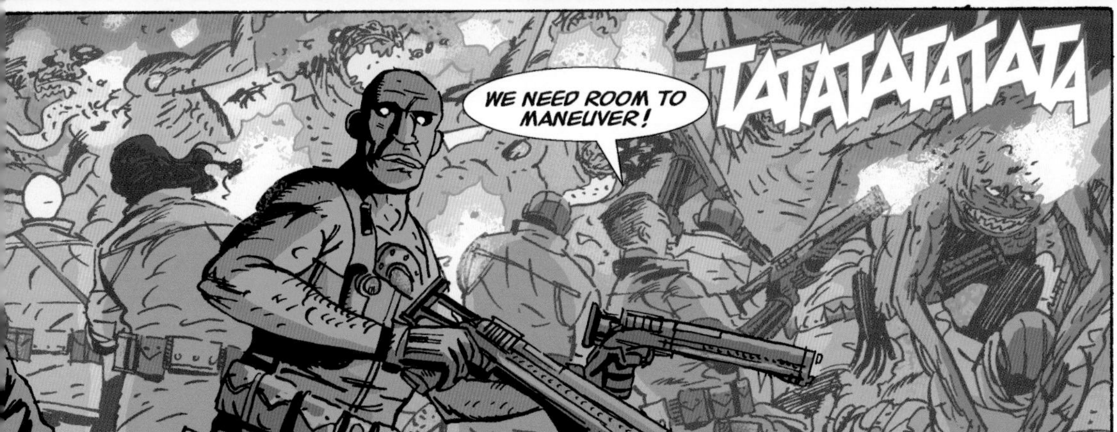
WE NEED ROOM TO MANEUVER!
TATATATATATA
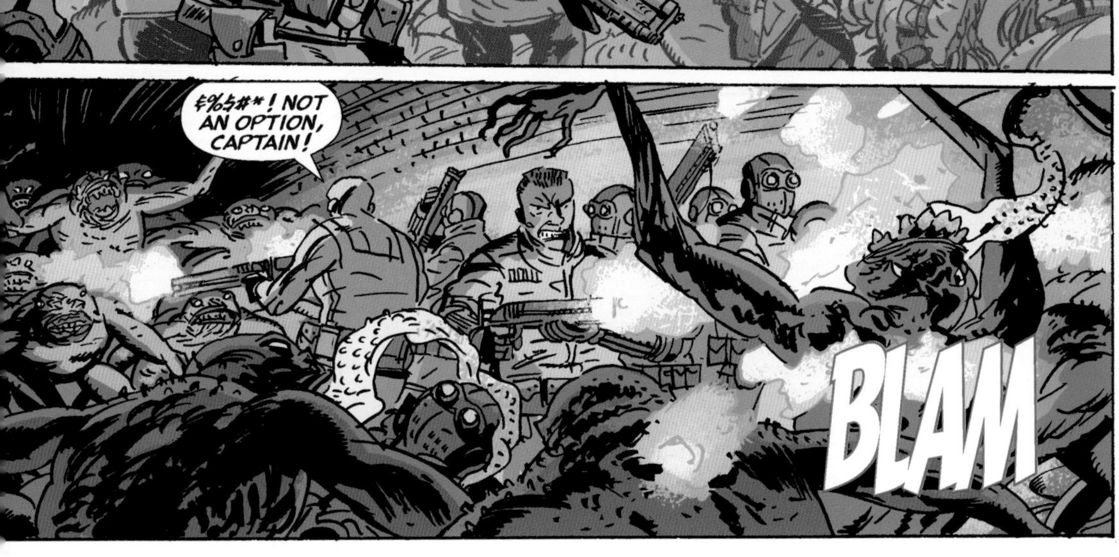
¢%$#*! NOT AN OPTION, CAPTAIN!
BLAM

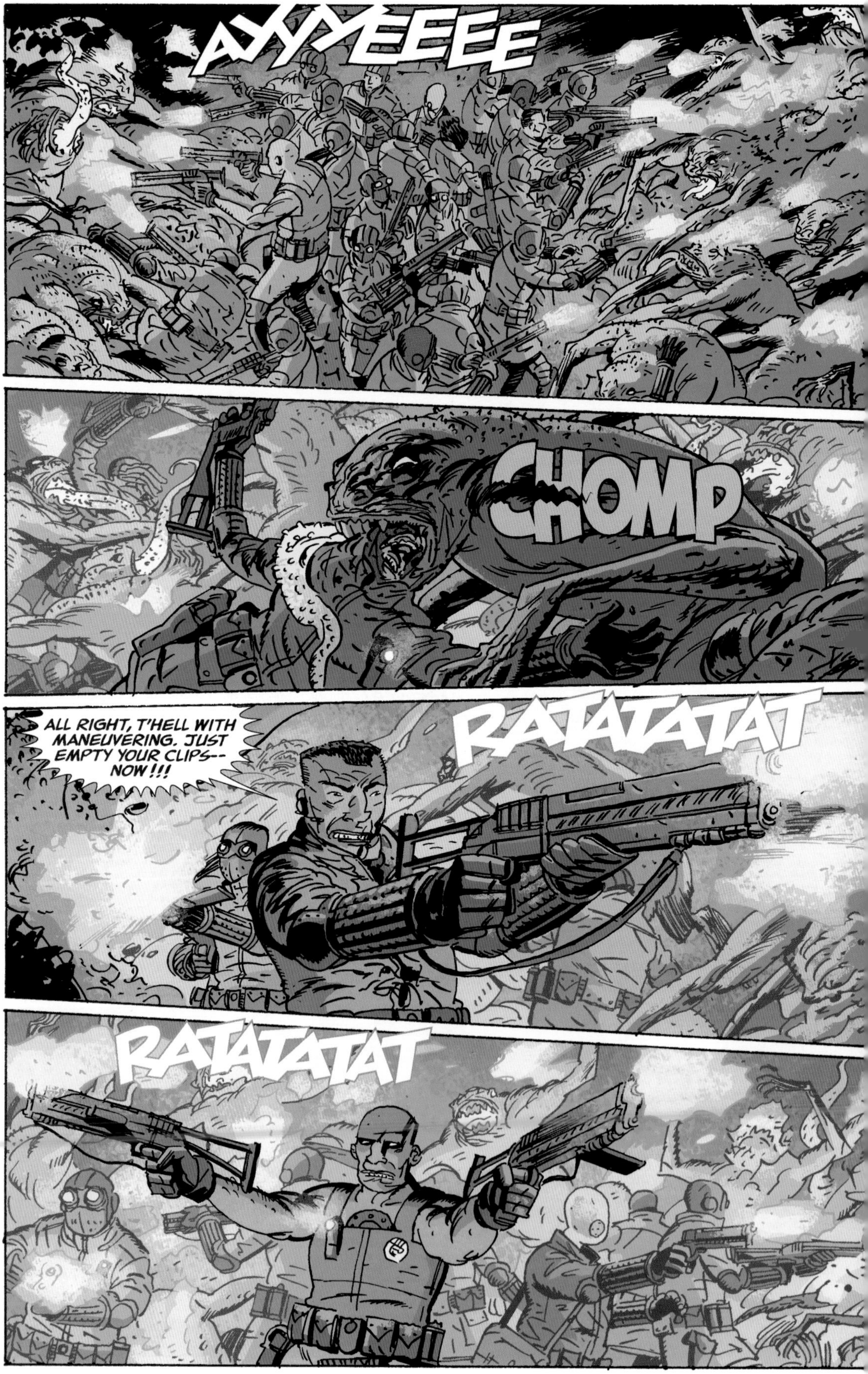
AYYEEEEE
CHOMP
ALL RIGHT, T'HELL WITH MANEUVERING. JUST EMPTY YOUR CLIPS-- NOW!!!
RATATATAT
RATATATAT

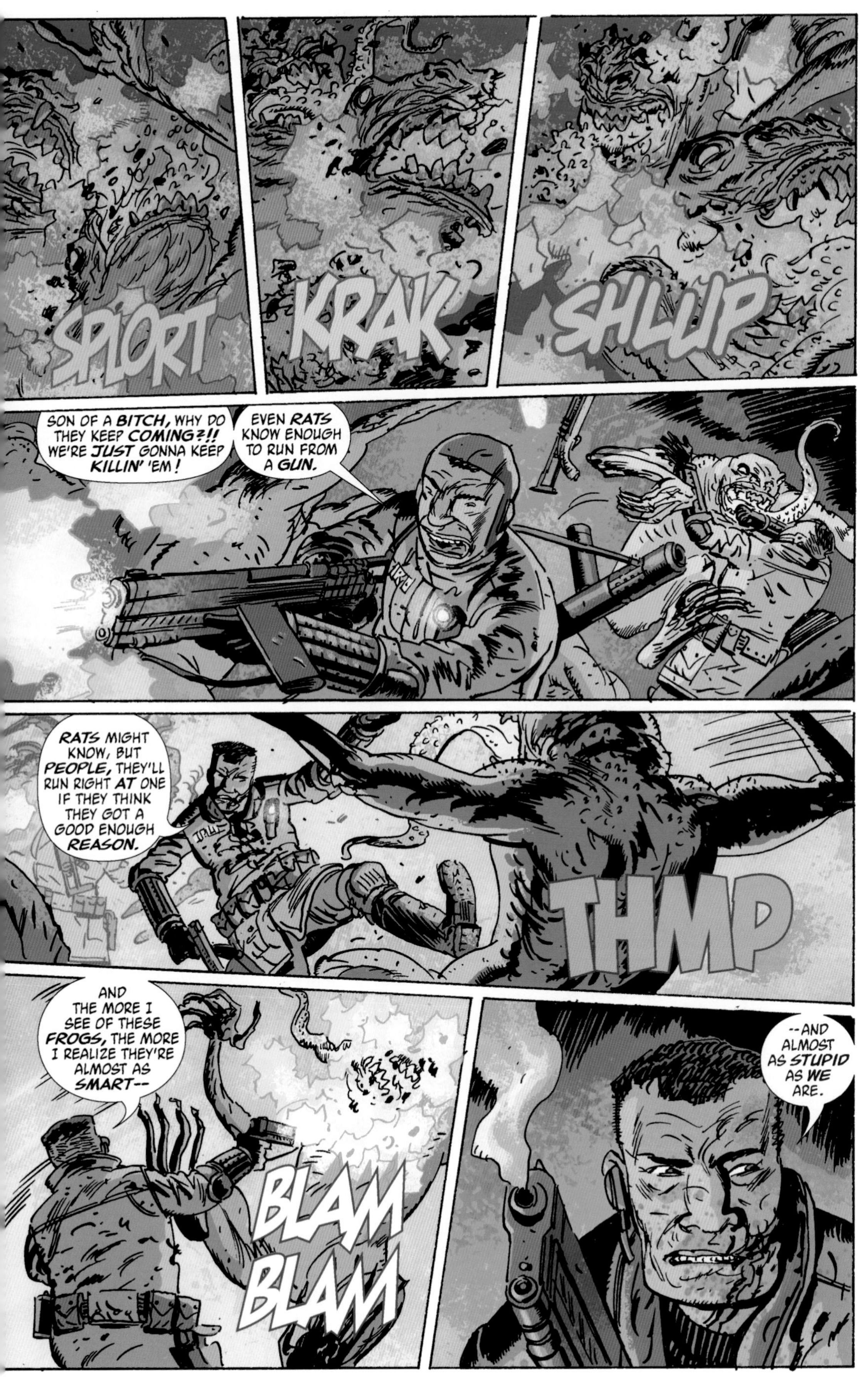
SPLORT
KRAK
SHLUP
SON OF A BITCH, WHY DO THEY KEEP COMING?!! WE'RE JUST GONNA KEEP KILLIN' 'EM!
EVEN RATS KNOW ENOUGH TO RUN FROM A GUN.
RATS MIGHT KNOW, BUT PEOPLE, THEY'LL RUN RIGHT AT ONE IF THEY THINK THEY GOT A GOOD ENOUGH REASON.
THMP
AND THE MORE I SEE OF THESE FROGS, THE MORE I REALIZE THEY'RE ALMOST AS SMART--
BLAM
BLAM
--AND ALMOST AS STUPID AS WE ARE.

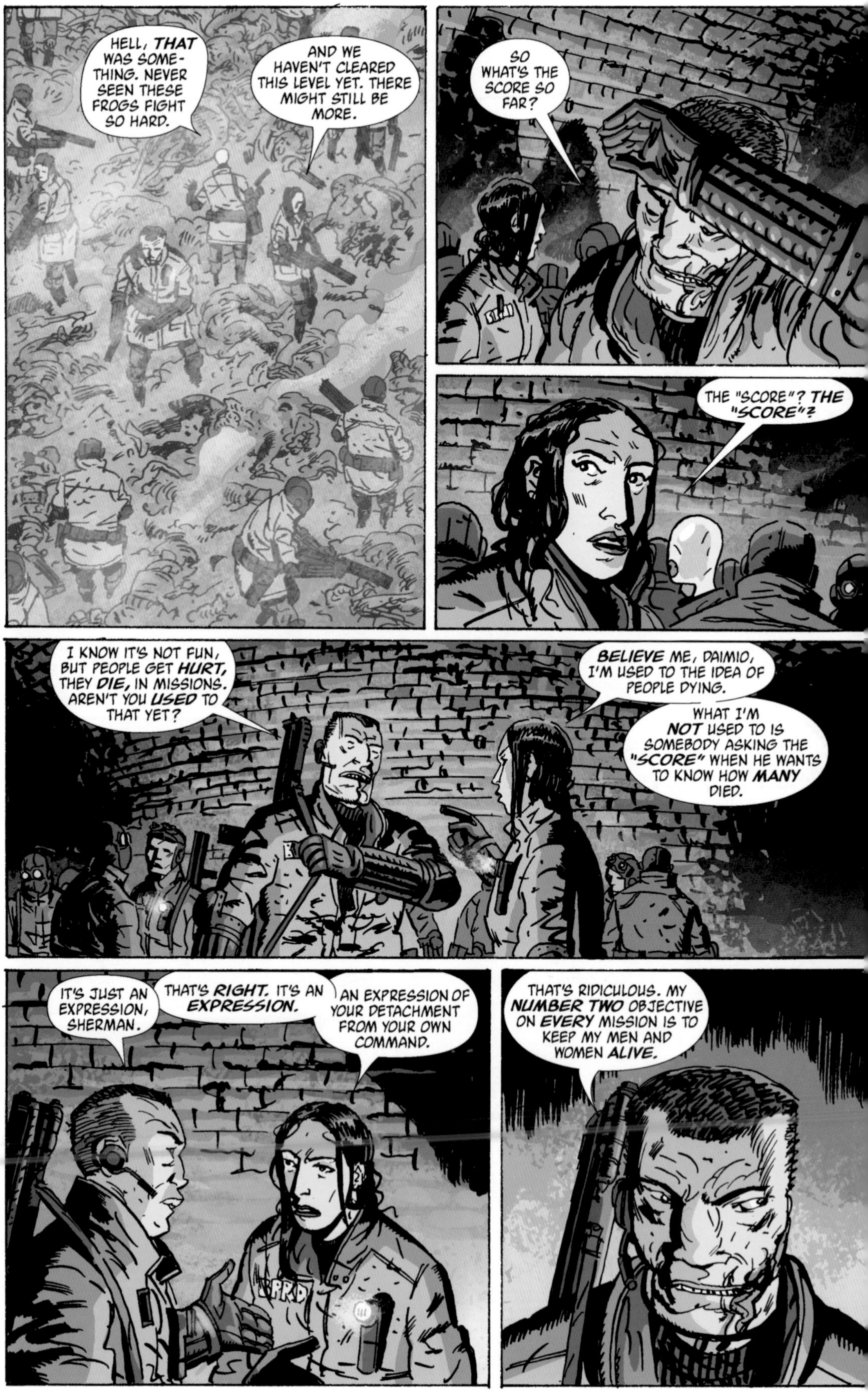
HELL, THAT WAS SOME-THING. NEVER SEEN THESE FROGS FIGHT SO HARD.
AND WE HAVEN'T CLEARED THIS LEVEL YET. THERE MIGHT STILL BE MORE.
SO WHAT'S THE SCORE SO FAR?
THE "SCORE"? THE "SCORE"?
I KNOW IT'S NOT FUN, BUT PEOPLE GET HURT, THEY DIE, IN MISSIONS. AREN'T YOU USED TO THAT YET?
BELIEVE ME, DAIMIO, I'M USED TO THE IDEA OF PEOPLE DYING.
WHAT I'M NOT USED TO IS SOMEBODY ASKING THE "SCORE" WHEN HE WANTS TO KNOW HOW MANY DIED.
IT'S JUST AN EXPRESSION, SHERMAN.
THAT'S RIGHT. IT'S AN EXPRESSION.
AN EXPRESSION OF YOUR DETACHMENT FROM YOUR OWN COMMAND.
THAT'S RIDICULOUS. MY NUMBER TWO OBJECTIVE ON EVERY MISSION IS TO KEEP MY MEN AND WOMEN ALIVE.

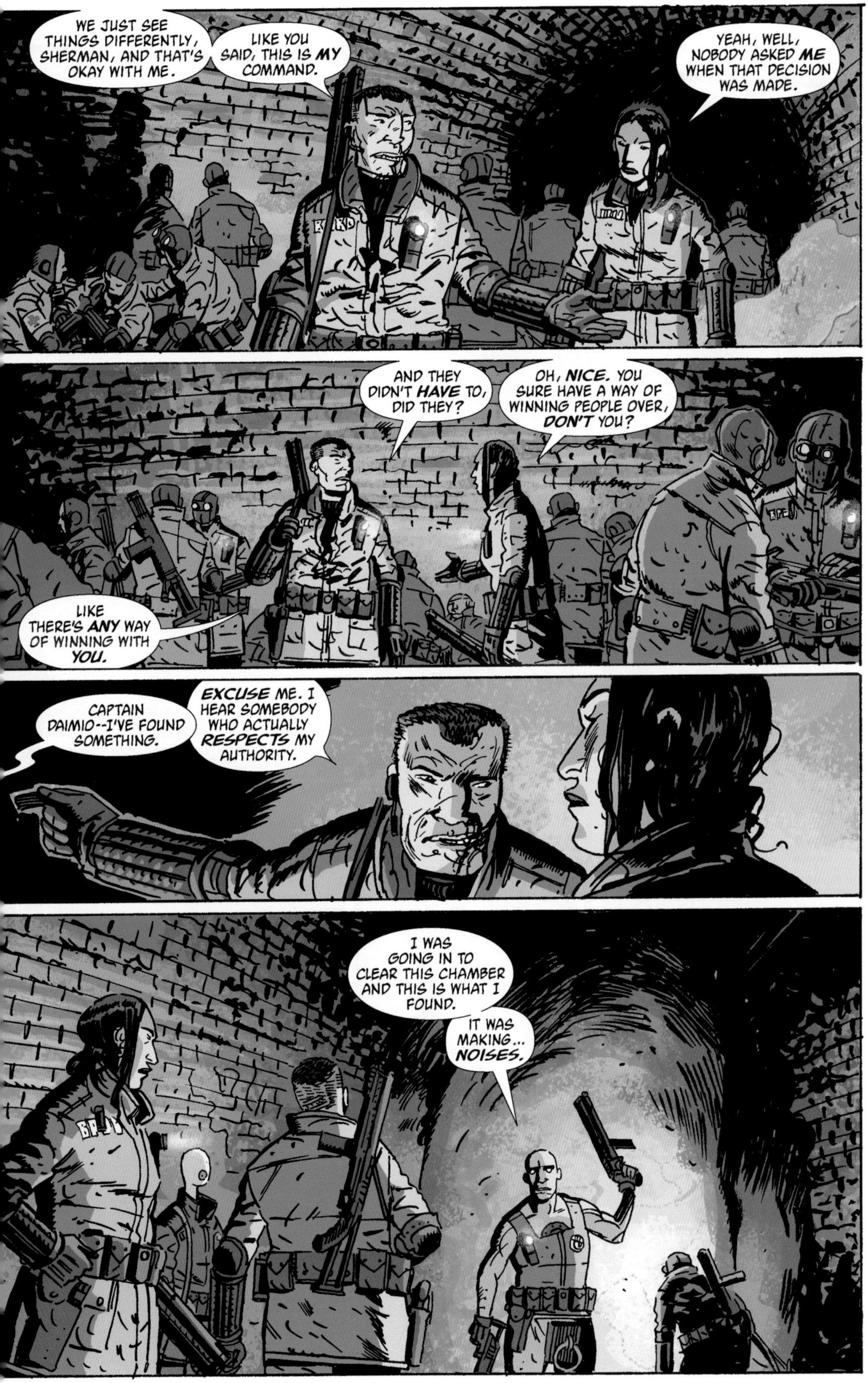

WE JUST SEE THINGS DIFFERENTLY, SHERMAN, AND THAT'S OKAY WITH ME.
LIKE YOU SAID, THIS IS *MY* COMMAND.
YEAH, WELL, NOBODY ASKED *ME* WHEN THAT DECISION WAS MADE.
AND THEY DIDN'T *HAVE* TO, DID THEY?
OH, *NICE.* YOU SURE HAVE A WAY OF WINNING PEOPLE OVER, *DON'T* YOU?
LIKE THERE'S *ANY* WAY OF WINNING WITH *YOU.*
CAPTAIN DAIMIO--I'VE FOUND SOMETHING.
*EXCUSE* ME. I HEAR SOMEBODY WHO ACTUALLY *RESPECTS* MY AUTHORITY.
I WAS GOING IN TO CLEAR THIS CHAMBER AND THIS IS WHAT I FOUND.
IT WAS MAKING... *NOISES.*

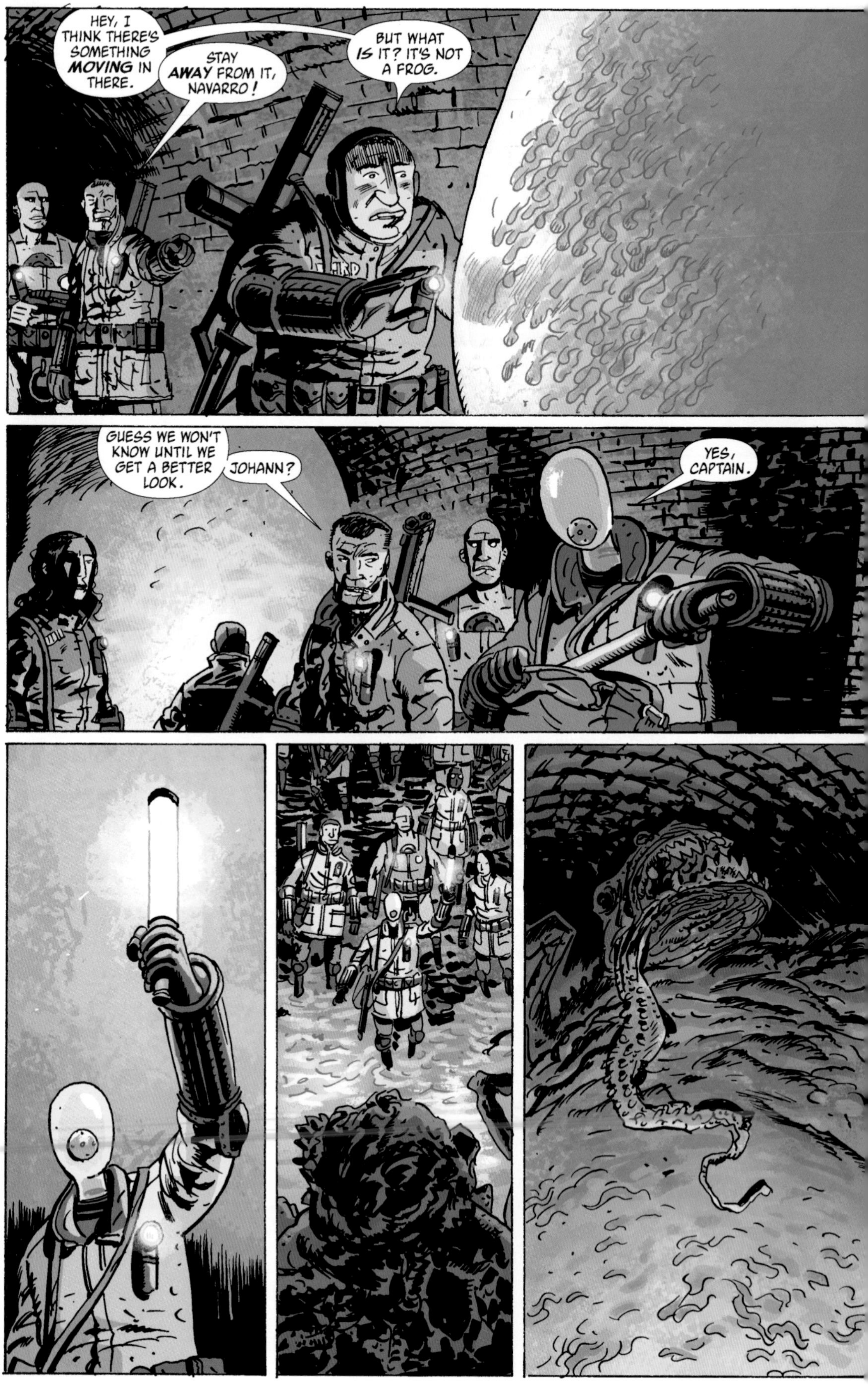
HEY, I THINK THERE'S SOMETHING MOVING IN THERE.
STAY AWAY FROM IT, NAVARRO!
BUT WHAT IS IT? IT'S NOT A FROG.
GUESS WE WON'T KNOW UNTIL WE GET A BETTER LOOK.
JOHANN?
YES, CAPTAIN.

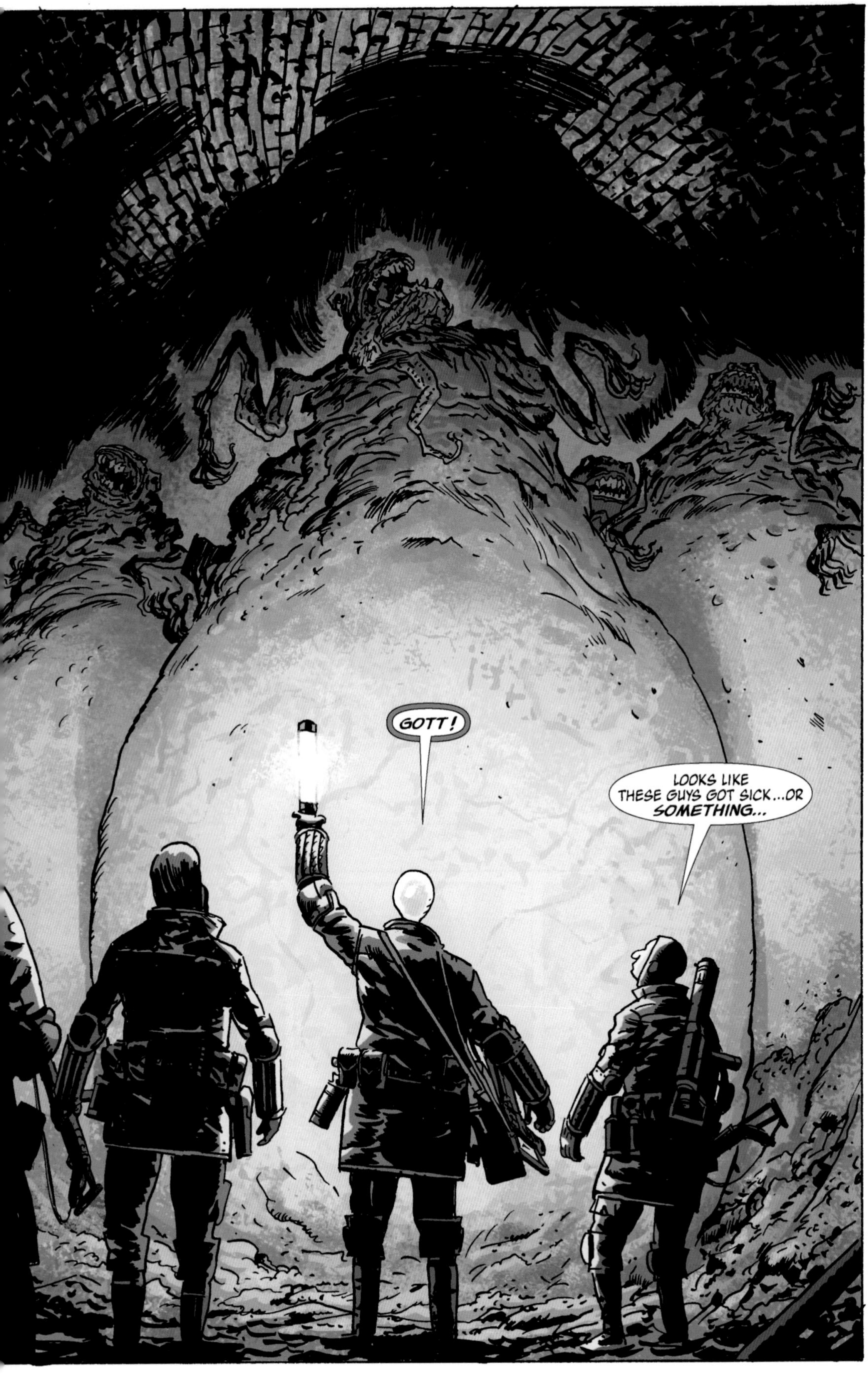
GOTT!
LOOKS LIKE THESE GUYS GOT SICK...OR SOMETHING...

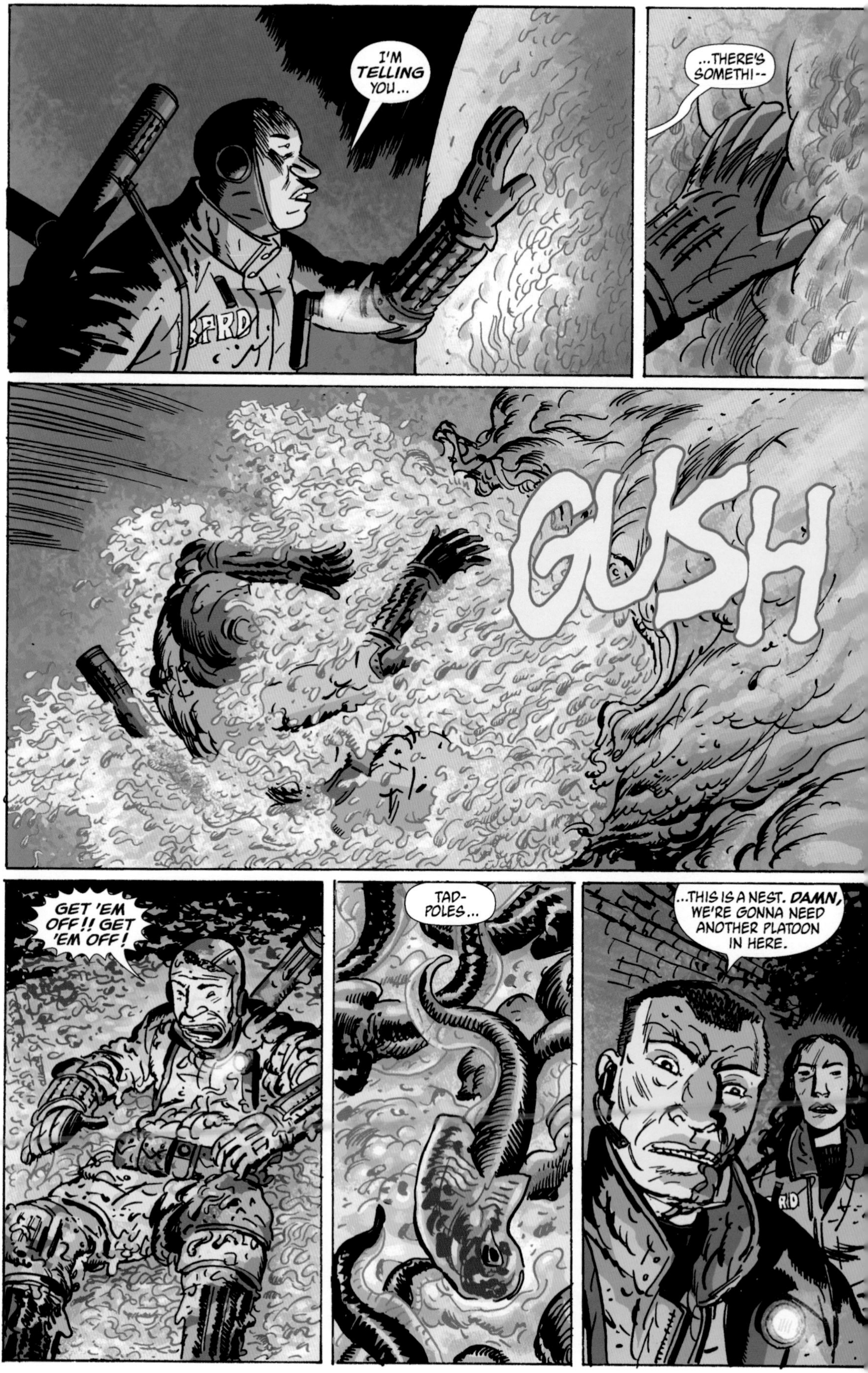
I'M TELLING YOU...
...THERE'S SOMETHI--
GUSH
GET 'EM OFF!! GET 'EM OFF!
TAD-POLES...
...THIS IS A NEST. DAMN, WE'RE GONNA NEED ANOTHER PLATOON IN HERE.

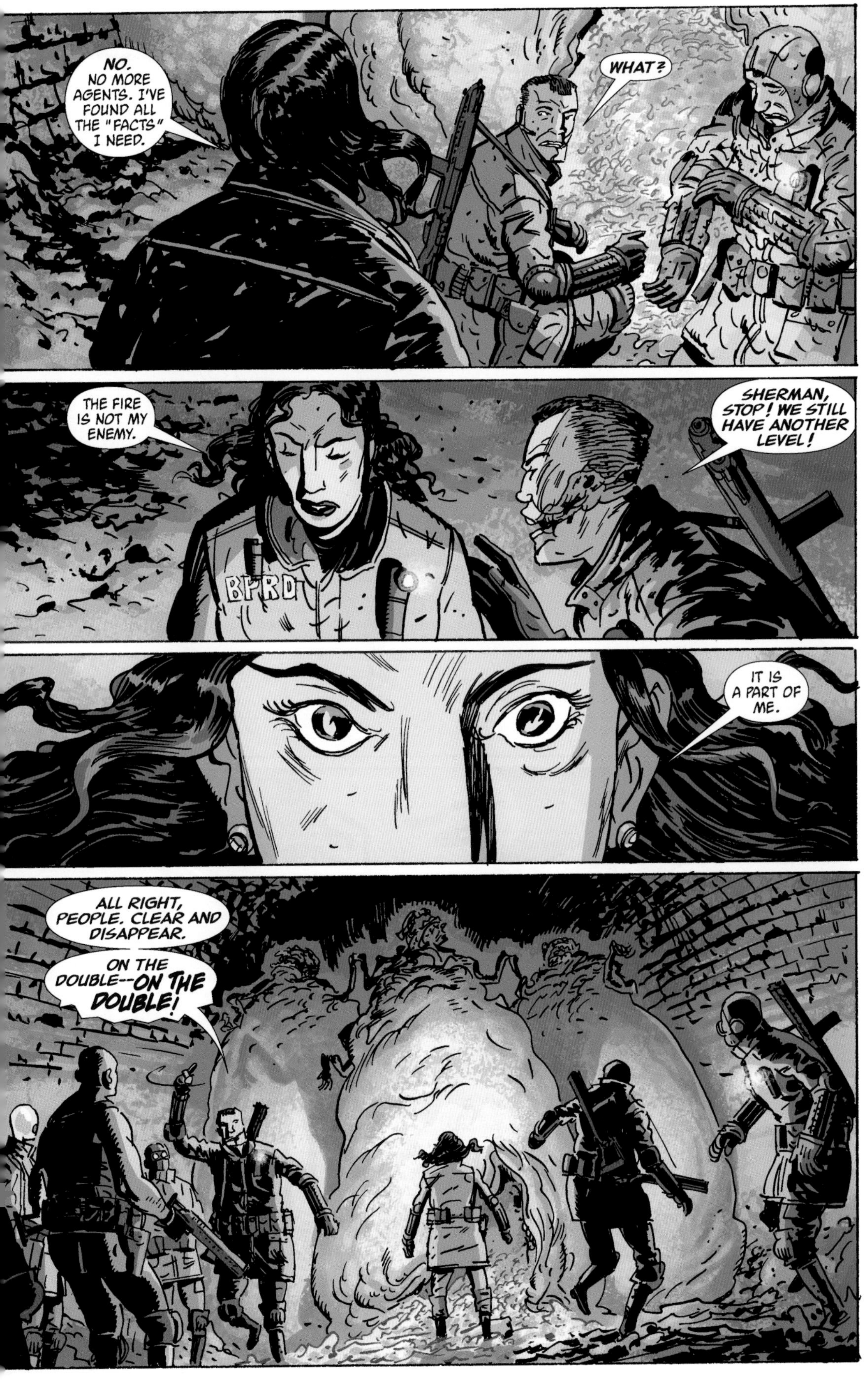

NO. NO MORE AGENTS. I'VE FOUND ALL THE "FACTS" I NEED.
WHAT?
THE FIRE IS NOT MY ENEMY.
SHERMAN, STOP! WE STILL HAVE ANOTHER LEVEL!
IT IS A PART OF ME.
ALL RIGHT, PEOPLE. CLEAR AND DISAPPEAR.
ON THE DOUBLE--ON THE DOUBLE!

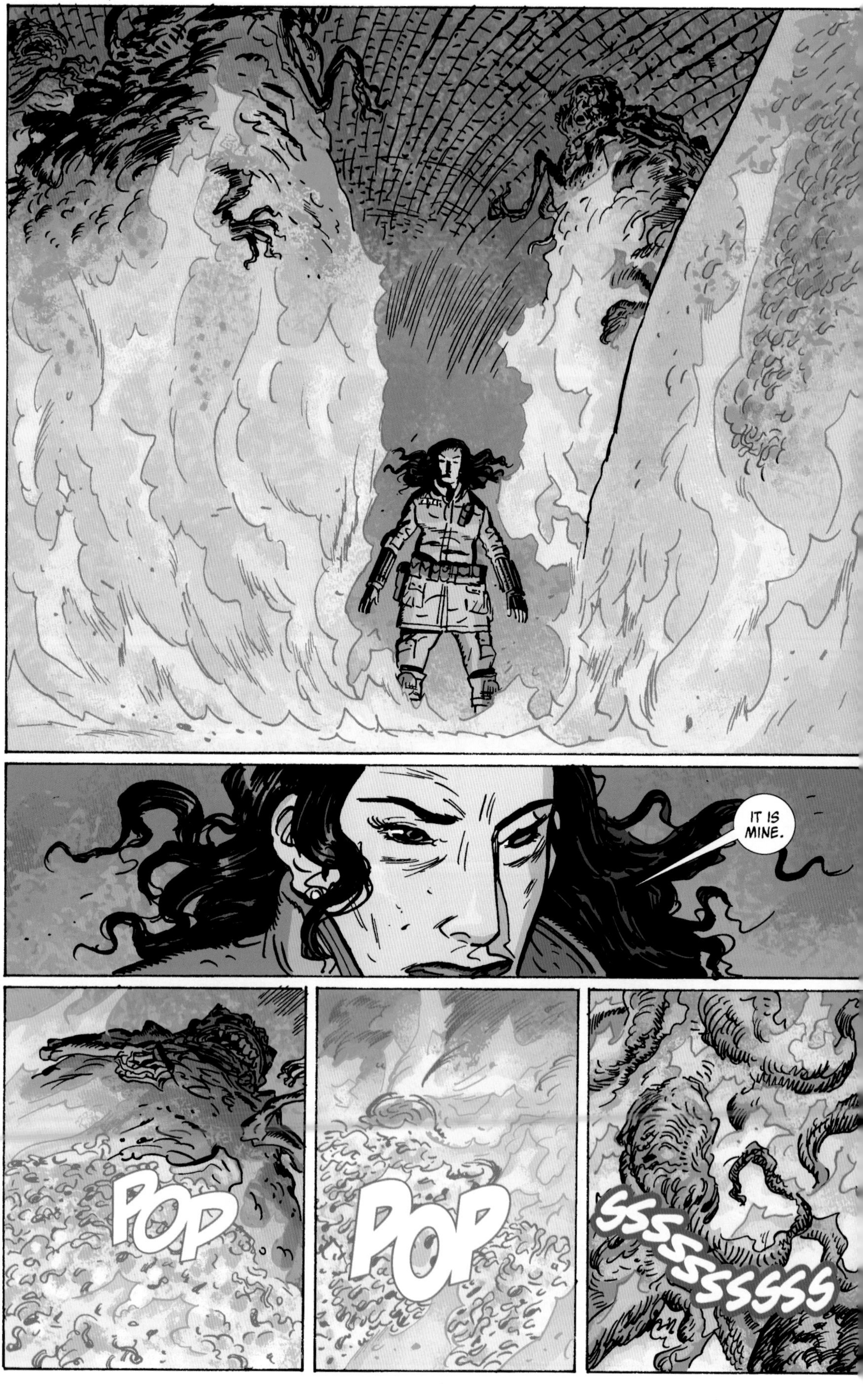
IT IS MINE.
POP
POP
SSSSSSSSSS

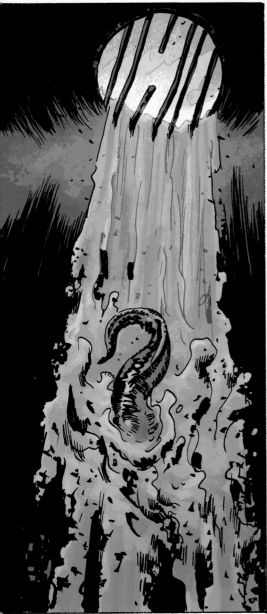

SPLOP

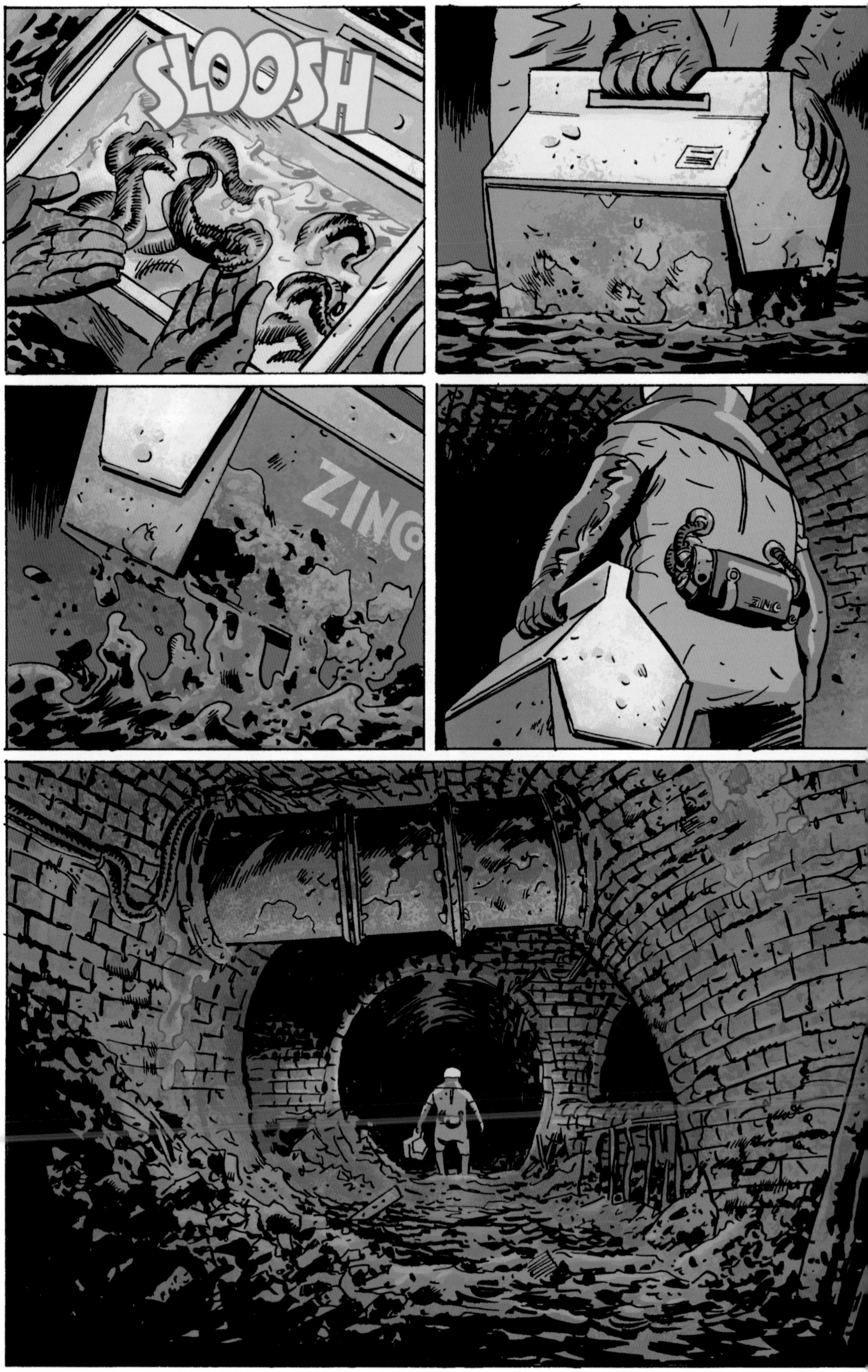
SLOOSH
ZINC
ZINC

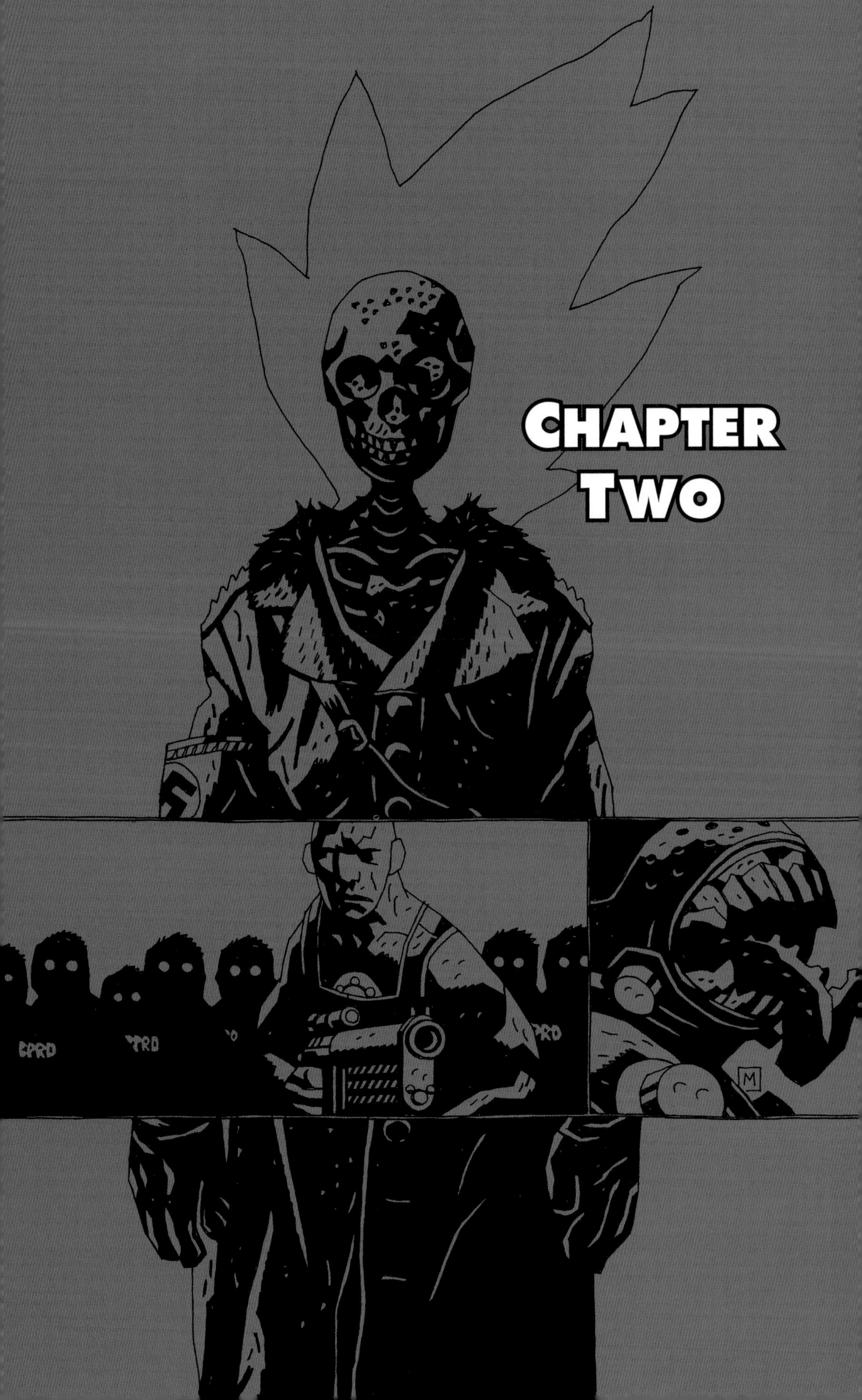
CHAPTER TWO
BPRD

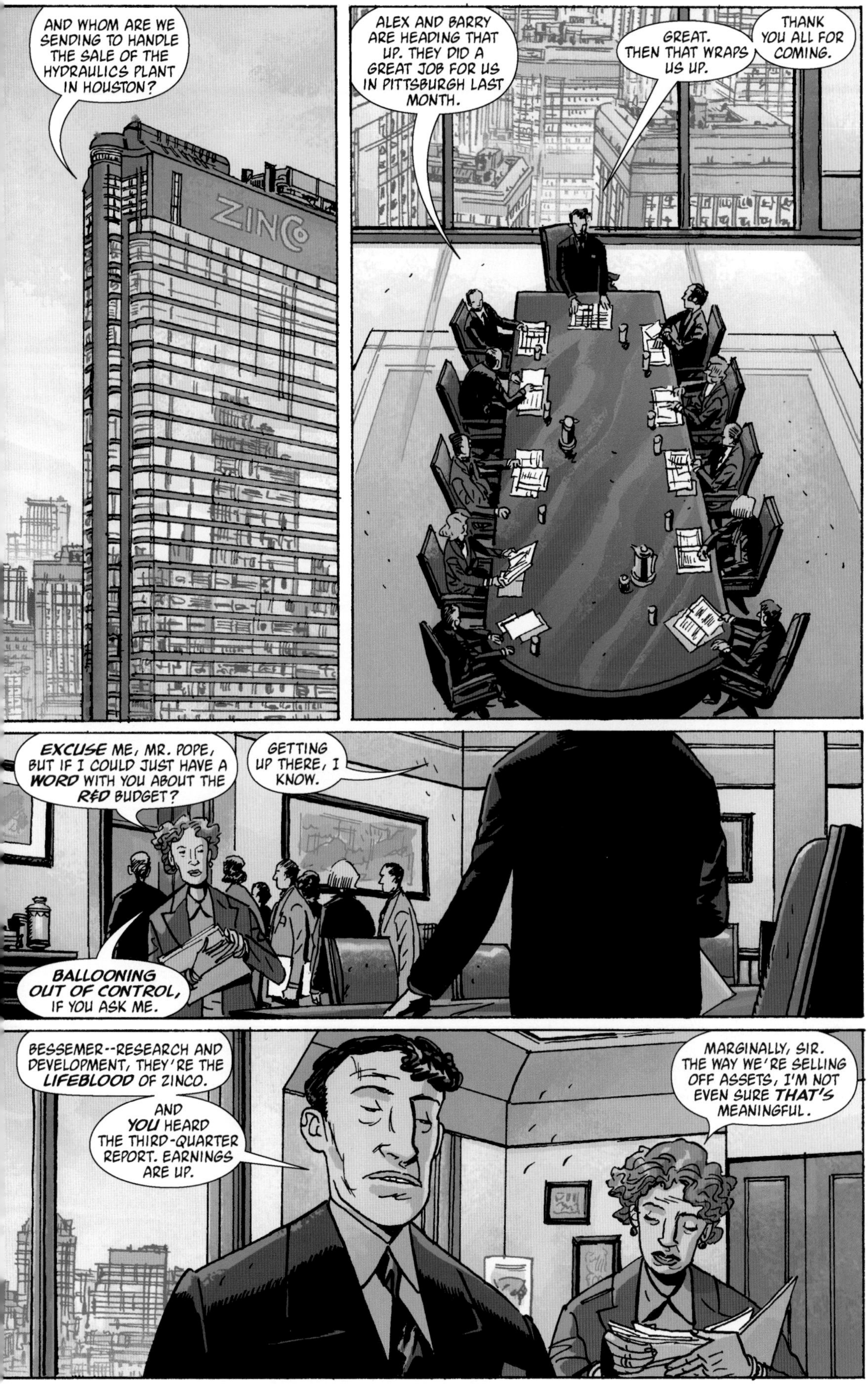
AND WHOM ARE WE SENDING TO HANDLE THE SALE OF THE HYDRAULICS PLANT IN HOUSTON?
ZINCo
ALEX AND BARRY ARE HEADING THAT UP. THEY DID A GREAT JOB FOR US IN PITTSBURGH LAST MONTH.
GREAT. THEN THAT WRAPS US UP.
THANK YOU ALL FOR COMING.
EXCUSE ME, MR. POPE, BUT IF I COULD JUST HAVE A WORD WITH YOU ABOUT THE R&D BUDGET?
GETTING UP THERE, I KNOW.
BALLOONING OUT OF CONTROL, IF YOU ASK ME.
BESSEMER--RESEARCH AND DEVELOPMENT, THEY'RE THE LIFEBLOOD OF ZINCO.
AND YOU HEARD THE THIRD-QUARTER REPORT. EARNINGS ARE UP.
MARGINALLY, SIR. THE WAY WE'RE SELLING OFF ASSETS, I'M NOT EVEN SURE THAT'S MEANINGFUL.

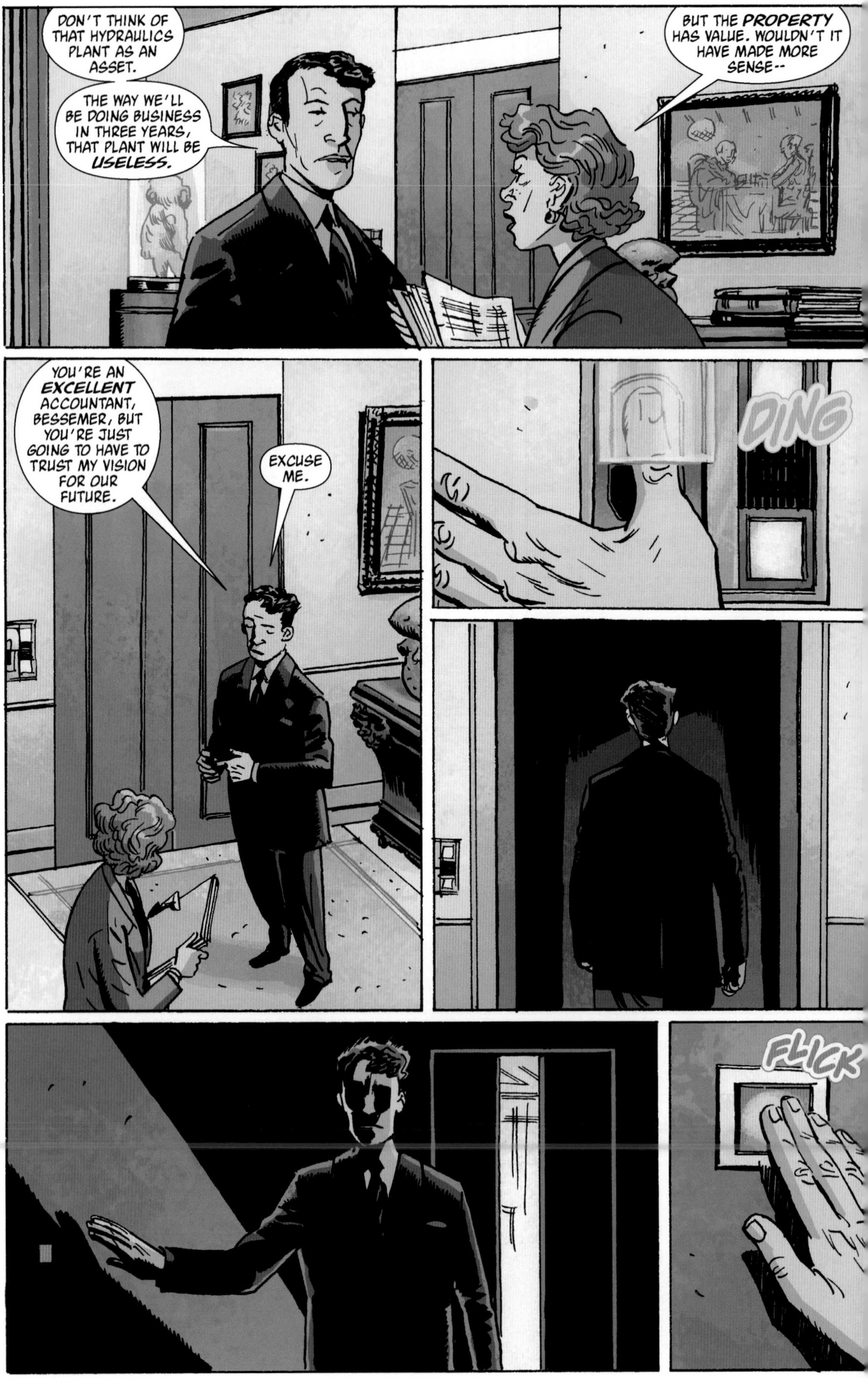
DON'T THINK OF THAT HYDRAULICS PLANT AS AN ASSET.
THE WAY WE'LL BE DOING BUSINESS IN THREE YEARS, THAT PLANT WILL BE USELESS.
BUT THE PROPERTY HAS VALUE. WOULDN'T IT HAVE MADE MORE SENSE--
YOU'RE AN EXCELLENT ACCOUNTANT, BESSEMER, BUT YOU'RE JUST GOING TO HAVE TO TRUST MY VISION FOR OUR FUTURE.
EXCUSE ME.
DING
FLICK

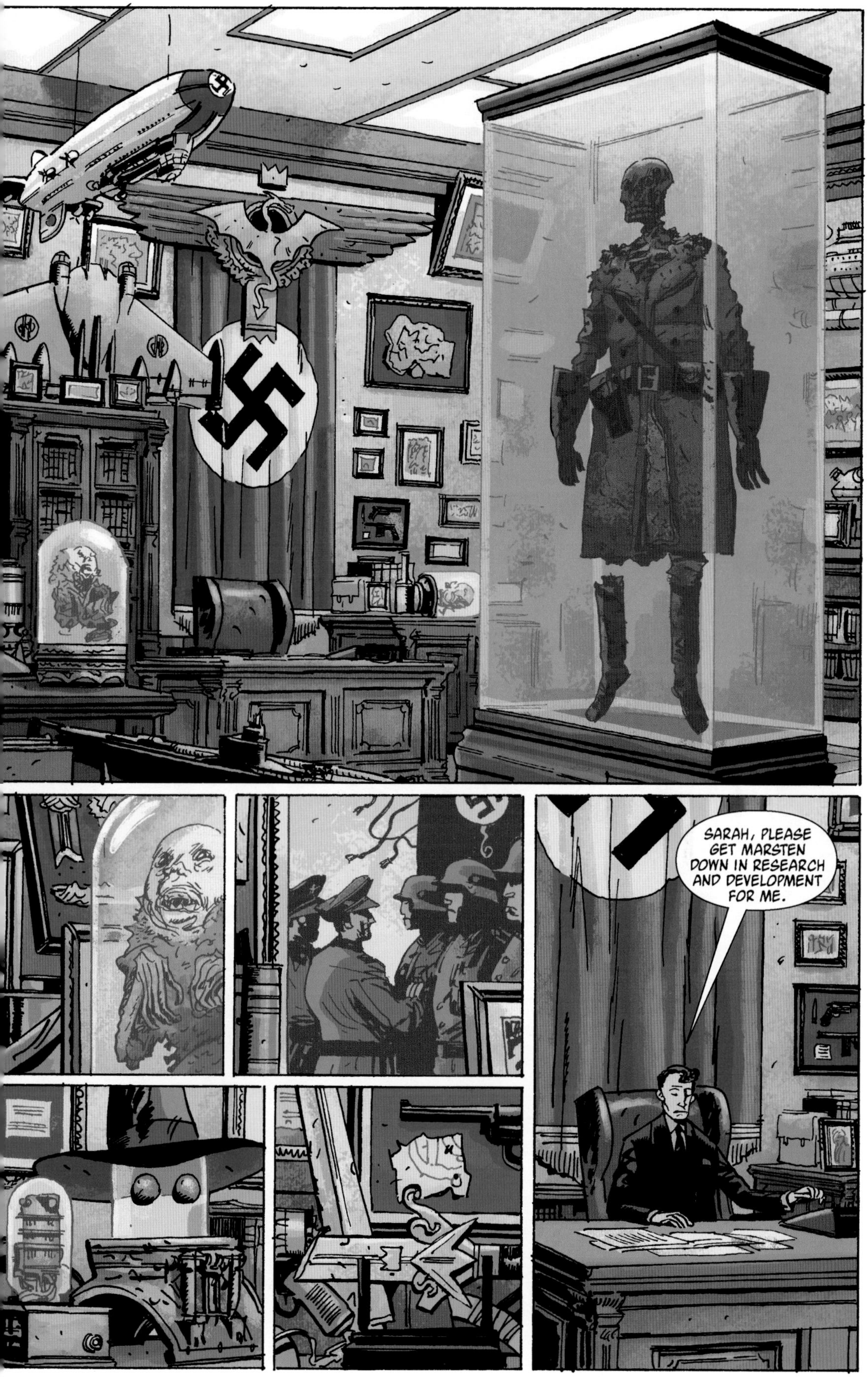
SARAH, PLEASE GET MARSTEN DOWN IN RESEARCH AND DEVELOPMENT FOR ME.

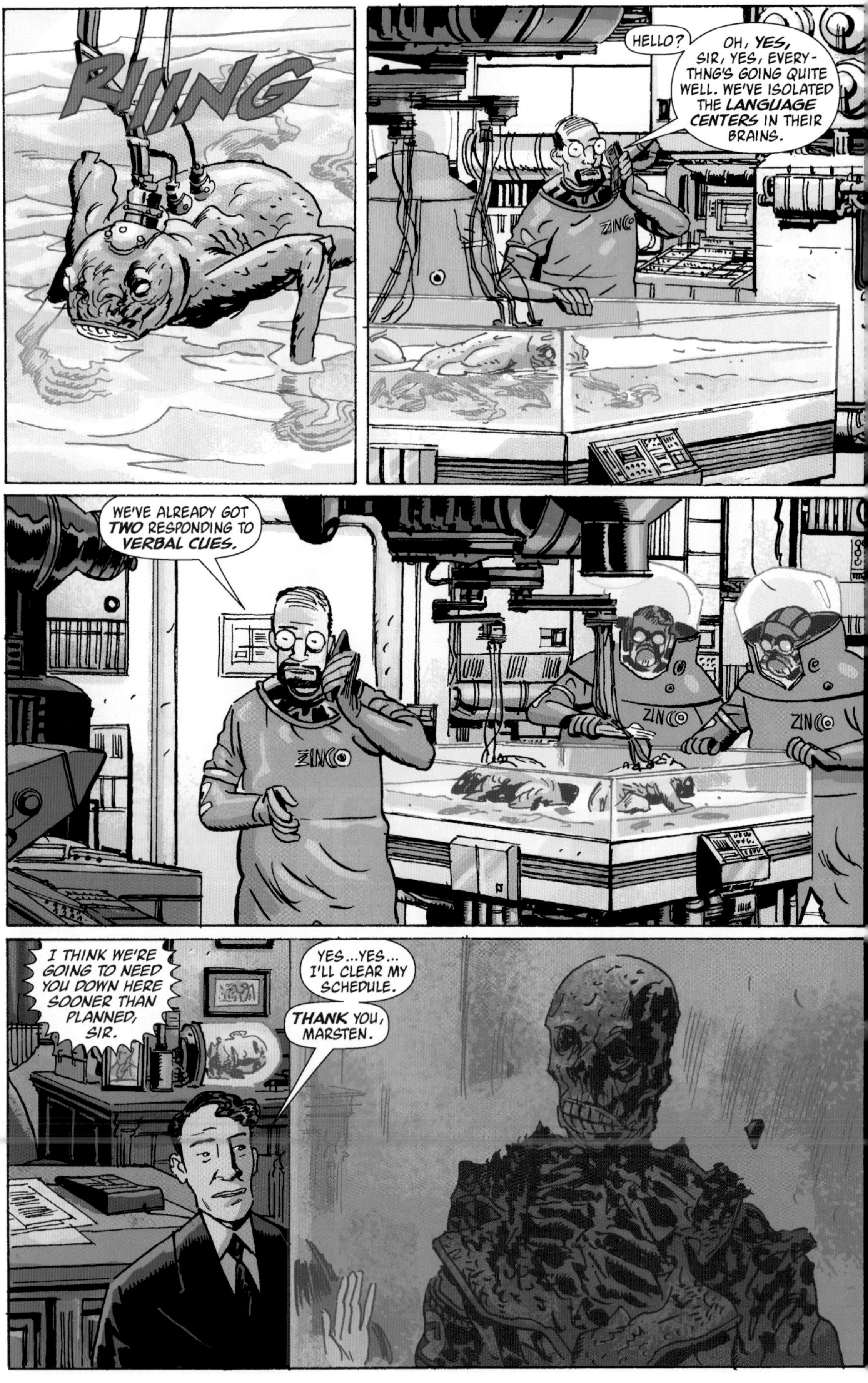
RIING
HELLO?
OH, YES, SIR, YES, EVERY-THNG'S GOING QUITE WELL. WE'VE ISOLATED THE LANGUAGE CENTERS IN THEIR BRAINS.
WE'VE ALREADY GOT TWO RESPONDING TO VERBAL CUES.
ZINCO
I THINK WE'RE GOING TO NEED YOU DOWN HERE SOONER THAN PLANNED, SIR.
YES...YES... I'LL CLEAR MY SCHEDULE.
THANK YOU, MARSTEN.

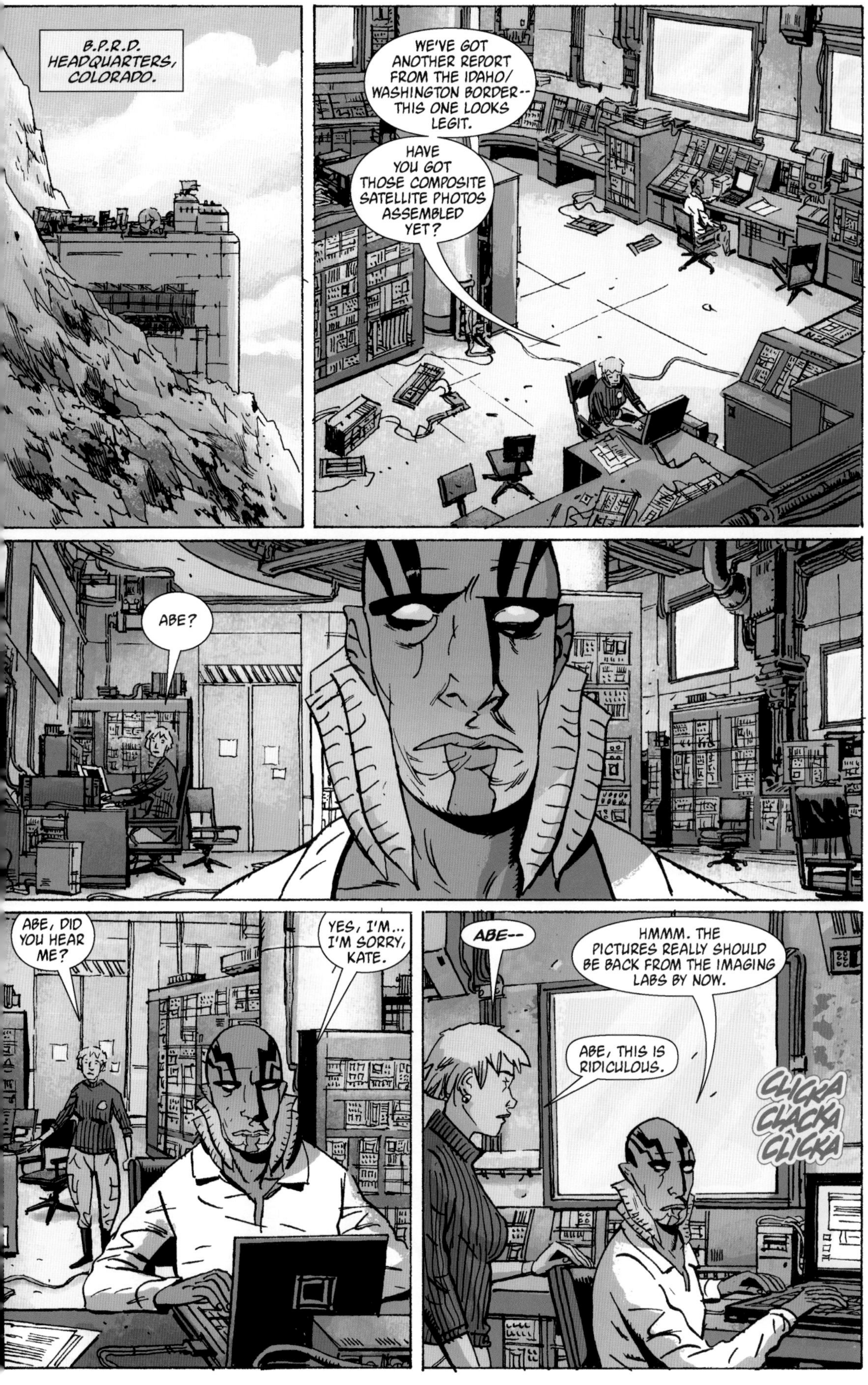
B.P.R.D. HEADQUARTERS, COLORADO.
WE'VE GOT ANOTHER REPORT FROM THE IDAHO/ WASHINGTON BORDER-- THIS ONE LOOKS LEGIT.
HAVE YOU GOT THOSE COMPOSITE SATELLITE PHOTOS ASSEMBLED YET?
ABE?
ABE, DID YOU HEAR ME?
YES, I'M... I'M SORRY, KATE.
ABE--
HMMM. THE PICTURES REALLY SHOULD BE BACK FROM THE IMAGING LABS BY NOW.
ABE, THIS IS RIDICULOUS.
CLICKA CLACKA CLICKA

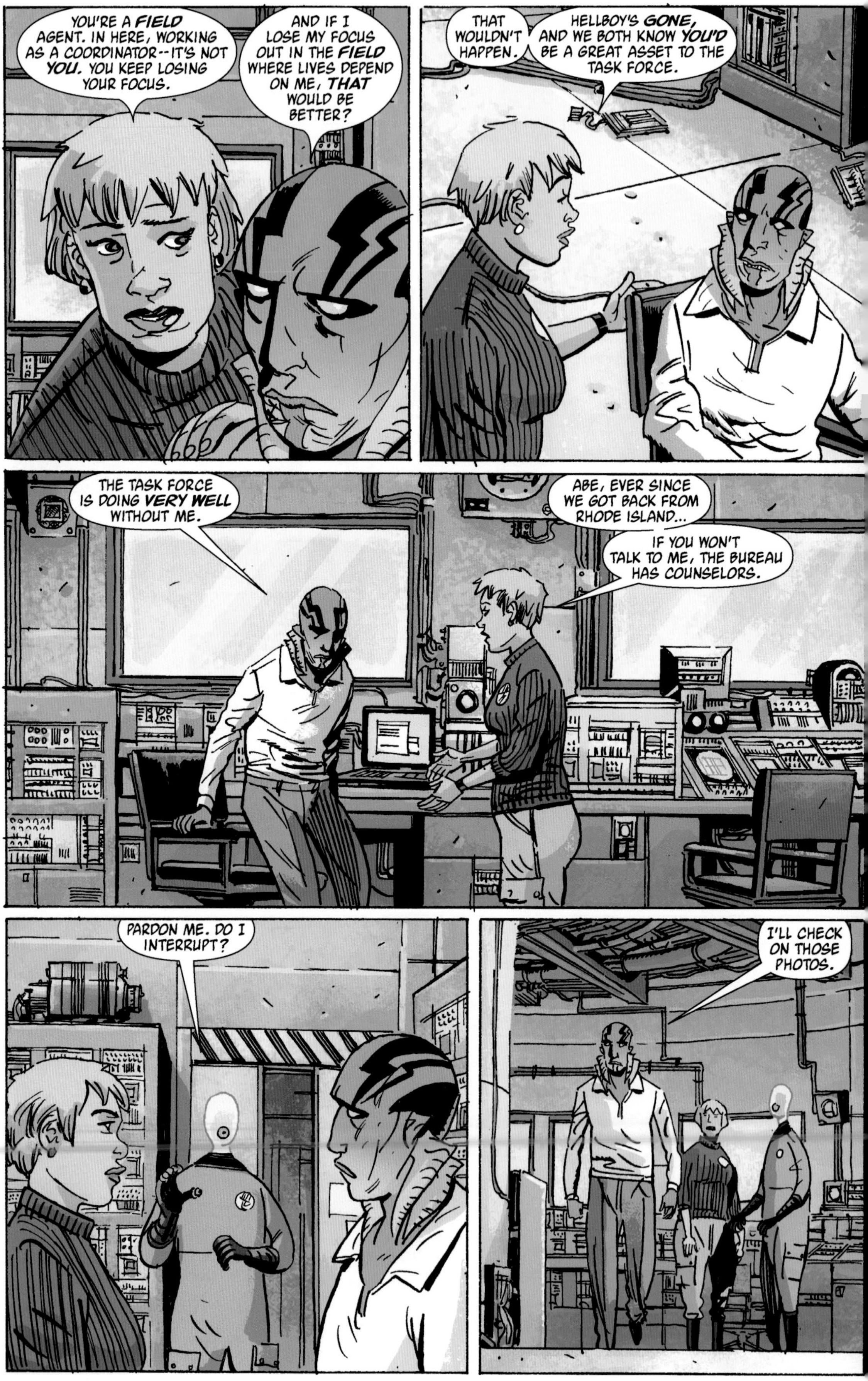
YOU'RE A FIELD AGENT. IN HERE, WORKING AS A COORDINATOR--IT'S NOT YOU. YOU KEEP LOSING YOUR FOCUS.
AND IF I LOSE MY FOCUS OUT IN THE FIELD WHERE LIVES DEPEND ON ME, THAT WOULD BE BETTER?
THAT WOULDN'T HAPPEN.
HELLBOY'S GONE, AND WE BOTH KNOW YOU'D BE A GREAT ASSET TO THE TASK FORCE.
THE TASK FORCE IS DOING VERY WELL WITHOUT ME.
ABE, EVER SINCE WE GOT BACK FROM RHODE ISLAND...
IF YOU WON'T TALK TO ME, THE BUREAU HAS COUNSELORS.
PARDON ME. DO I INTERRUPT?
I'LL CHECK ON THOSE PHOTOS.

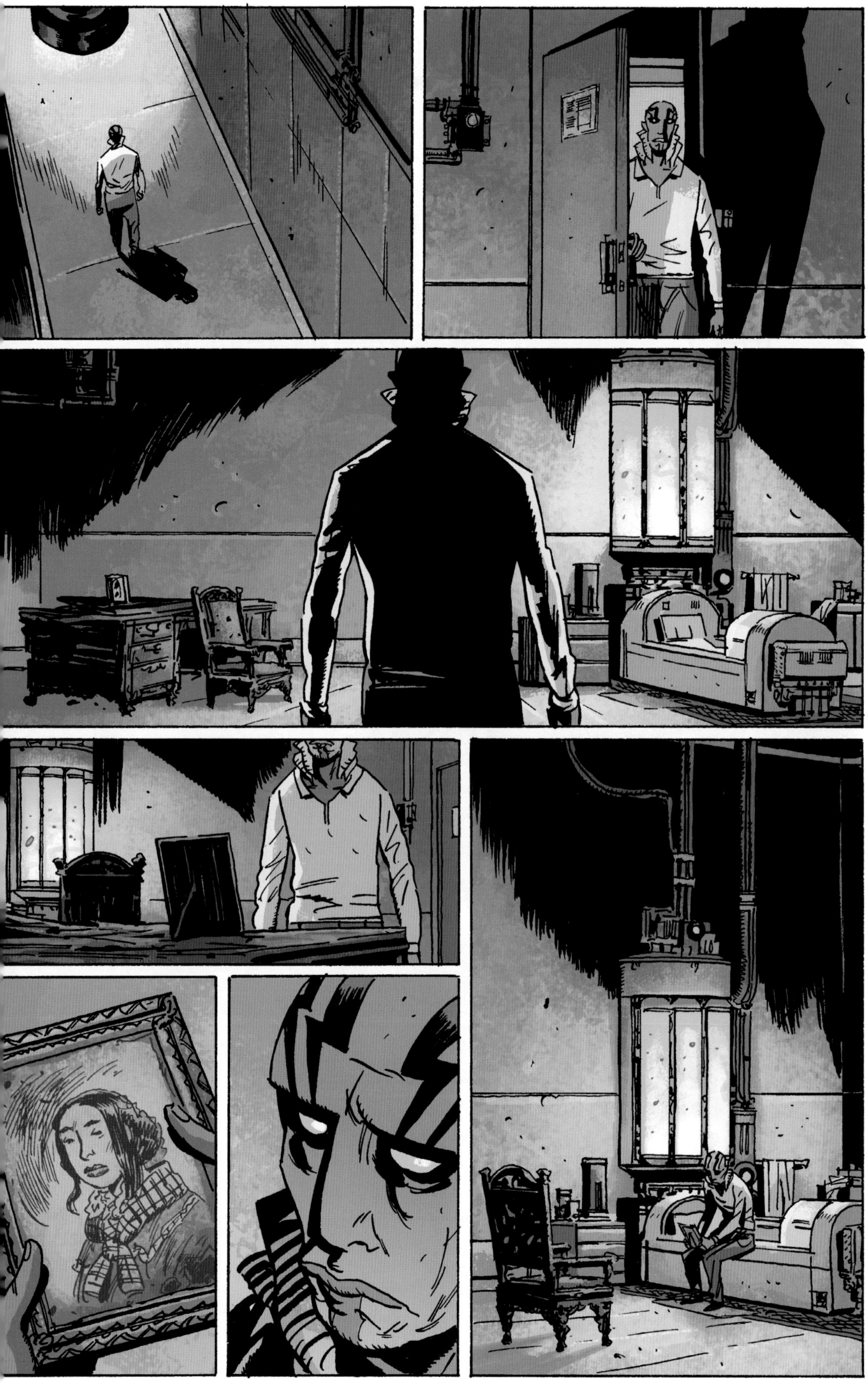

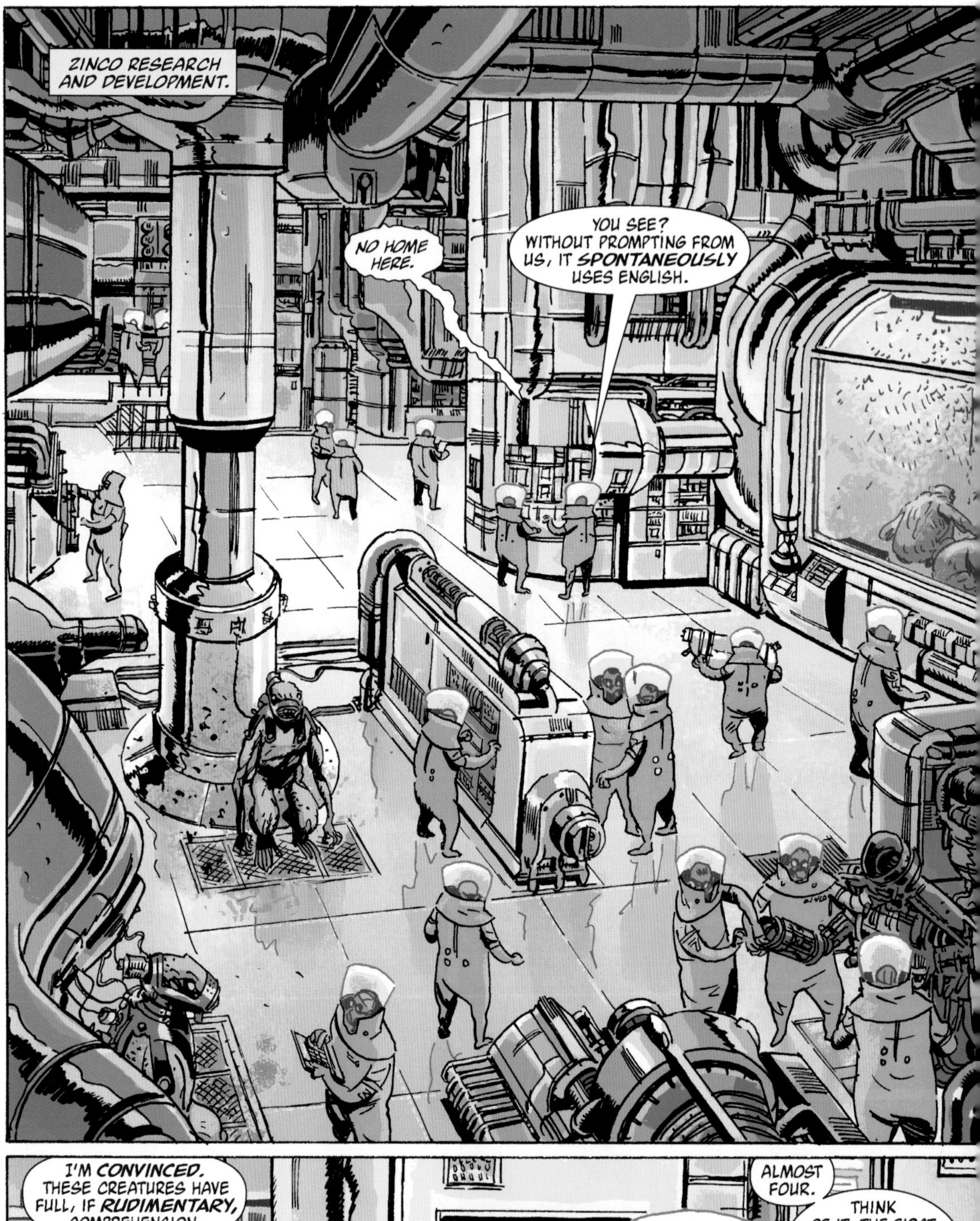
ZINCO RESEARCH AND DEVELOPMENT.
NO HOME HERE.
YOU SEE? WITHOUT PROMPTING FROM US, IT SPONTANEOUSLY USES ENGLISH.

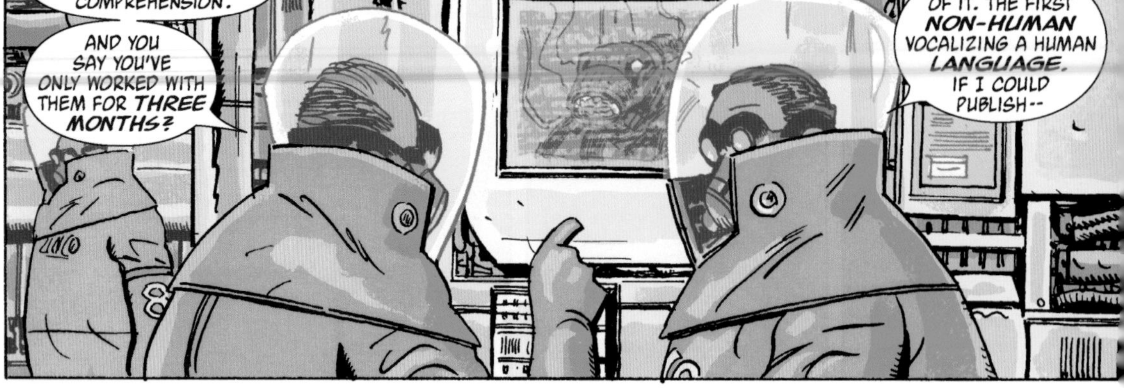
I'M CONVINCED. THESE CREATURES HAVE FULL, IF RUDIMENTARY, COMPREHENSION.
AND YOU SAY YOU'VE ONLY WORKED WITH THEM FOR THREE MONTHS?
ALMOST FOUR.
THINK OF IT. THE FIRST NON-HUMAN VOCALIZING A HUMAN LANGUAGE. IF I COULD PUBLISH--

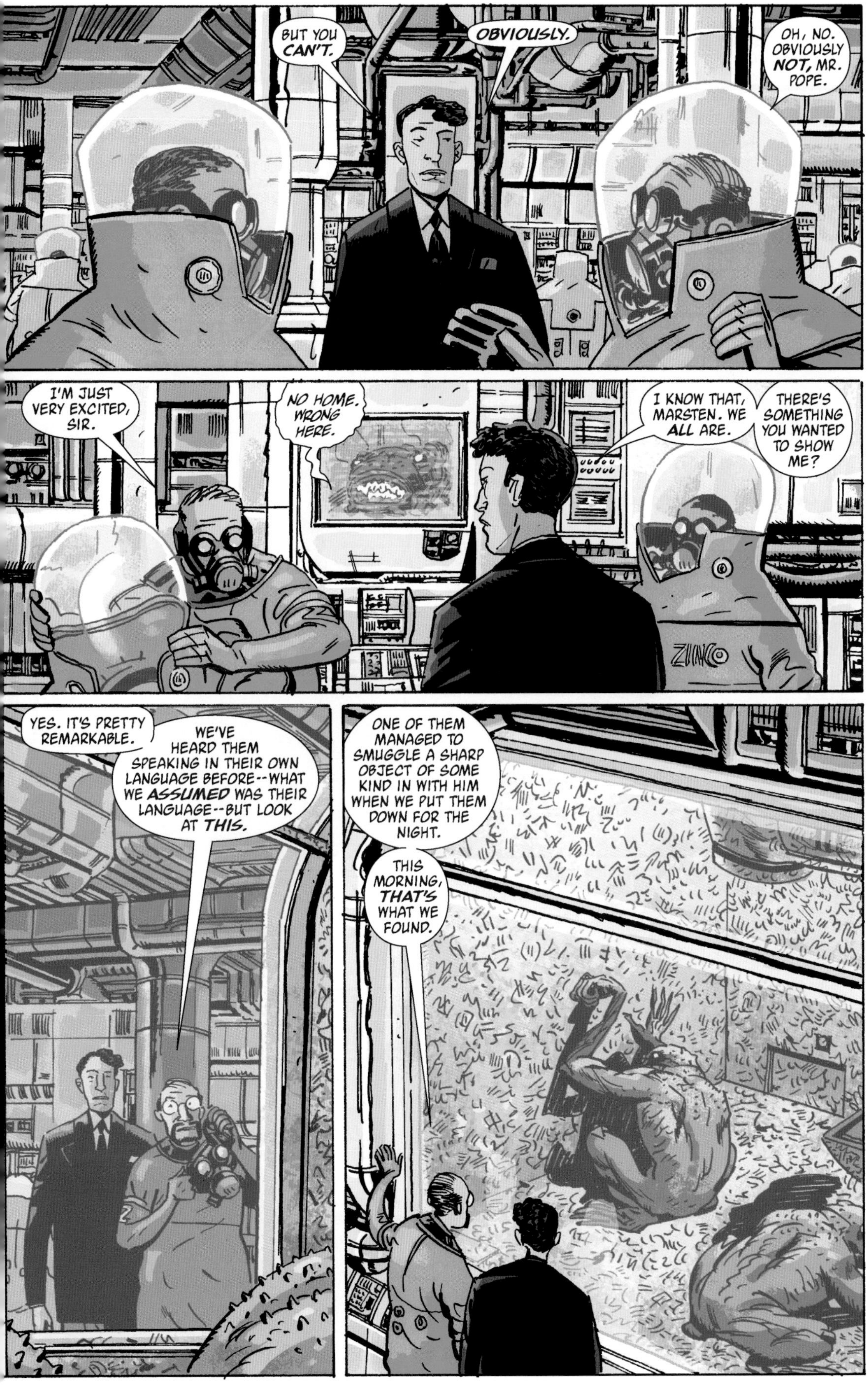
BUT YOU CAN'T.
OBVIOUSLY.
OH, NO. OBVIOUSLY NOT, MR. POPE.
I'M JUST VERY EXCITED, SIR.
NO HOME. WRONG HERE.
I KNOW THAT, MARSTEN. WE ALL ARE.
THERE'S SOMETHING YOU WANTED TO SHOW ME?
ZINCO
YES. IT'S PRETTY REMARKABLE.
WE'VE HEARD THEM SPEAKING IN THEIR OWN LANGUAGE BEFORE--WHAT WE ASSUMED WAS THEIR LANGUAGE--BUT LOOK AT THIS.
ONE OF THEM MANAGED TO SMUGGLE A SHARP OBJECT OF SOME KIND IN WITH HIM WHEN WE PUT THEM DOWN FOR THE NIGHT.
THIS MORNING, THAT'S WHAT WE FOUND.

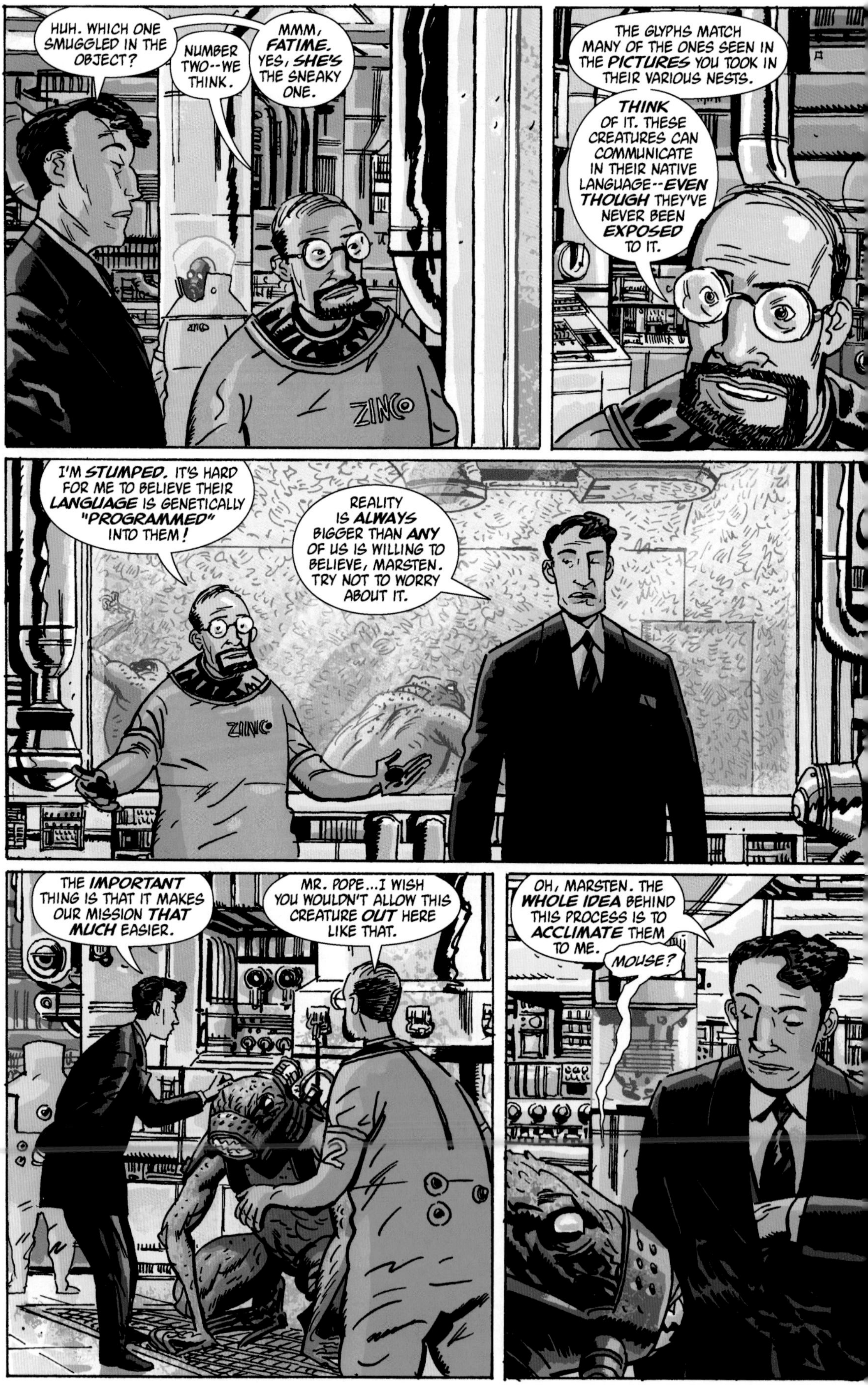
HUH. WHICH ONE SMUGGLED IN THE OBJECT?
NUMBER TWO--WE THINK.
MMM, FATIME. YES, SHE'S THE SNEAKY ONE.
ZINCO
THE GLYPHS MATCH MANY OF THE ONES SEEN IN THE PICTURES YOU TOOK IN THEIR VARIOUS NESTS.
THINK OF IT. THESE CREATURES CAN COMMUNICATE IN THEIR NATIVE LANGUAGE--EVEN THOUGH THEY'VE NEVER BEEN EXPOSED TO IT.
I'M STUMPED. IT'S HARD FOR ME TO BELIEVE THEIR LANGUAGE IS GENETICALLY "PROGRAMMED" INTO THEM!
REALITY IS ALWAYS BIGGER THAN ANY OF US IS WILLING TO BELIEVE, MARSTEN. TRY NOT TO WORRY ABOUT IT.
ZINCO
THE IMPORTANT THING IS THAT IT MAKES OUR MISSION THAT MUCH EASIER.
MR. POPE...I WISH YOU WOULDN'T ALLOW THIS CREATURE OUT HERE LIKE THAT.
OH, MARSTEN. THE WHOLE IDEA BEHIND THIS PROCESS IS TO ACCLIMATE THEM TO ME.
MOUSE?

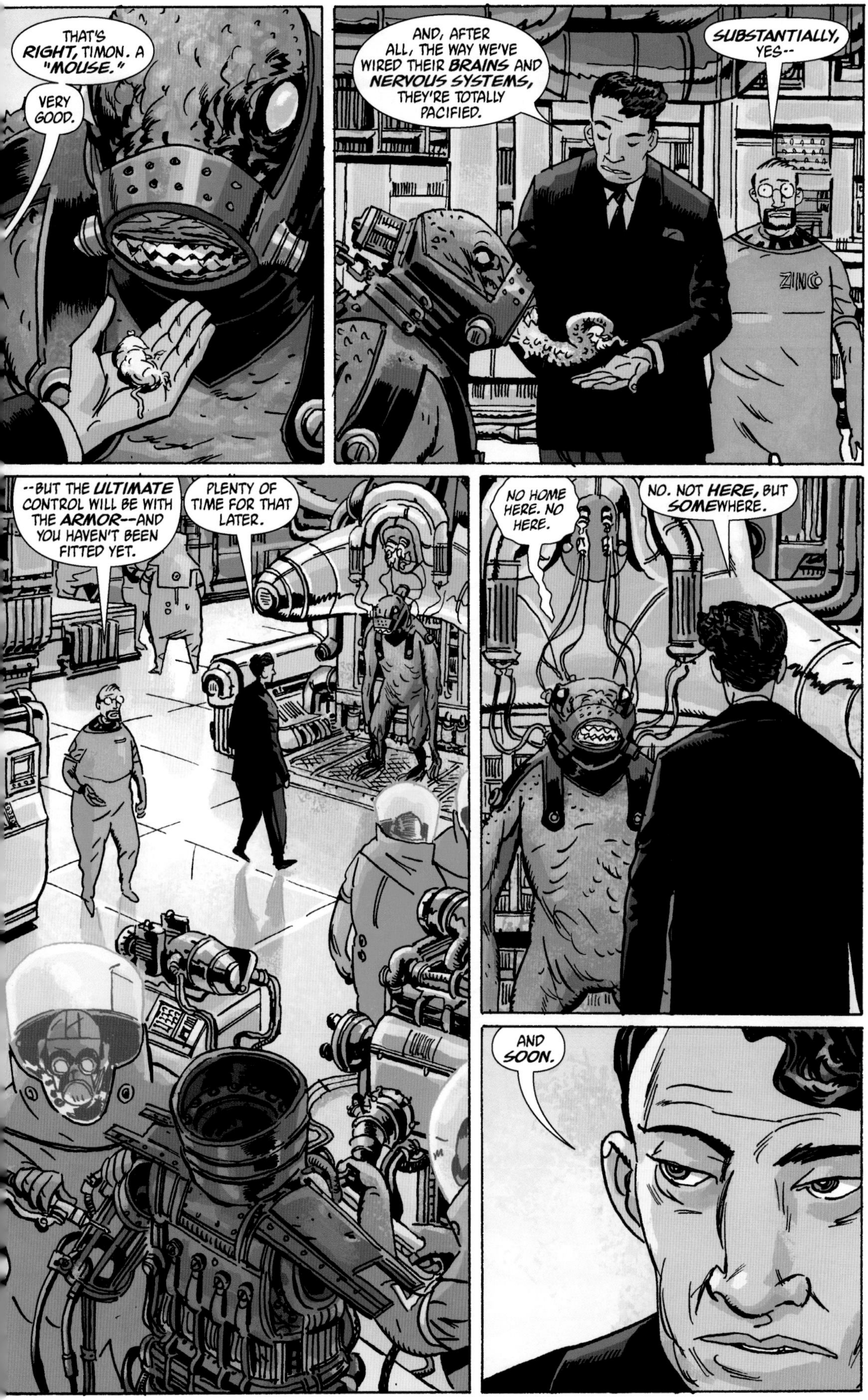
THAT'S RIGHT, TIMON. A "MOUSE."
VERY GOOD.
AND, AFTER ALL, THE WAY WE'VE WIRED THEIR BRAINS AND NERVOUS SYSTEMS, THEY'RE TOTALLY PACIFIED.
SUBSTANTIALLY, YES--
ZINCO
--BUT THE ULTIMATE CONTROL WILL BE WITH THE ARMOR--AND YOU HAVEN'T BEEN FITTED YET.
PLENTY OF TIME FOR THAT LATER.
NO HOME HERE. NO HERE.
NO. NOT HERE, BUT SOMEWHERE.
AND SOON.

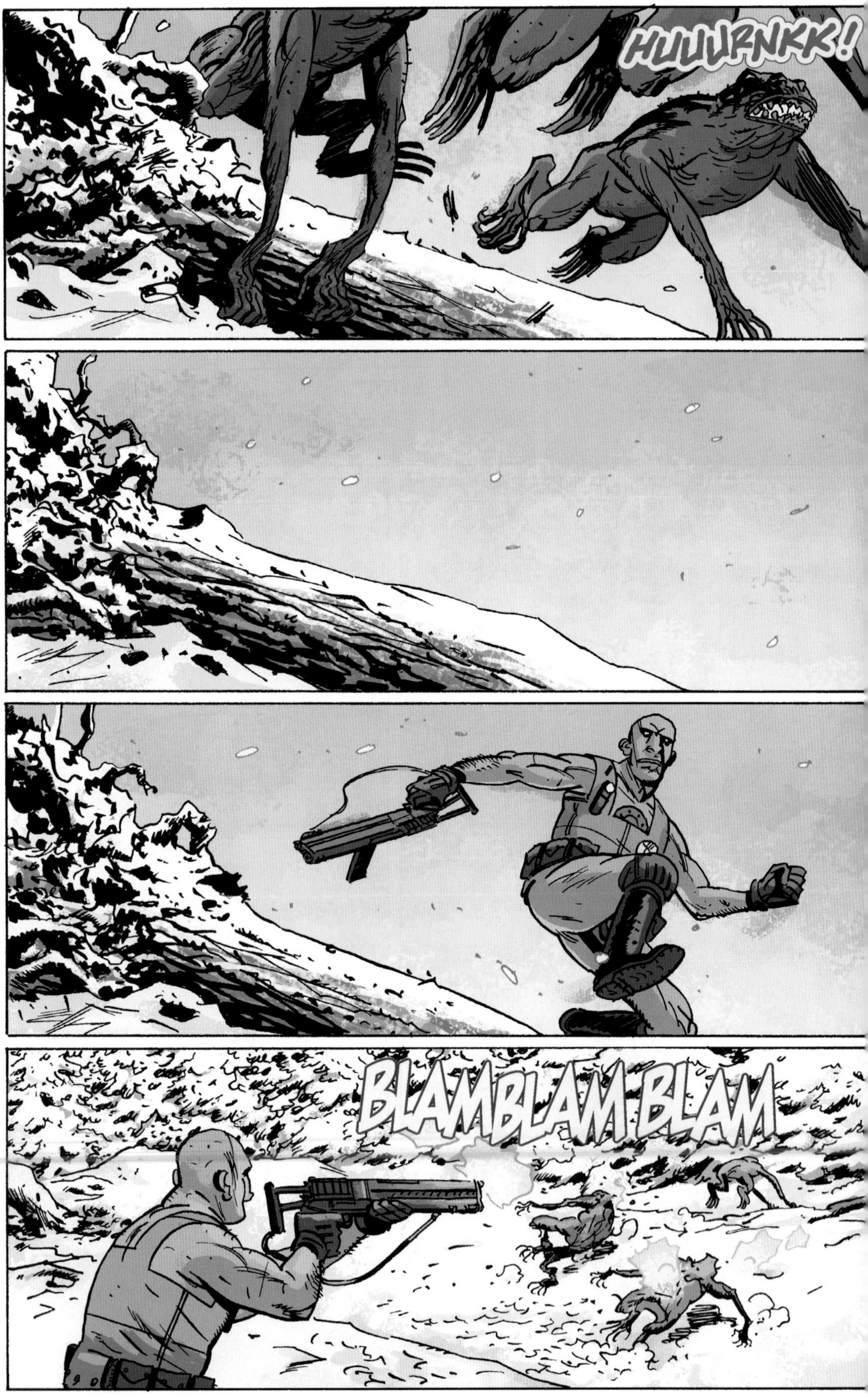
HUUURNKK!
BLAMBLAM BLAM

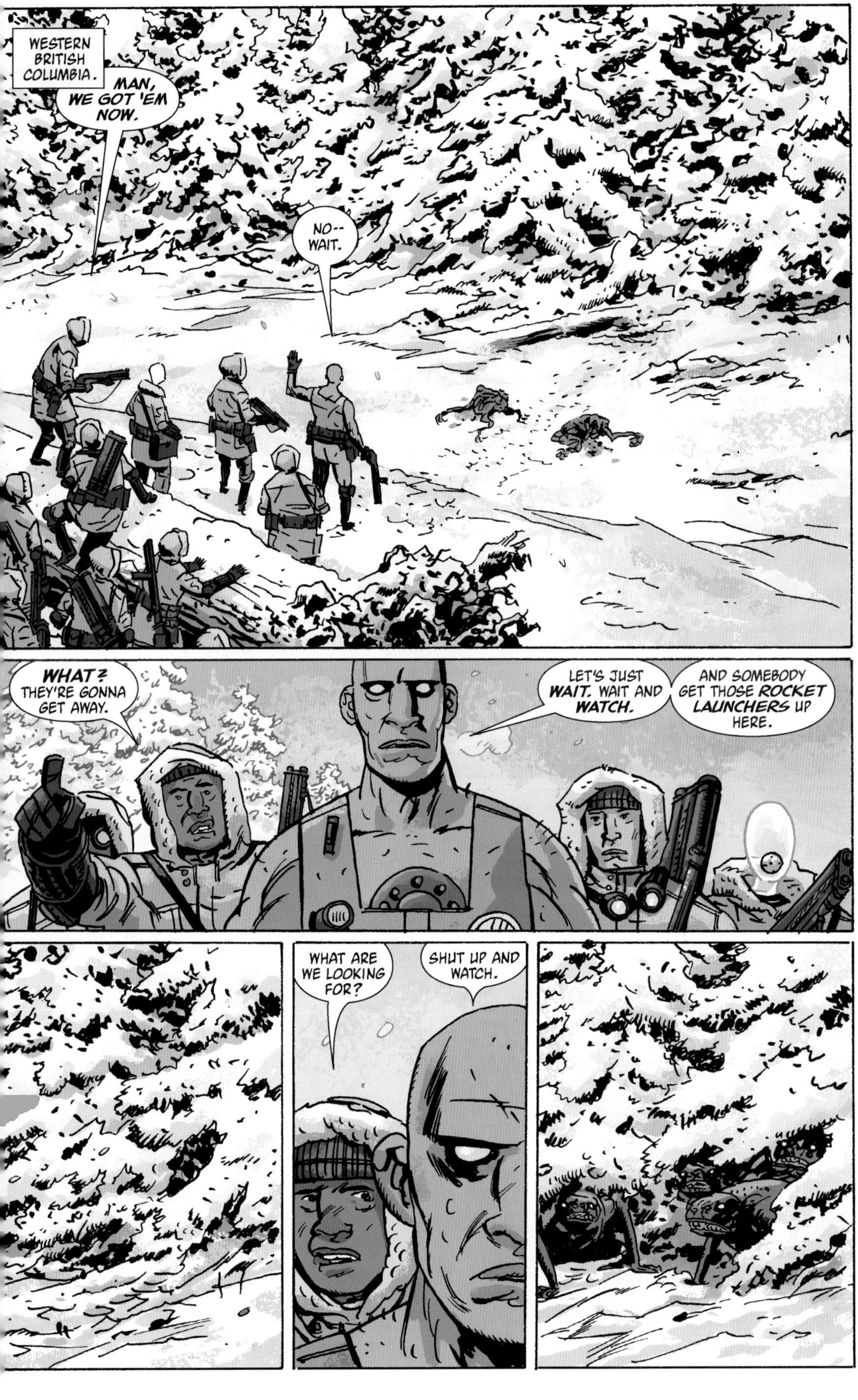
WESTERN BRITISH COLUMBIA.
MAN, WE GOT 'EM NOW.
NO-- WAIT.
WHAT? THEY'RE GONNA GET AWAY.
LET'S JUST WAIT. WAIT AND WATCH.
AND SOMEBODY GET THOSE ROCKET LAUNCHERS UP HERE.
WHAT ARE WE LOOKING FOR?
SHUT UP AND WATCH.

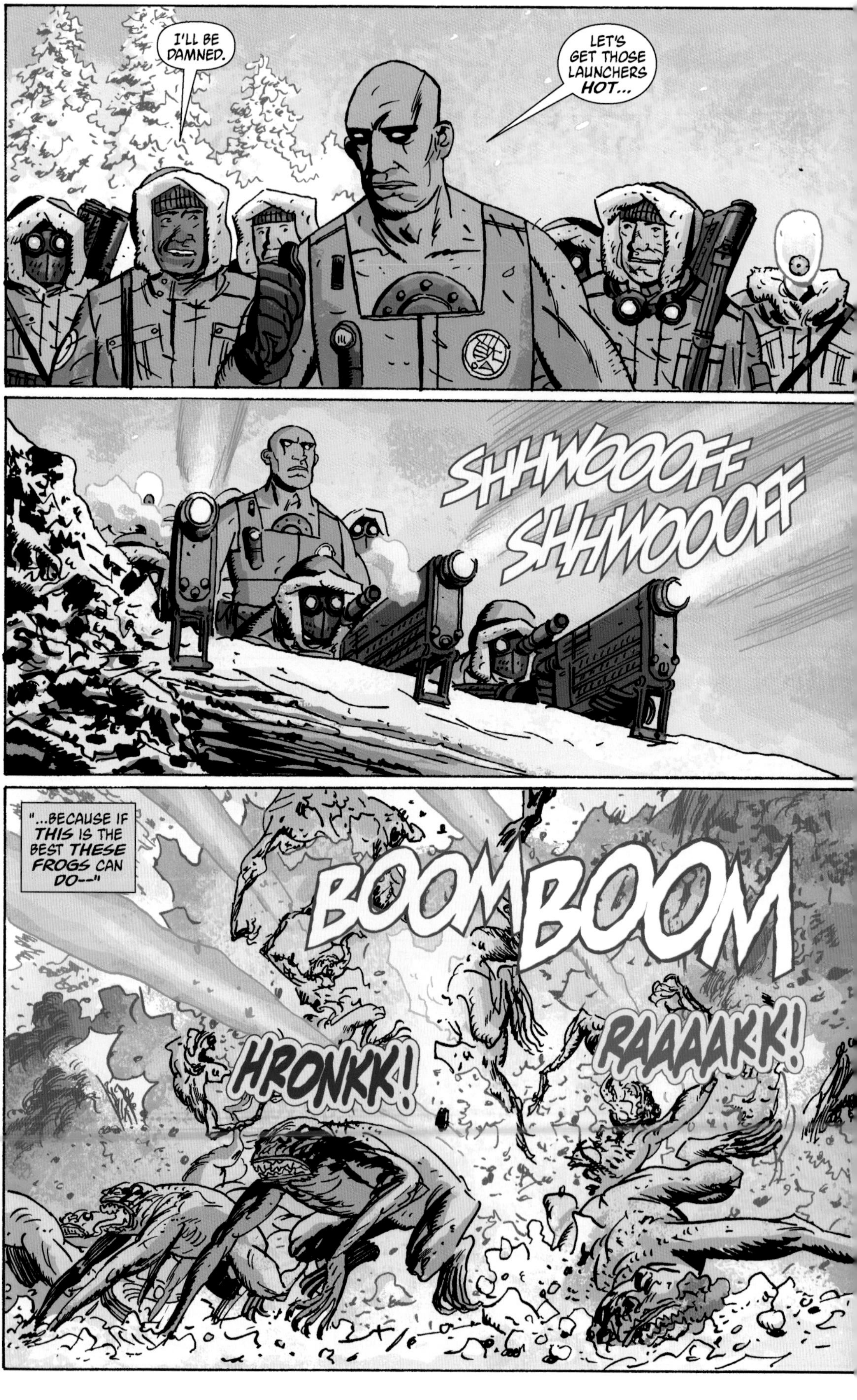
I'LL BE DAMNED.
LET'S GET THOSE LAUNCHERS HOT...
SHHWOOOFF
SHHWOOOFF
"...BECAUSE IF THIS IS THE BEST THESE FROGS CAN DO--"
BOOM
BOOM
HRONKK!
RAAAAKK!

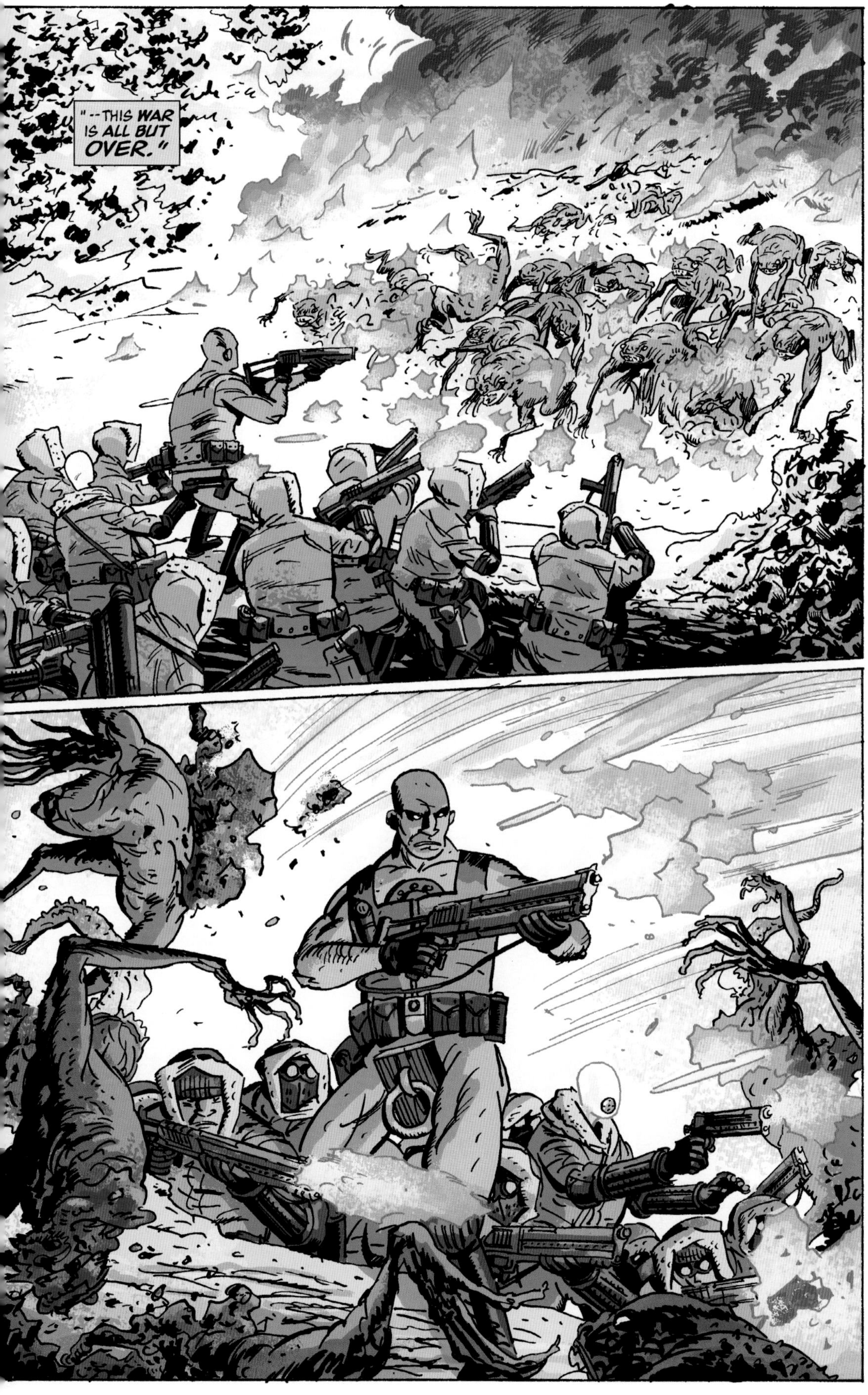
"--THIS WAR IS ALL BUT OVER."

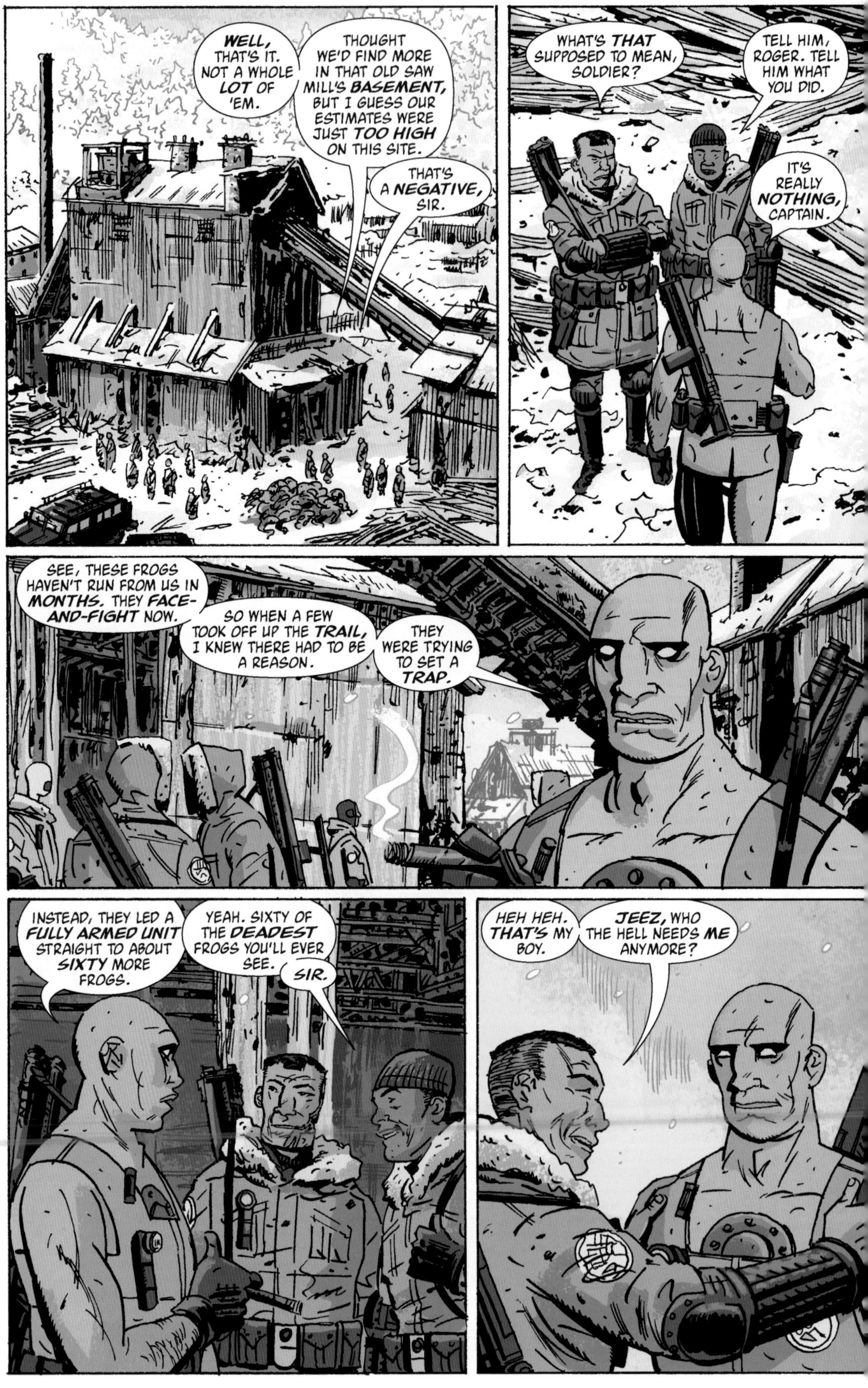
WELL, THAT'S IT. NOT A WHOLE LOT OF 'EM.
THOUGHT WE'D FIND MORE IN THAT OLD SAW MILL'S BASEMENT, BUT I GUESS OUR ESTIMATES WERE JUST TOO HIGH ON THIS SITE.
THAT'S A NEGATIVE, SIR.
WHAT'S THAT SUPPOSED TO MEAN, SOLDIER?
TELL HIM, ROGER. TELL HIM WHAT YOU DID.
IT'S REALLY NOTHING, CAPTAIN.
SEE, THESE FROGS HAVEN'T RUN FROM US IN MONTHS. THEY FACE-AND-FIGHT NOW.
SO WHEN A FEW TOOK OFF UP THE TRAIL, I KNEW THERE HAD TO BE A REASON.
THEY WERE TRYING TO SET A TRAP.
INSTEAD, THEY LED A FULLY ARMED UNIT STRAIGHT TO ABOUT SIXTY MORE FROGS.
YEAH. SIXTY OF THE DEADEST FROGS YOU'LL EVER SEE.
SIR.
HEH HEH. THAT'S MY BOY.
JEEZ, WHO THE HELL NEEDS ME ANYMORE?

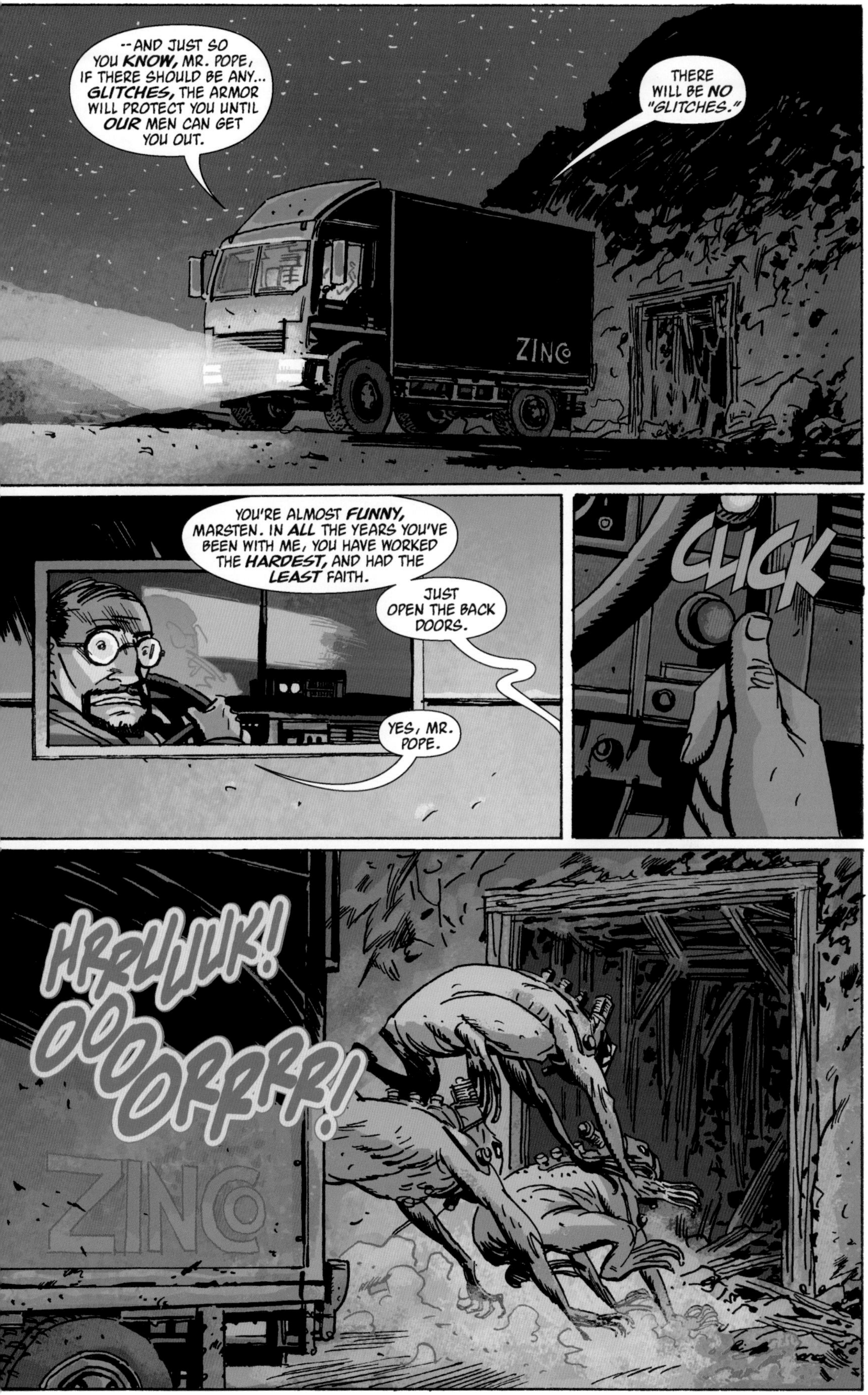
--AND JUST SO YOU KNOW, MR. POPE, IF THERE SHOULD BE ANY... GLITCHES, THE ARMOR WILL PROTECT YOU UNTIL OUR MEN CAN GET YOU OUT.
THERE WILL BE NO "GLITCHES."
ZINC
YOU'RE ALMOST FUNNY, MARSTEN. IN ALL THE YEARS YOU'VE BEEN WITH ME, YOU HAVE WORKED THE HARDEST, AND HAD THE LEAST FAITH.
JUST OPEN THE BACK DOORS.
YES, MR. POPE.
CLICK
HRRUUUK!
OOOOORRRR!
ZINC

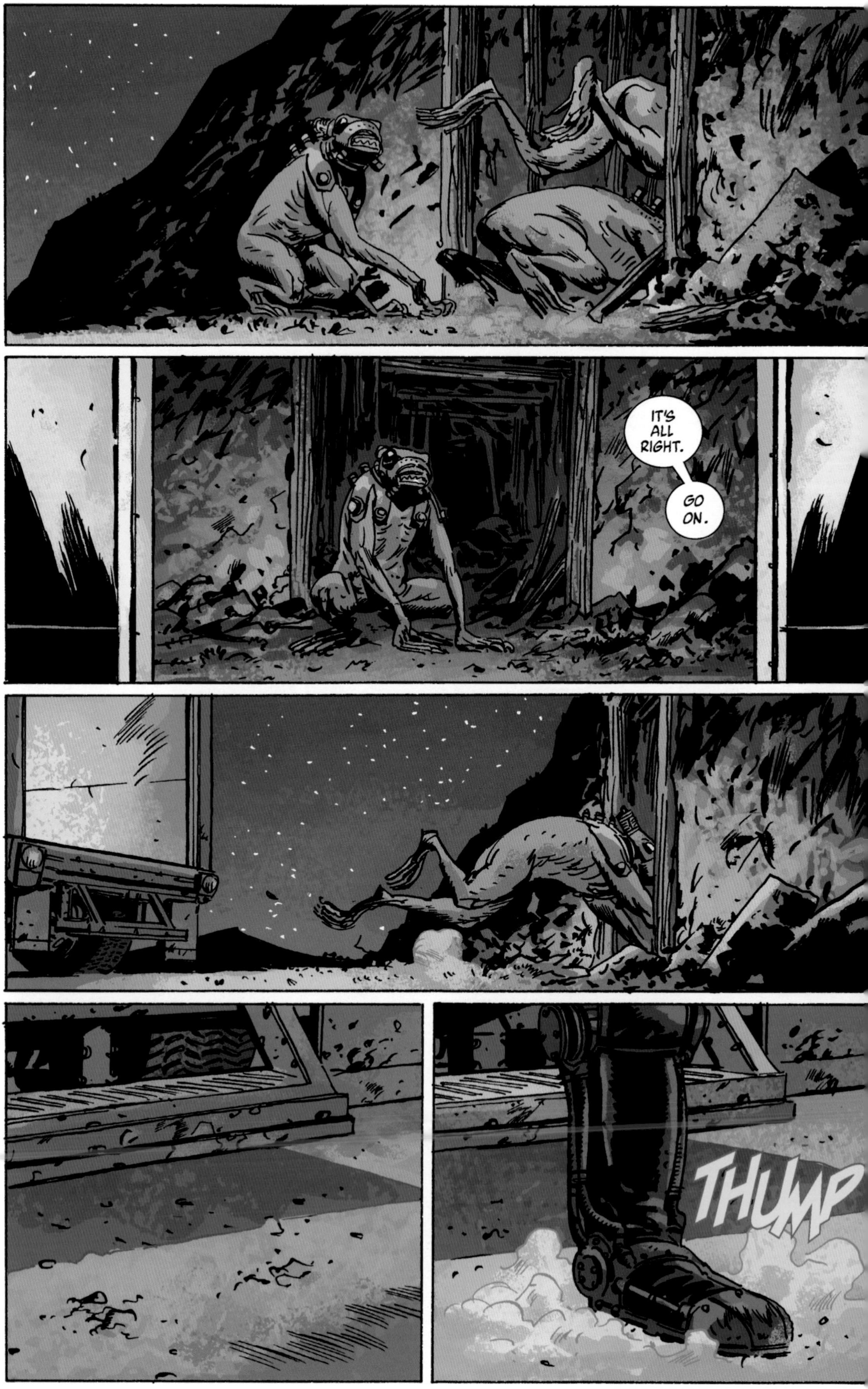
IT'S ALL RIGHT.
GO ON.
THUMP

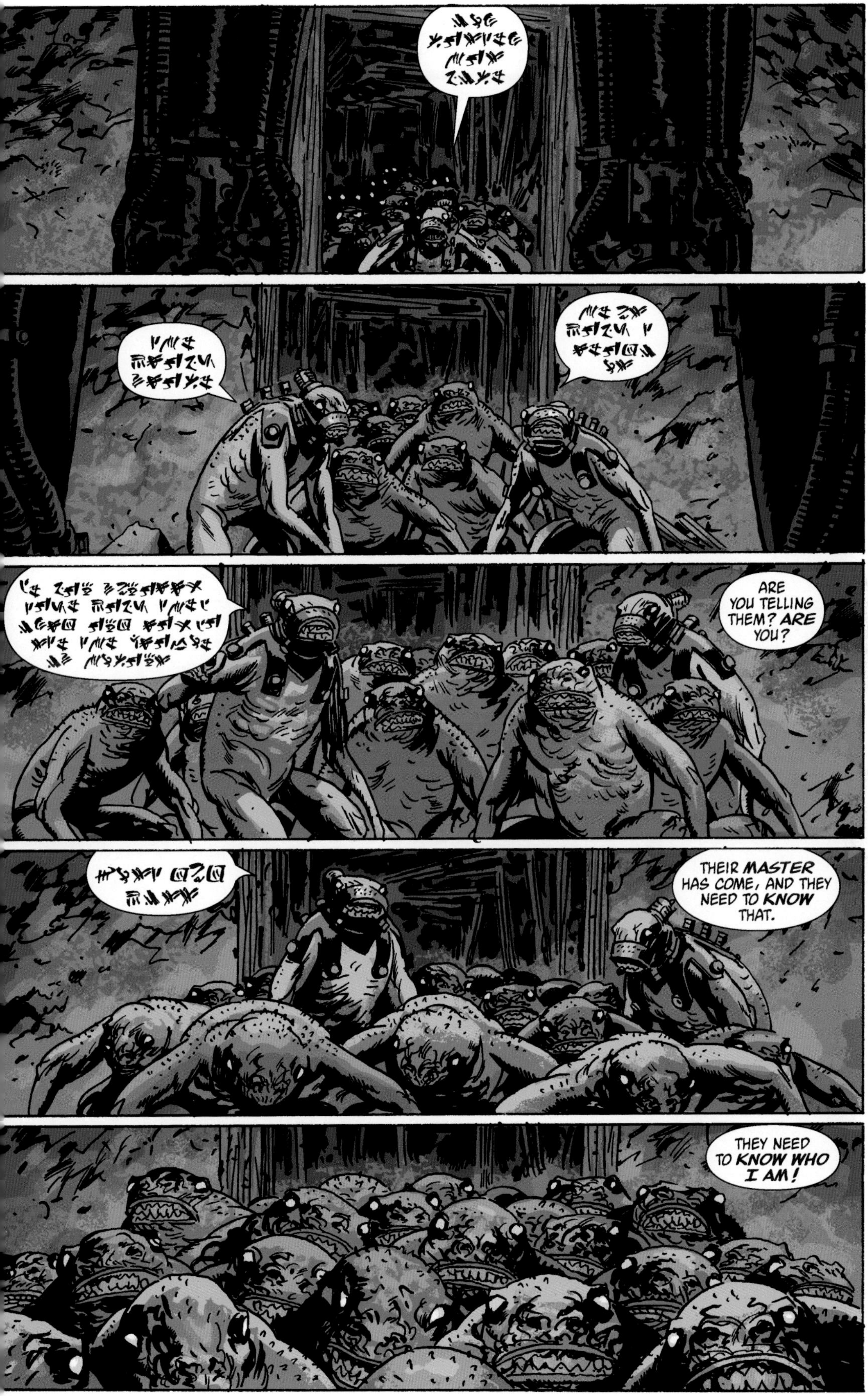
ARE YOU TELLING THEM? ARE YOU?
THEIR MASTER HAS COME, AND THEY NEED TO KNOW THAT.
THEY NEED TO KNOW WHO I AM!

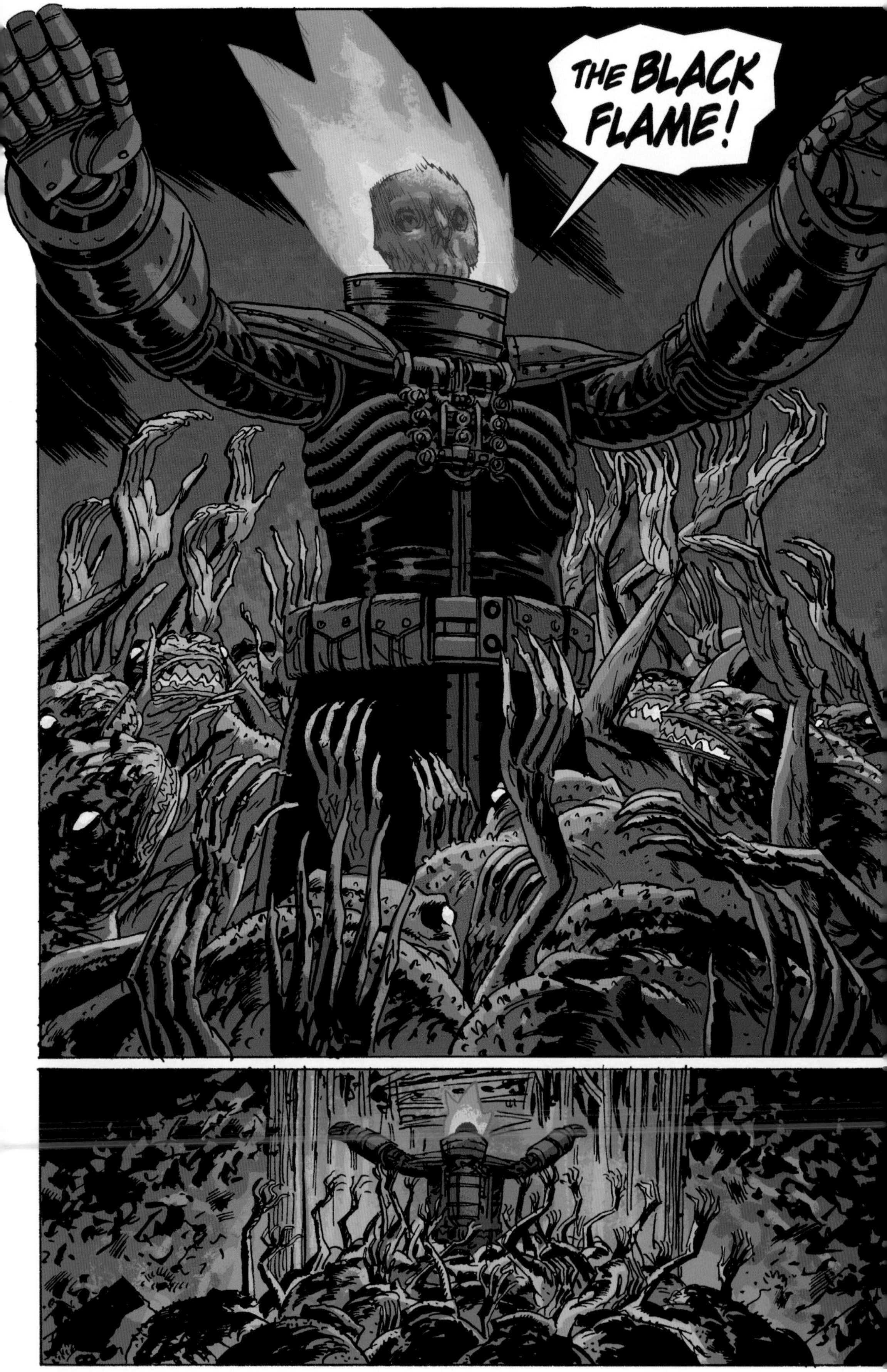
THE BLACK FLAME!

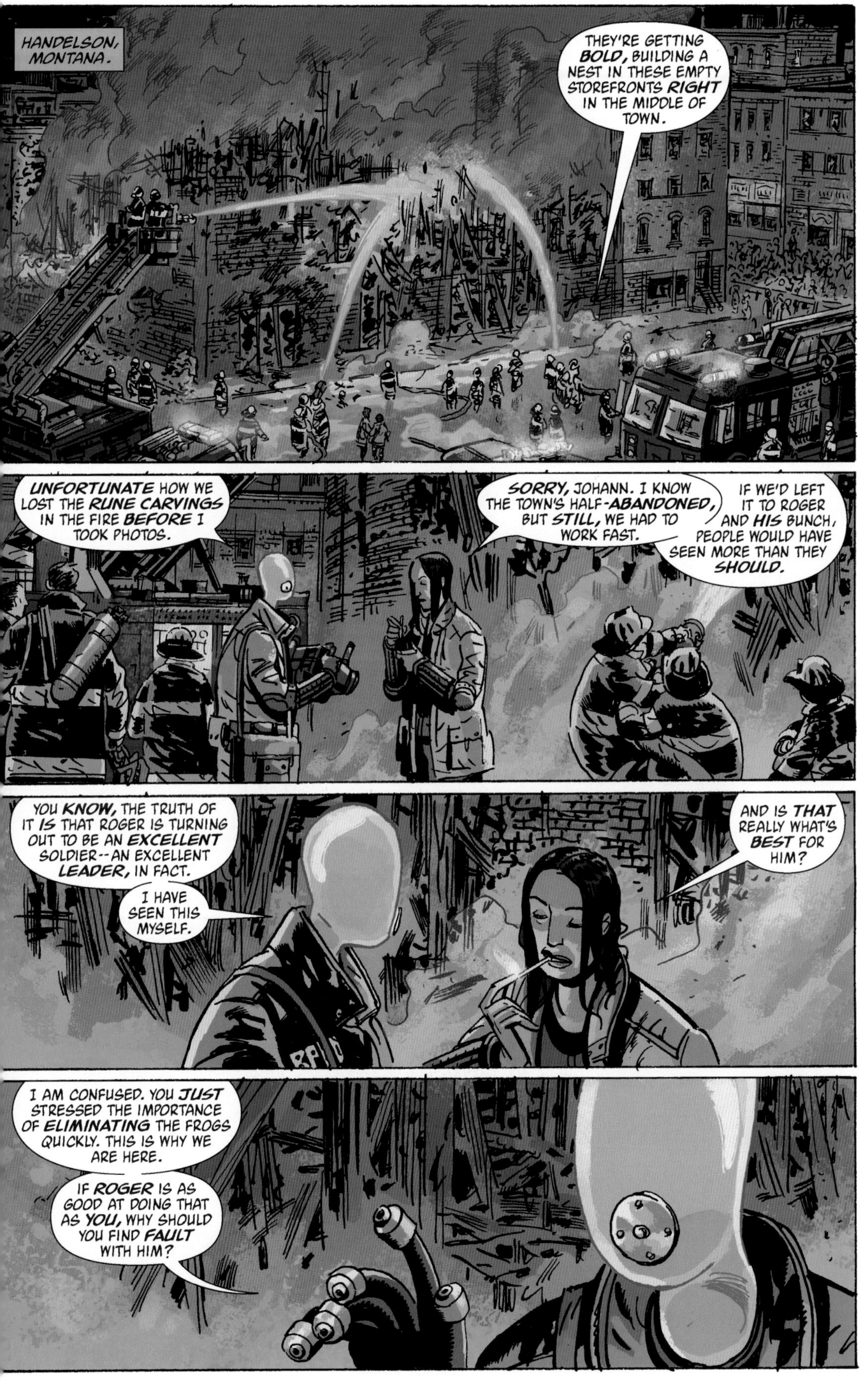
HANDELSON, MONTANA.
THEY'RE GETTING BOLD, BUILDING A NEST IN THESE EMPTY STOREFRONTS RIGHT IN THE MIDDLE OF TOWN.
UNFORTUNATE HOW WE LOST THE RUNE CARVINGS IN THE FIRE BEFORE I TOOK PHOTOS.
SORRY, JOHANN. I KNOW THE TOWN'S HALF-ABANDONED, BUT STILL, WE HAD TO WORK FAST.
IF WE'D LEFT IT TO ROGER AND HIS BUNCH, PEOPLE WOULD HAVE SEEN MORE THAN THEY SHOULD.
YOU KNOW, THE TRUTH OF IT IS THAT ROGER IS TURNING OUT TO BE AN EXCELLENT SOLDIER--AN EXCELLENT LEADER, IN FACT.
I HAVE SEEN THIS MYSELF.
AND IS THAT REALLY WHAT'S BEST FOR HIM?
I AM CONFUSED. YOU JUST STRESSED THE IMPORTANCE OF ELIMINATING THE FROGS QUICKLY. THIS IS WHY WE ARE HERE.
IF ROGER IS AS GOOD AT DOING THAT AS YOU, WHY SHOULD YOU FIND FAULT WITH HIM?

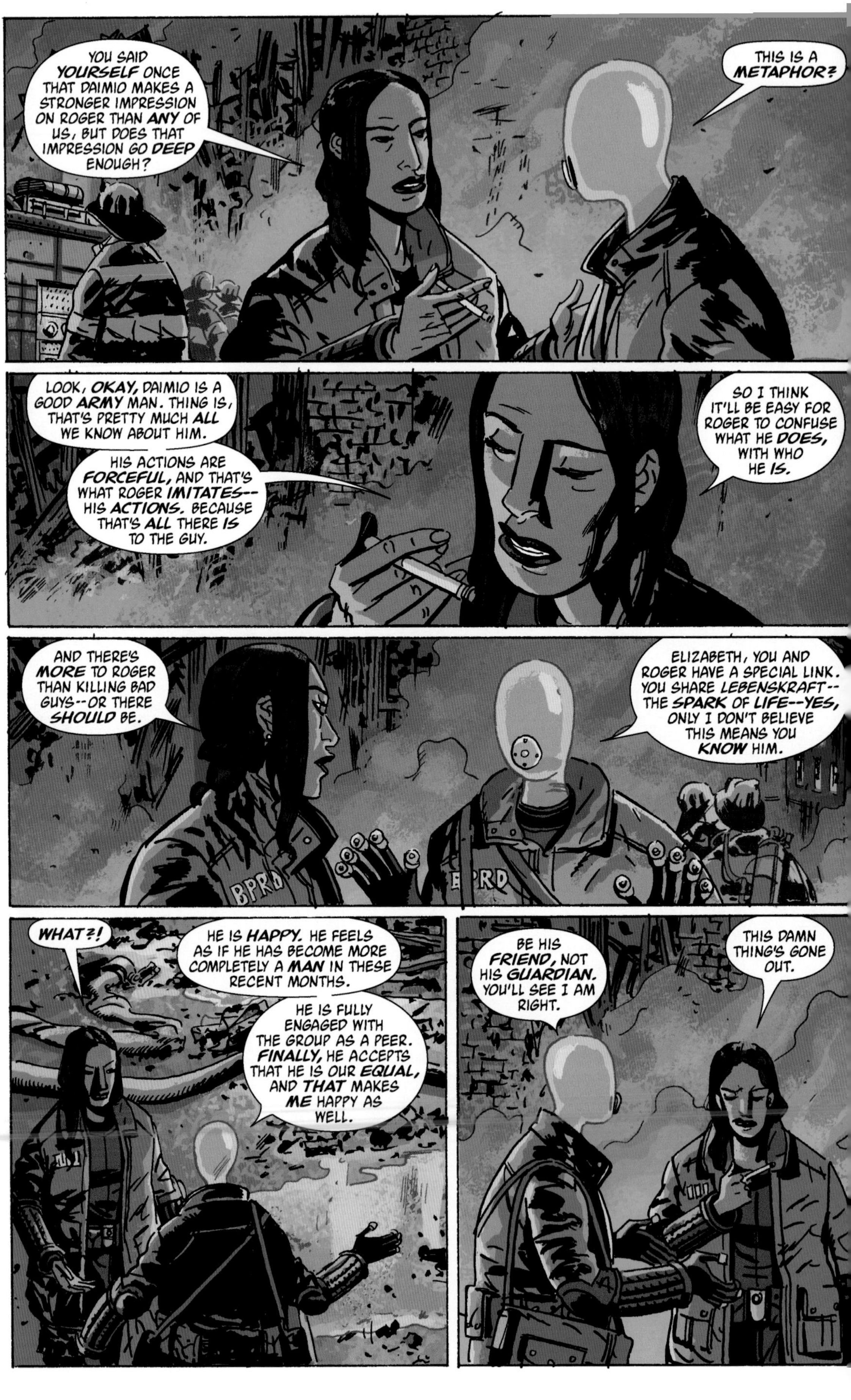
YOU SAID YOURSELF ONCE THAT DAIMIO MAKES A STRONGER IMPRESSION ON ROGER THAN ANY OF US, BUT DOES THAT IMPRESSION GO DEEP ENOUGH?
THIS IS A METAPHOR?
LOOK, OKAY, DAIMIO IS A GOOD ARMY MAN. THING IS, THAT'S PRETTY MUCH ALL WE KNOW ABOUT HIM.
HIS ACTIONS ARE FORCEFUL, AND THAT'S WHAT ROGER IMITATES-- HIS ACTIONS. BECAUSE THAT'S ALL THERE IS TO THE GUY.
SO I THINK IT'LL BE EASY FOR ROGER TO CONFUSE WHAT HE DOES, WITH WHO HE IS.
AND THERE'S MORE TO ROGER THAN KILLING BAD GUYS--OR THERE SHOULD BE.
ELIZABETH, YOU AND ROGER HAVE A SPECIAL LINK. YOU SHARE LEBENSKRAFT-- THE SPARK OF LIFE--YES, ONLY I DON'T BELIEVE THIS MEANS YOU KNOW HIM.
BPRD
BPRD
WHAT?!
HE IS HAPPY. HE FEELS AS IF HE HAS BECOME MORE COMPLETELY A MAN IN THESE RECENT MONTHS.
HE IS FULLY ENGAGED WITH THE GROUP AS A PEER. FINALLY, HE ACCEPTS THAT HE IS OUR EQUAL, AND THAT MAKES ME HAPPY AS WELL.
BE HIS FRIEND, NOT HIS GUARDIAN. YOU'LL SEE I AM RIGHT.
THIS DAMN THING'S GONE OUT.

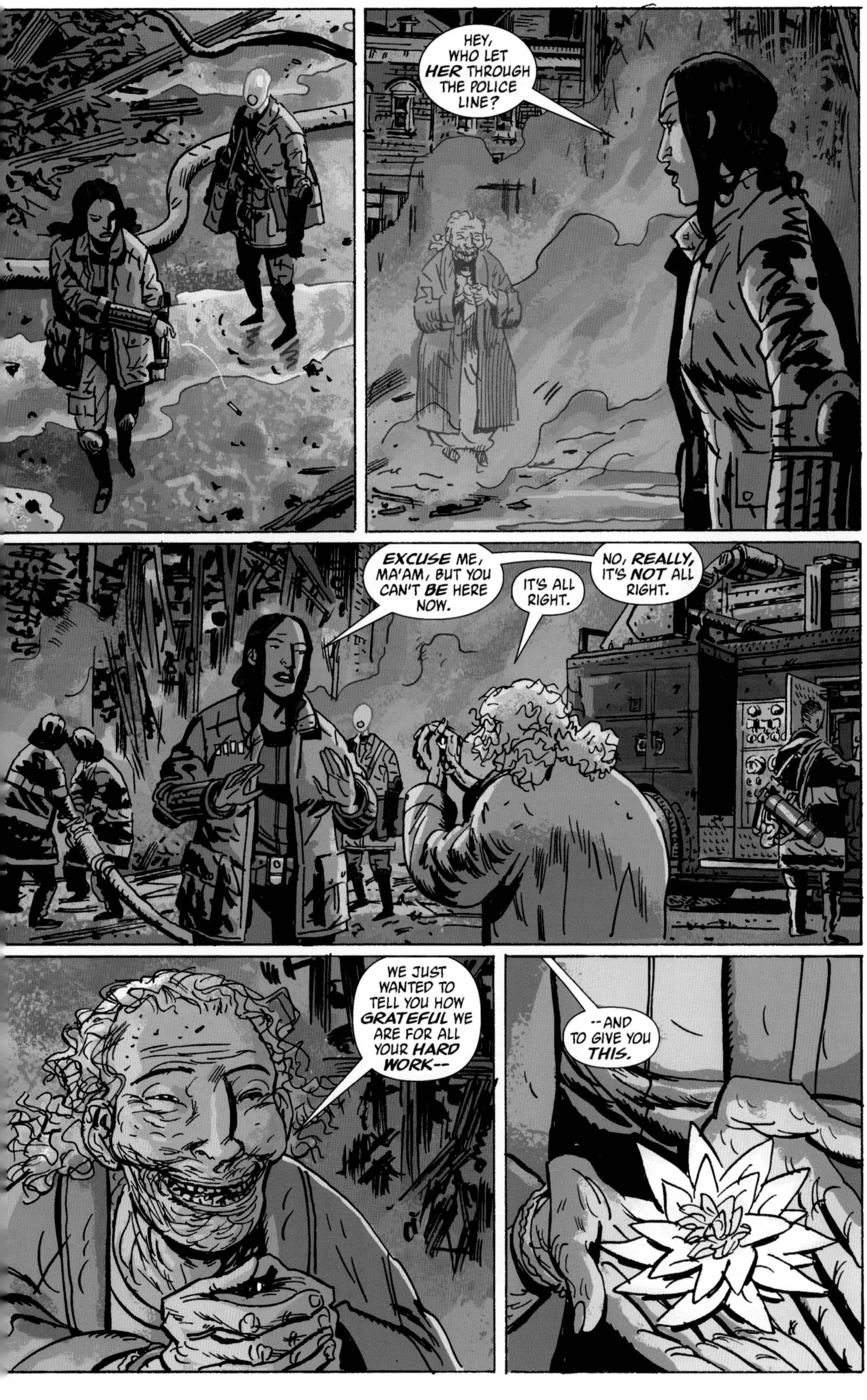
HEY, WHO LET HER THROUGH THE POLICE LINE?
EXCUSE ME, MA'AM, BUT YOU CAN'T BE HERE NOW.
IT'S ALL RIGHT.
NO, REALLY, IT'S NOT ALL RIGHT.
WE JUST WANTED TO TELL YOU HOW GRATEFUL WE ARE FOR ALL YOUR HARD WORK--
--AND TO GIVE YOU THIS.

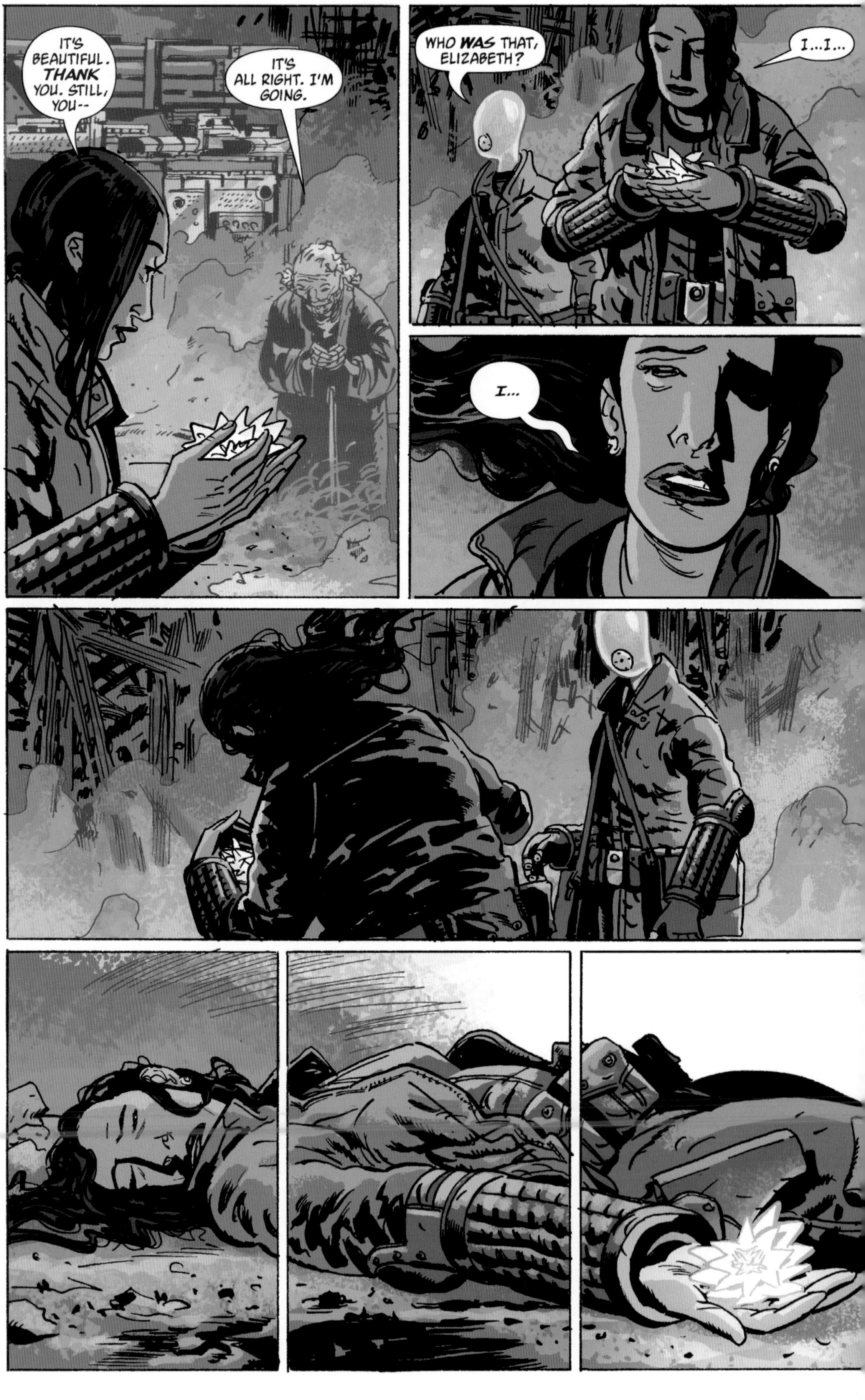
IT'S BEAUTIFUL. THANK YOU. STILL, YOU--
IT'S ALL RIGHT. I'M GOING.
WHO WAS THAT, ELIZABETH?
I...I...
I...

# CHAPTER THREE

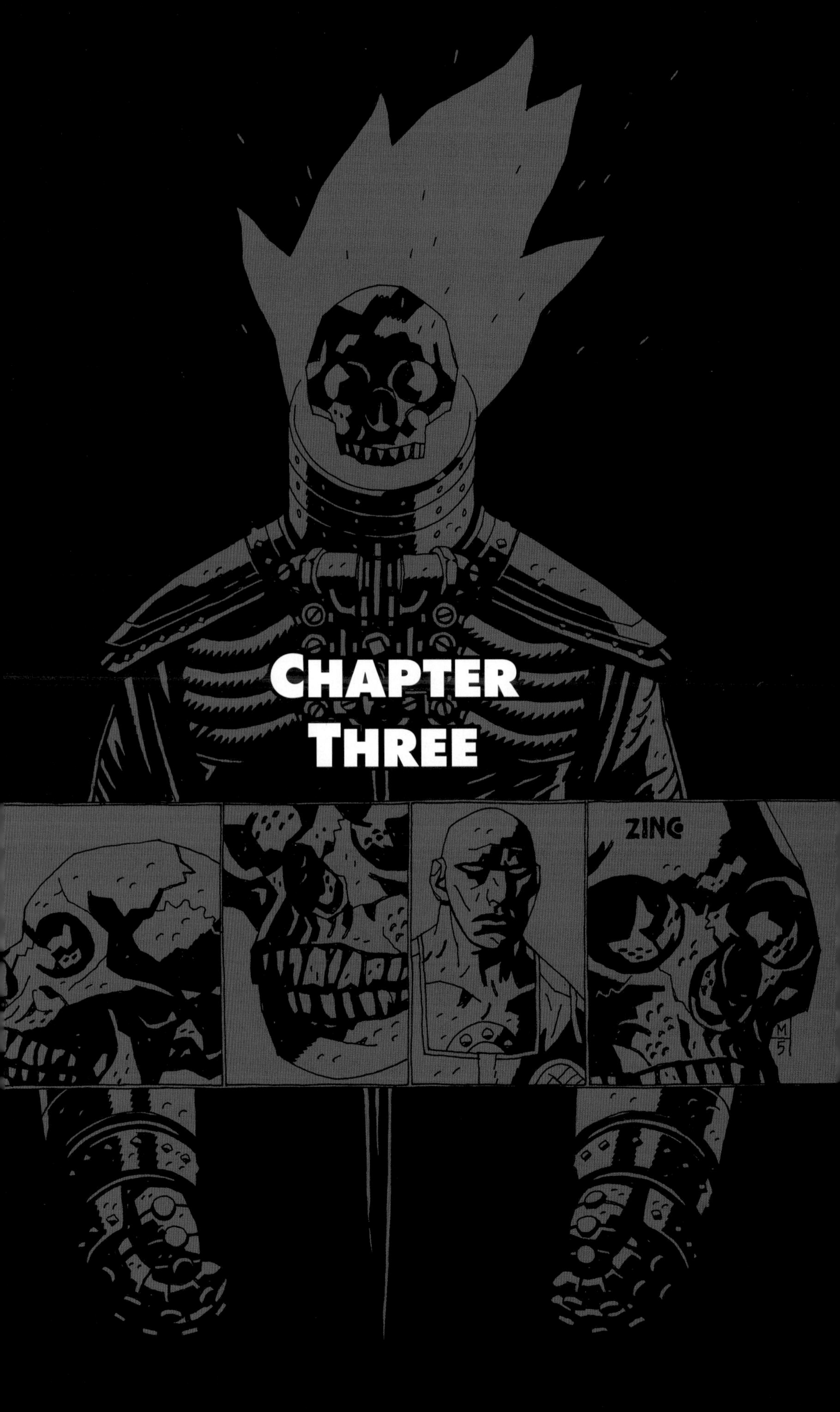
ZINC

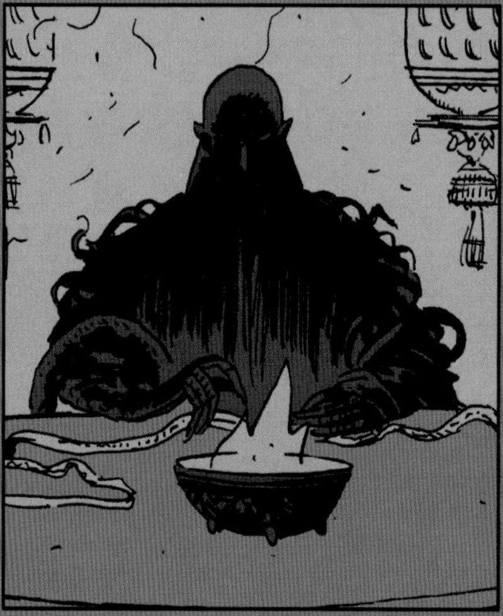

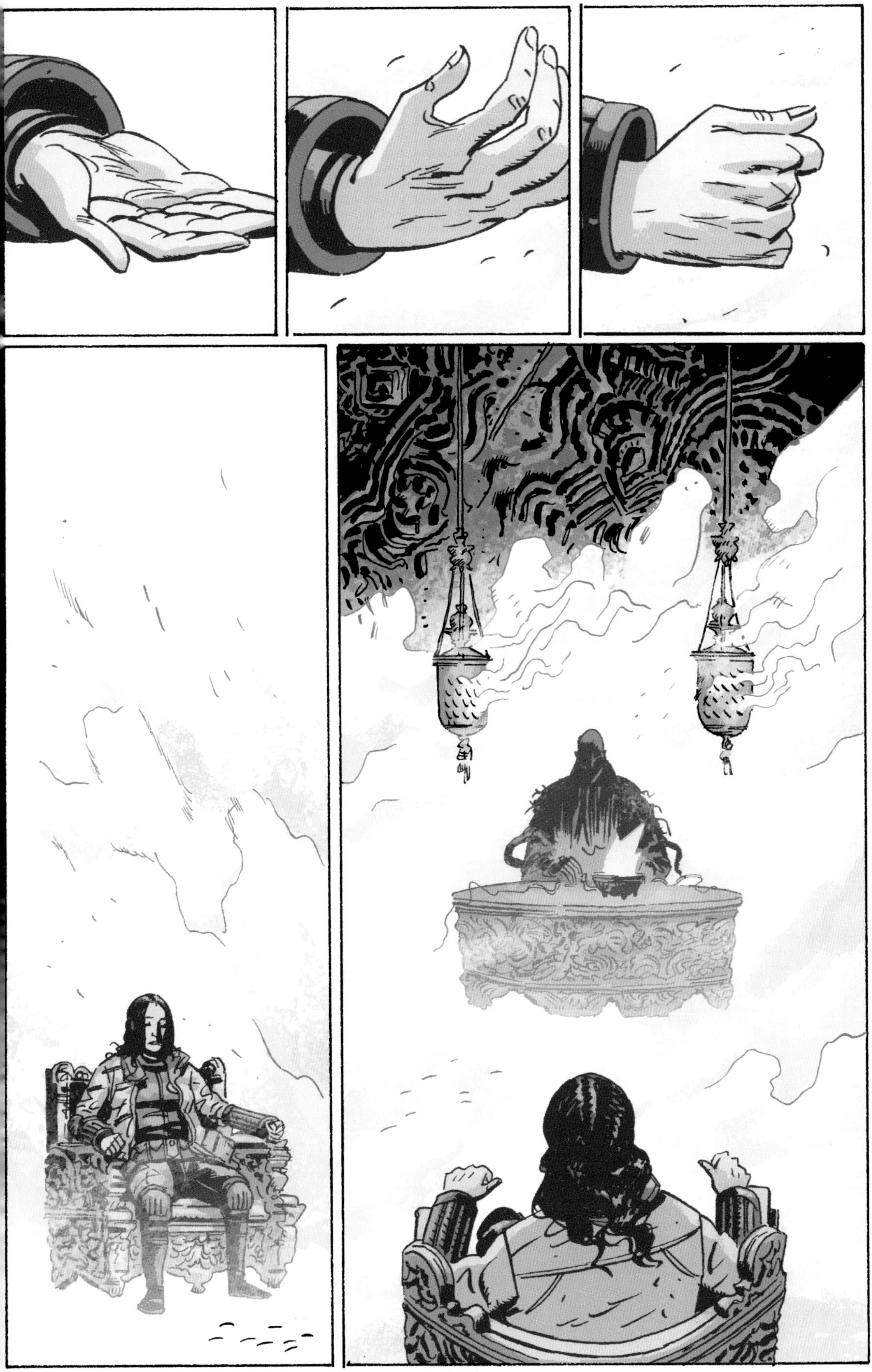

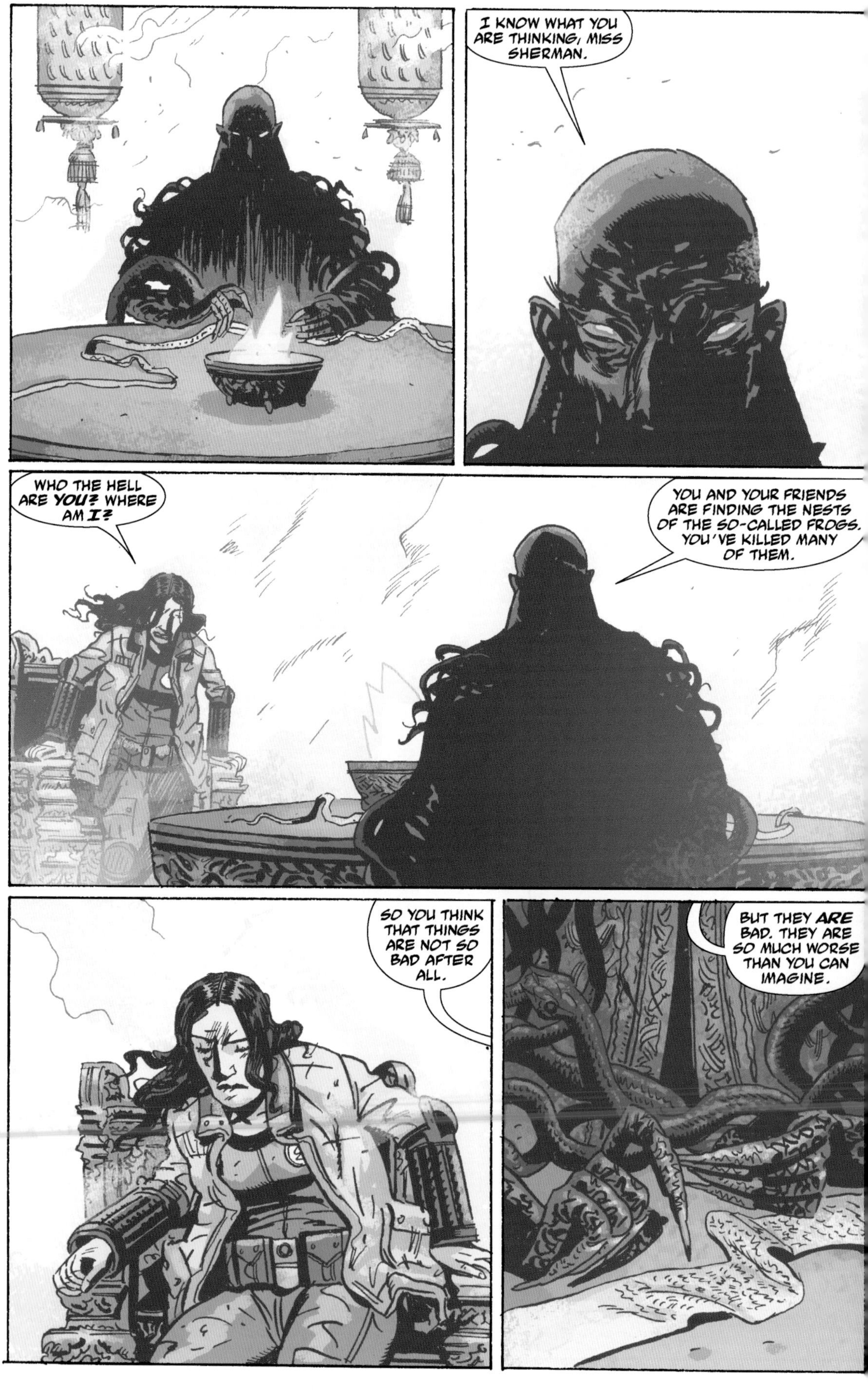
I KNOW WHAT YOU ARE THINKING, MISS SHERMAN.
WHO THE HELL ARE *YOU?* WHERE AM *I?*
YOU AND YOUR FRIENDS ARE FINDING THE NESTS OF THE SO-CALLED FROGS. YOU'VE KILLED MANY OF THEM.
SO YOU THINK THAT THINGS ARE NOT SO BAD AFTER ALL.
BUT THEY *ARE* BAD. THEY ARE SO MUCH WORSE THAN YOU CAN IMAGINE.

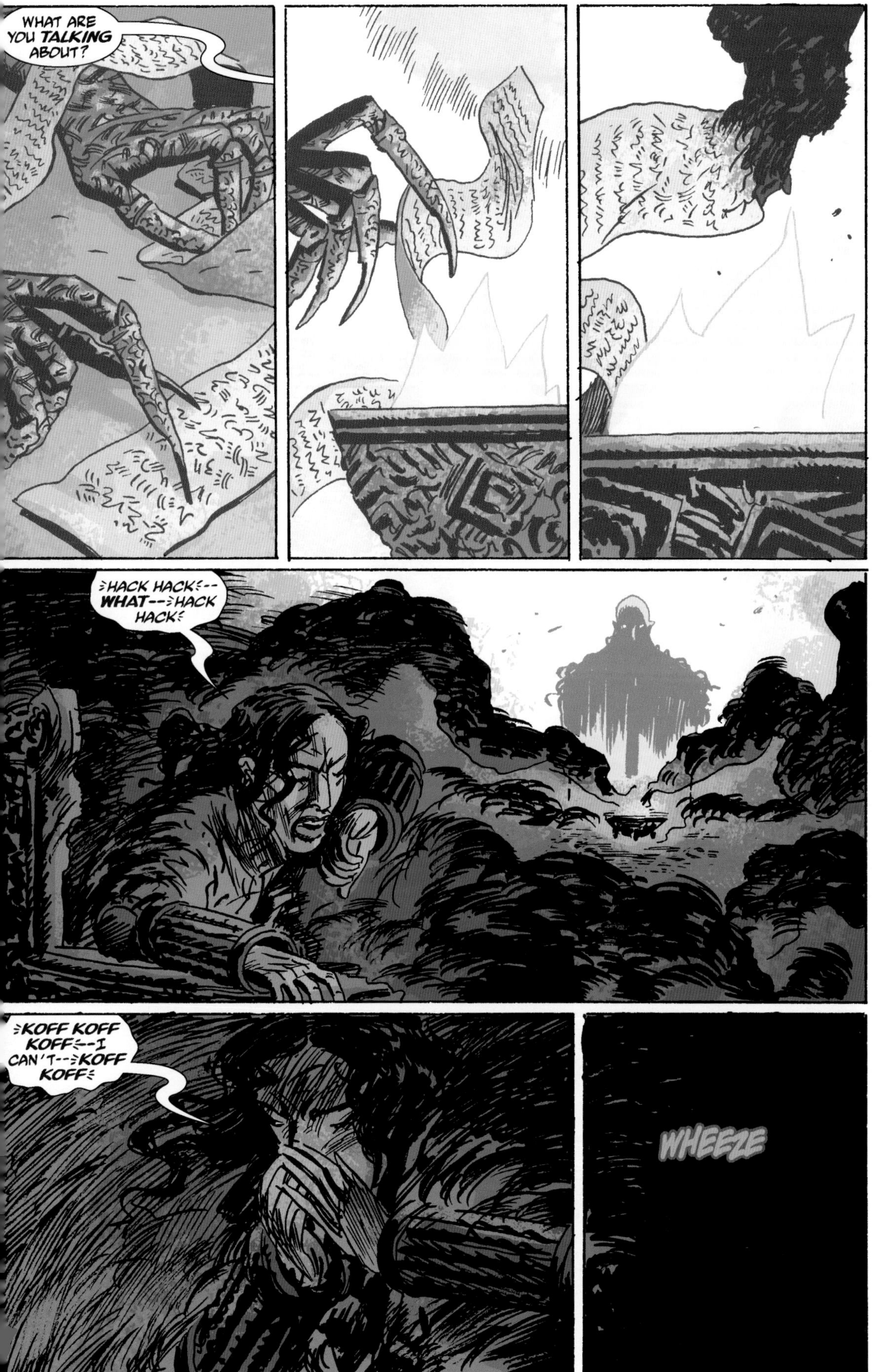
WHAT ARE YOU TALKING ABOUT?
HACK HACK-- WHAT-- HACK HACK
KOFF KOFF KOFF--I CAN'T-- KOFF KOFF
WHEEZE

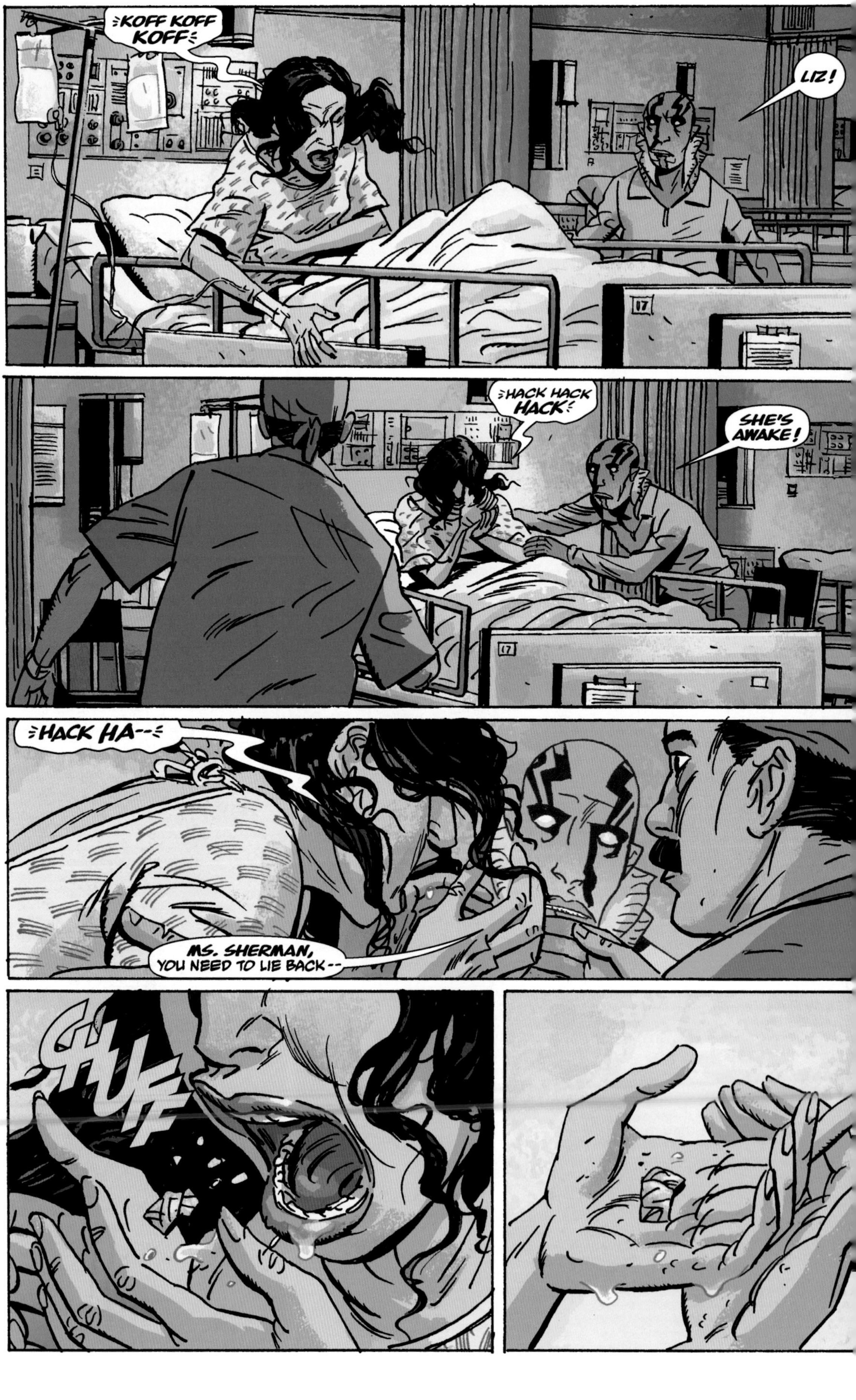
KOFF KOFF KOFF
LIZ!
HACK HACK HACK
SHE'S AWAKE!
HACK HA--
MS. SHERMAN, YOU NEED TO LIE BACK--
CHUFF

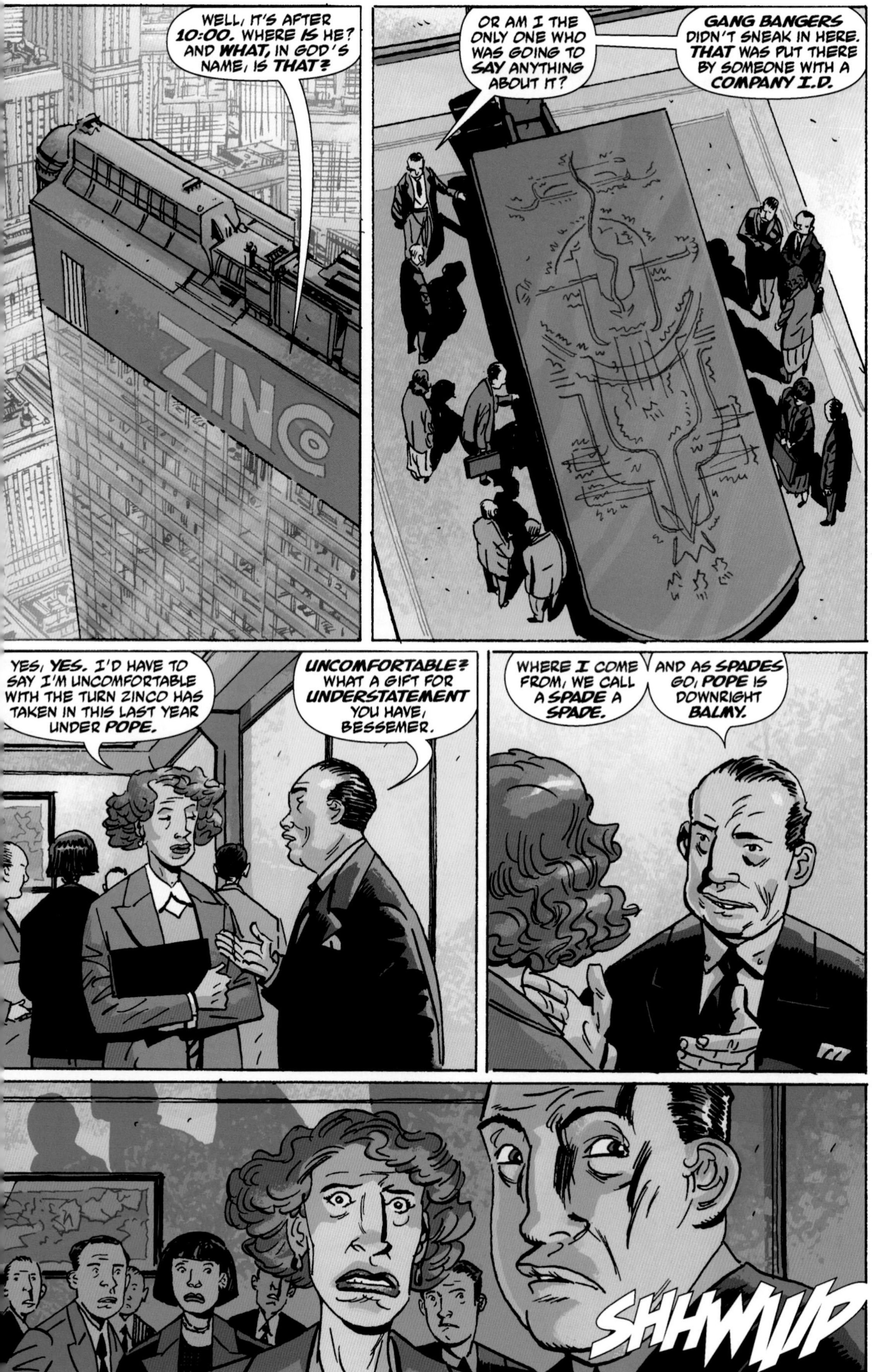
WELL, IT'S AFTER 10:00. WHERE IS HE? AND WHAT, IN GOD'S NAME, IS THAT?
ZINCO
OR AM I THE ONLY ONE WHO WAS GOING TO SAY ANYTHING ABOUT IT?
GANG BANGERS DIDN'T SNEAK IN HERE. THAT WAS PUT THERE BY SOMEONE WITH A COMPANY I.D.
YES, YES. I'D HAVE TO SAY I'M UNCOMFORTABLE WITH THE TURN ZINCO HAS TAKEN IN THIS LAST YEAR UNDER POPE.
UNCOMFORTABLE? WHAT A GIFT FOR UNDERSTATEMENT YOU HAVE, BESSEMER.
WHERE I COME FROM, WE CALL A SPADE A SPADE.
AND AS SPADES GO, POPE IS DOWNRIGHT BALMY.
SHHWUP

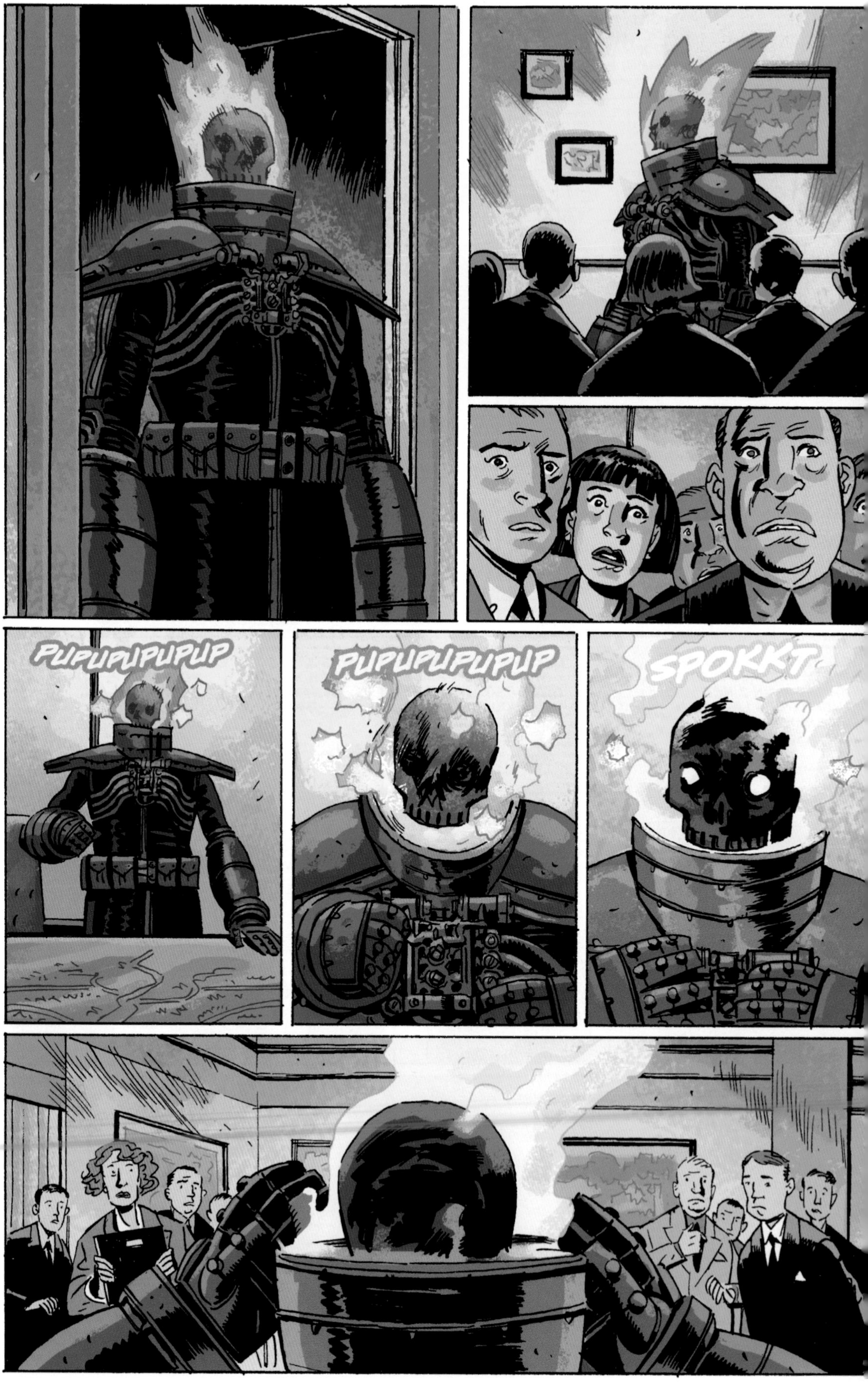
PUPUPUPUPUP
PUPUPUPUPUP
SPOKKT

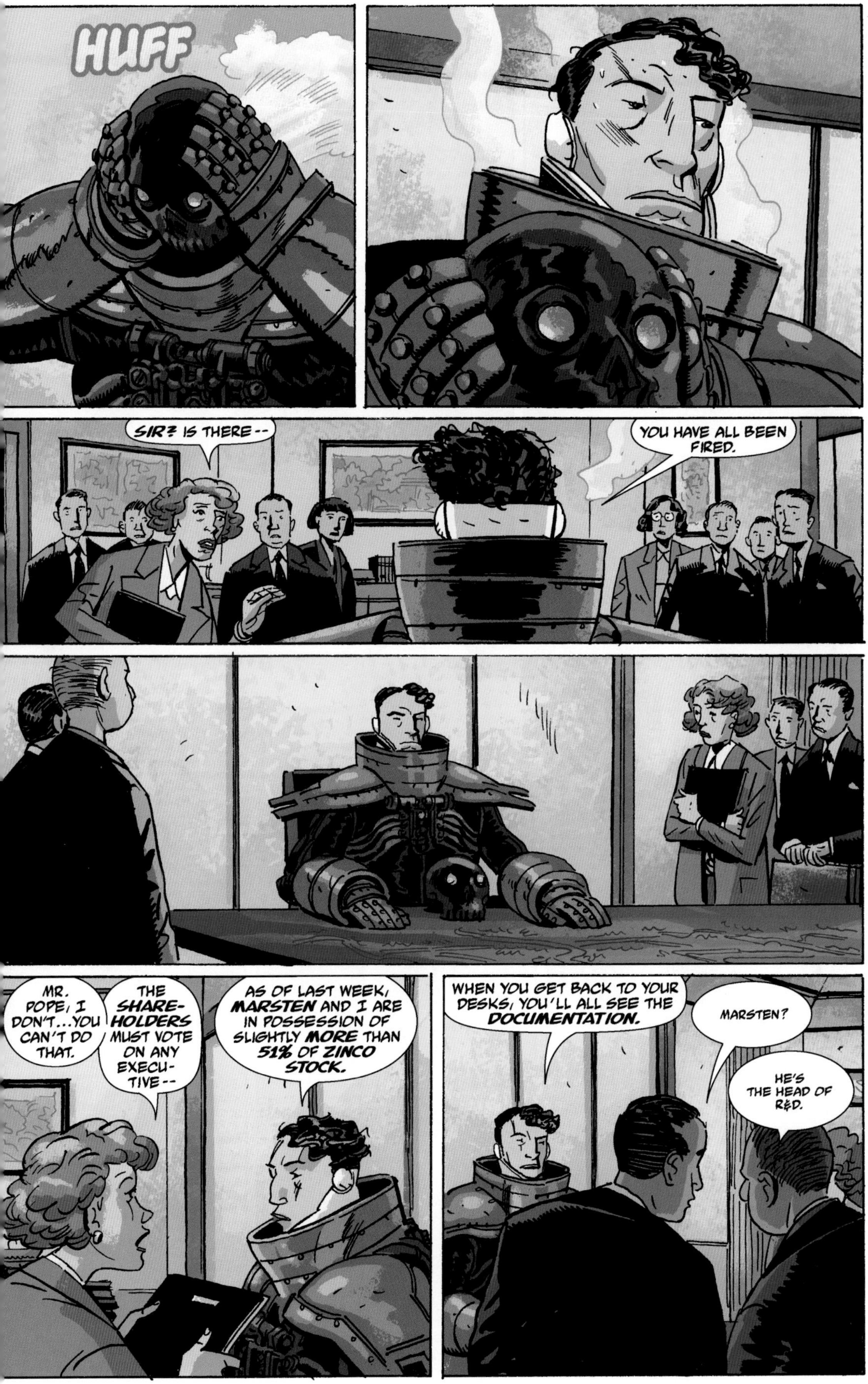
HUFF
SIR? IS THERE --
YOU HAVE ALL BEEN FIRED.
MR. POPE, I DON'T...YOU CAN'T DO THAT.
THE SHAREHOLDERS MUST VOTE ON ANY EXECUTIVE --
AS OF LAST WEEK, MARSTEN AND I ARE IN POSSESSION OF SLIGHTLY MORE THAN 51% OF ZINCO STOCK.
WHEN YOU GET BACK TO YOUR DESKS, YOU'LL ALL SEE THE DOCUMENTATION.
MARSTEN?
HE'S THE HEAD OF R&D.

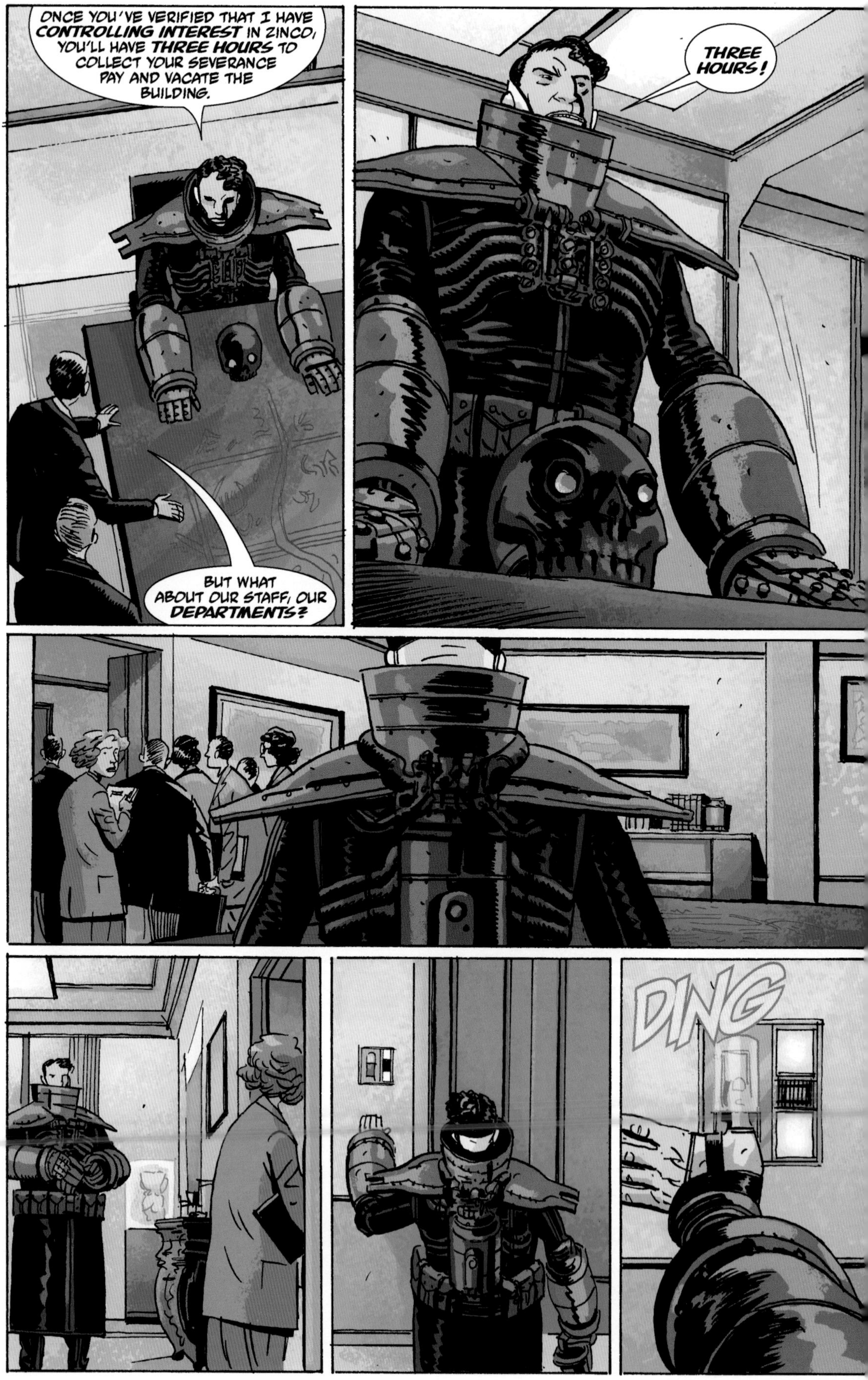
ONCE YOU'VE VERIFIED THAT I HAVE CONTROLLING INTEREST IN ZINCO, YOU'LL HAVE THREE HOURS TO COLLECT YOUR SEVERANCE PAY AND VACATE THE BUILDING.
BUT WHAT ABOUT OUR STAFF, OUR DEPARTMENTS?
THREE HOURS!
DING

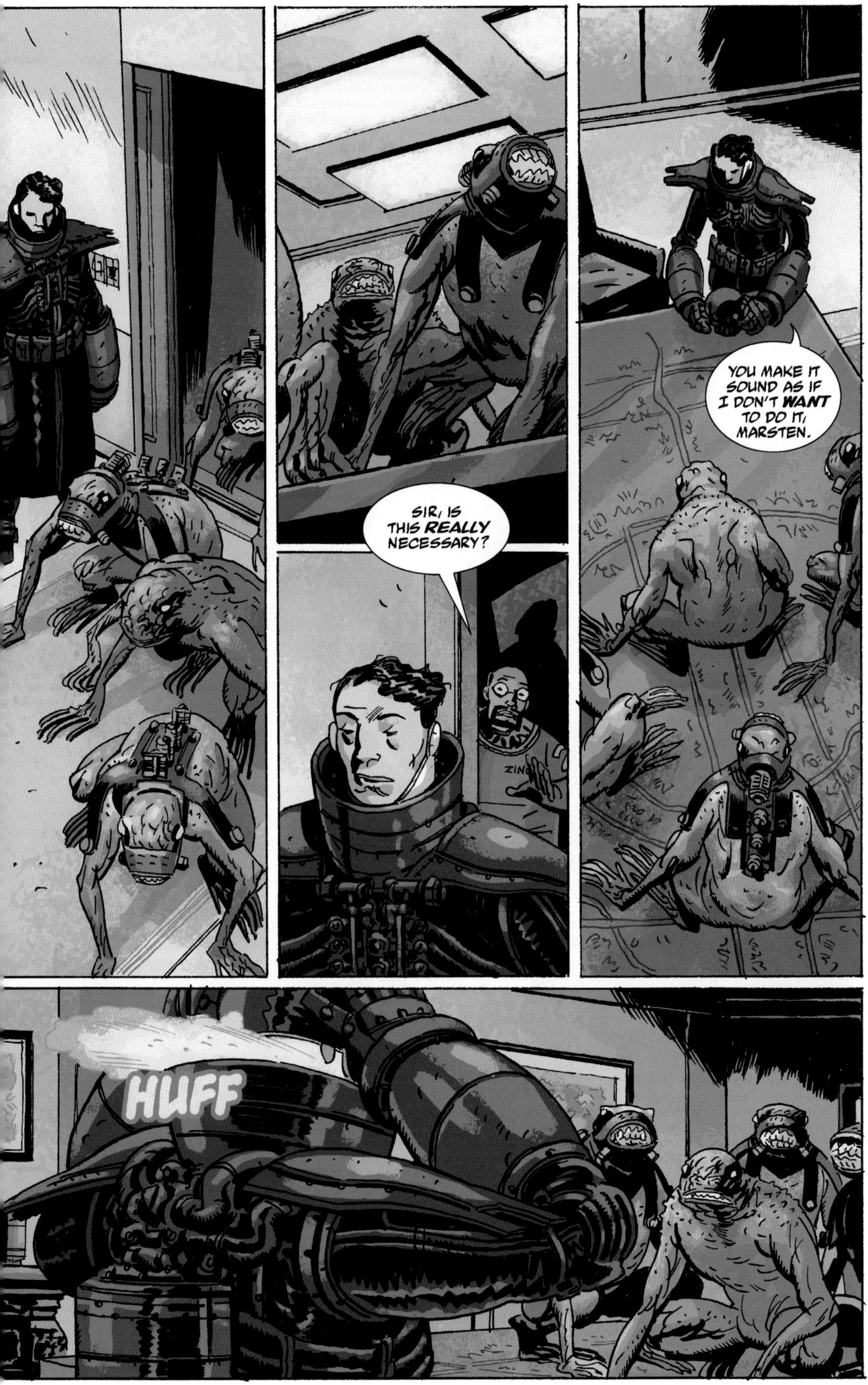
SIR, IS THIS REALLY NECESSARY?
ZINC
YOU MAKE IT SOUND AS IF I DON'T WANT TO DO IT, MARSTEN.
HUFF

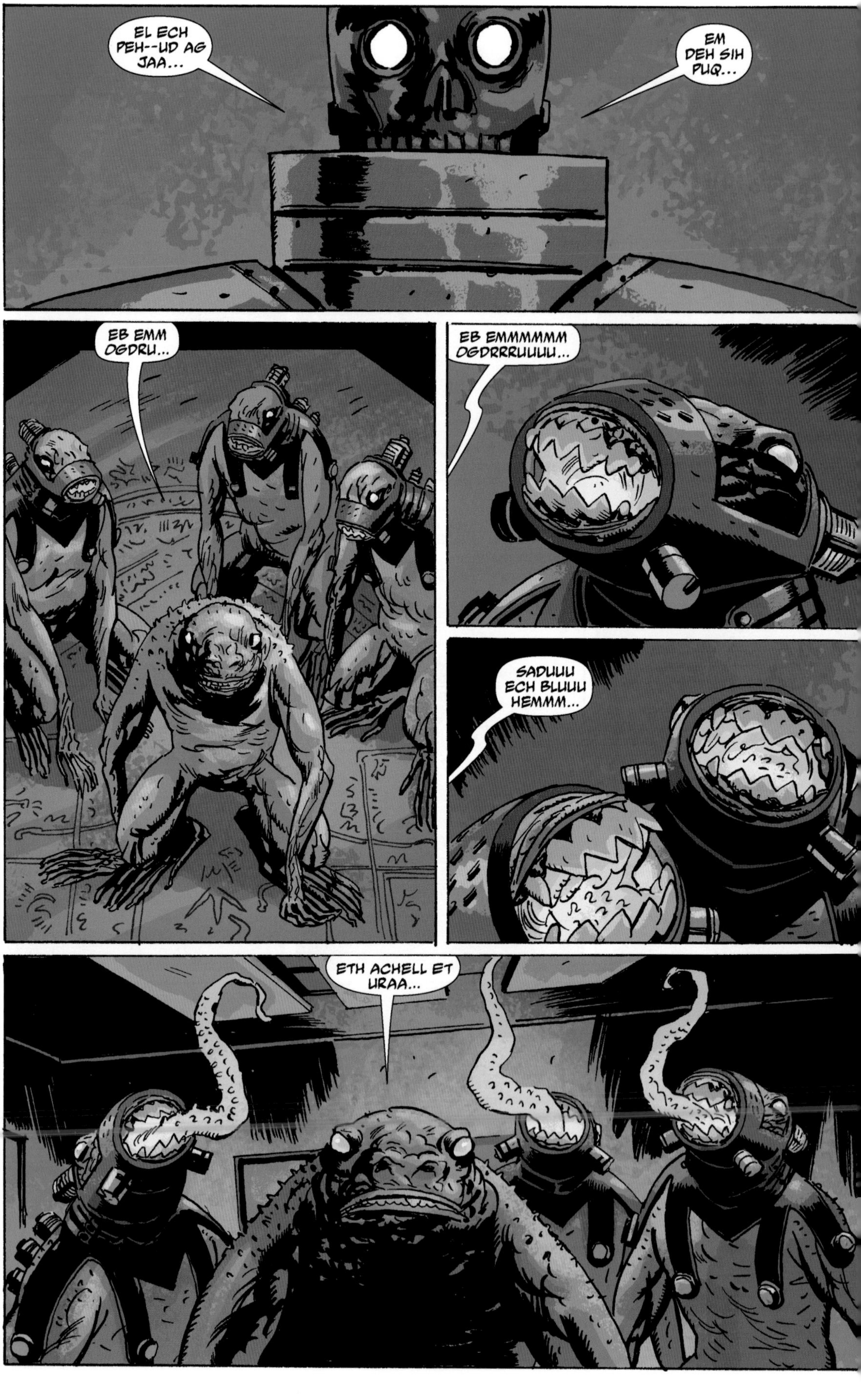

EL ECH PEH--UD AG JAA...
EM DEH SIH PUQ...
EB EMM OGDRU...
EB EMMMMMM OGDRRRUUUU...
SADUUU ECH BLUUU HEMMM...
ETH ACHELL ET URAA...

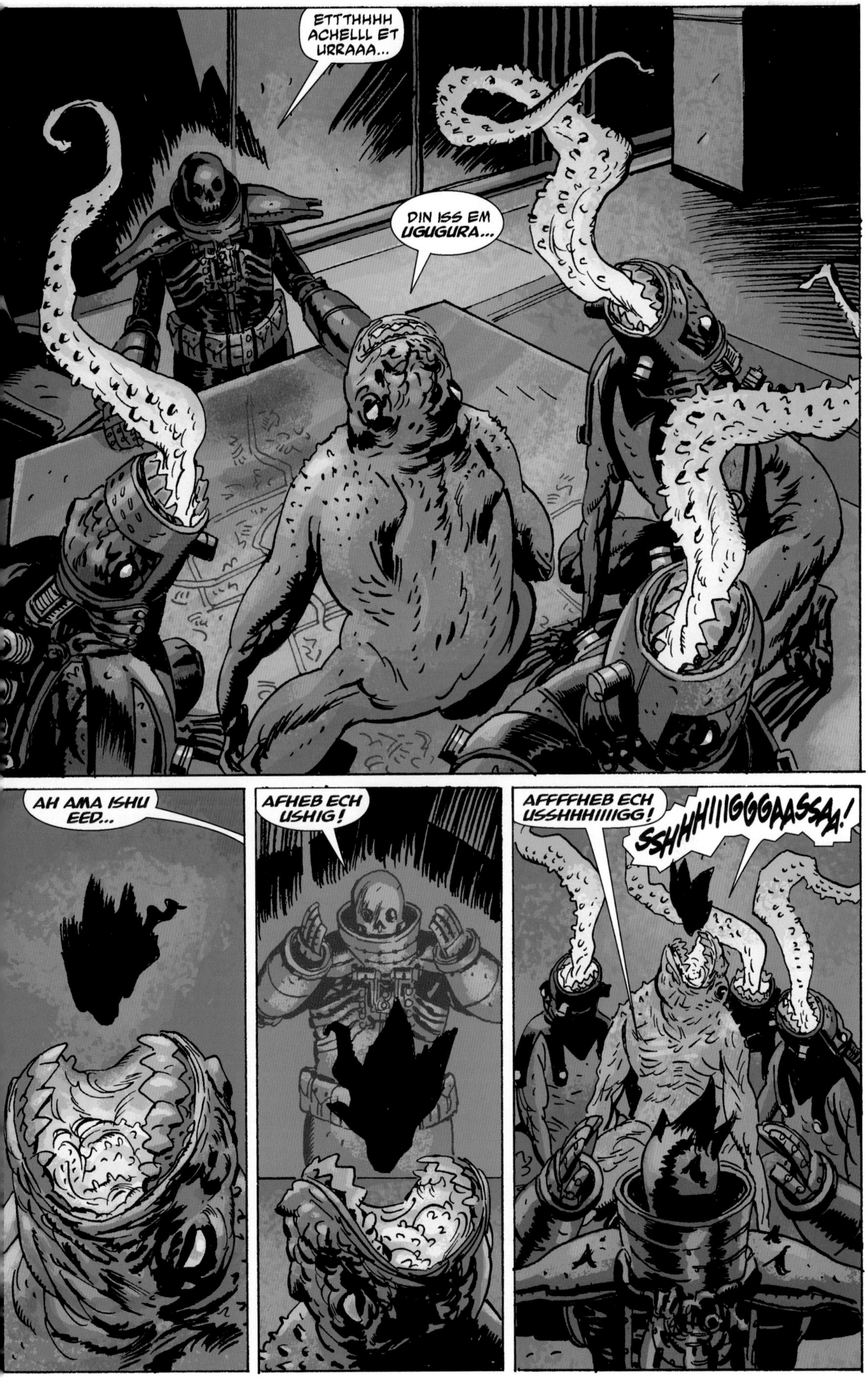
ETTTHHHH ACHELLL ET URRAAA...
DIN ISS EM UGUGURA...
AH AMA ISHU EED...
AFHEB ECH USHIG!
AFFFFHEB ECH USSHHHIIIIGG!
SSHHHIIIGGGAASSAA!

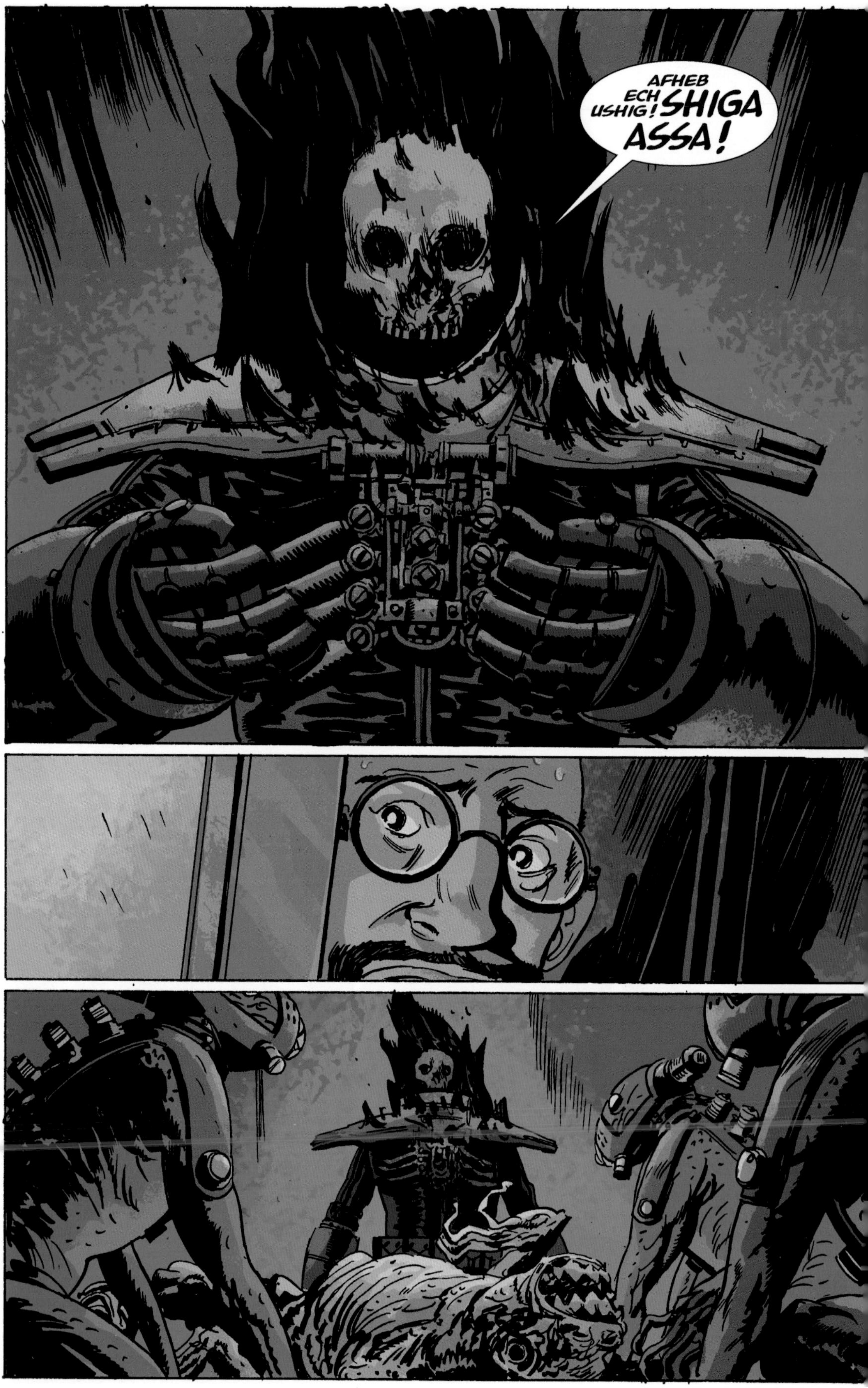
AFHEB ECH USHIG! SHIGA ASSA!

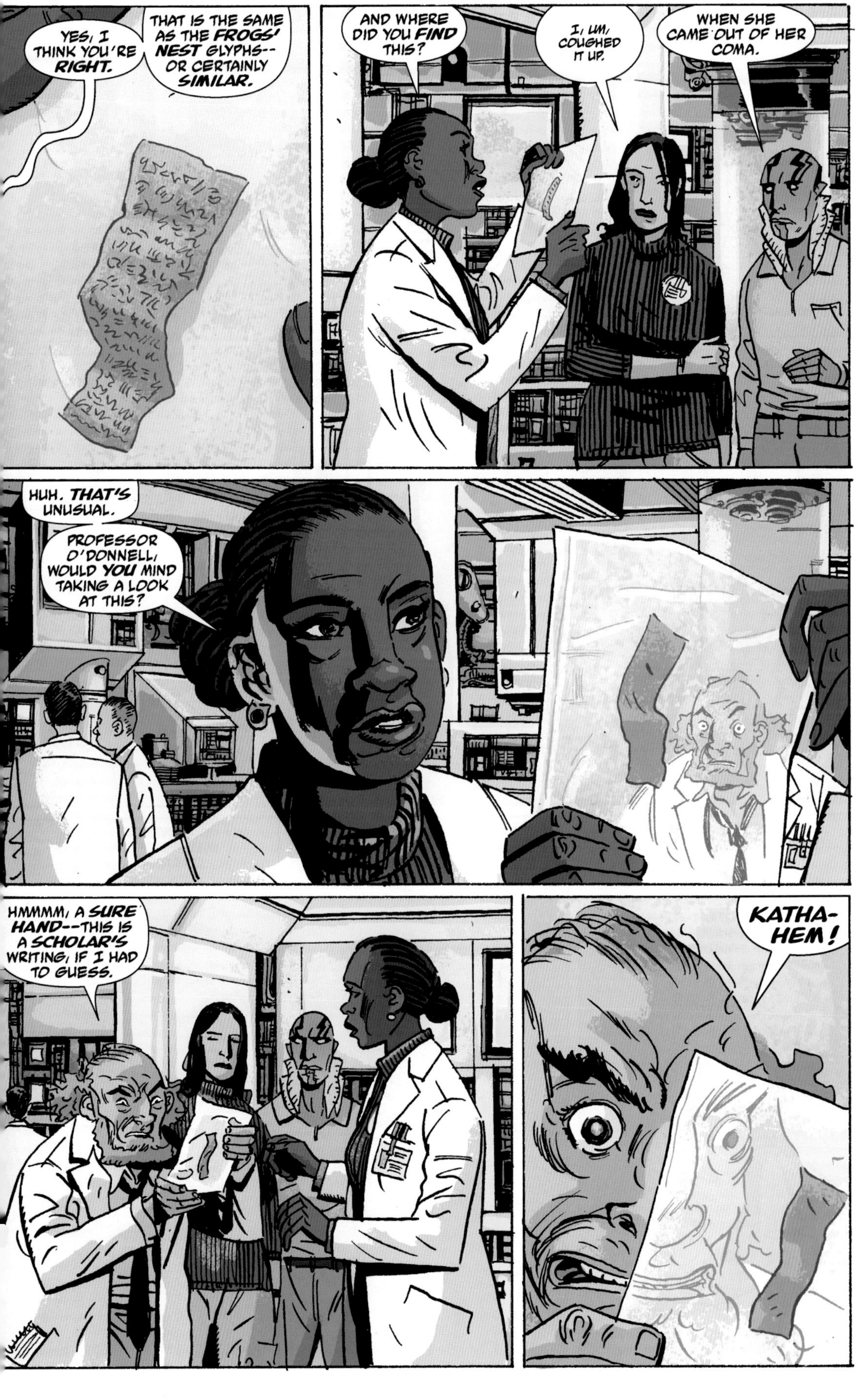
YES, I THINK YOU'RE RIGHT.
THAT IS THE SAME AS THE FROGS' NEST GLYPHS-- OR CERTAINLY SIMILAR.
AND WHERE DID YOU FIND THIS?
I, UM, COUGHED IT UP.
WHEN SHE CAME OUT OF HER COMA.
HUH. THAT'S UNUSUAL.
PROFESSOR O'DONNELL, WOULD YOU MIND TAKING A LOOK AT THIS?
HMMMM, A SURE HAND--THIS IS A SCHOLAR'S WRITING, IF I HAD TO GUESS.
KATHA-HEM!

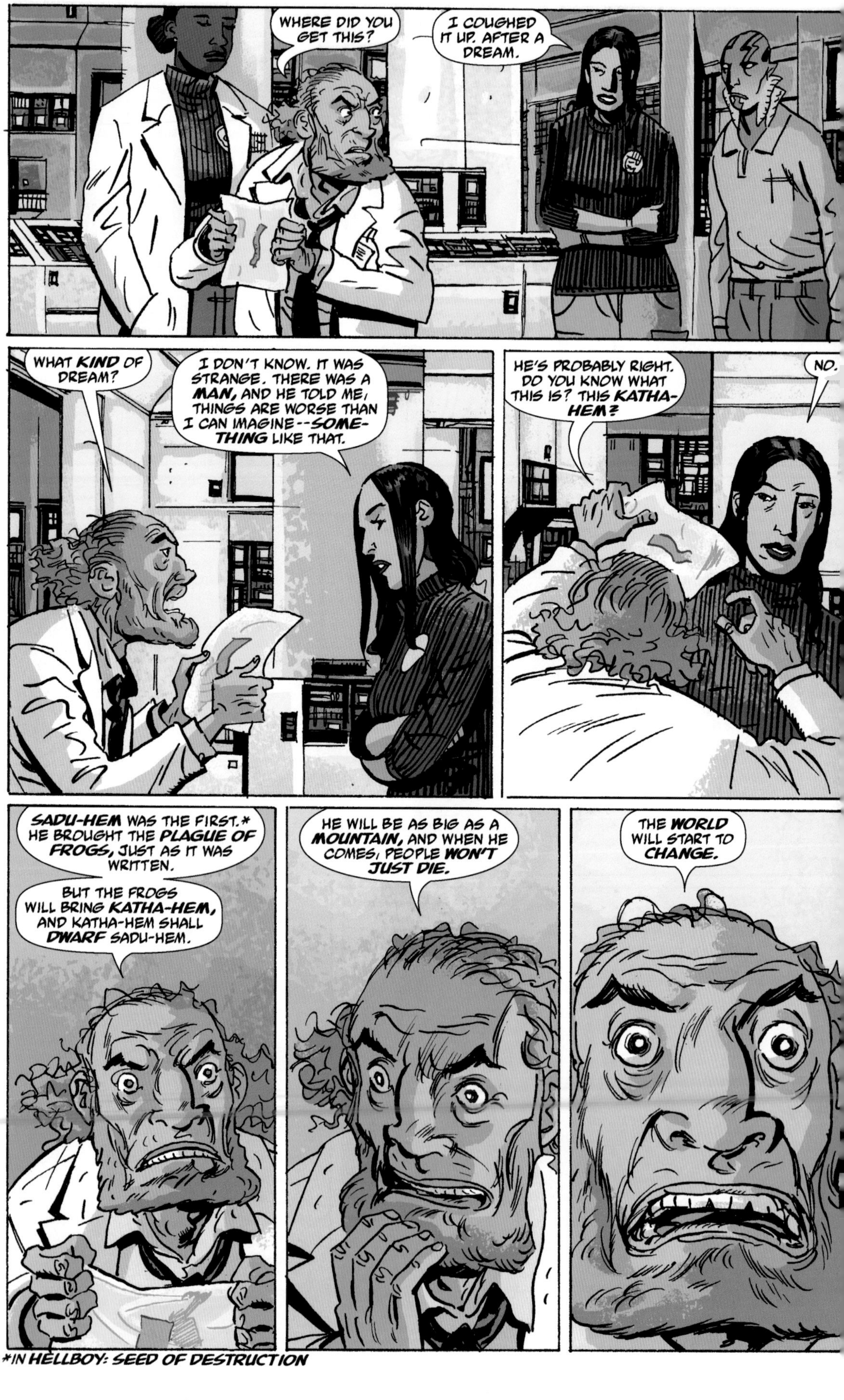
WHERE DID YOU GET THIS?
I COUGHED IT UP. AFTER A DREAM.
WHAT KIND OF DREAM?
I DON'T KNOW. IT WAS STRANGE. THERE WAS A MAN, AND HE TOLD ME; THINGS ARE WORSE THAN I CAN IMAGINE--SOMETHING LIKE THAT.
HE'S PROBABLY RIGHT. DO YOU KNOW WHAT THIS IS? THIS KATHA-HEM?
NO.
SADU-HEM WAS THE FIRST.* HE BROUGHT THE PLAGUE OF FROGS, JUST AS IT WAS WRITTEN.
BUT THE FROGS WILL BRING KATHA-HEM, AND KATHA-HEM SHALL DWARF SADU-HEM.
HE WILL BE AS BIG AS A MOUNTAIN, AND WHEN HE COMES, PEOPLE WON'T JUST DIE.
THE WORLD WILL START TO CHANGE.

*IN HELLBOY: SEED OF DESTRUCTION

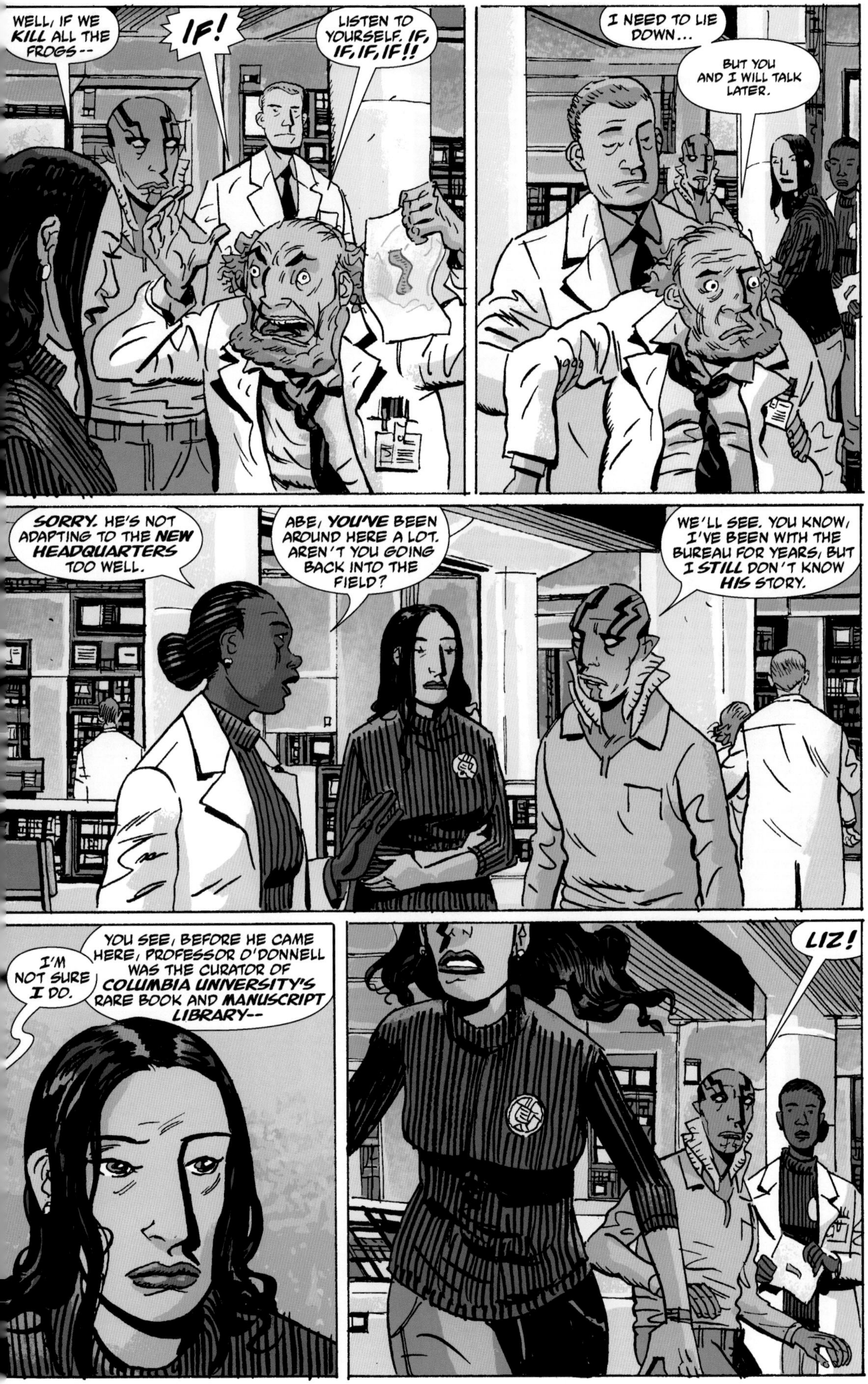

WELL, IF WE KILL ALL THE FROGS--
IF!
LISTEN TO YOURSELF. IF, IF, IF, IF!!
I NEED TO LIE DOWN...
BUT YOU AND I WILL TALK LATER.
SORRY. HE'S NOT ADAPTING TO THE NEW HEADQUARTERS TOO WELL.
ABE, YOU'VE BEEN AROUND HERE A LOT. AREN'T YOU GOING BACK INTO THE FIELD?
WE'LL SEE. YOU KNOW, I'VE BEEN WITH THE BUREAU FOR YEARS, BUT I STILL DON'T KNOW HIS STORY.
I'M NOT SURE I DO.
YOU SEE, BEFORE HE CAME HERE, PROFESSOR O'DONNELL WAS THE CURATOR OF COLUMBIA UNIVERSITY'S RARE BOOK AND MANUSCRIPT LIBRARY--
LIZ!

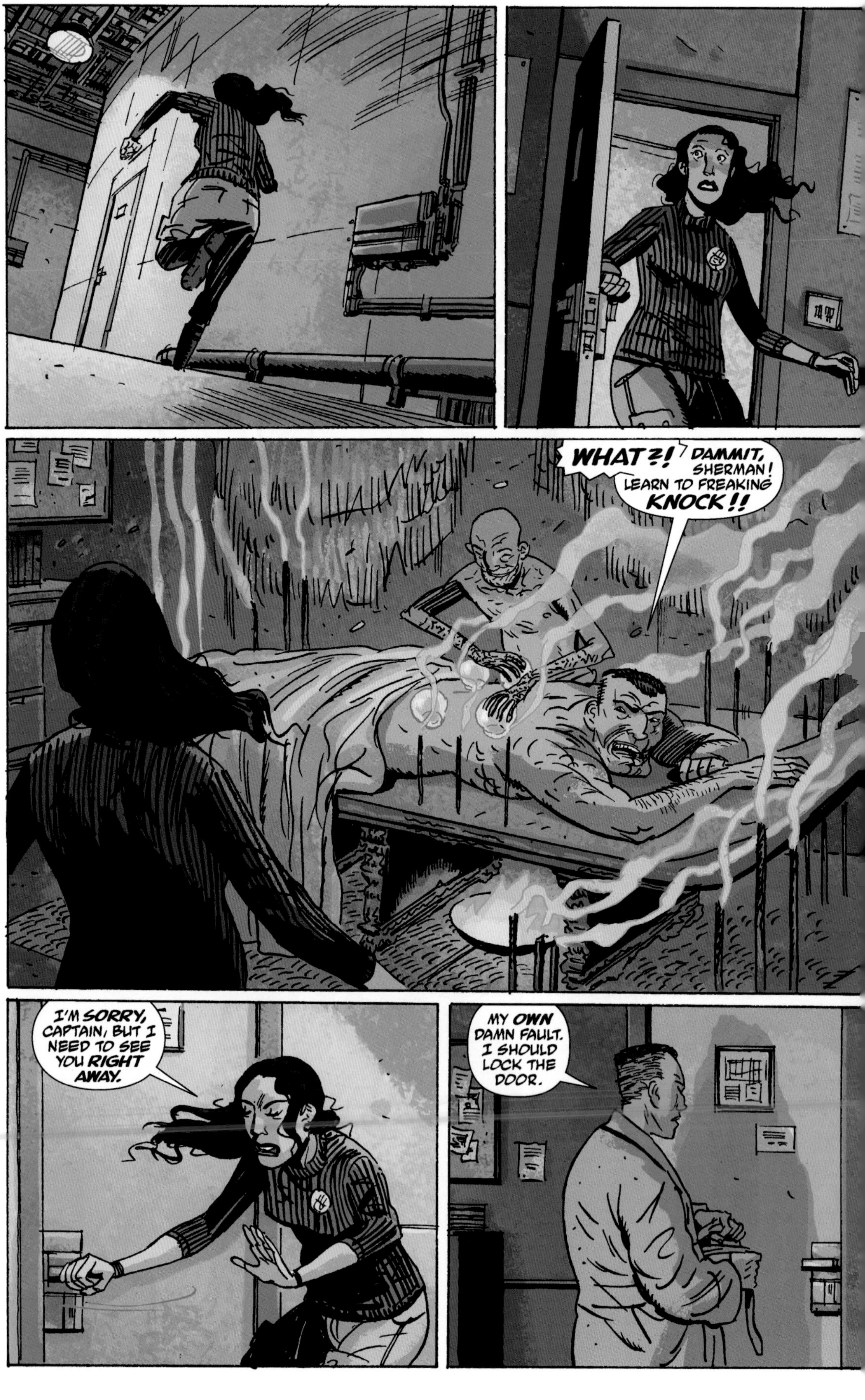
WHAT?! DAMMIT, SHERMAN! LEARN TO FREAKING KNOCK!!
I'M SORRY, CAPTAIN, BUT I NEED TO SEE YOU RIGHT AWAY.
MY OWN DAMN FAULT. I SHOULD LOCK THE DOOR.

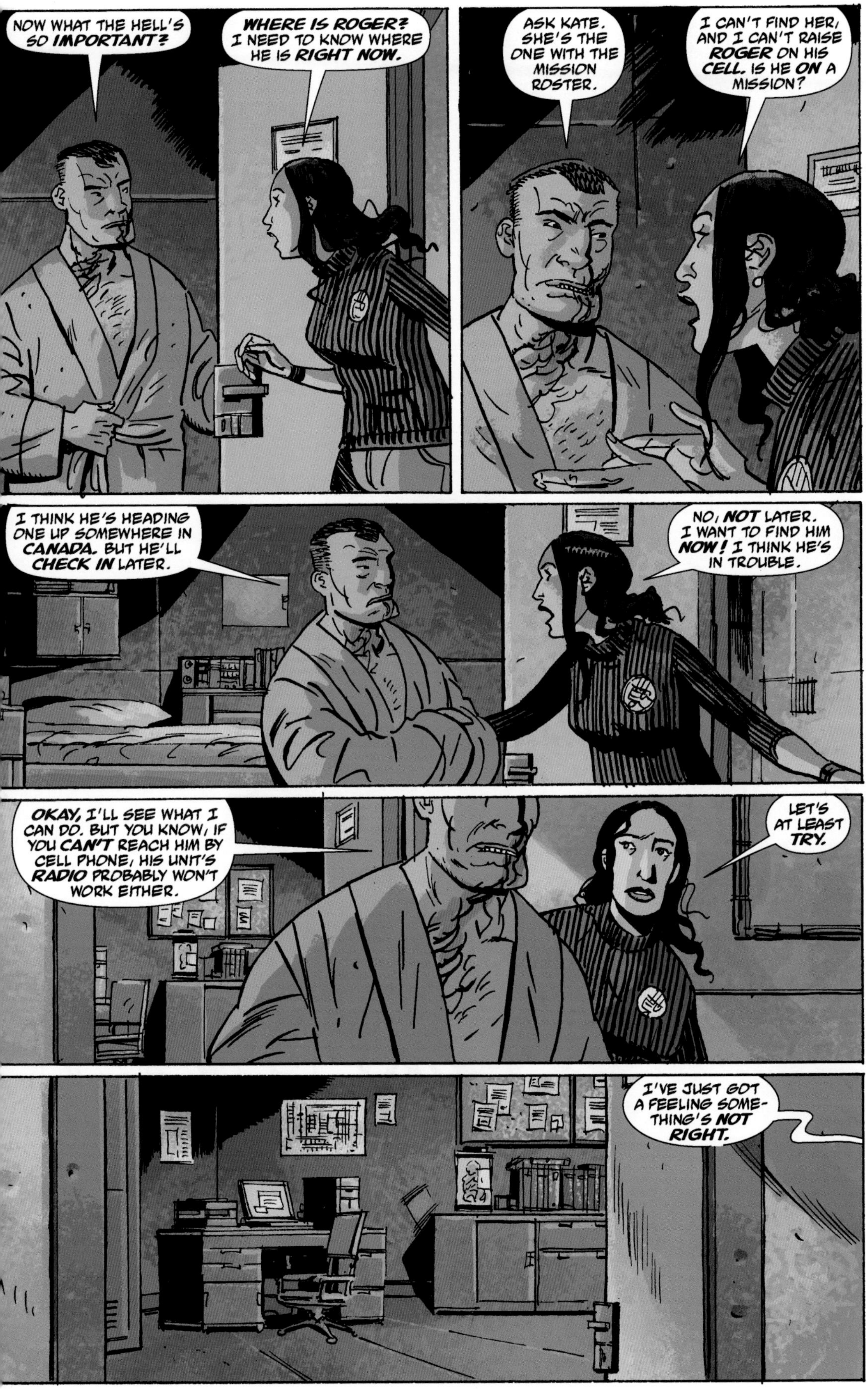
NOW WHAT THE HELL'S SO IMPORTANT?
WHERE IS ROGER? I NEED TO KNOW WHERE HE IS RIGHT NOW.
ASK KATE. SHE'S THE ONE WITH THE MISSION ROSTER.
I CAN'T FIND HER, AND I CAN'T RAISE ROGER ON HIS CELL. IS HE ON A MISSION?
I THINK HE'S HEADING ONE UP SOMEWHERE IN CANADA. BUT HE'LL CHECK IN LATER.
NO, NOT LATER. I WANT TO FIND HIM NOW! I THINK HE'S IN TROUBLE.
OKAY, I'LL SEE WHAT I CAN DO. BUT YOU KNOW, IF YOU CAN'T REACH HIM BY CELL PHONE, HIS UNIT'S RADIO PROBABLY WON'T WORK EITHER.
LET'S AT LEAST TRY.
I'VE JUST GOT A FEELING SOME-THING'S NOT RIGHT.

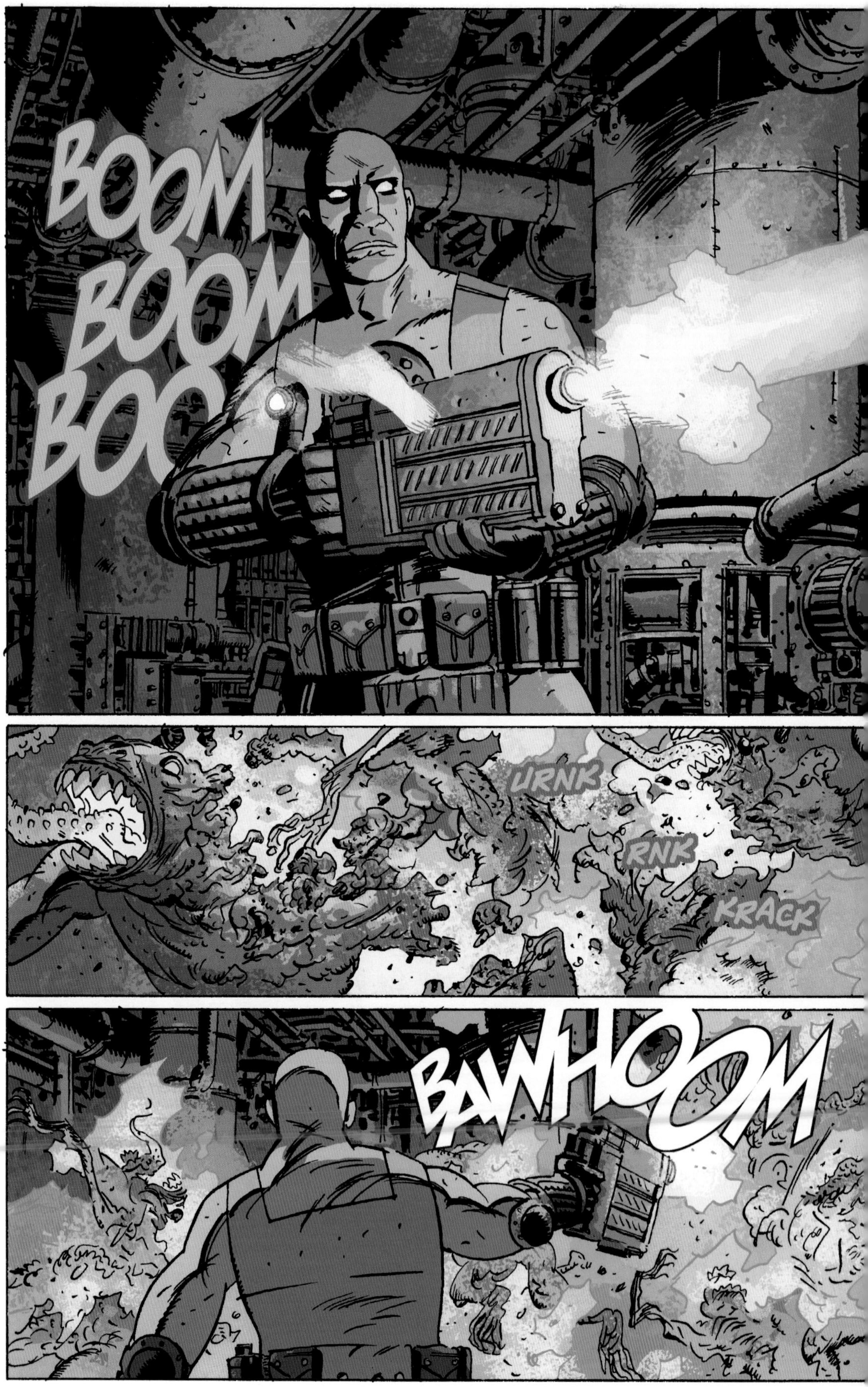
BOOM
BOOM
BOO
URNK
RNK
KRACK
BAWHOOM

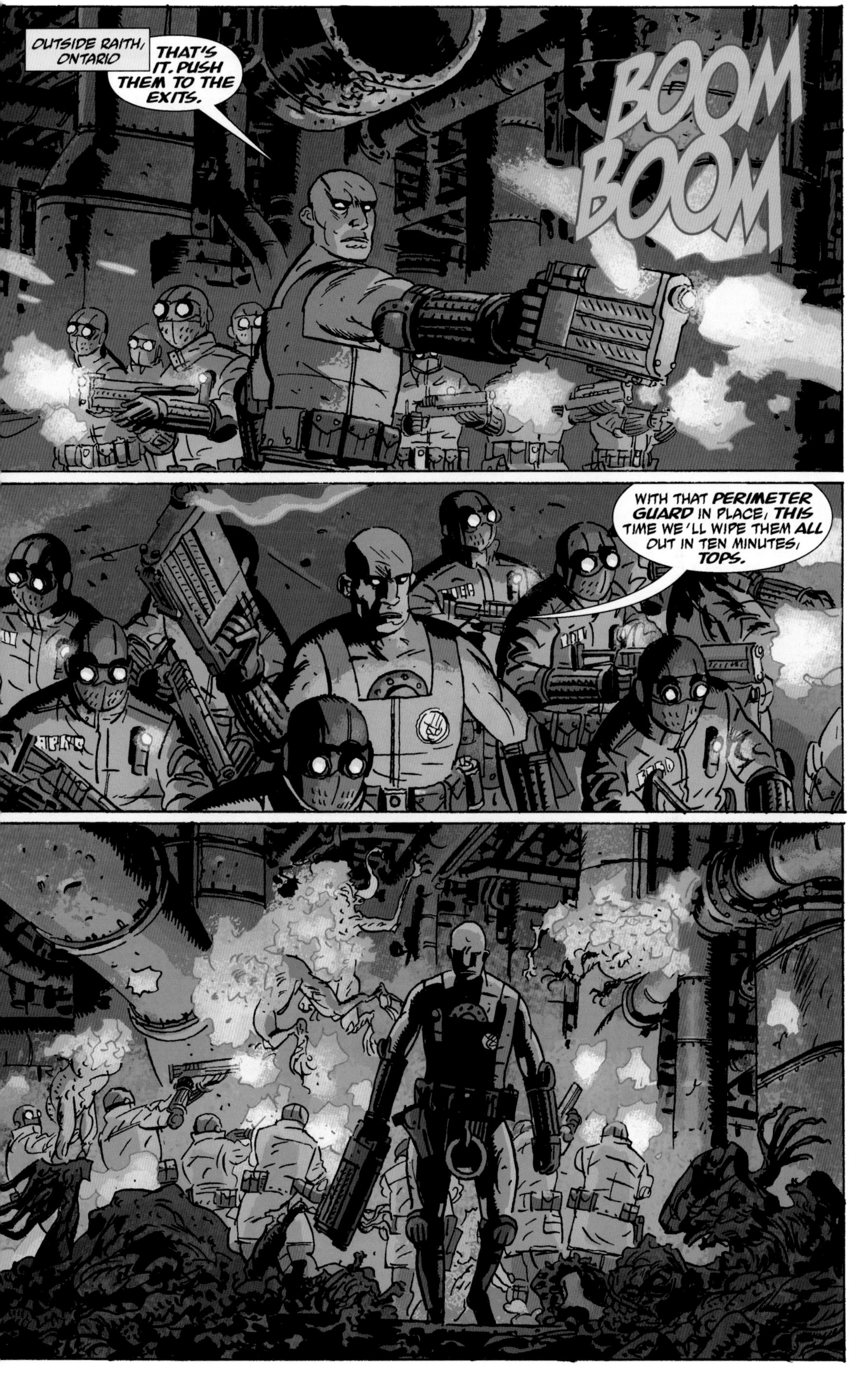
OUTSIDE RAITH, ONTARIO
THAT'S IT. PUSH THEM TO THE EXITS.
BOOM BOOM
WITH THAT PERIMETER GUARD IN PLACE, THIS TIME WE'LL WIPE THEM ALL OUT IN TEN MINUTES, TOPS.

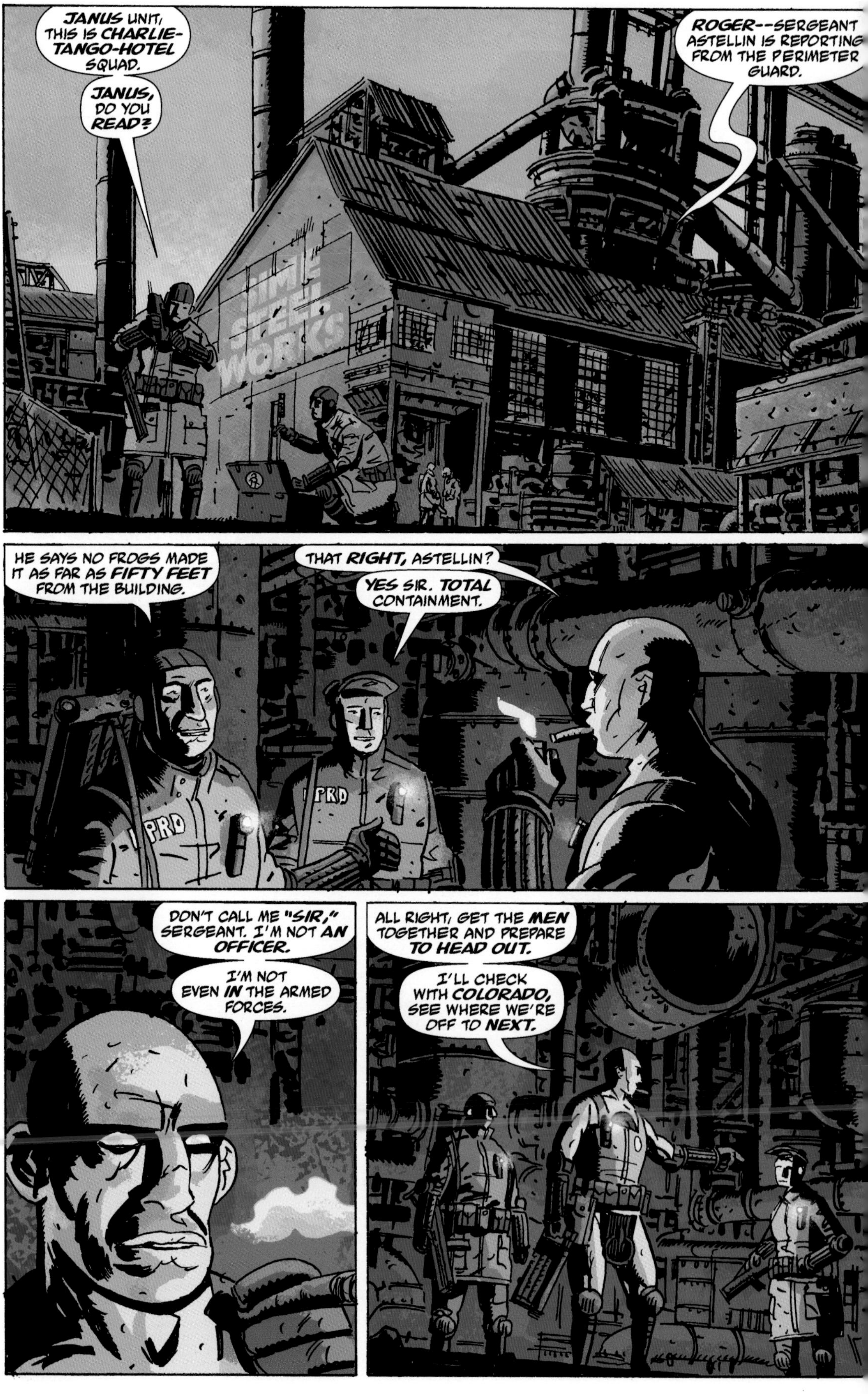
JANUS UNIT, THIS IS CHARLIE-TANGO-HOTEL SQUAD.
JANUS, DO YOU READ?
ROGER--SERGEANT ASTELLIN IS REPORTING FROM THE PERIMETER GUARD.
SIMI STEEL WORKS
HE SAYS NO FROGS MADE IT AS FAR AS FIFTY FEET FROM THE BUILDING.
THAT RIGHT, ASTELLIN?
YES SIR. TOTAL CONTAINMENT.
DON'T CALL ME "SIR," SERGEANT. I'M NOT AN OFFICER.
I'M NOT EVEN IN THE ARMED FORCES.
ALL RIGHT, GET THE MEN TOGETHER AND PREPARE TO HEAD OUT.
I'LL CHECK WITH COLORADO, SEE WHERE WE'RE OFF TO NEXT.

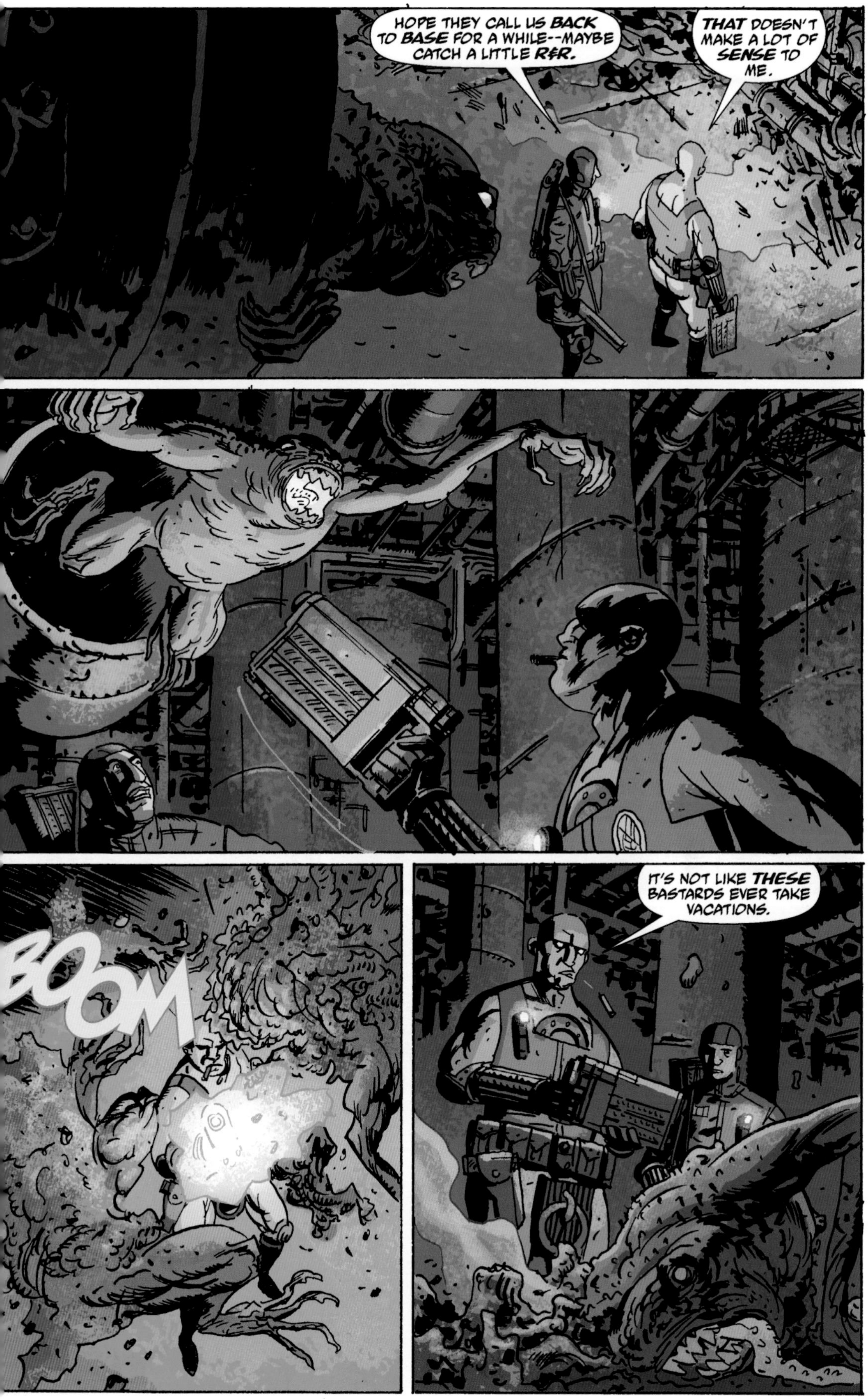
HOPE THEY CALL US BACK TO BASE FOR A WHILE--MAYBE CATCH A LITTLE R&R.
THAT DOESN'T MAKE A LOT OF SENSE TO ME.
BOOM
IT'S NOT LIKE THESE BASTARDS EVER TAKE VACATIONS.

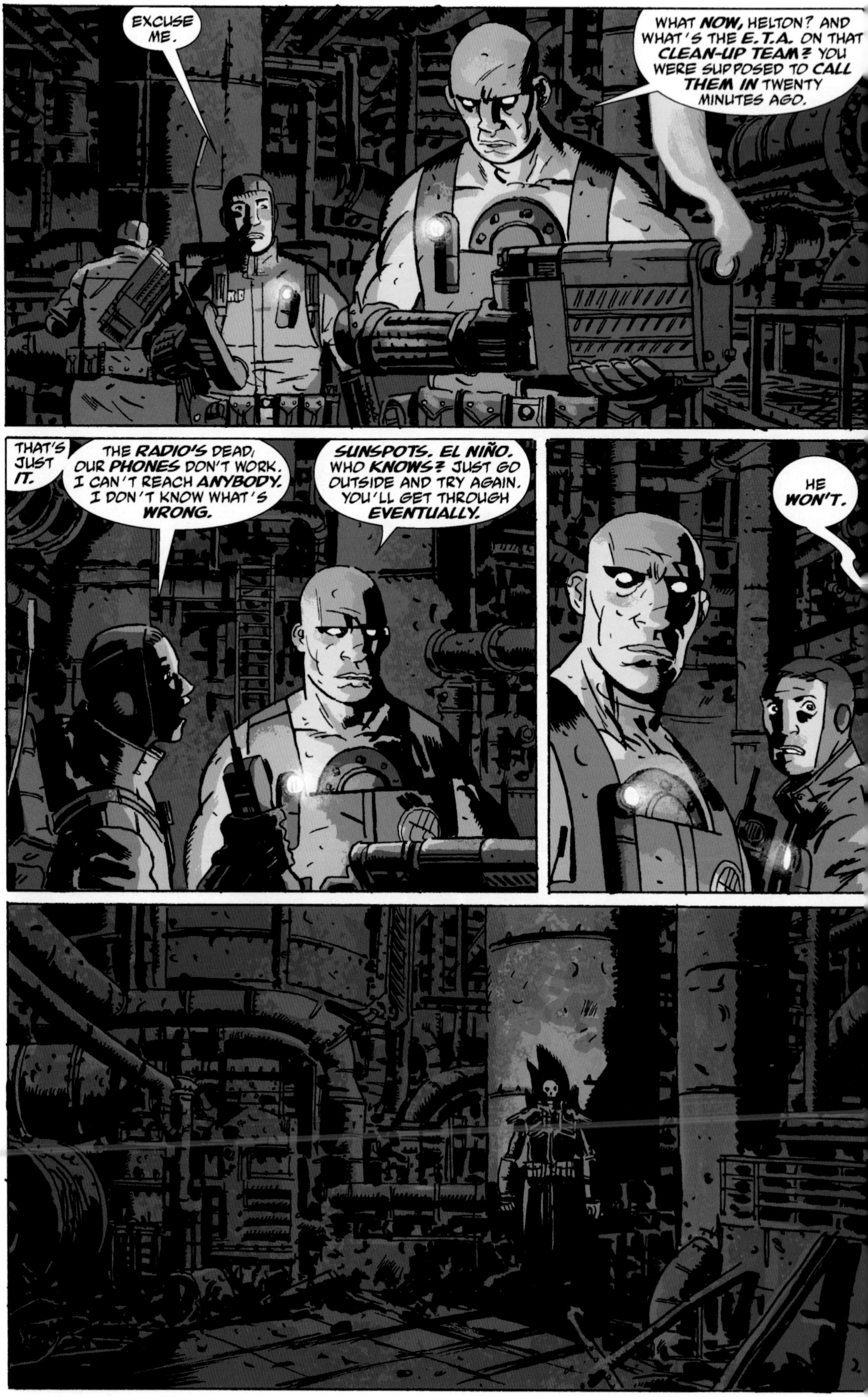
EXCUSE ME.
WHAT NOW, HELTON? AND WHAT'S THE E.T.A. ON THAT CLEAN-UP TEAM? YOU WERE SUPPOSED TO CALL THEM IN TWENTY MINUTES AGO.
THAT'S JUST IT.
THE RADIO'S DEAD, OUR PHONES DON'T WORK. I CAN'T REACH ANYBODY. I DON'T KNOW WHAT'S WRONG.
SUNSPOTS. EL NIÑO. WHO KNOWS? JUST GO OUTSIDE AND TRY AGAIN. YOU'LL GET THROUGH EVENTUALLY.
HE WON'T.

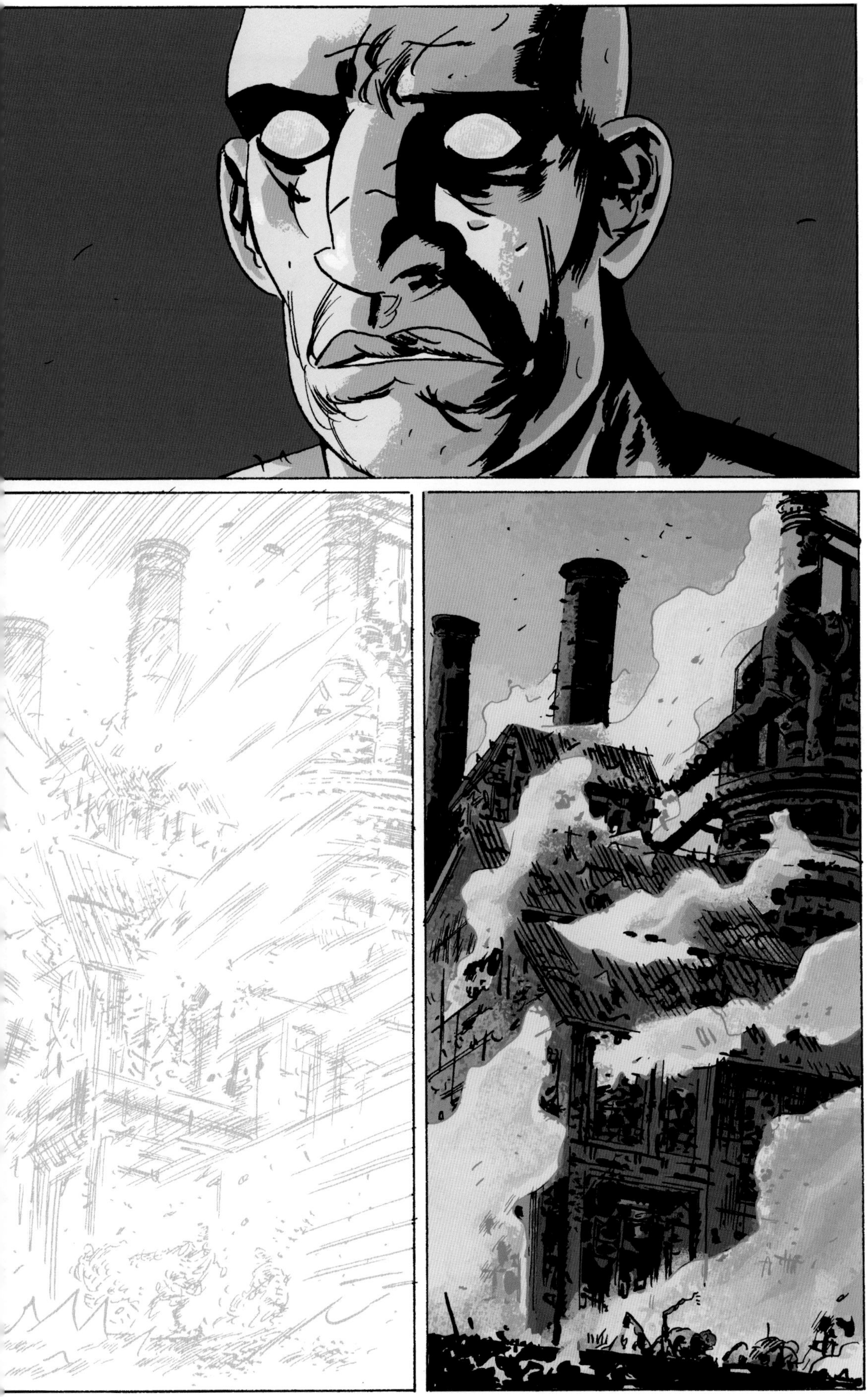

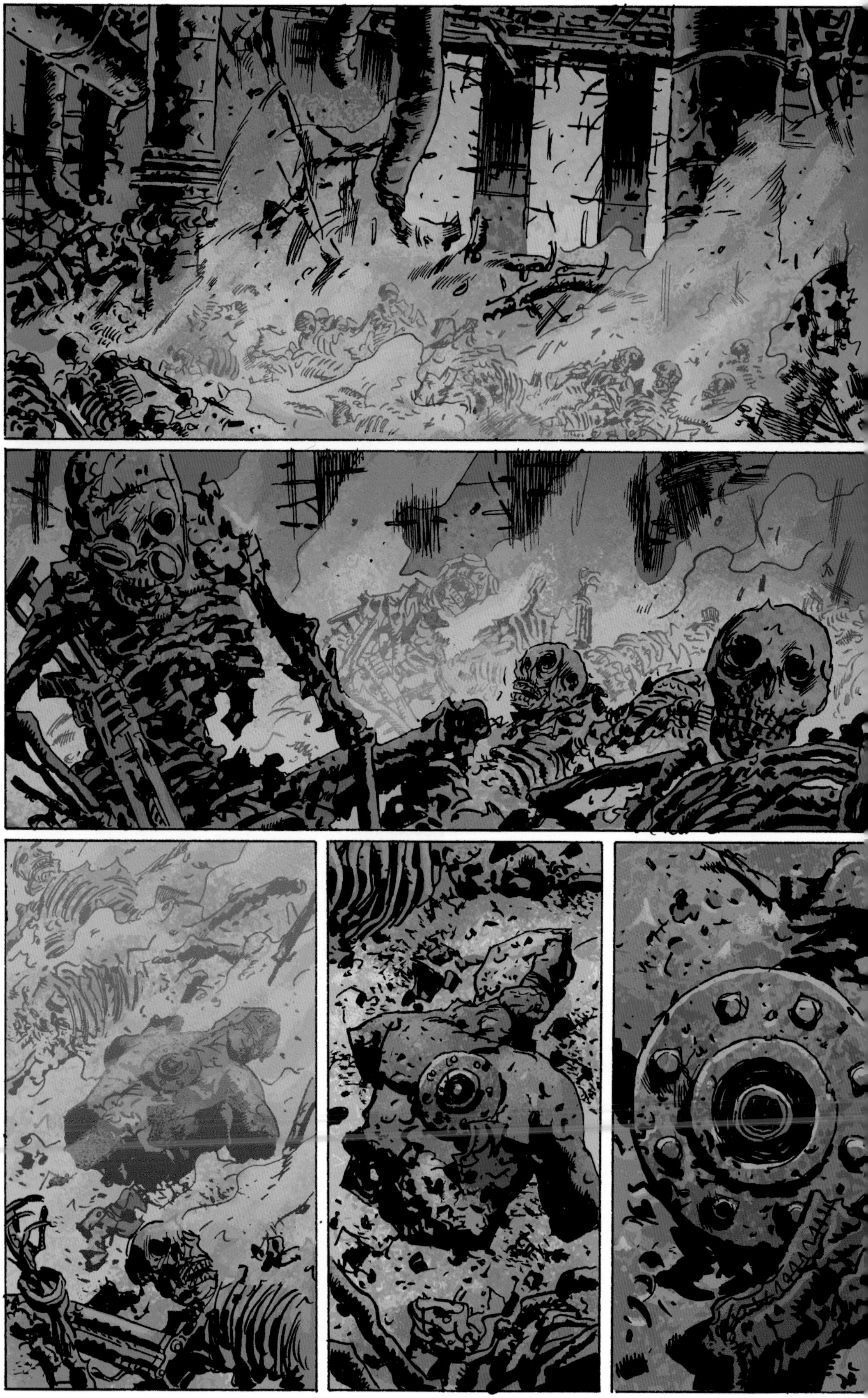

# CHAPTER FOUR

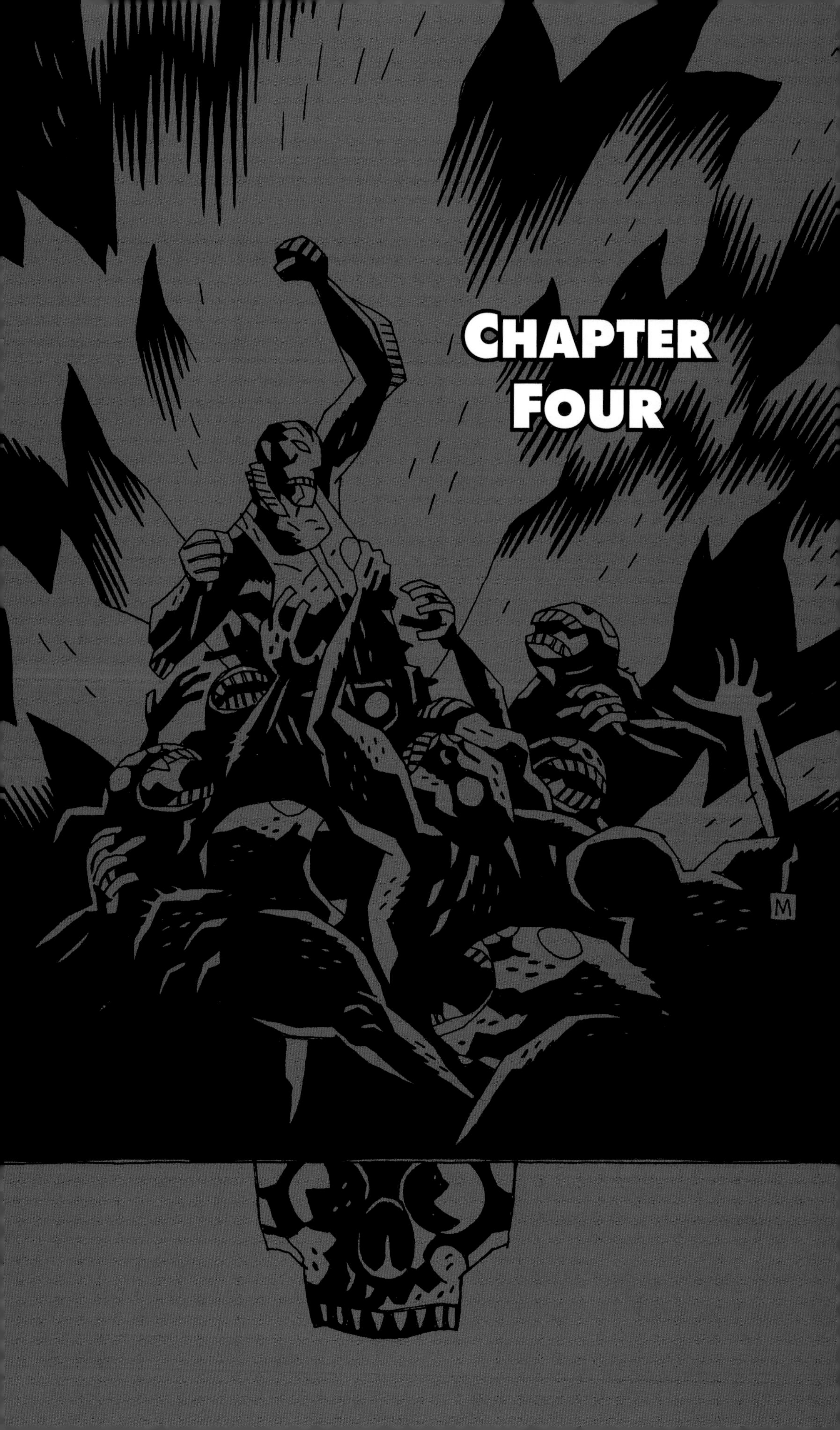

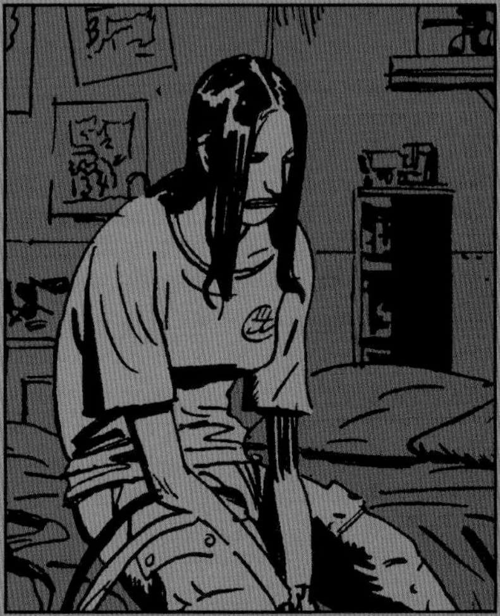

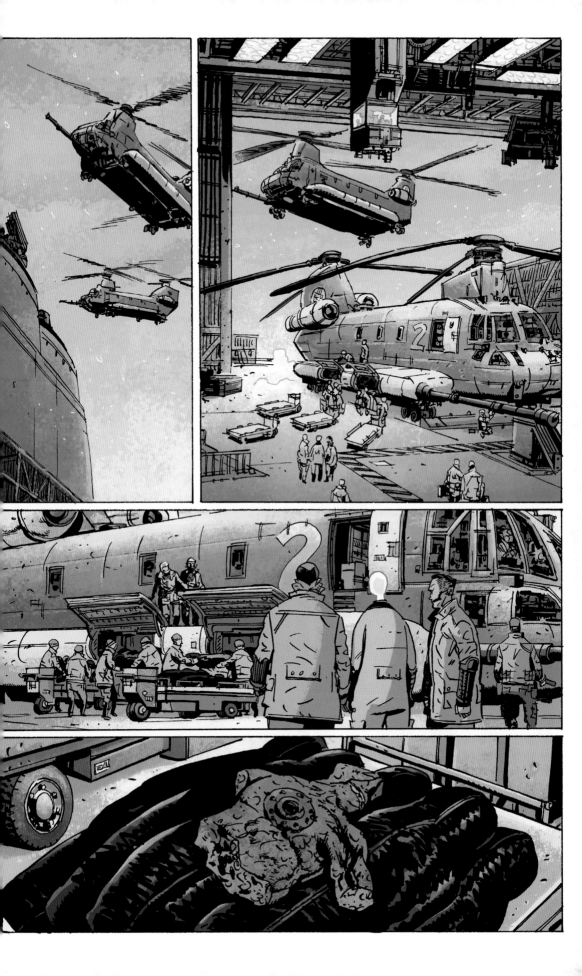

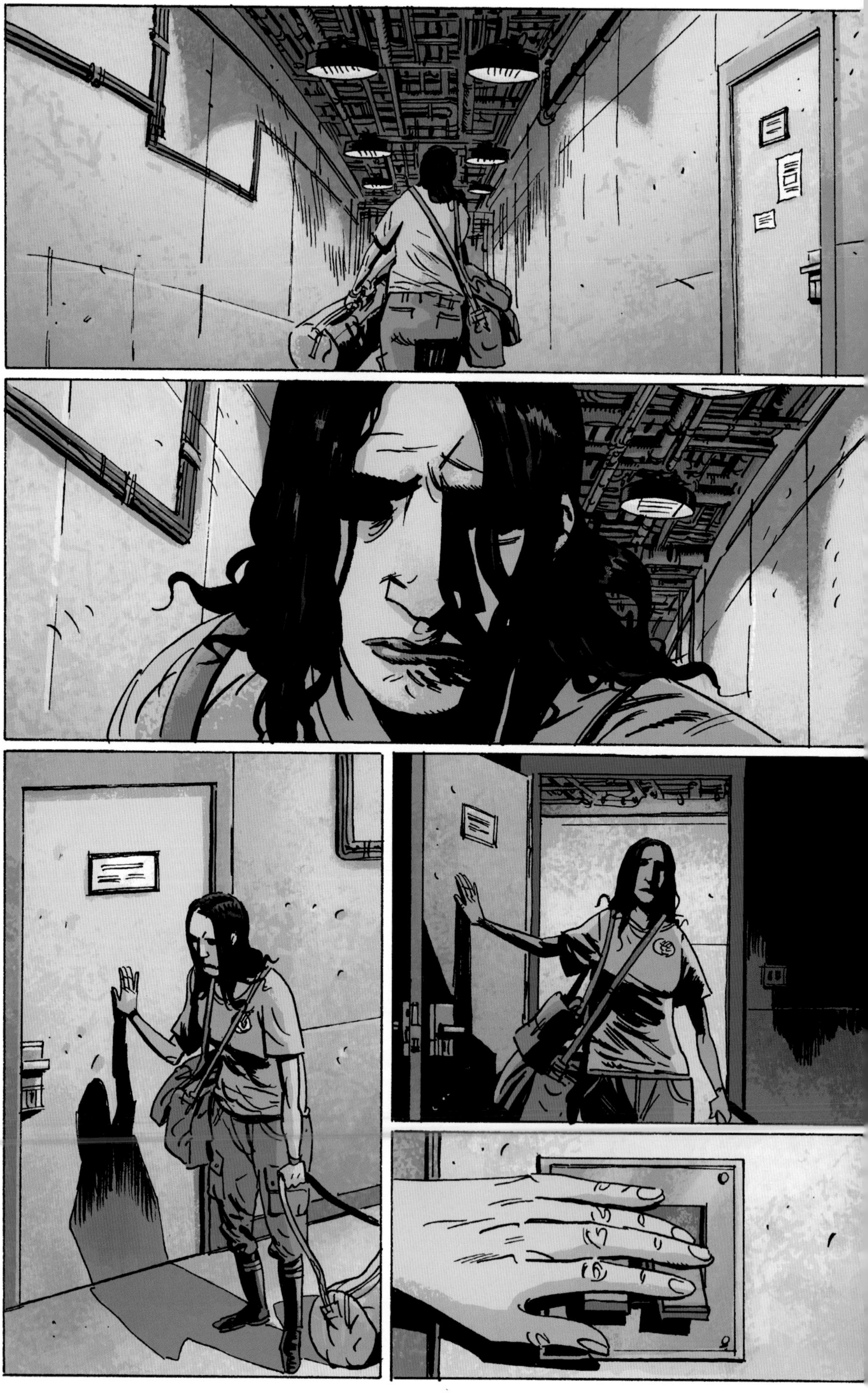

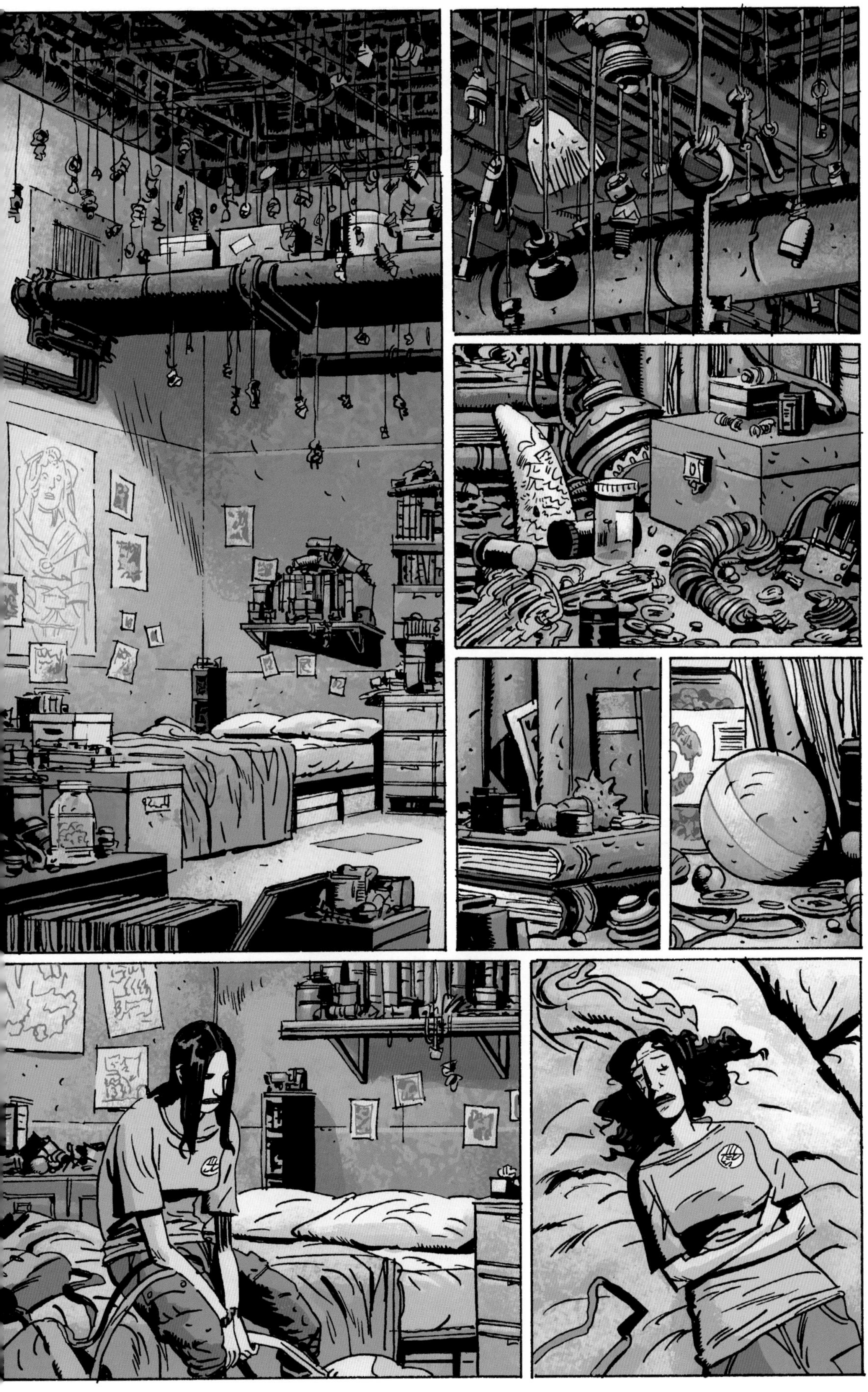

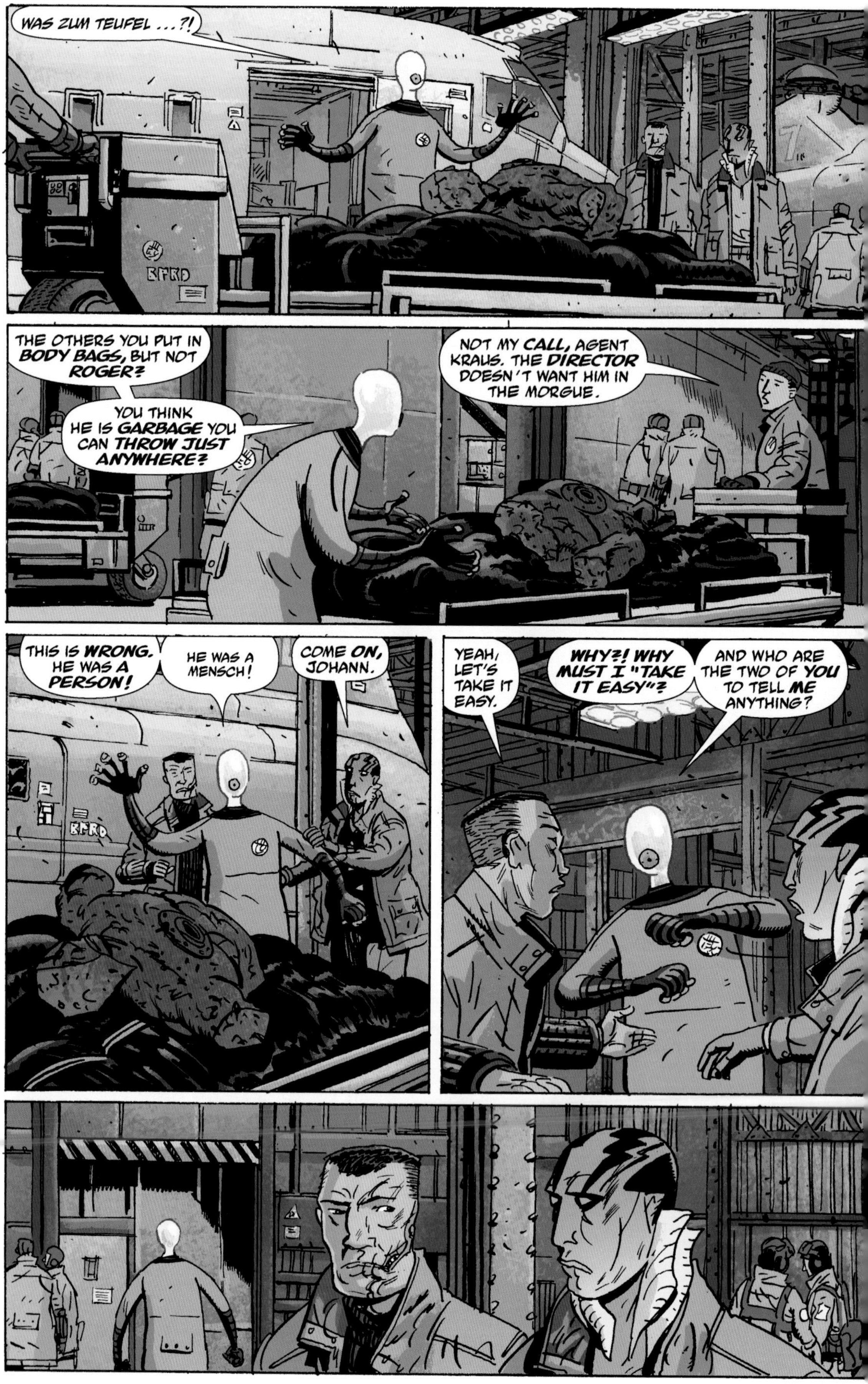
WAS ZUM TEUFEL . . . ?!
THE OTHERS YOU PUT IN BODY BAGS, BUT NOT ROGER?
YOU THINK HE IS GARBAGE YOU CAN THROW JUST ANYWHERE?
NOT MY CALL, AGENT KRAUS. THE DIRECTOR DOESN'T WANT HIM IN THE MORGUE.
THIS IS WRONG. HE WAS A PERSON!
HE WAS A MENSCH!
COME ON, JOHANN.
YEAH, LET'S TAKE IT EASY.
WHY?! WHY MUST I "TAKE IT EASY"?
AND WHO ARE THE TWO OF YOU TO TELL ME ANYTHING?

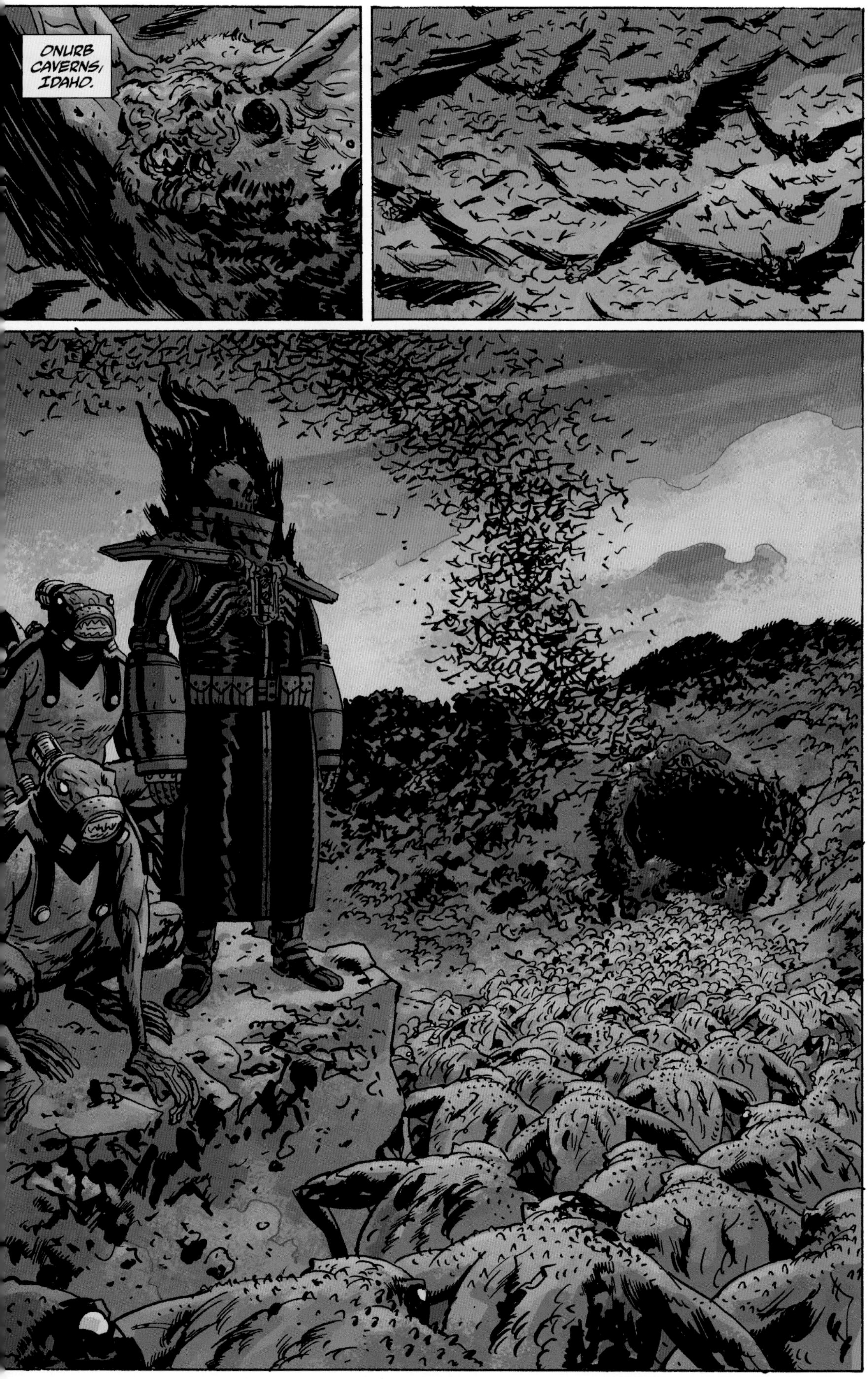
ONURB CAVERNS, IDAHO.

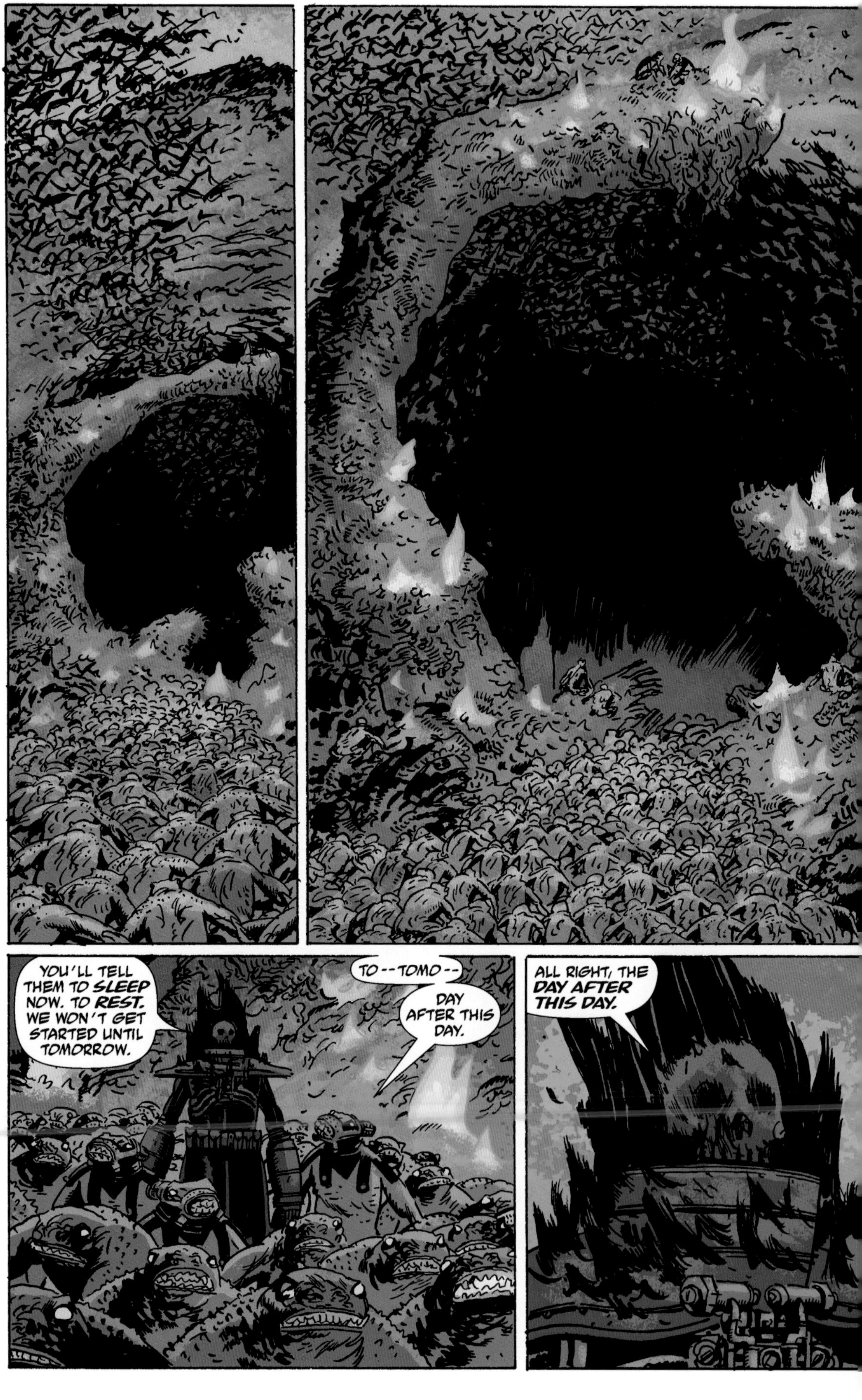
YOU'LL TELL THEM TO SLEEP NOW. TO REST. WE WON'T GET STARTED UNTIL TOMORROW.
TO--TOMO--
DAY AFTER THIS DAY.
ALL RIGHT, THE DAY AFTER THIS DAY.

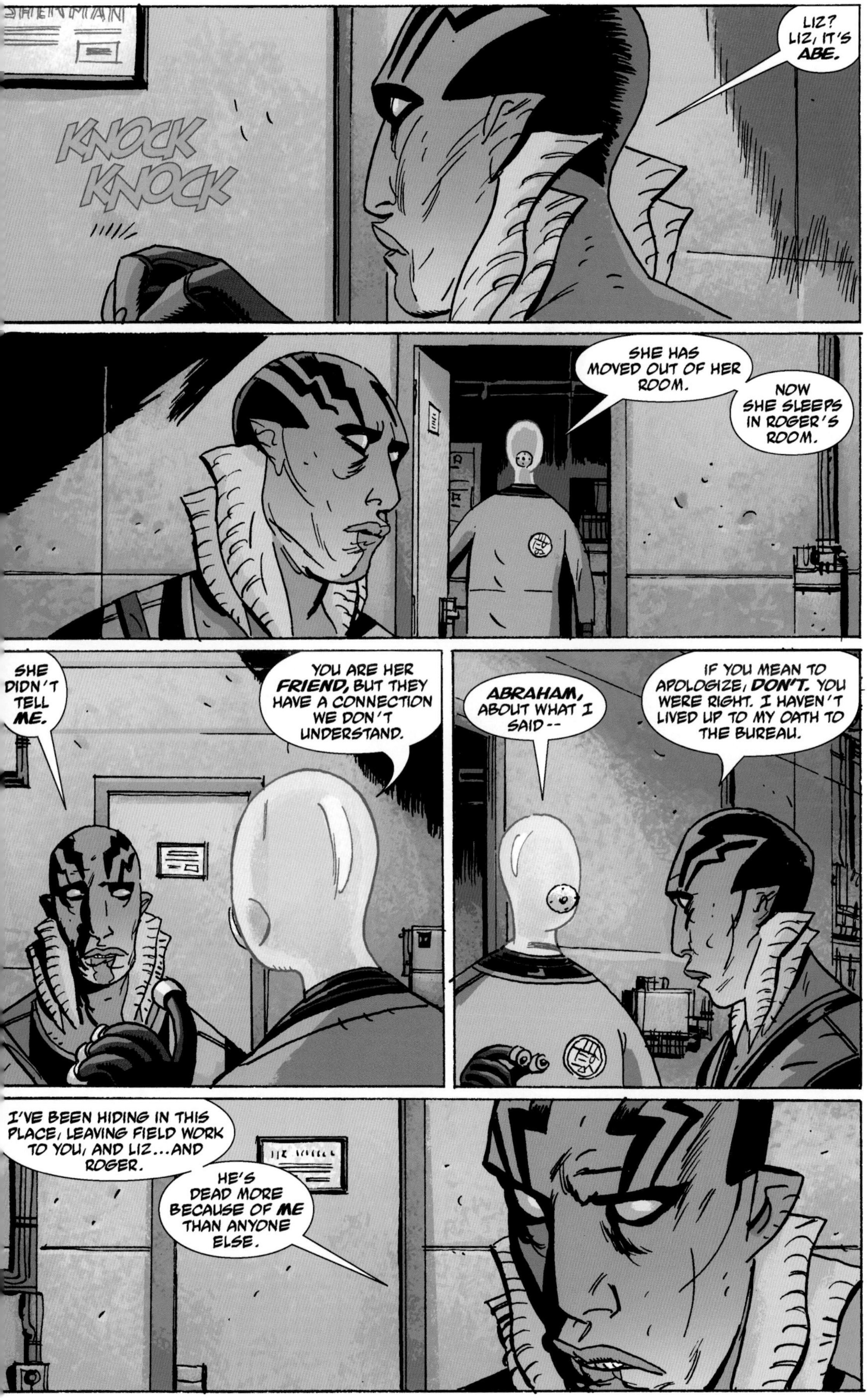
KNOCK KNOCK
LIZ? LIZ, IT'S **ABE.**
SHE HAS MOVED OUT OF HER ROOM.
NOW SHE SLEEPS IN ROGER'S ROOM.
SHE DIDN'T TELL **ME.**
YOU ARE HER **FRIEND,** BUT THEY HAVE A CONNECTION WE DON'T UNDERSTAND.
**ABRAHAM,** ABOUT WHAT I SAID--
IF YOU MEAN TO APOLOGIZE, **DON'T.** YOU WERE RIGHT. I HAVEN'T LIVED UP TO MY OATH TO THE BUREAU.
I'VE BEEN HIDING IN THIS PLACE, LEAVING FIELD WORK TO YOU, AND LIZ...AND ROGER.
HE'S DEAD MORE BECAUSE OF **ME** THAN ANYONE ELSE.

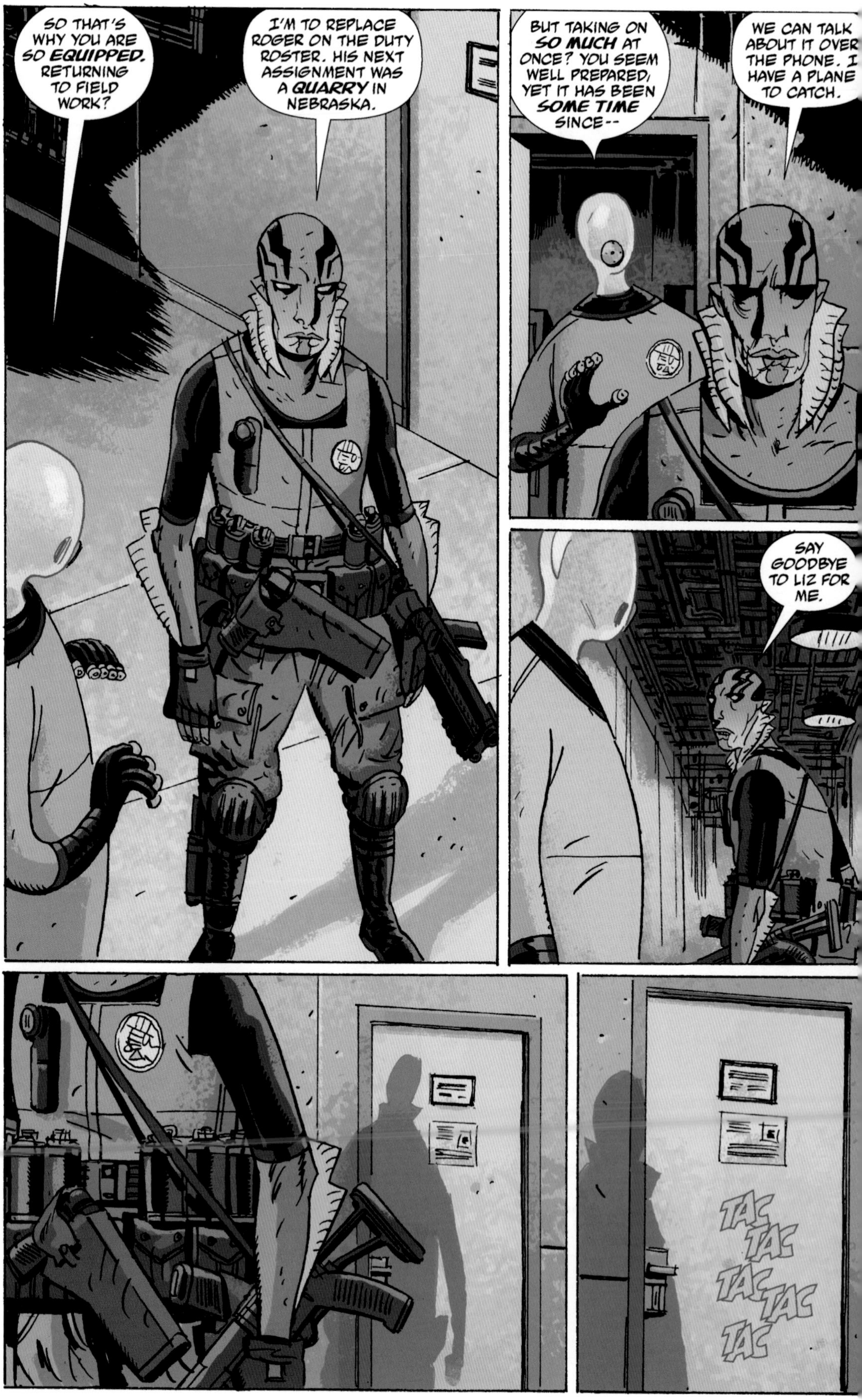
SO THAT'S WHY YOU ARE SO **EQUIPPED.** RETURNING TO FIELD WORK?
I'M TO REPLACE ROGER ON THE DUTY ROSTER. HIS NEXT ASSIGNMENT WAS A **QUARRY** IN NEBRASKA.
BUT TAKING ON **SO MUCH** AT ONCE? YOU SEEM WELL PREPARED, YET IT HAS BEEN **SOME TIME** SINCE--
WE CAN TALK ABOUT IT OVER THE PHONE. I HAVE A PLANE TO CATCH.
SAY GOODBYE TO LIZ FOR ME.
TAC TAC TAC TAC TAC

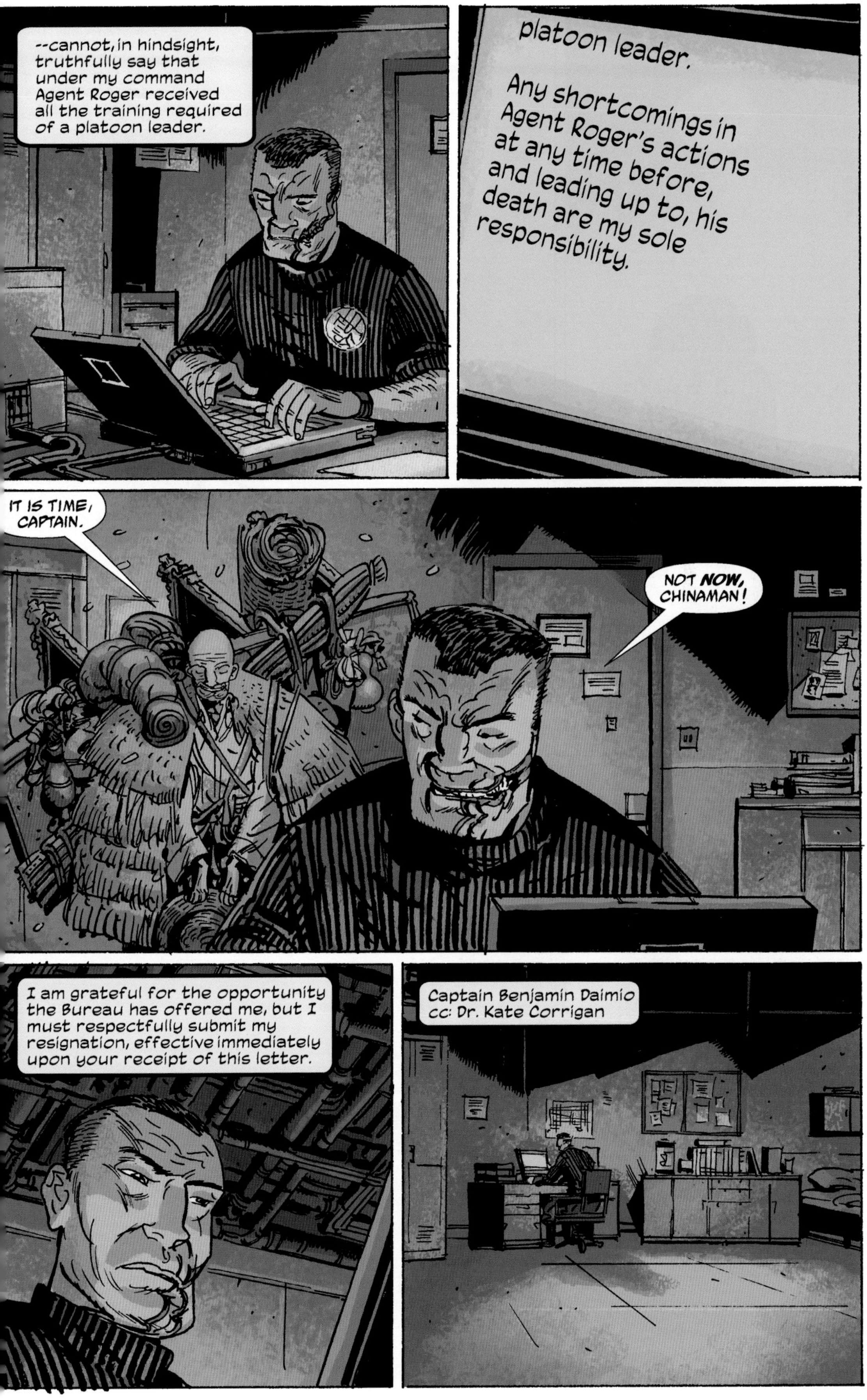
--cannot, in hindsight, truthfully say that under my command Agent Roger received all the training required of a platoon leader.
platoon leader.
Any shortcomings in Agent Roger's actions at any time before, and leading up to, his death are my sole responsibility.
IT IS TIME, CAPTAIN.
NOT NOW, CHINAMAN!
I am grateful for the opportunity the Bureau has offered me, but I must respectfully submit my resignation, effective immediately upon your receipt of this letter.
Captain Benjamin Daimio
cc: Dr. Kate Corrigan

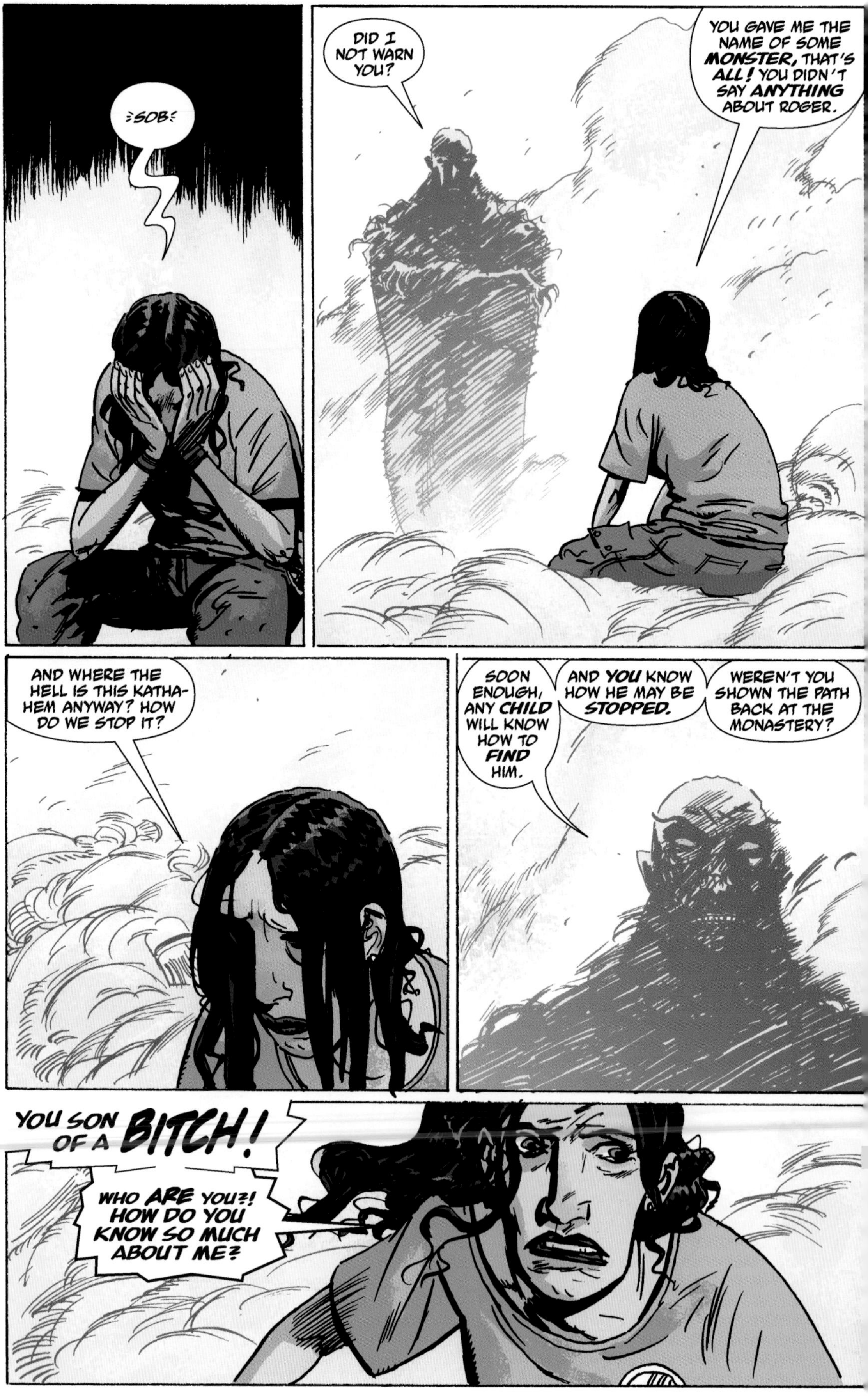
SOB
DID I NOT WARN YOU?
YOU GAVE ME THE NAME OF SOME MONSTER, THAT'S ALL! YOU DIDN'T SAY ANYTHING ABOUT ROGER.
AND WHERE THE HELL IS THIS KATHA-HEM ANYWAY? HOW DO WE STOP IT?
WEREN'T YOU SHOWN THE PATH BACK AT THE MONASTERY?
AND YOU KNOW HOW HE MAY BE STOPPED.
SOON ENOUGH, ANY CHILD WILL KNOW HOW TO FIND HIM.
YOU SON OF A BITCH!
WHO ARE YOU?! HOW DO YOU KNOW SO MUCH ABOUT ME?

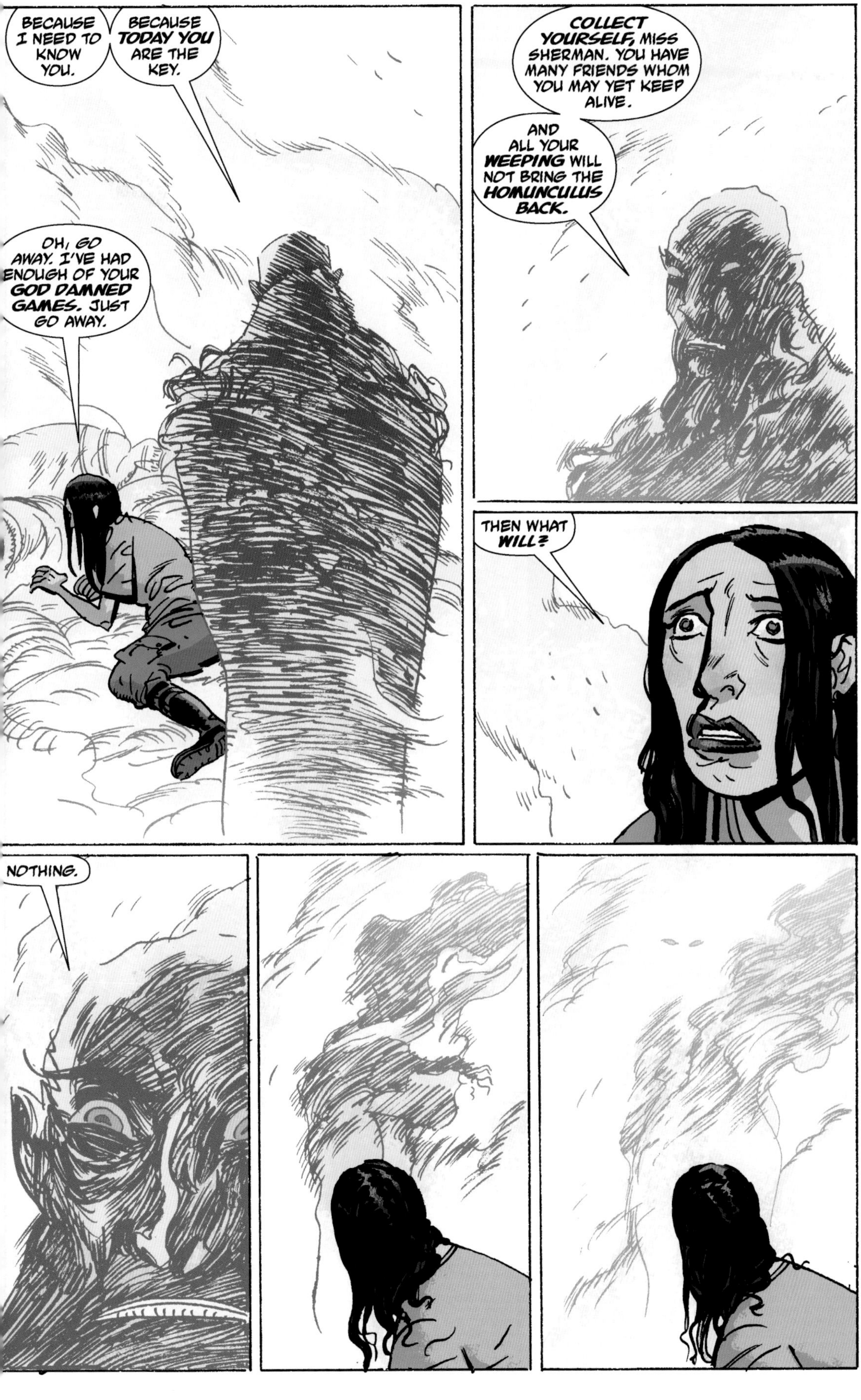
BECAUSE I NEED TO KNOW YOU.
BECAUSE TODAY YOU ARE THE KEY.
OH, GO AWAY. I'VE HAD ENOUGH OF YOUR GOD DAMNED GAMES. JUST GO AWAY.
COLLECT YOURSELF, MISS SHERMAN. YOU HAVE MANY FRIENDS WHOM YOU MAY YET KEEP ALIVE.
AND ALL YOUR WEEPING WILL NOT BRING THE HOMUNCULUS BACK.
THEN WHAT WILL?
NOTHING.

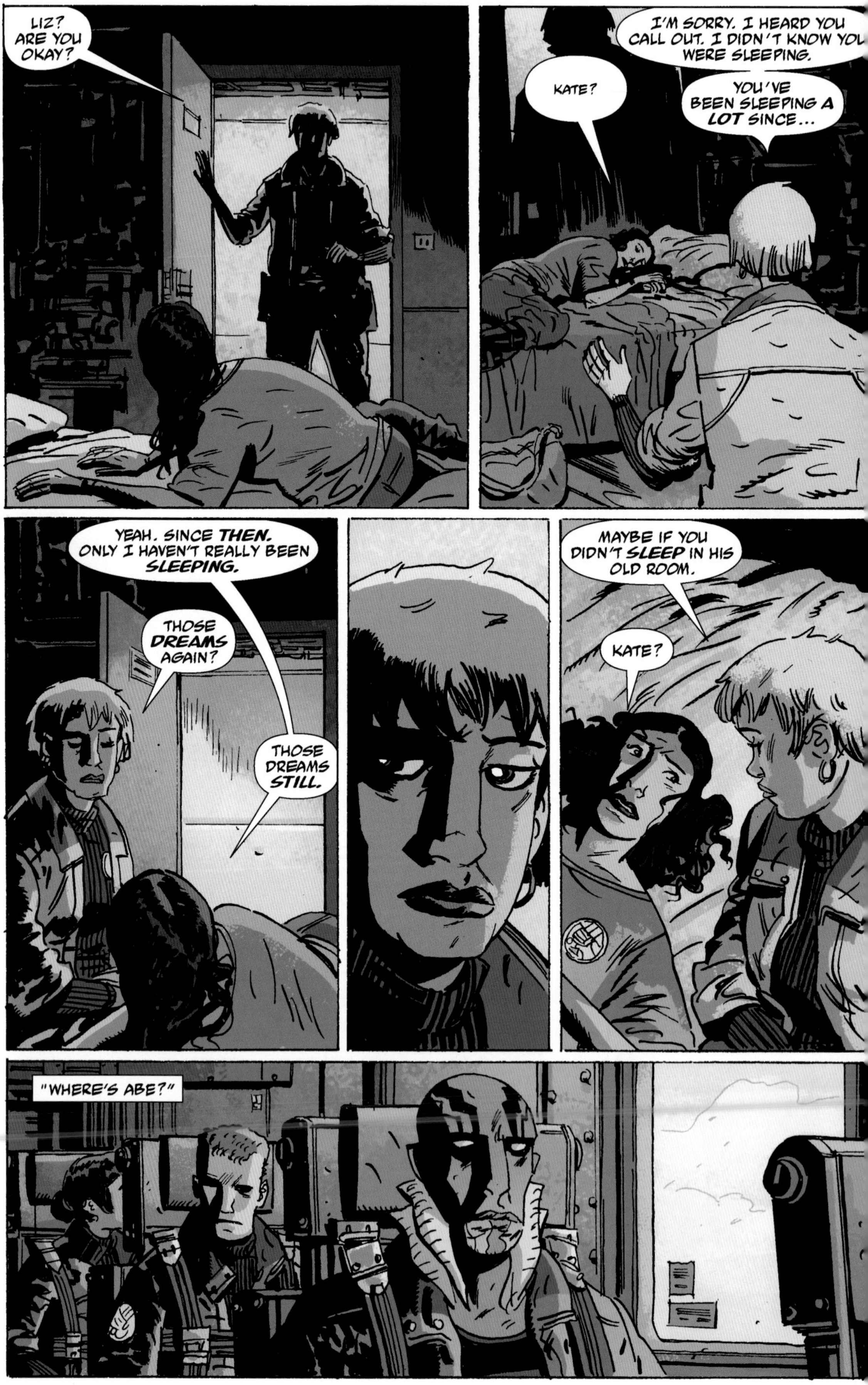

LIZ? ARE YOU OKAY?
KATE?
I'M SORRY. I HEARD YOU CALL OUT. I DIDN'T KNOW YOU WERE SLEEPING.
YOU'VE BEEN SLEEPING A LOT SINCE...
YEAH. SINCE THEN. ONLY I HAVEN'T REALLY BEEN SLEEPING.
THOSE DREAMS AGAIN?
THOSE DREAMS STILL.
MAYBE IF YOU DIDN'T SLEEP IN HIS OLD ROOM.
KATE?
"WHERE'S ABE?"

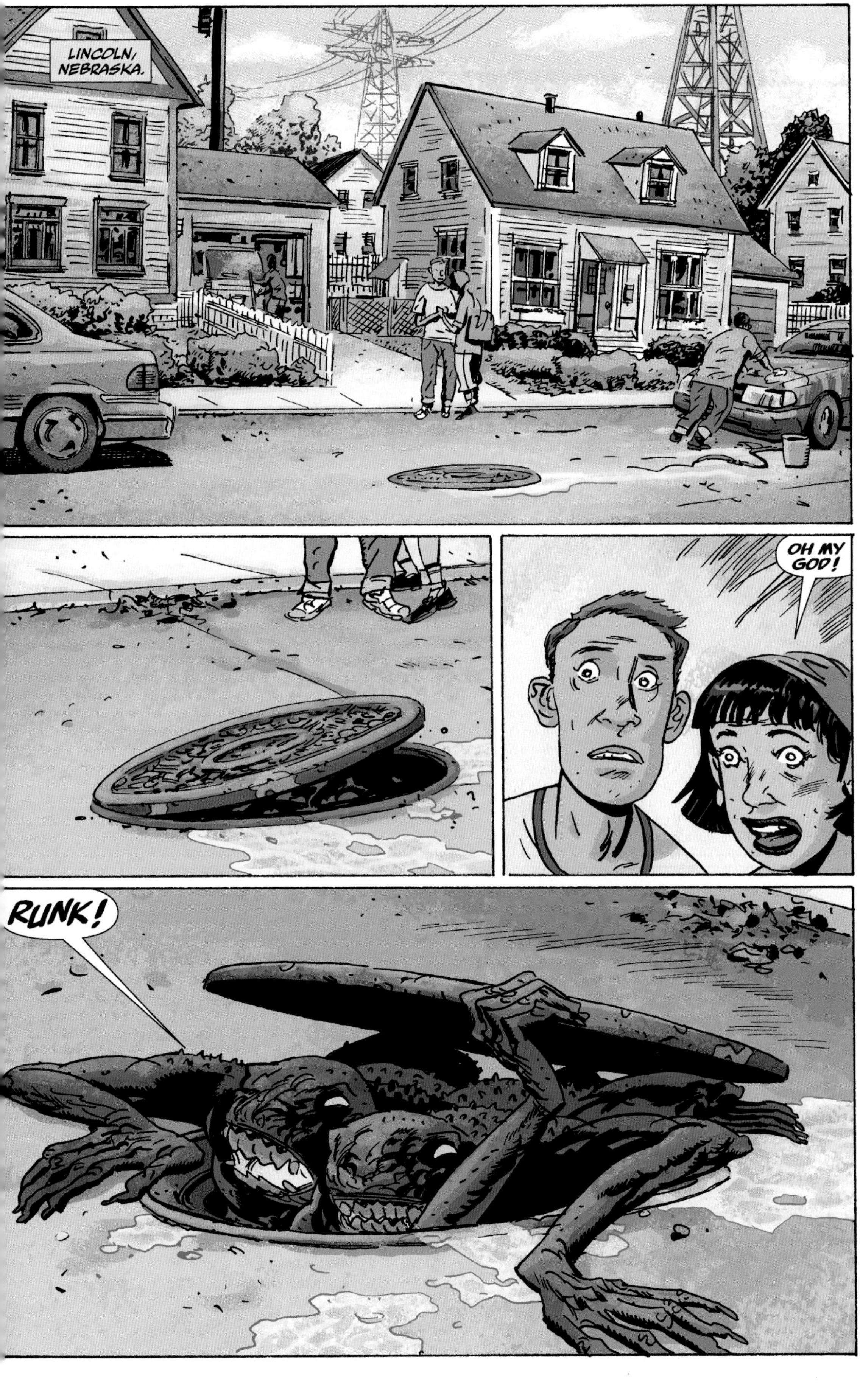
LINCOLN, NEBRASKA.
OH MY GOD!
RUNK!

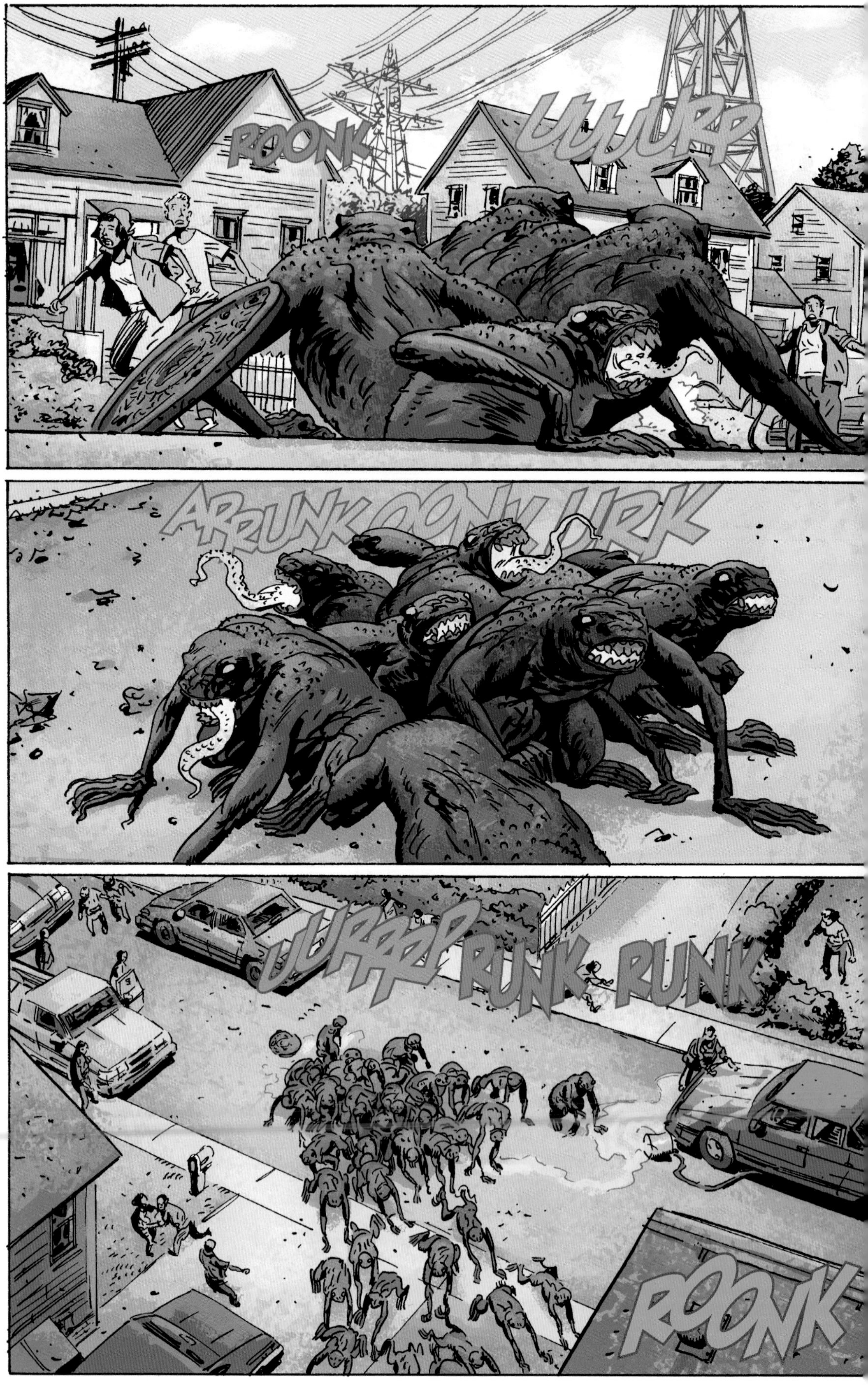
ROONK
UUUURP
ARRUNKOONKURK
UURRRP
RUNK
RUNK
ROONK

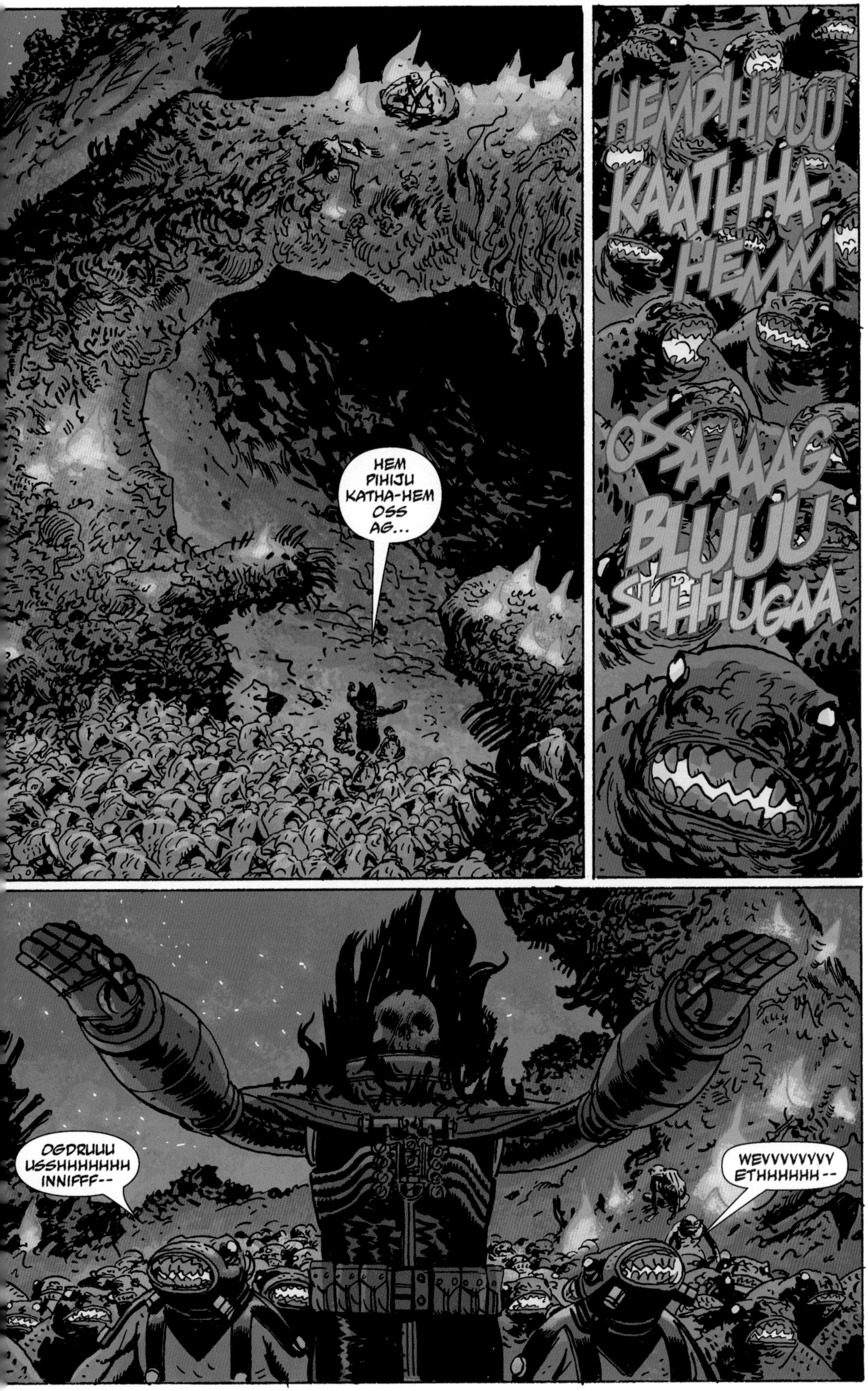
HEM PIHIJU KATHA-HEM OSS AG...
HEMPIHIJUU KAATHHA-HEMM
OSSAAAAG BLUUU SHHHUGAA
OGDRUUU USSHHHHHHH INNIFFF--
WEVVVVVVVY ETHHHHHH--

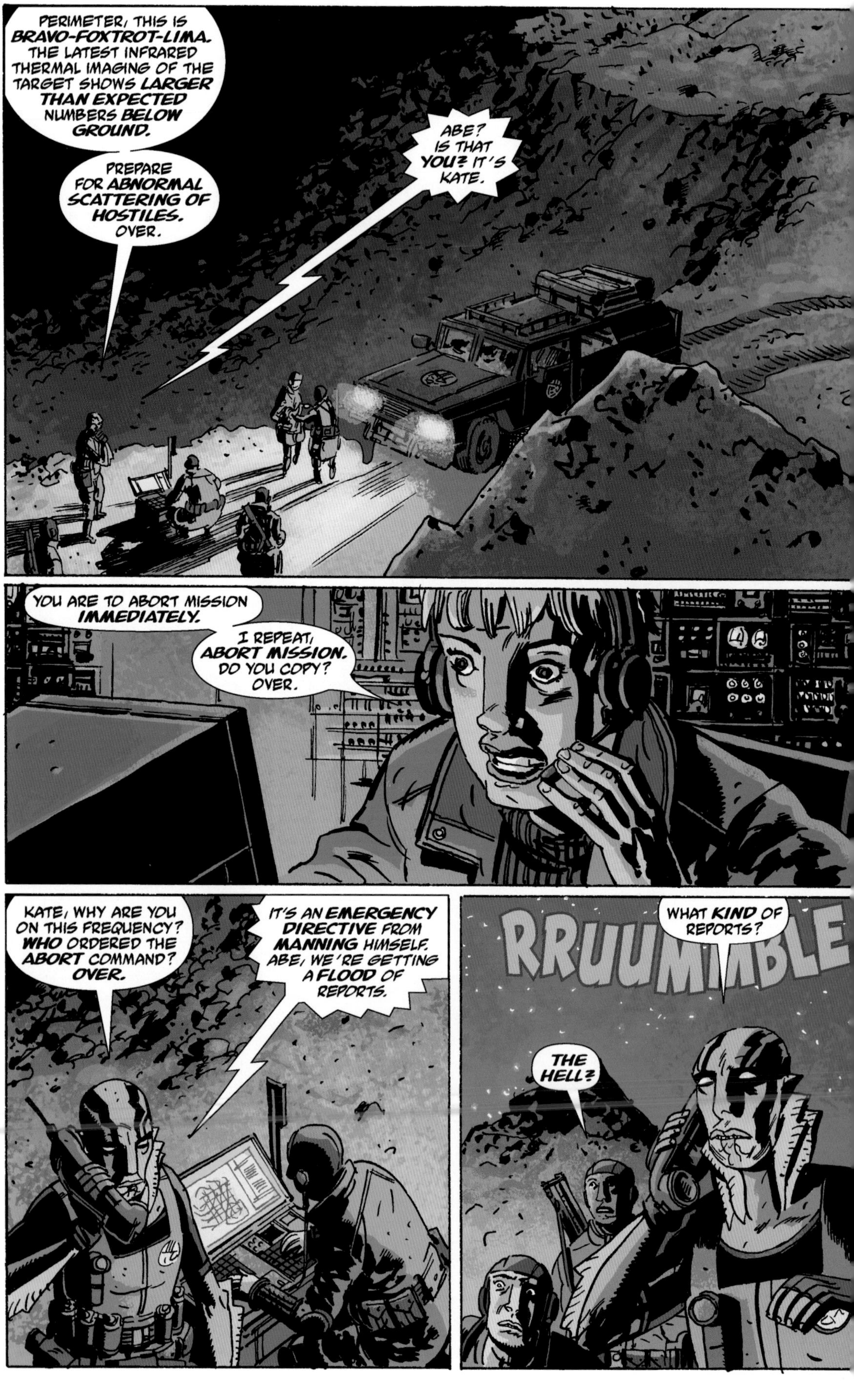
PERIMETER, THIS IS BRAVO-FOXTROT-LIMA. THE LATEST INFRARED THERMAL IMAGING OF THE TARGET SHOWS LARGER THAN EXPECTED NUMBERS BELOW GROUND.
PREPARE FOR ABNORMAL SCATTERING OF HOSTILES. OVER.
ABE? IS THAT YOU? IT'S KATE.
YOU ARE TO ABORT MISSION IMMEDIATELY.
I REPEAT, ABORT MISSION. DO YOU COPY? OVER.
KATE, WHY ARE YOU ON THIS FREQUENCY? WHO ORDERED THE ABORT COMMAND? OVER.
IT'S AN EMERGENCY DIRECTIVE FROM MANNING HIMSELF. ABE, WE'RE GETTING A FLOOD OF REPORTS.
RRUUMMBLE
WHAT KIND OF REPORTS?
THE HELL?

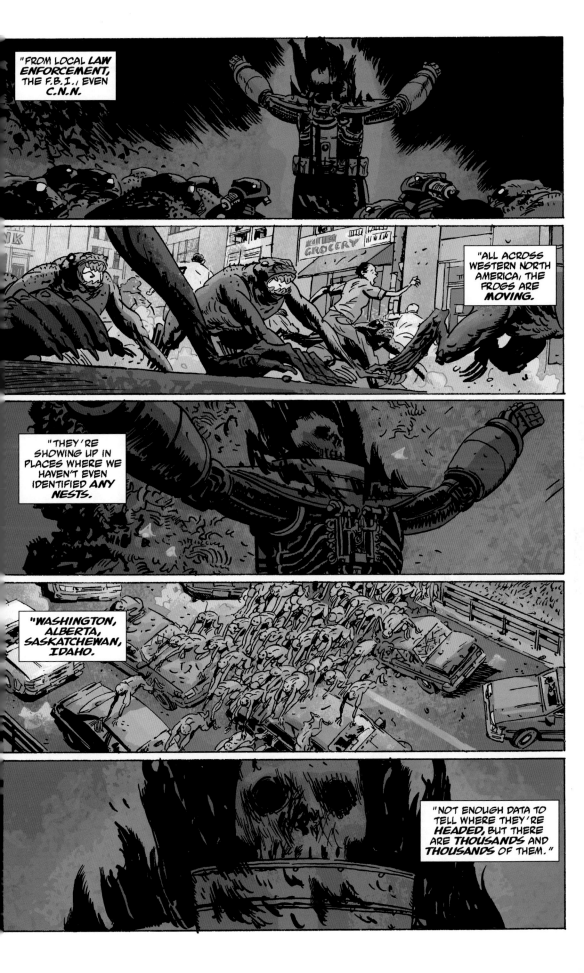

"FROM LOCAL *LAW ENFORCEMENT*, THE *F.B.I.*, EVEN *C.N.N.*

"ALL ACROSS WESTERN NORTH AMERICA, THE FROGS ARE *MOVING.*

"THEY'RE SHOWING UP IN PLACES WHERE WE HAVEN'T EVEN IDENTIFIED *ANY NESTS.*

"*WASHINGTON, ALBERTA, SASKATCHEWAN, IDAHO.*

"NOT ENOUGH DATA TO TELL WHERE THEY'RE *HEADED,* BUT THERE ARE *THOUSANDS* AND *THOUSANDS* OF THEM."

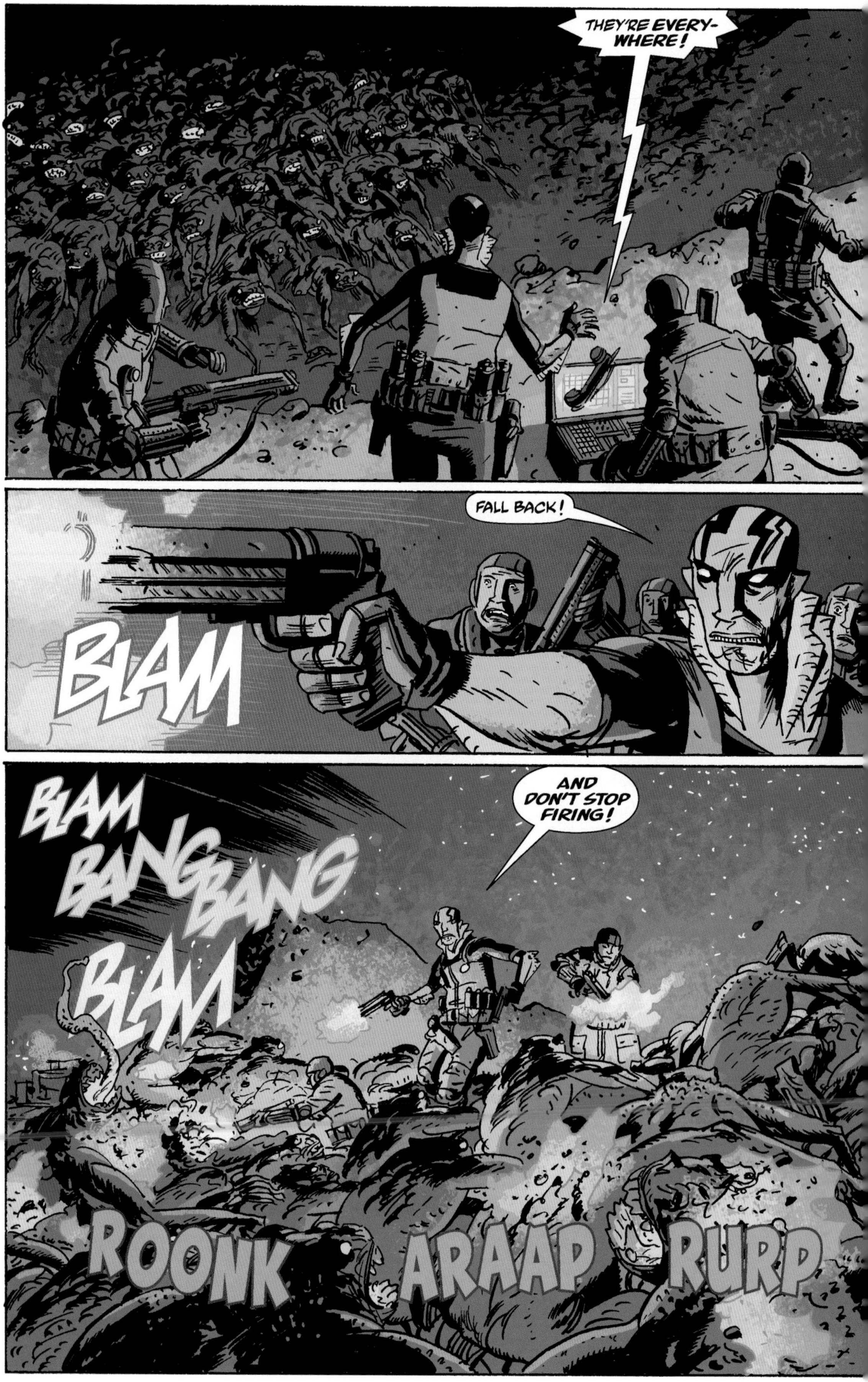
THEY'RE EVERY-WHERE!
FALL BACK!
BLAM
AND DON'T STOP FIRING!
BLAM
BANG BANG
BLAM
ROONK
ARAAP
RURP

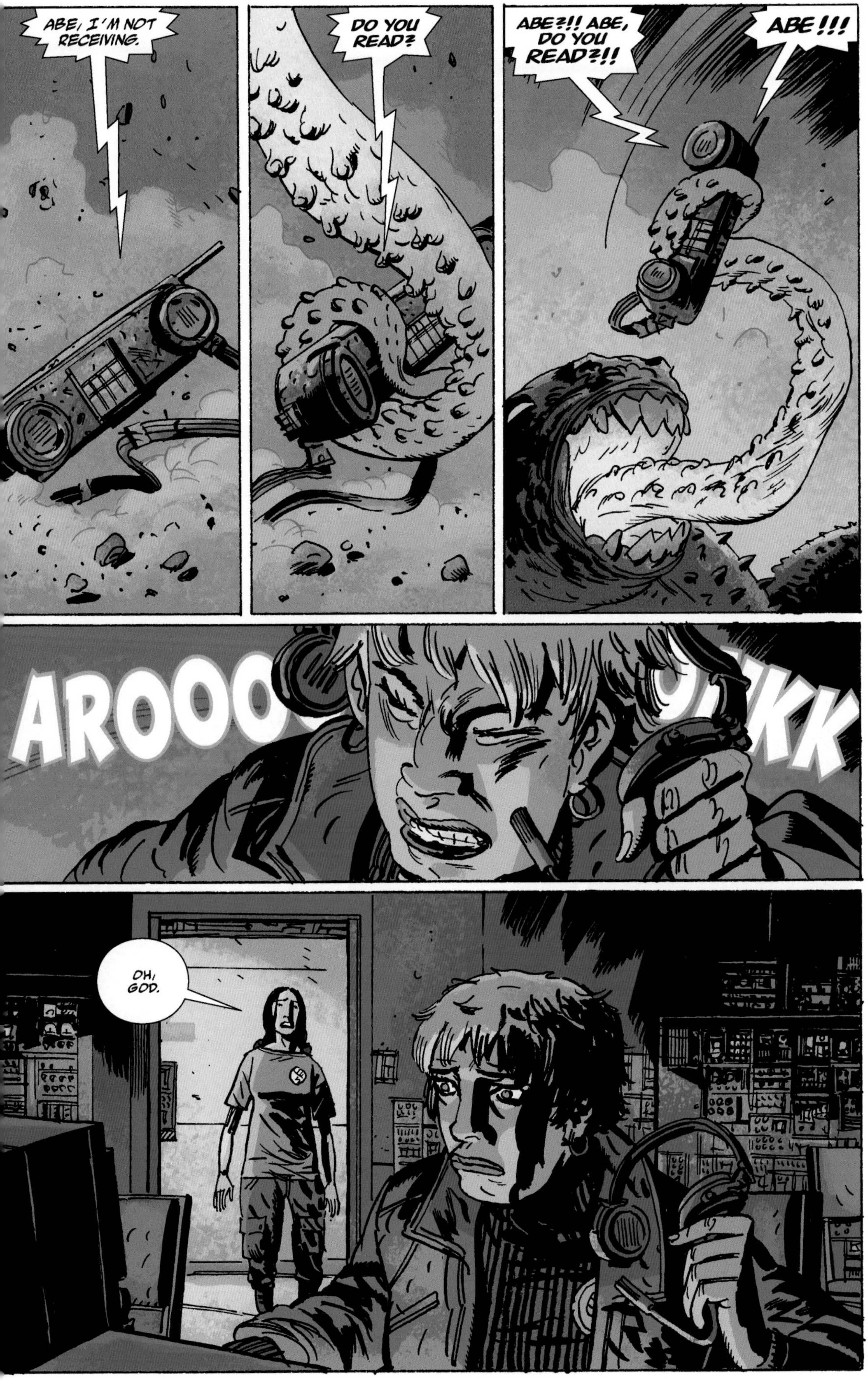
ABE, I'M NOT RECEIVING.
DO YOU READ?
ABE?!! ABE, DO YOU READ?!!
ABE!!!
AROOO
KK
OH, GOD.

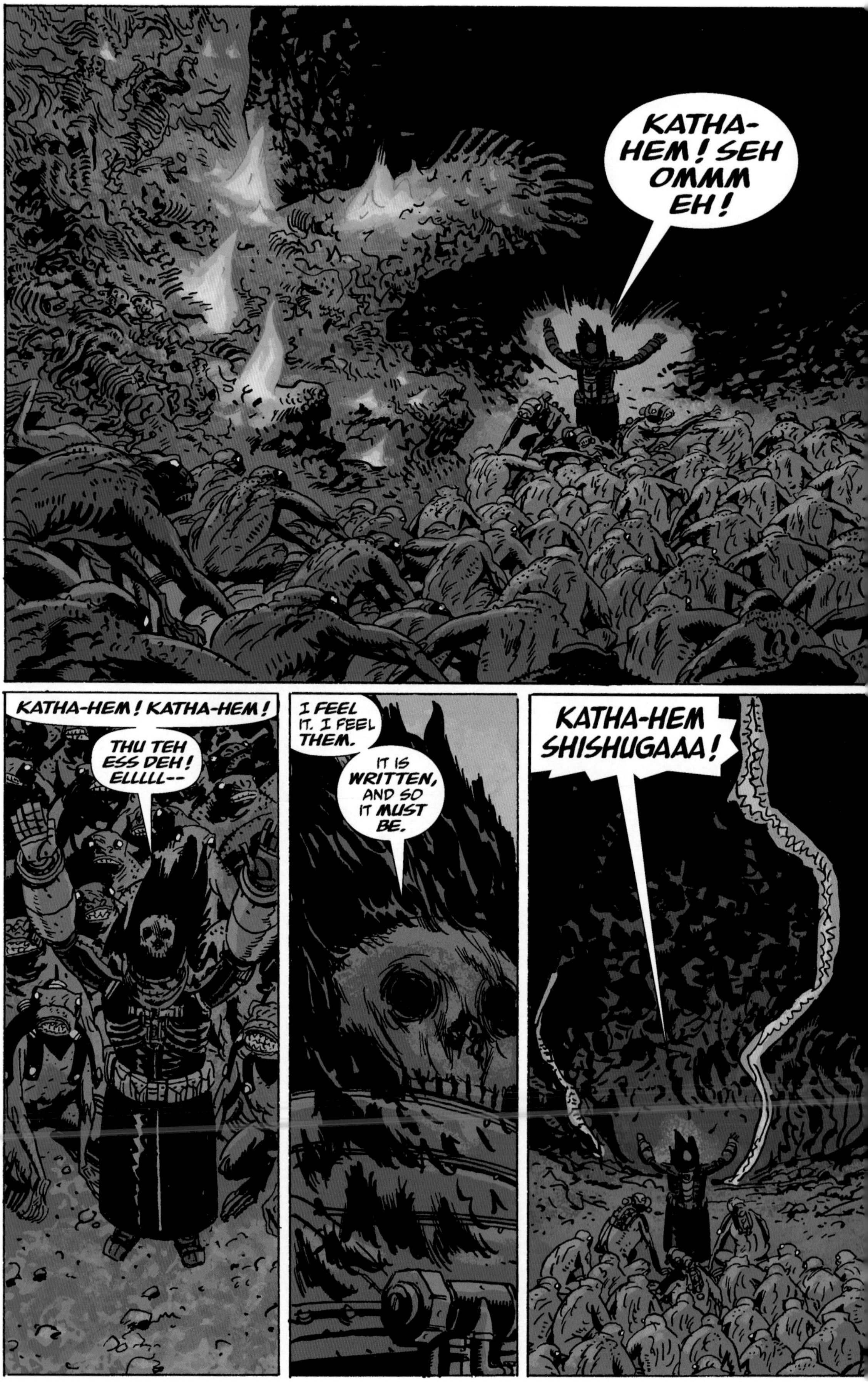
KATHA-HEM! SEH OMMM EH!
KATHA-HEM! KATHA-HEM!
THU TEH ESS DEH! ELLLLL--
I FEEL IT. I FEEL THEM.
IT IS WRITTEN, AND SO IT MUST BE.
KATHA-HEM SHISHUGAAA!

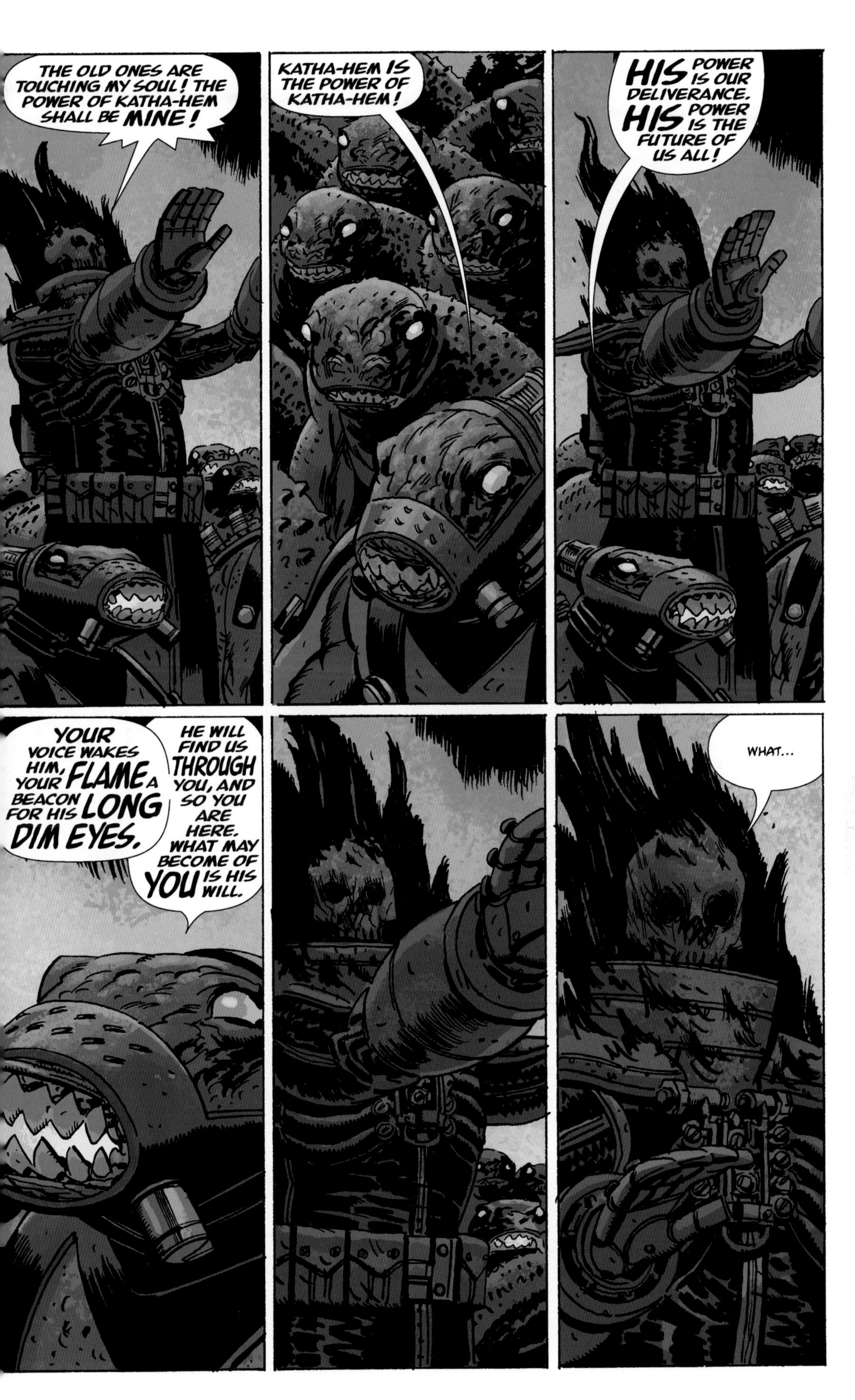
THE OLD ONES ARE TOUCHING MY SOUL! THE POWER OF KATHA-HEM SHALL BE MINE!
KATHA-HEM IS THE POWER OF KATHA-HEM!
HIS POWER IS OUR DELIVERANCE. HIS POWER IS THE FUTURE OF US ALL!
YOUR VOICE WAKES HIM, YOUR FLAME A BEACON FOR HIS LONG DIM EYES.
HE WILL FIND US THROUGH YOU, AND SO YOU ARE HERE. WHAT MAY BECOME OF YOU IS HIS WILL.
WHAT...

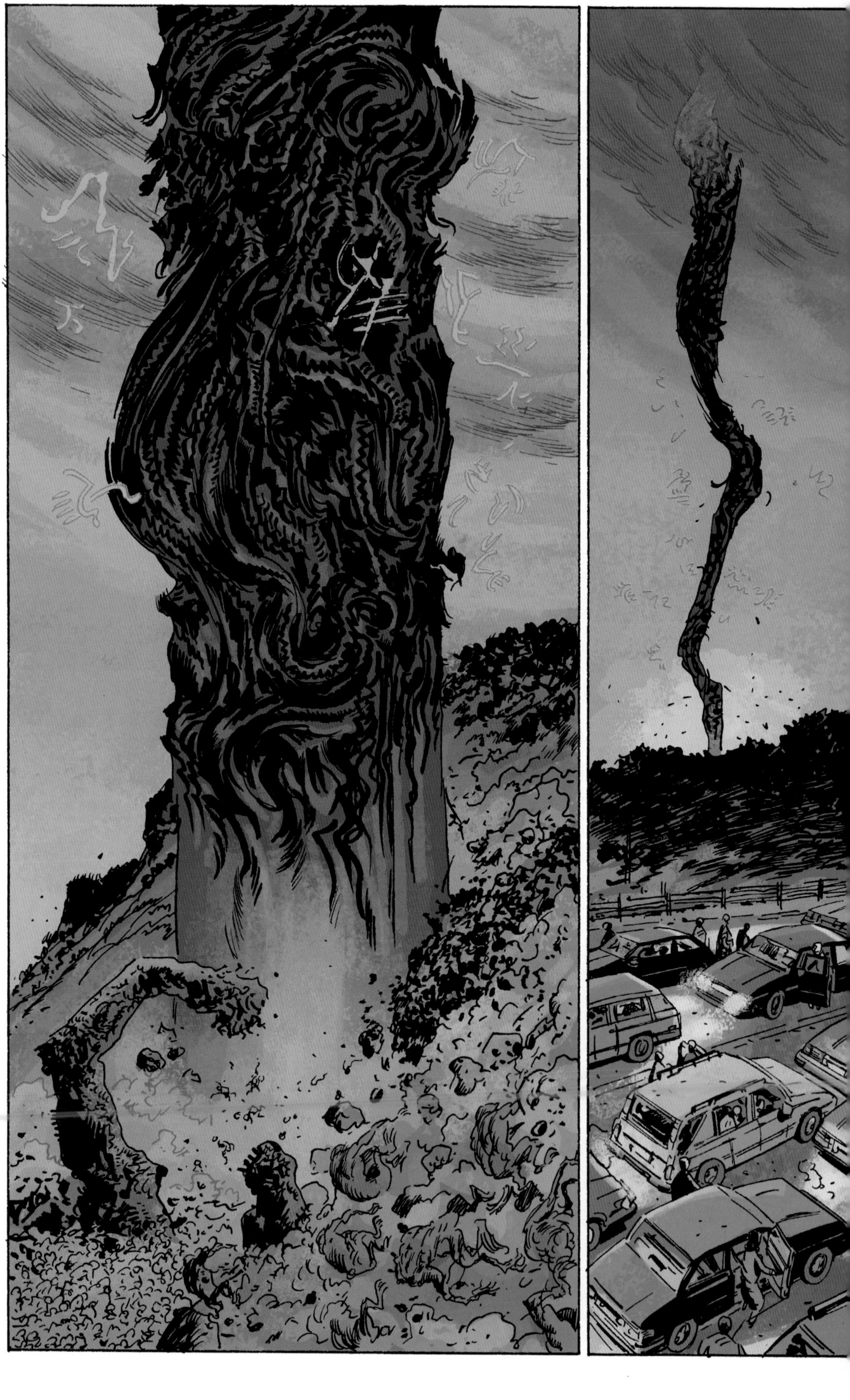

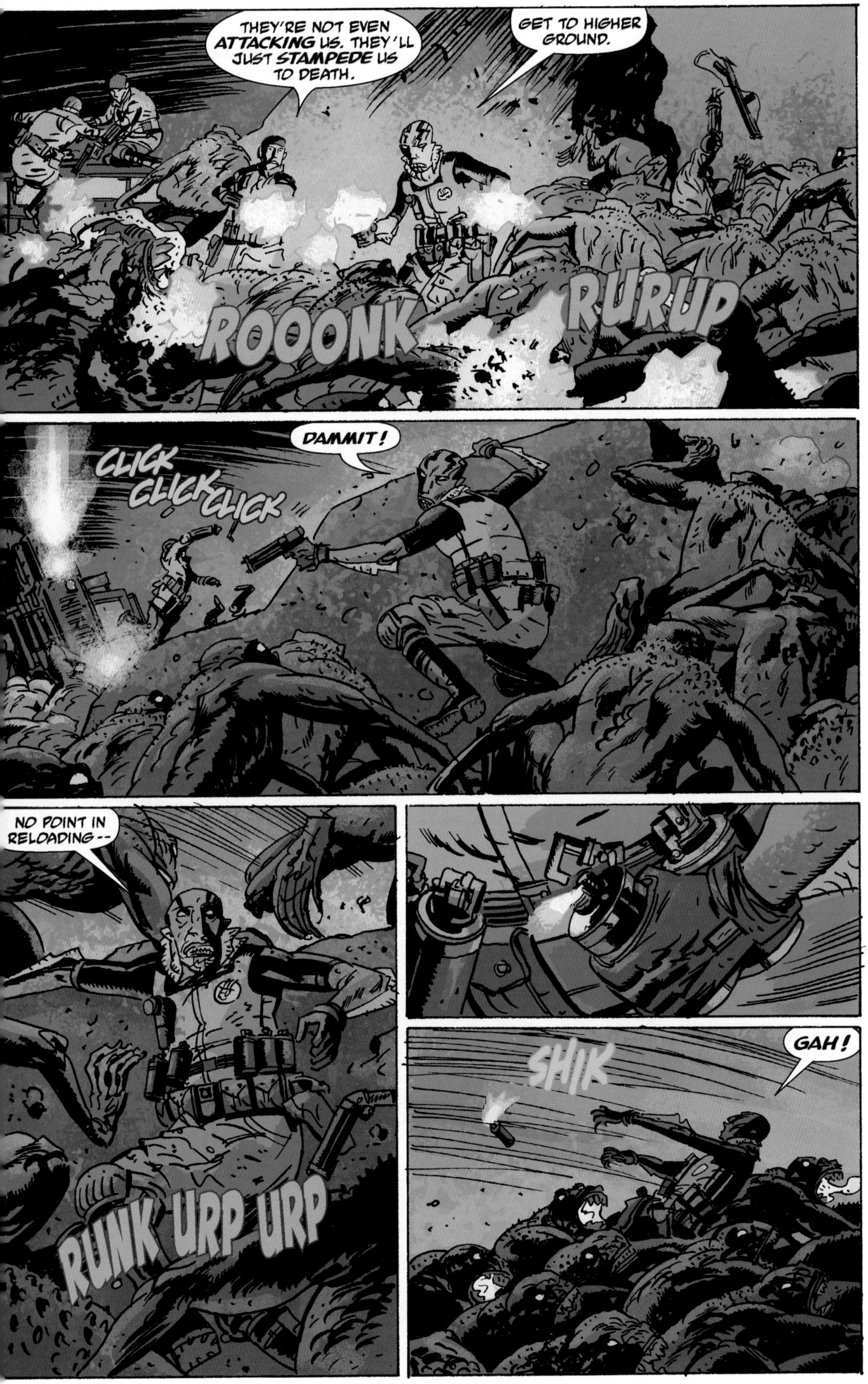

THEY'RE NOT EVEN ATTACKING US. THEY'LL JUST STAMPEDE US TO DEATH.
GET TO HIGHER GROUND.
ROOONK
RURUP
DAMMIT!
CLICK CLICK CLICK
NO POINT IN RELOADING --
RUNK URP URP
SHIK
GAH!

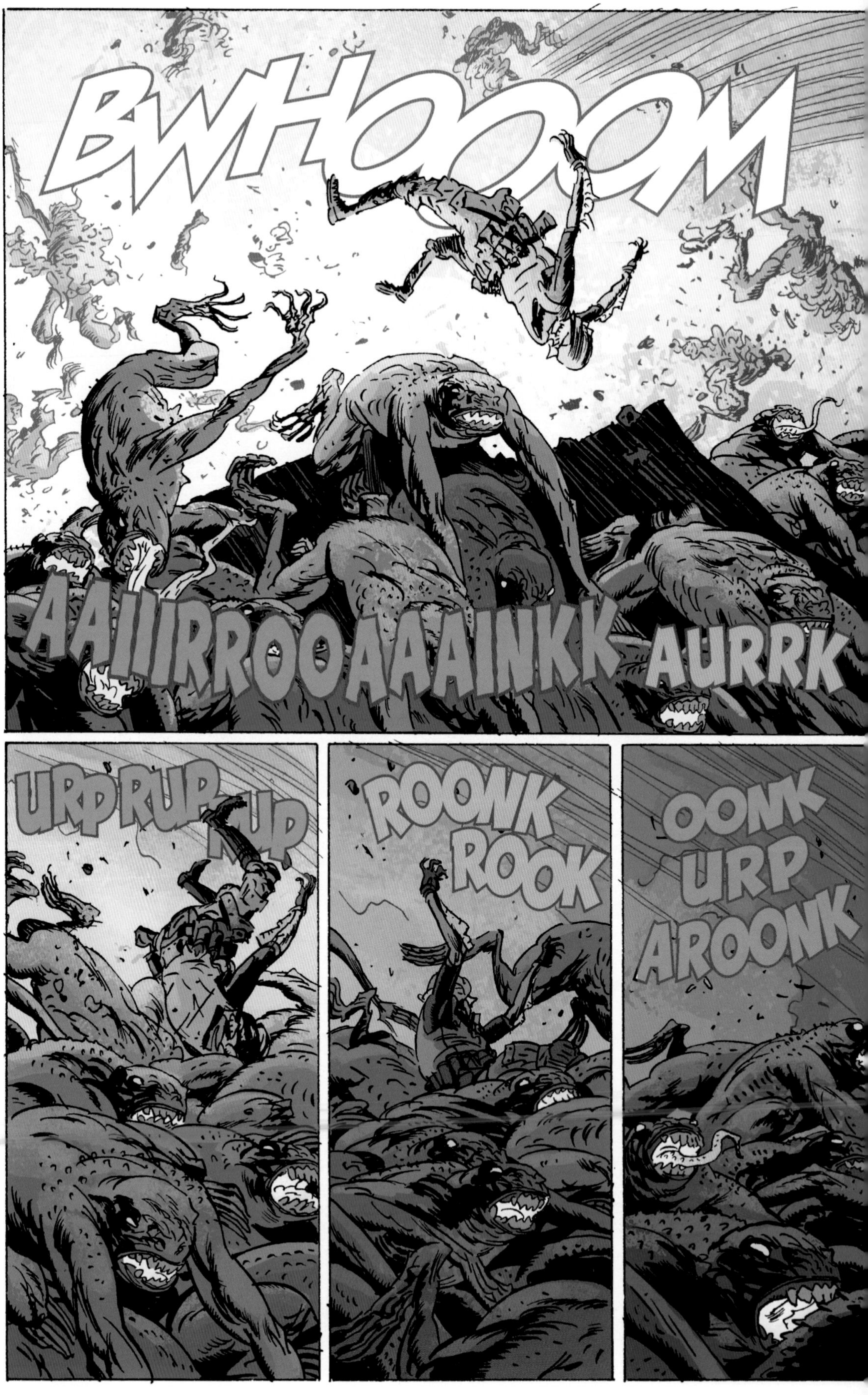
BWHOOOOM
AAIIIRROOAAAINKK
AURRK
URP RUP
UP
ROONK
ROOK
OONK
URP
AROONK

# CHAPTER FIVE

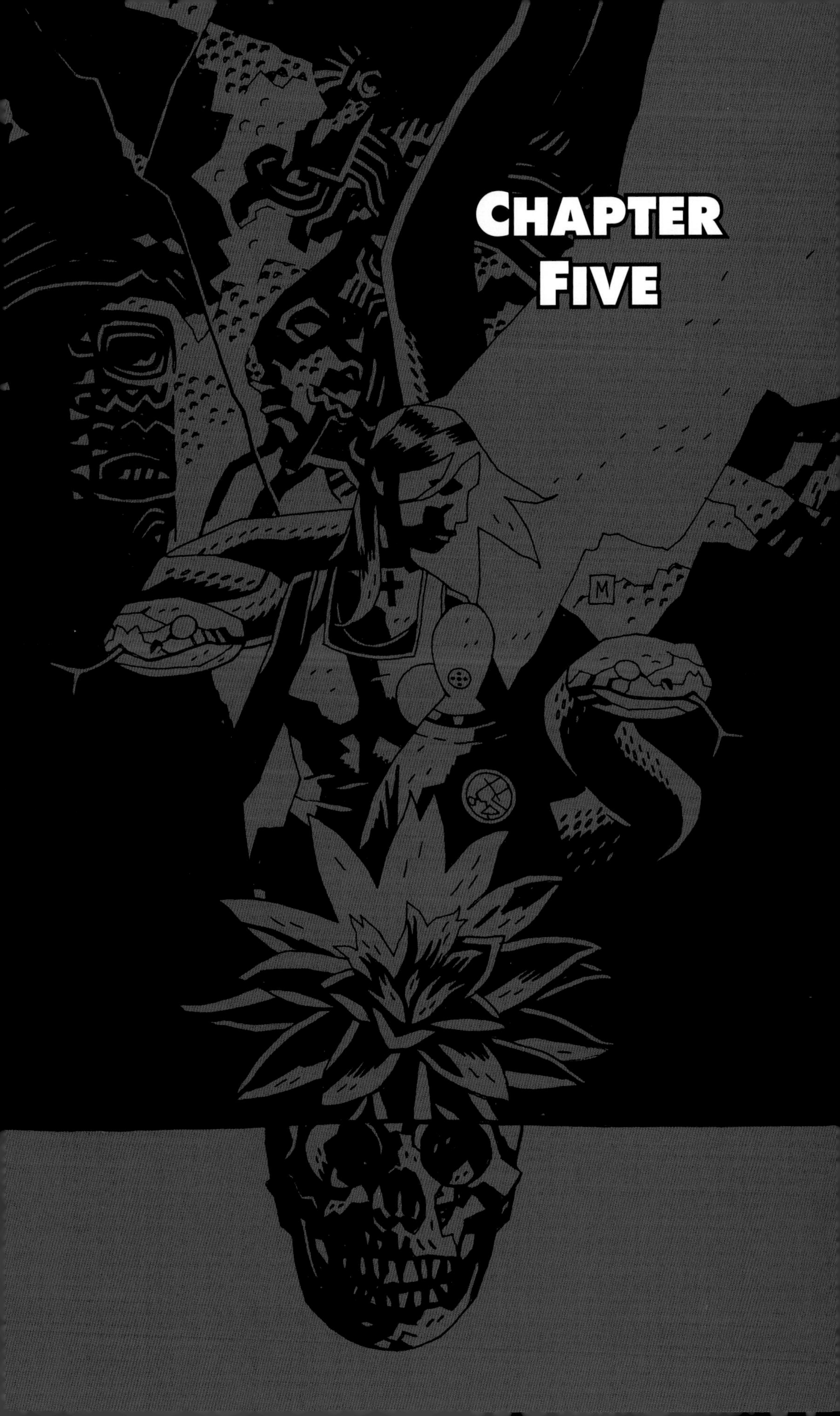

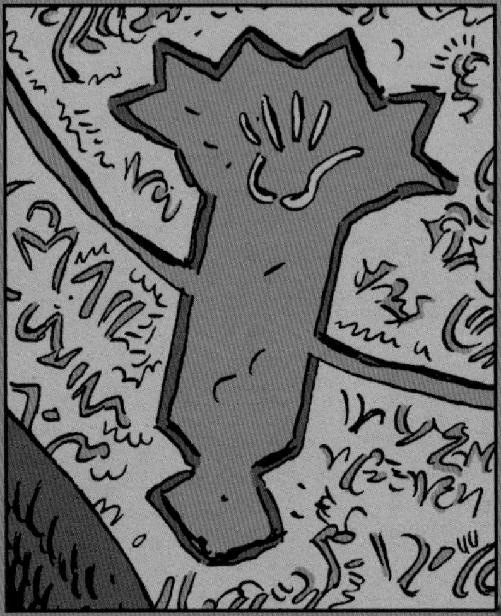

...UHHHH...

I...

I THINK I MADE A MISTAKE.

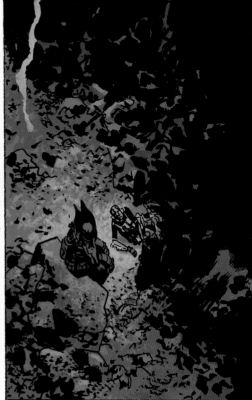

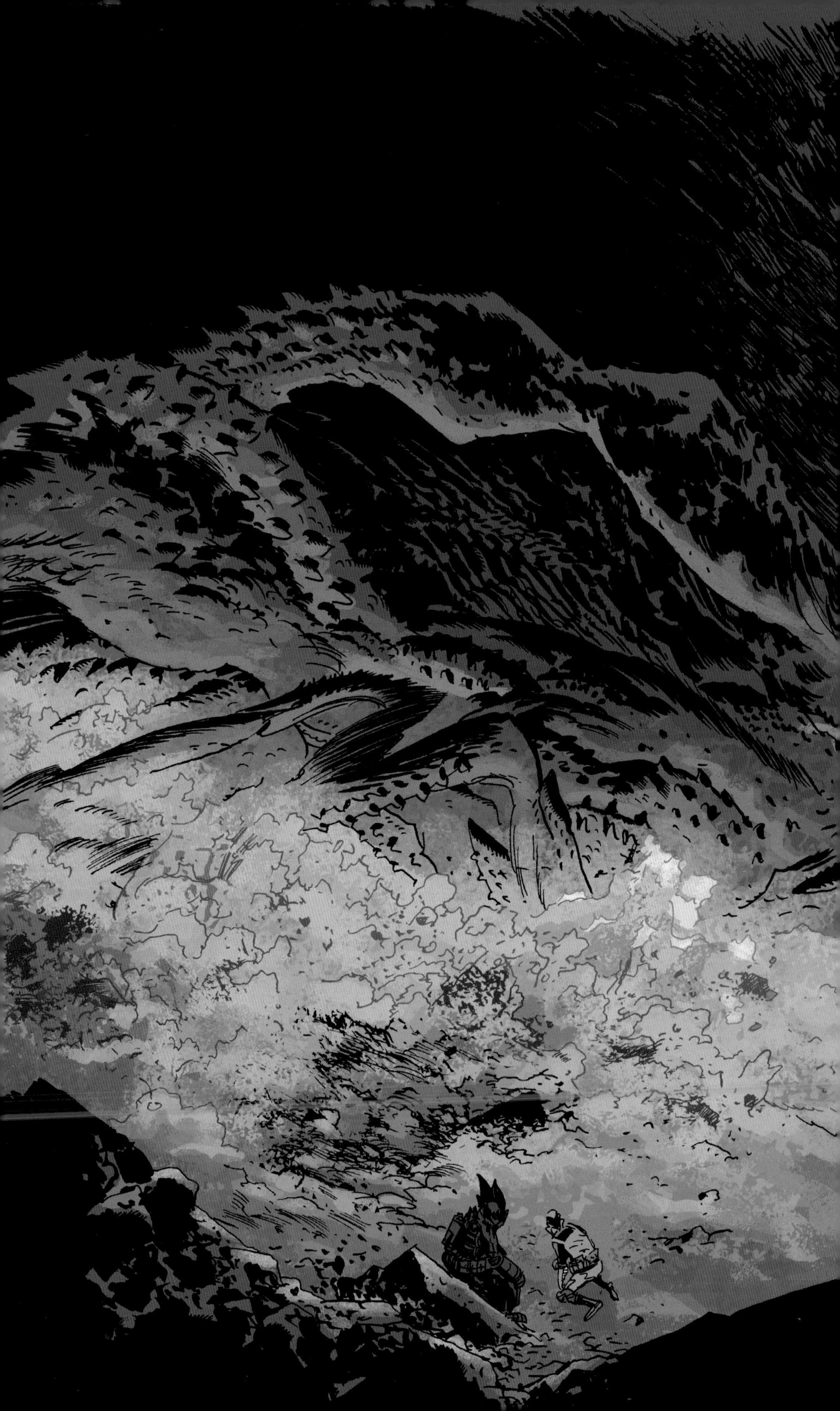

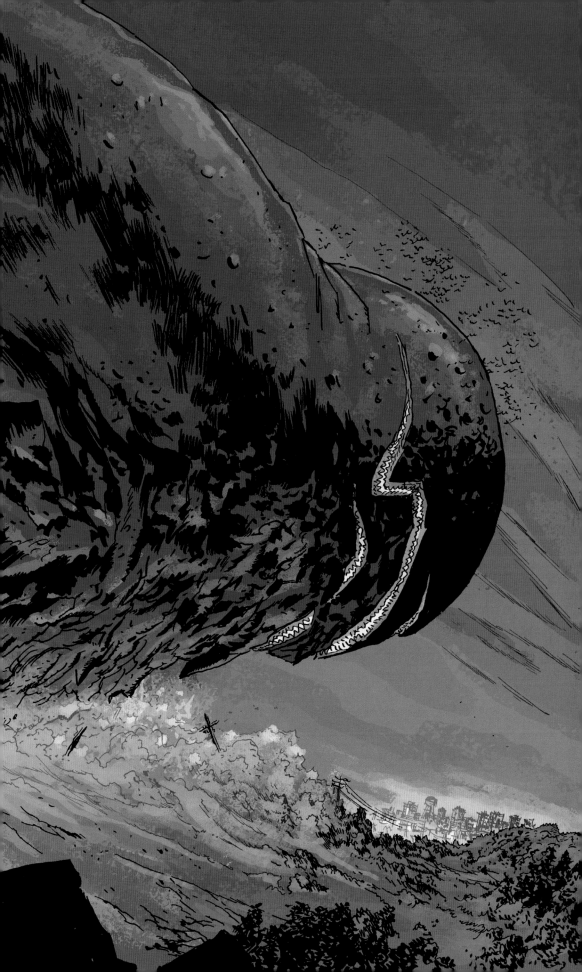

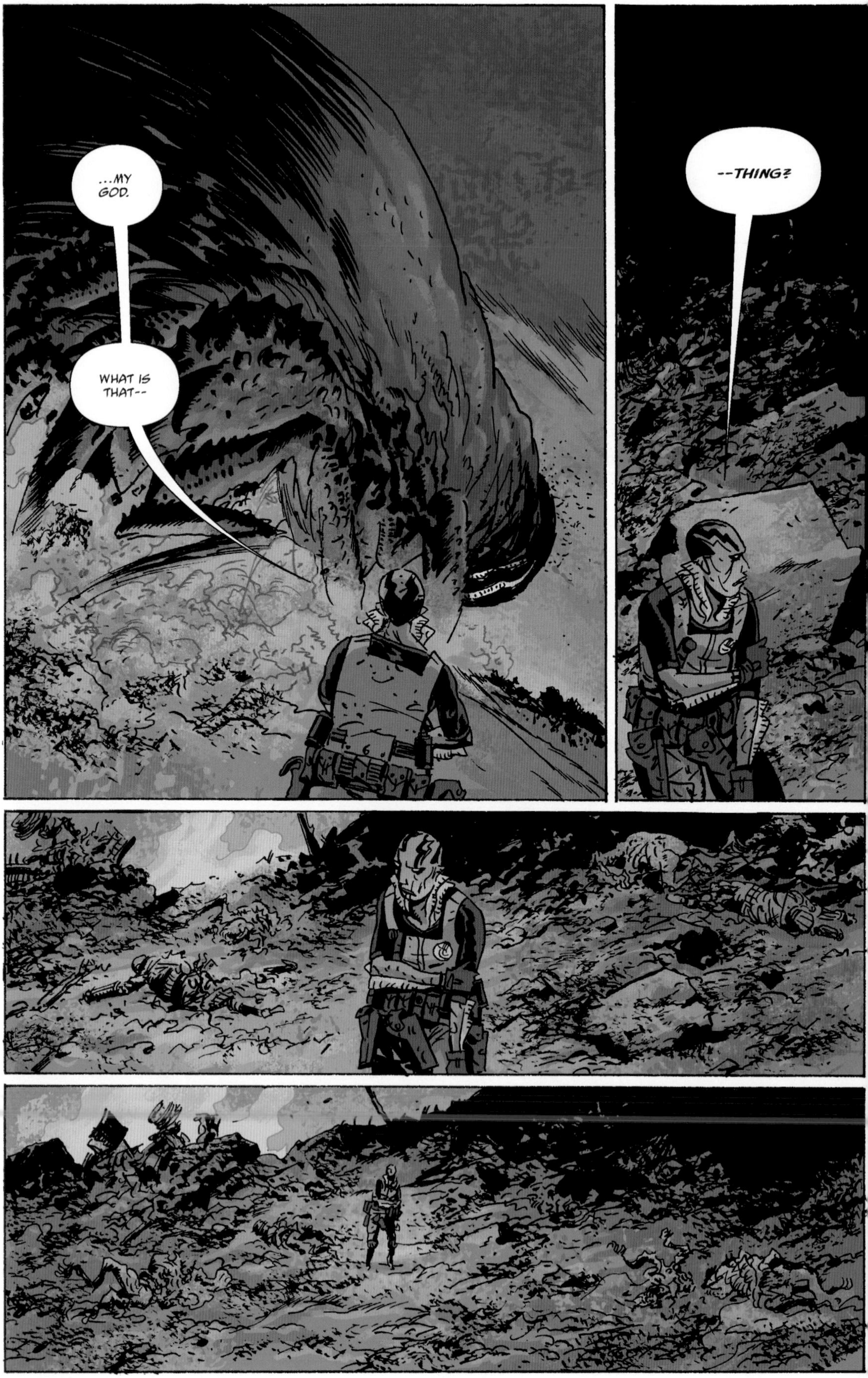
...MY GOD.
WHAT IS THAT--
--THING?

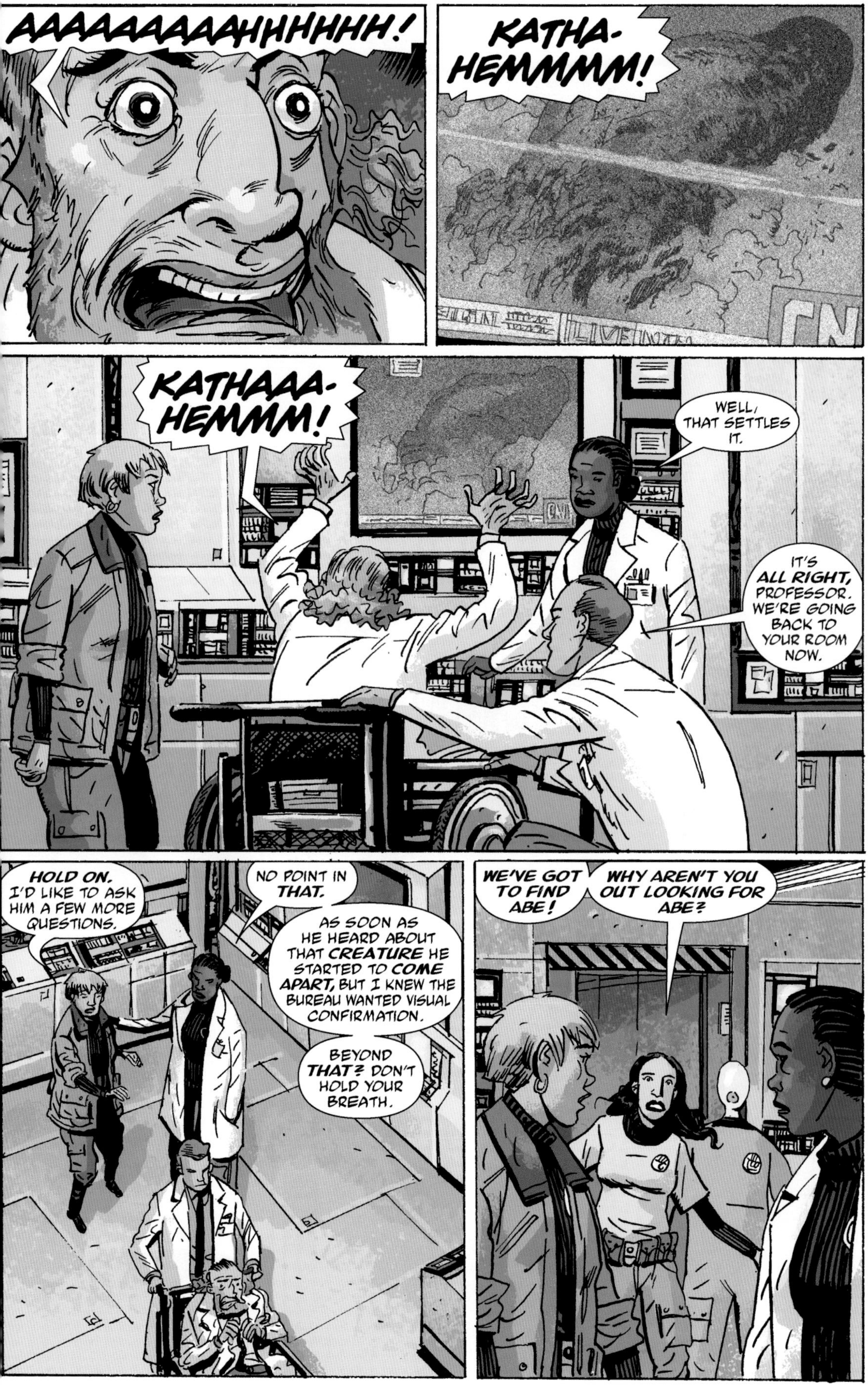
AAAAAAAAAHHHHHH!
KATHA-HEMMMM!
KATHAAA-HEMMM!
WELL, THAT SETTLES IT.
IT'S ALL RIGHT, PROFESSOR. WE'RE GOING BACK TO YOUR ROOM NOW.
HOLD ON. I'D LIKE TO ASK HIM A FEW MORE QUESTIONS.
NO POINT IN THAT.
AS SOON AS HE HEARD ABOUT THAT CREATURE HE STARTED TO COME APART, BUT I KNEW THE BUREAU WANTED VISUAL CONFIRMATION.
BEYOND THAT? DON'T HOLD YOUR BREATH.
WE'VE GOT TO FIND ABE!
WHY AREN'T YOU OUT LOOKING FOR ABE?

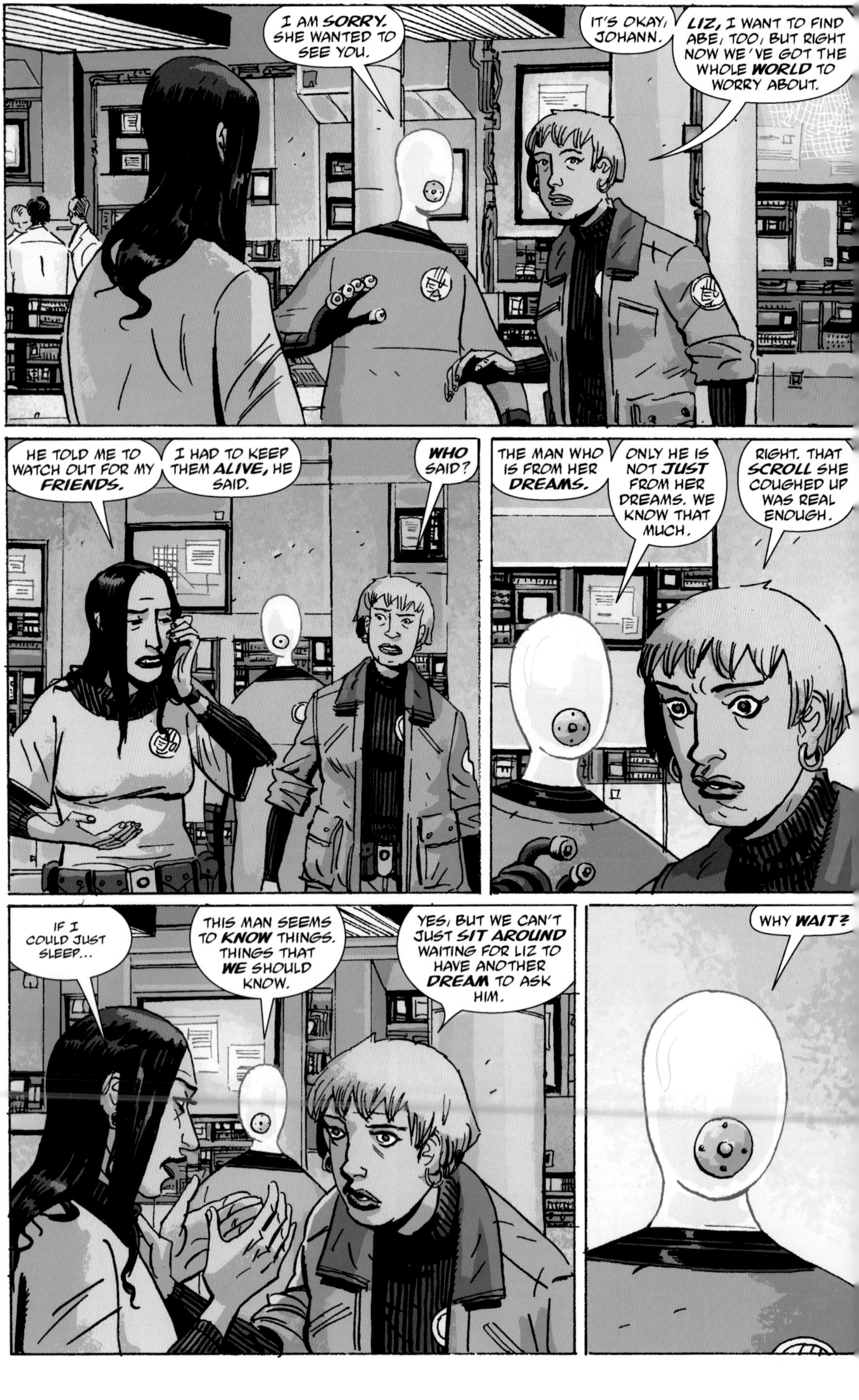
I AM **SORRY.** SHE WANTED TO SEE YOU.
IT'S OKAY, JOHANN.
**LIZ,** I WANT TO FIND ABE, TOO, BUT RIGHT NOW WE'VE GOT THE WHOLE **WORLD** TO WORRY ABOUT.
HE TOLD ME TO WATCH OUT FOR MY **FRIENDS.**
I HAD TO KEEP THEM **ALIVE,** HE SAID.
**WHO** SAID?
THE MAN WHO IS FROM HER **DREAMS.**
ONLY HE IS NOT **JUST** FROM HER DREAMS. WE KNOW THAT MUCH.
RIGHT. THAT **SCROLL** SHE COUGHED UP WAS REAL ENOUGH.
IF I COULD JUST SLEEP...
THIS MAN SEEMS TO **KNOW** THINGS. THINGS THAT **WE** SHOULD KNOW.
YES, BUT WE CAN'T JUST **SIT AROUND** WAITING FOR LIZ TO HAVE ANOTHER **DREAM** TO ASK HIM.
WHY **WAIT?**

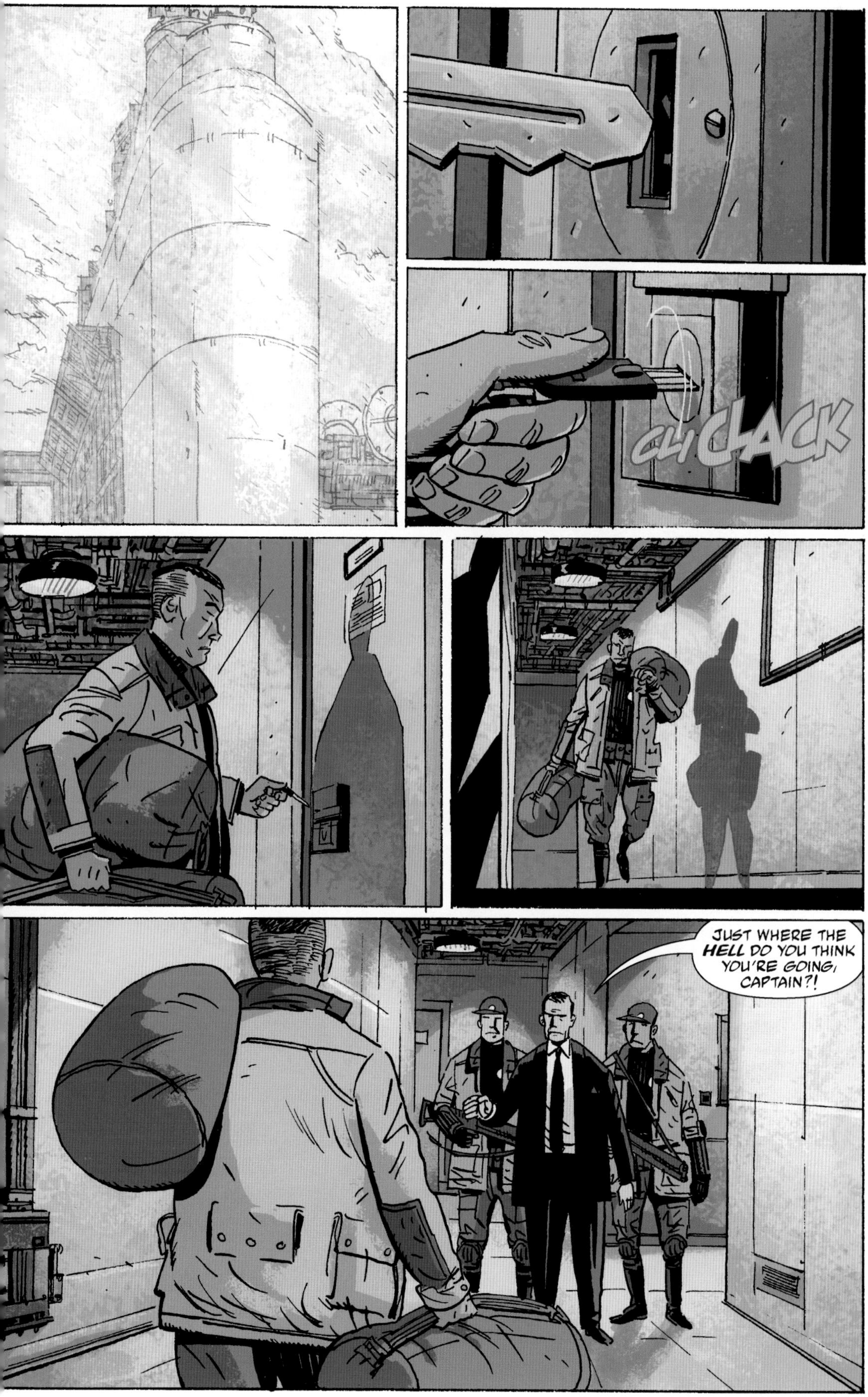
CLI CLACK
JUST WHERE THE **HELL** DO YOU THINK YOU'RE GOING, CAPTAIN?!

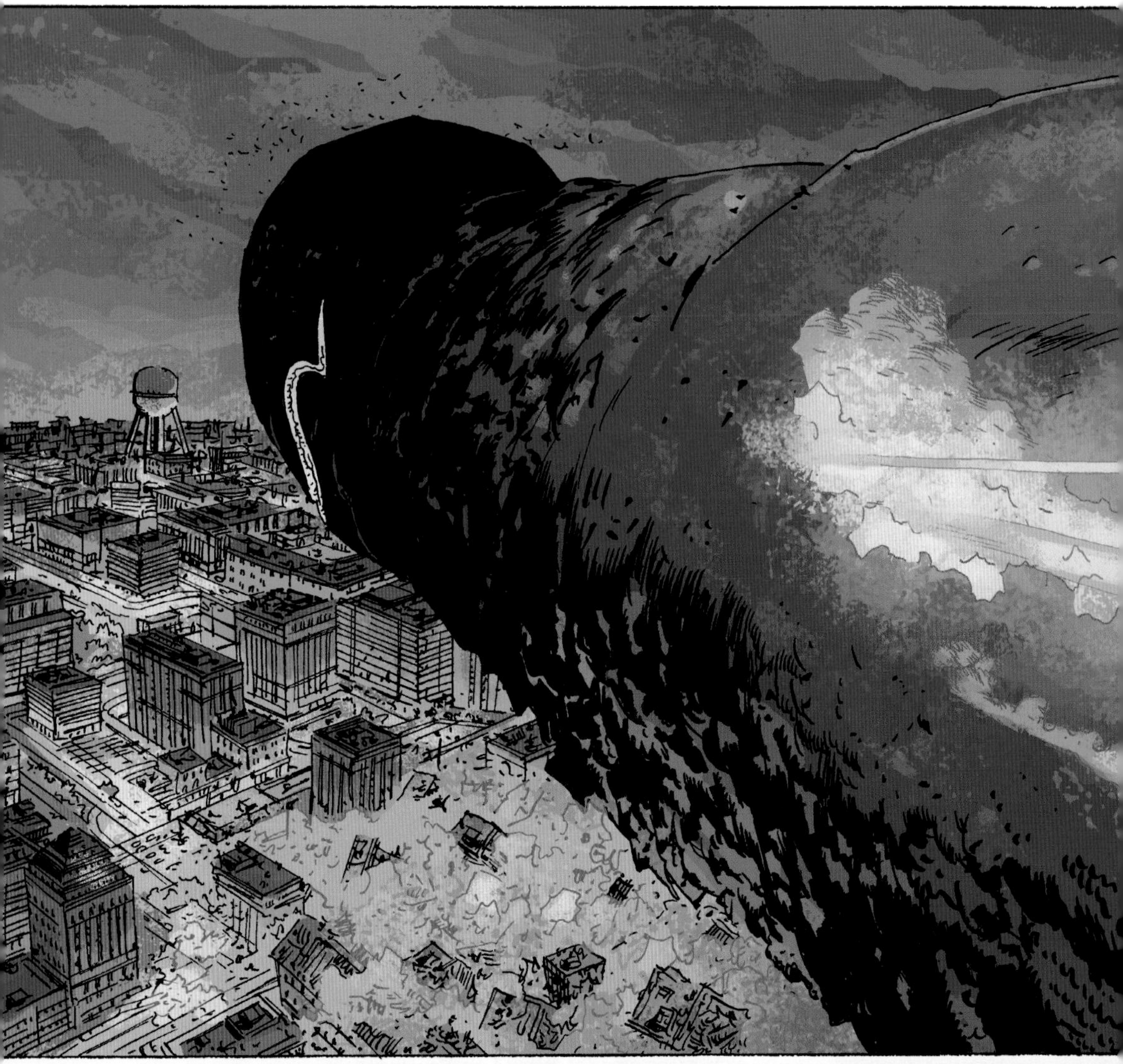

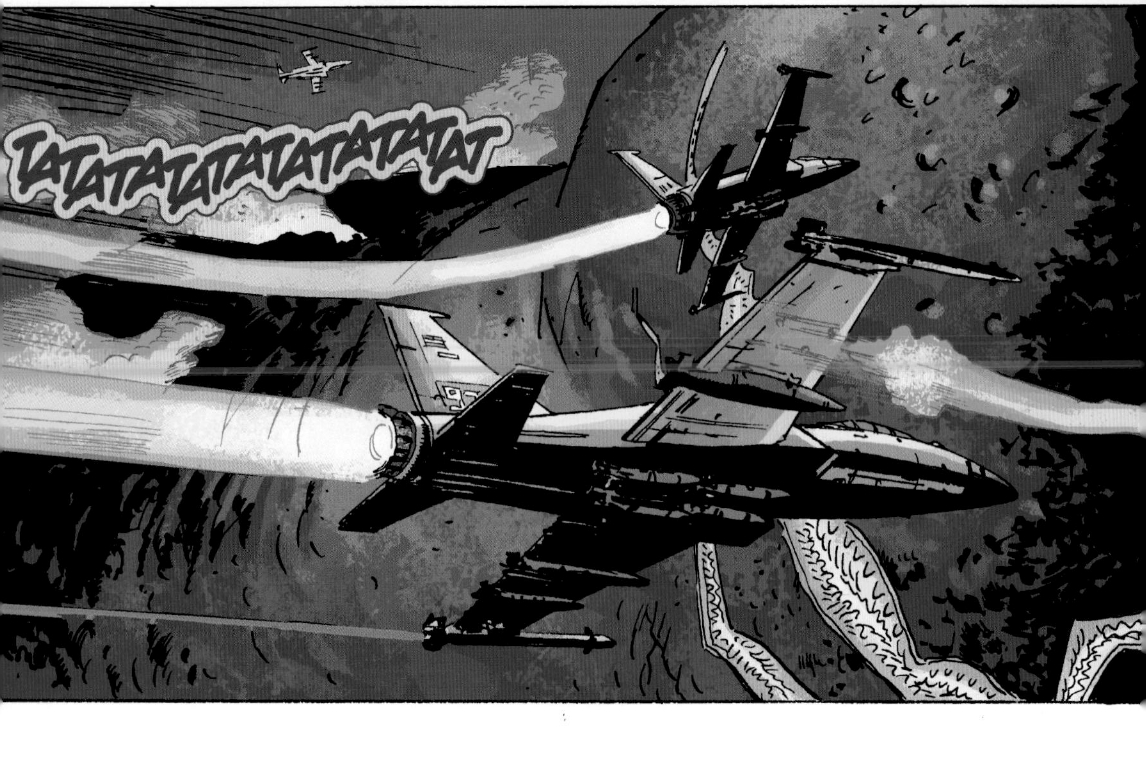
TATATATATATATATATATAT

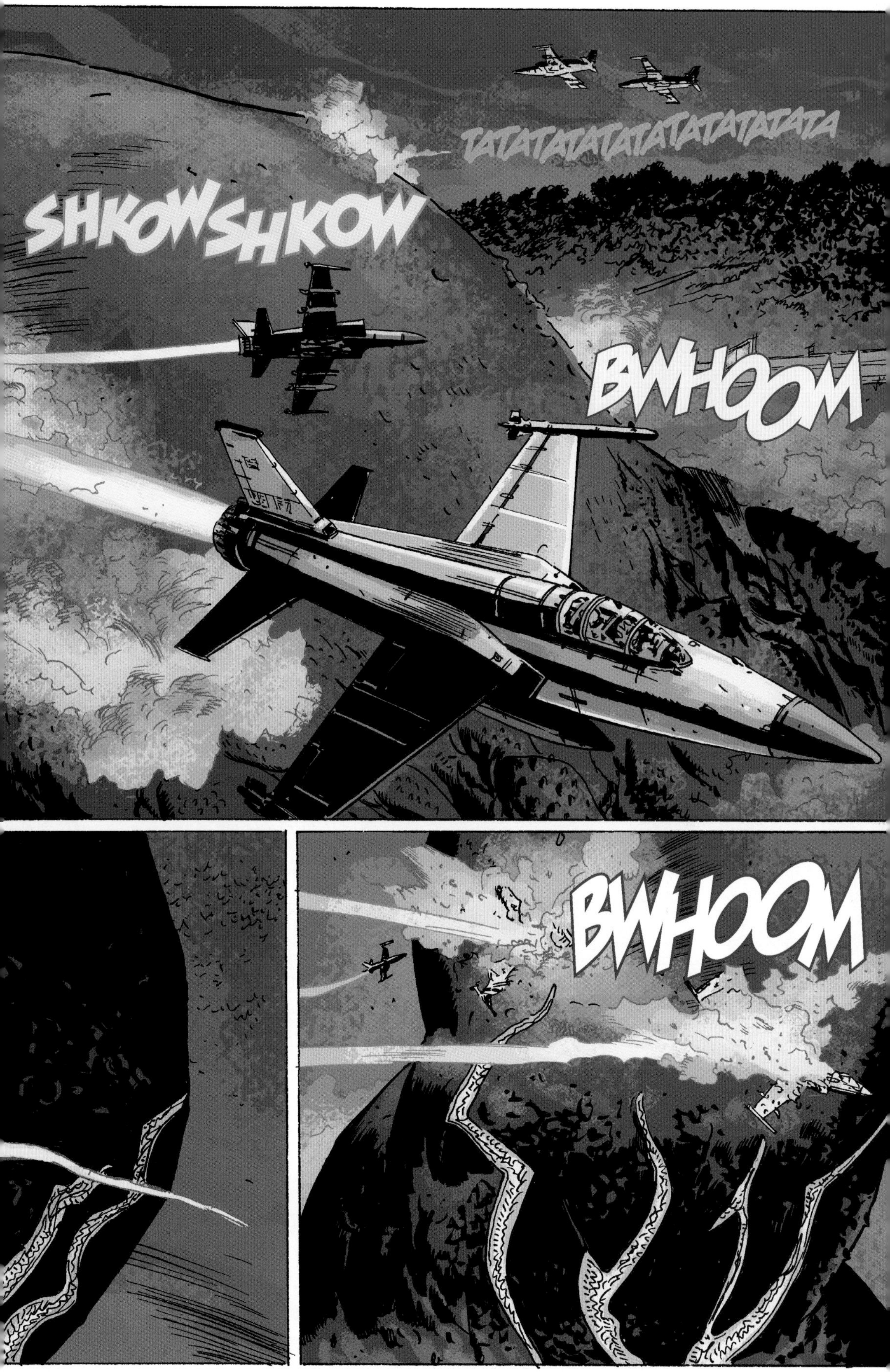
TATATATATATATATATATATATA
SHKOW SHKOW
BWHOOM
BWHOOM

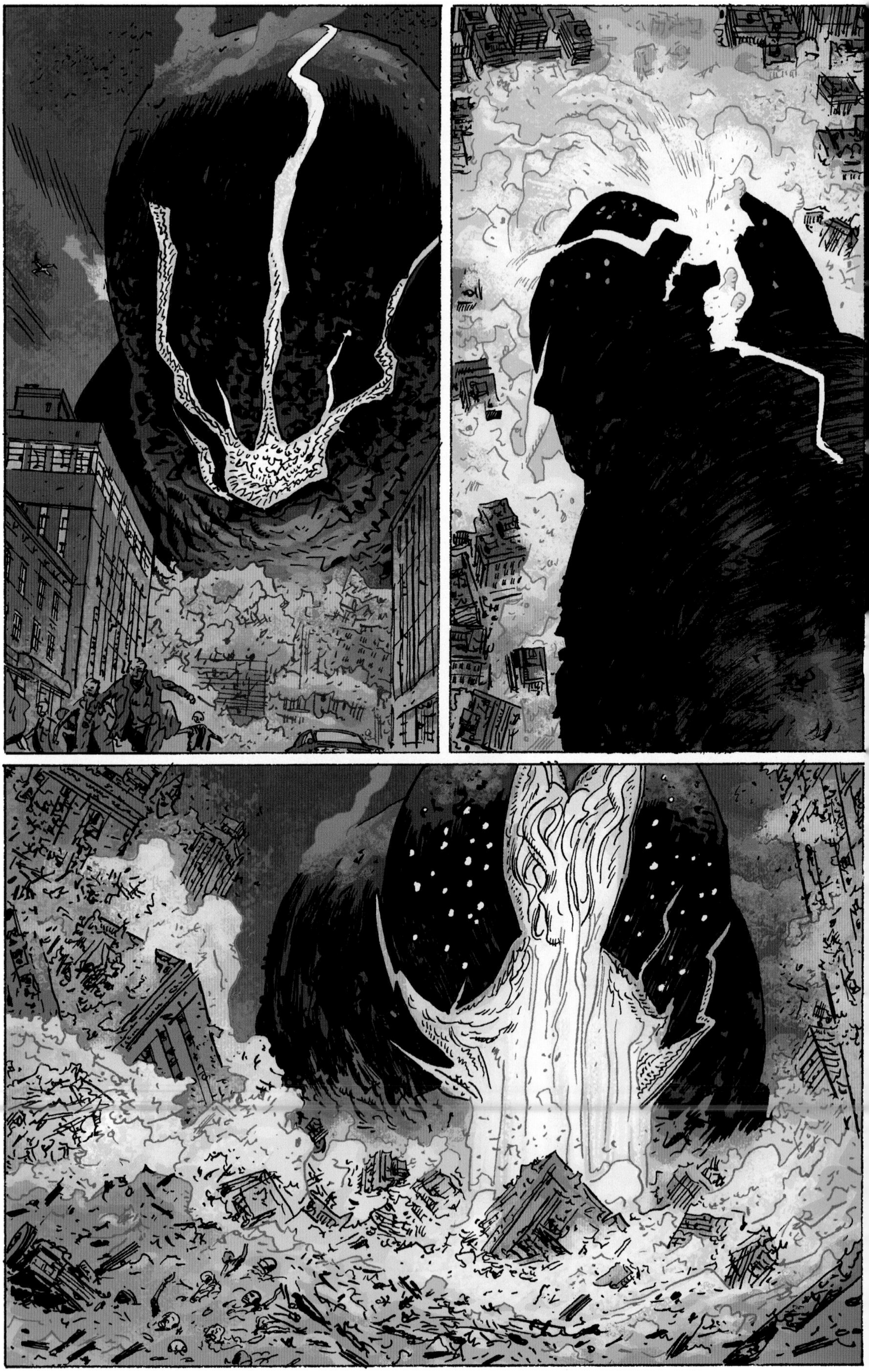

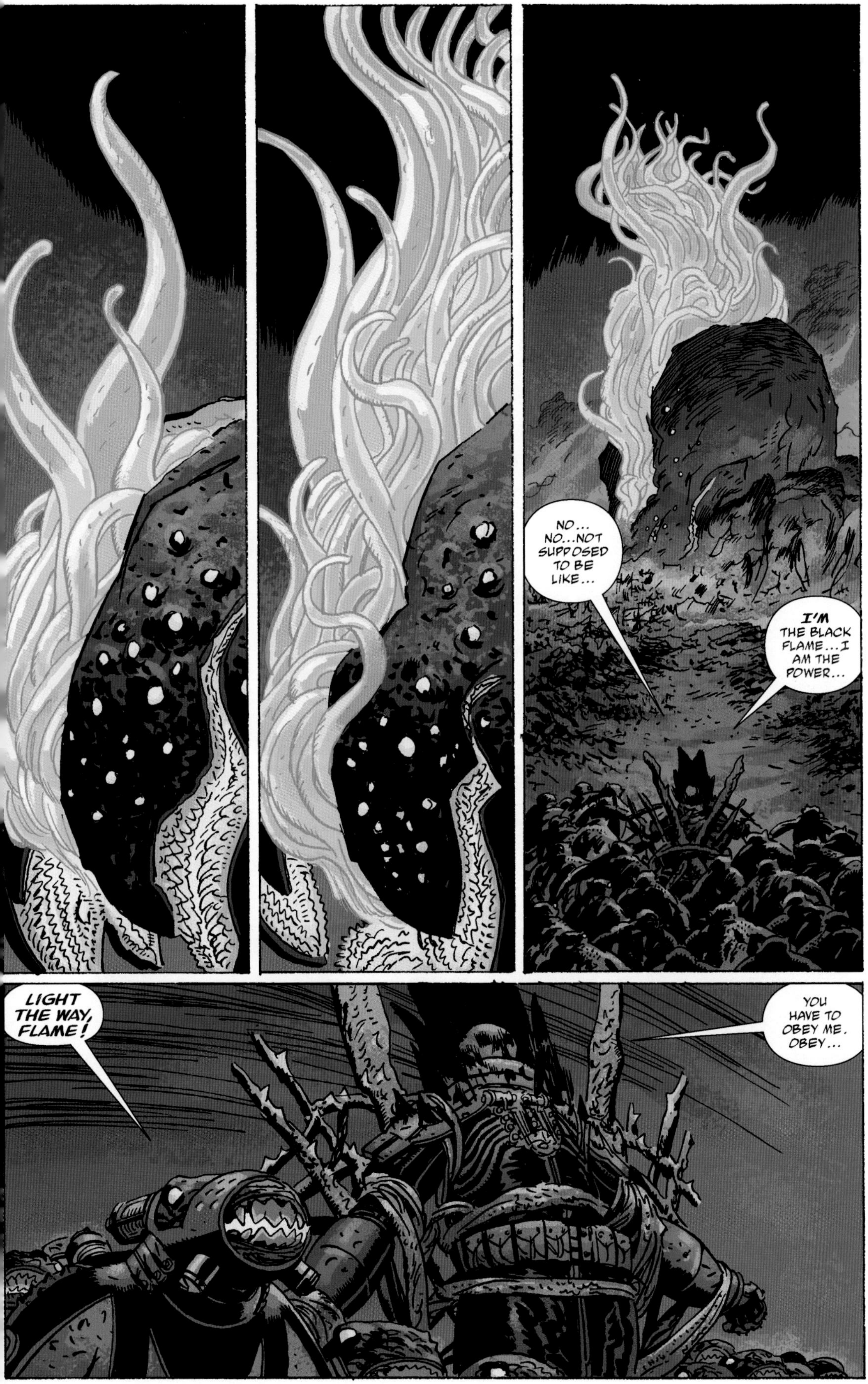
NO... NO...NOT SUPPOSED TO BE LIKE...
I'M THE BLACK FLAME... I AM THE POWER...
LIGHT THE WAY, FLAME!
YOU HAVE TO OBEY ME. OBEY...

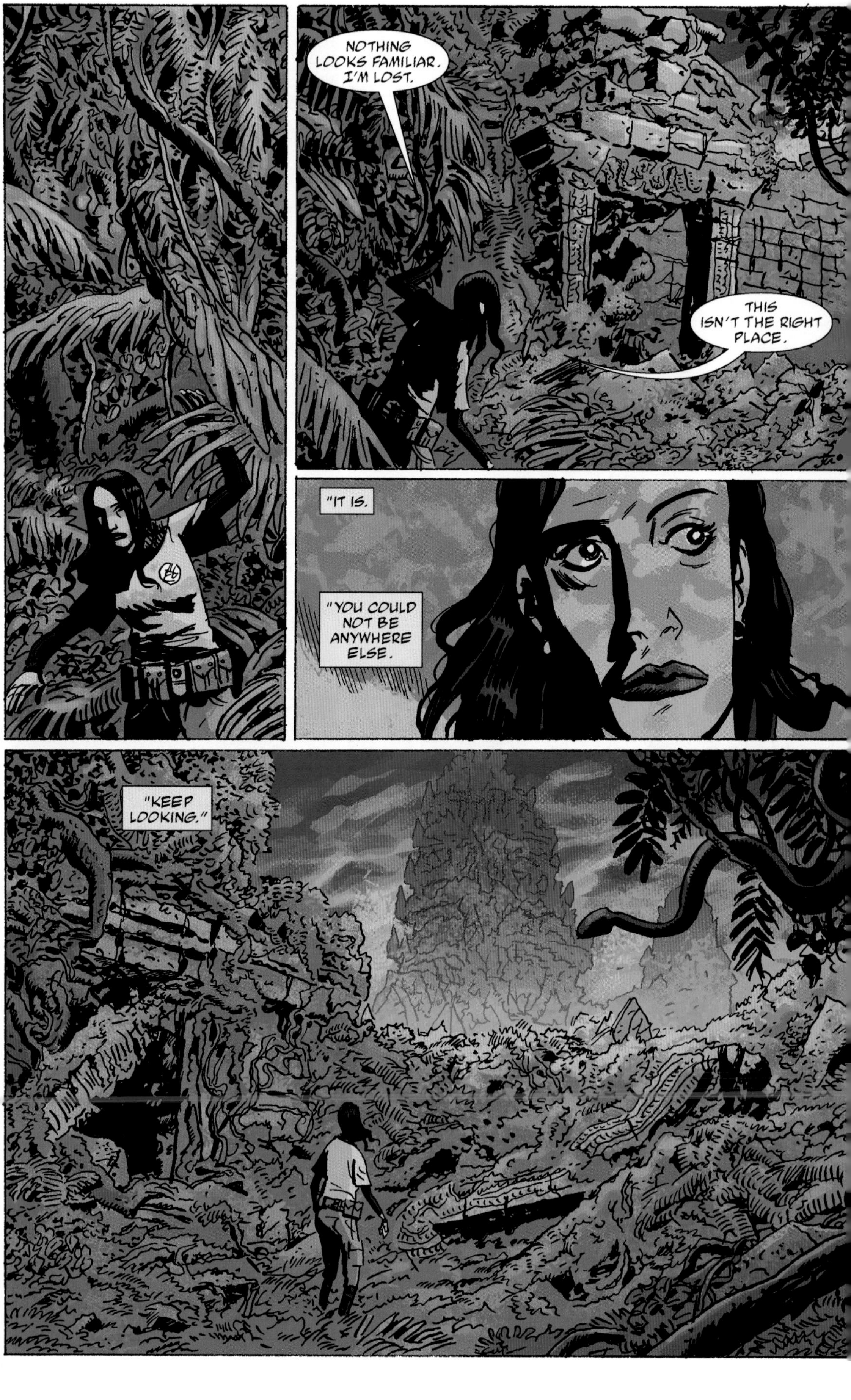
NOTHING LOOKS FAMILIAR. I'M LOST.
THIS ISN'T THE RIGHT PLACE.
"IT IS.
"YOU COULD NOT BE ANYWHERE ELSE.
"KEEP LOOKING."

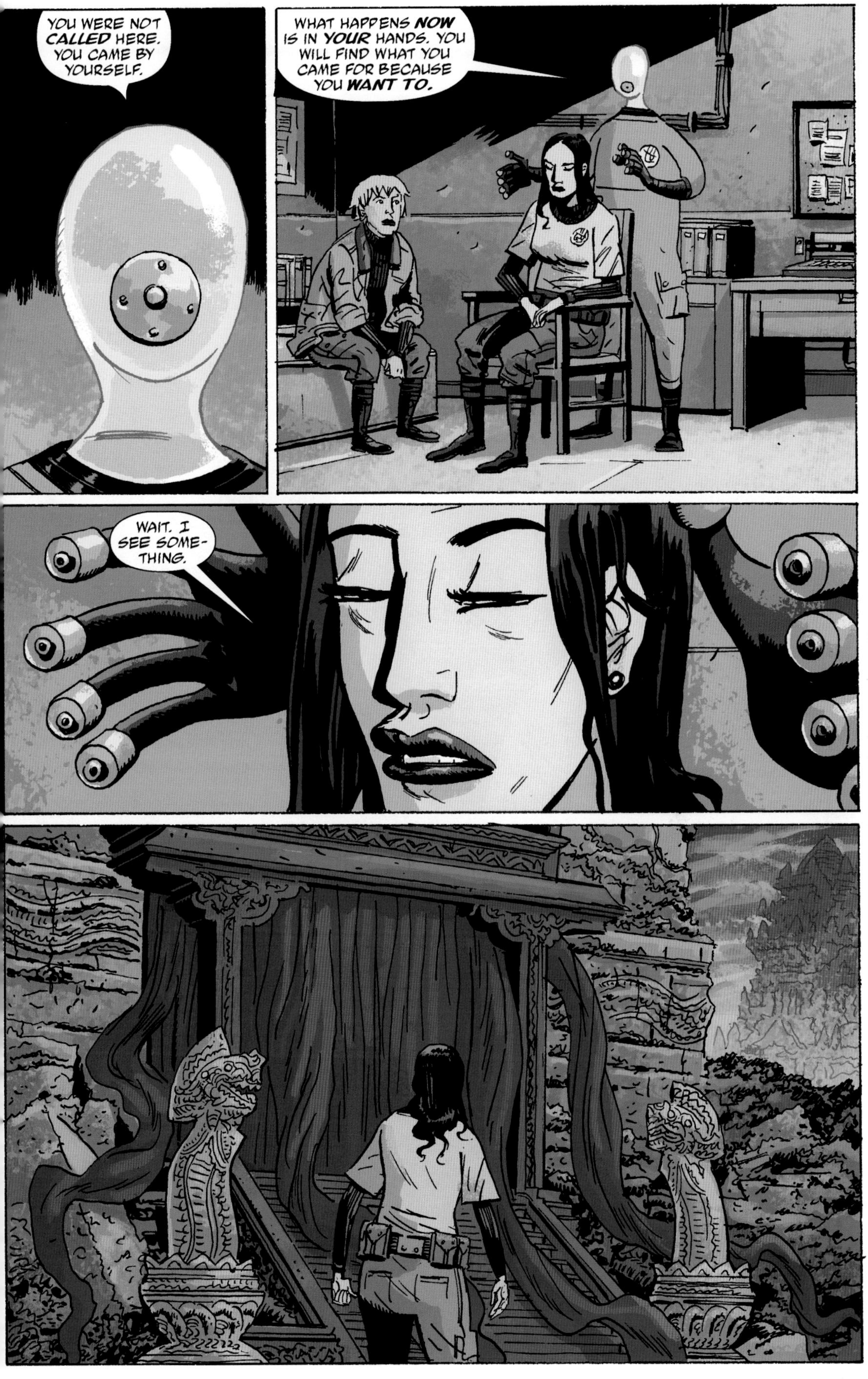
YOU WERE NOT CALLED HERE. YOU CAME BY YOURSELF.
WHAT HAPPENS NOW IS IN YOUR HANDS. YOU WILL FIND WHAT YOU CAME FOR BECAUSE YOU WANT TO.
WAIT. I SEE SOME-THING.

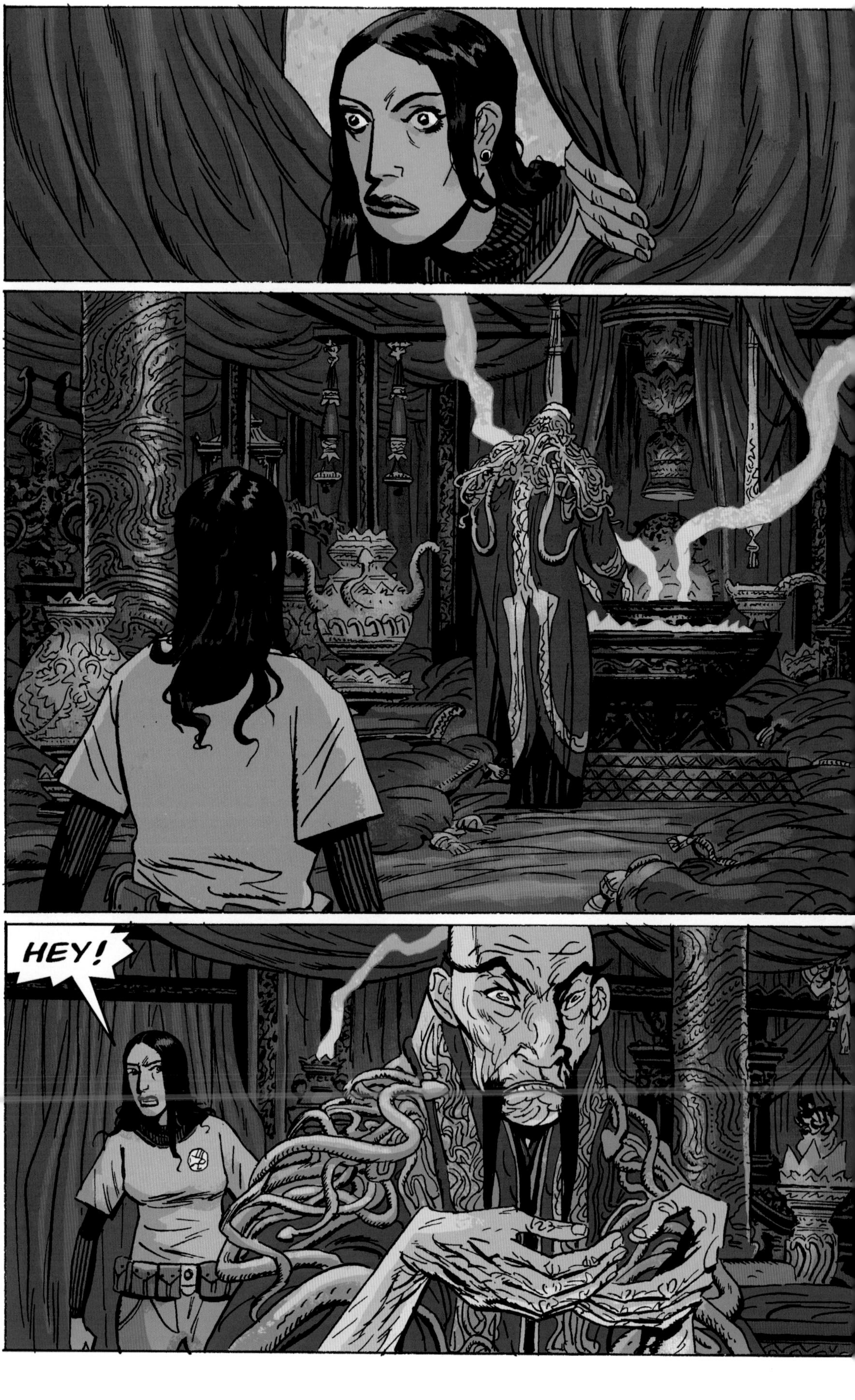
HEY!

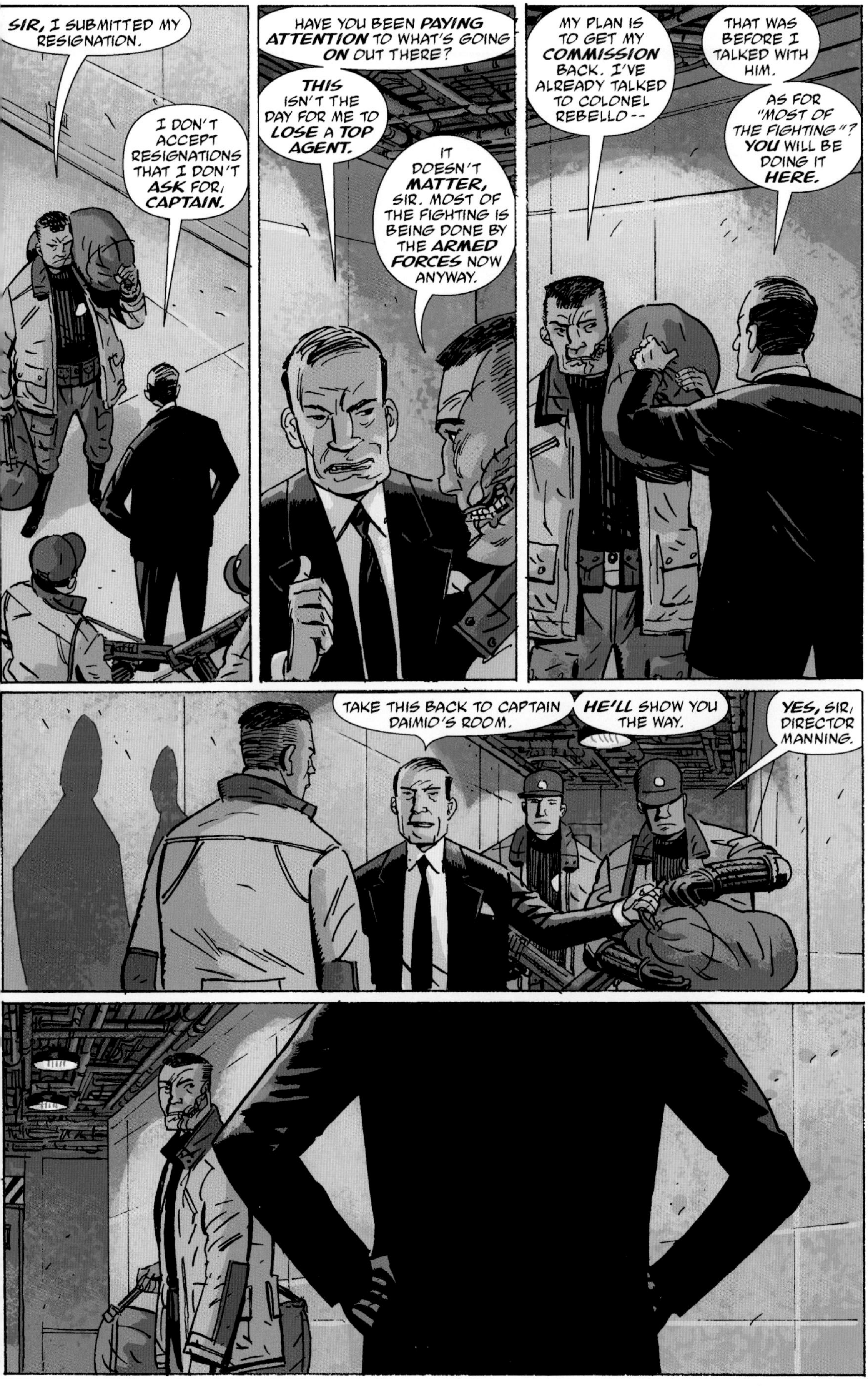
SIR, I SUBMITTED MY RESIGNATION.
I DON'T ACCEPT RESIGNATIONS THAT I DON'T ASK FOR, CAPTAIN.
HAVE YOU BEEN PAYING ATTENTION TO WHAT'S GOING ON OUT THERE?
THIS ISN'T THE DAY FOR ME TO LOSE A TOP AGENT.
IT DOESN'T MATTER, SIR. MOST OF THE FIGHTING IS BEING DONE BY THE ARMED FORCES NOW ANYWAY.
MY PLAN IS TO GET MY COMMISSION BACK. I'VE ALREADY TALKED TO COLONEL REBELLO--
THAT WAS BEFORE I TALKED WITH HIM.
AS FOR "MOST OF THE FIGHTING"? YOU WILL BE DOING IT HERE.
TAKE THIS BACK TO CAPTAIN DAIMIO'S ROOM.
HE'LL SHOW YOU THE WAY.
YES, SIR, DIRECTOR MANNING.

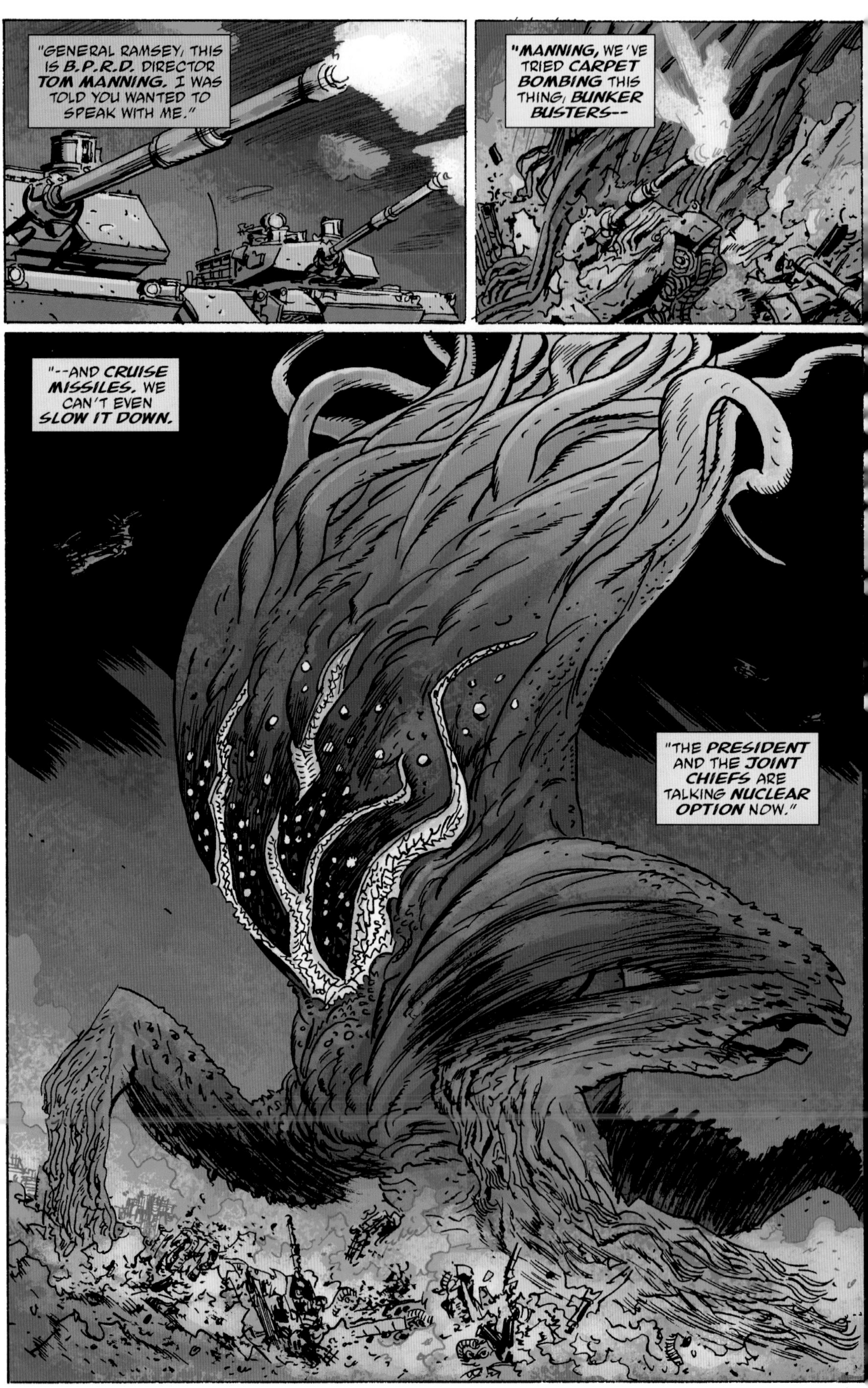
"GENERAL RAMSEY, THIS IS B.P.R.D. DIRECTOR TOM MANNING. I WAS TOLD YOU WANTED TO SPEAK WITH ME."
"MANNING, WE'VE TRIED CARPET BOMBING THIS THING, BUNKER BUSTERS--
"--AND CRUISE MISSILES. WE CAN'T EVEN SLOW IT DOWN.
"THE PRESIDENT AND THE JOINT CHIEFS ARE TALKING NUCLEAR OPTION NOW."

"NUCLEAR, SIR?"

"MANNING, DO YOU KNOW HOW MANY AMERICANS HAVE BEEN KILLED BY THAT THING SINCE YESTERDAY MORNING?"

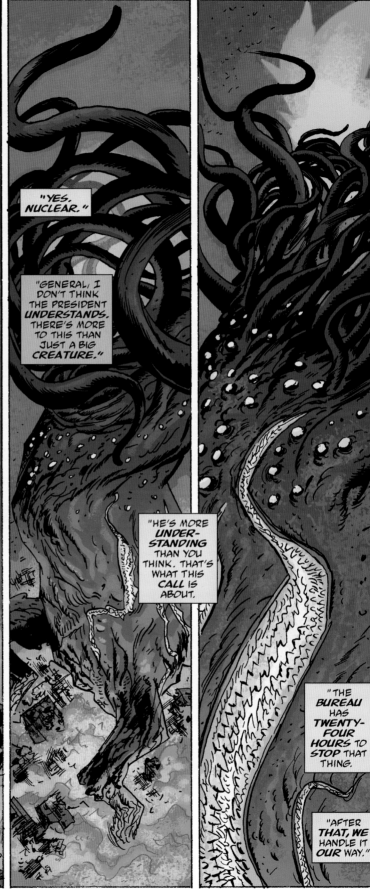

"YES. NUCLEAR."

"GENERAL, I DON'T THINK THE PRESIDENT UNDERSTANDS. THERE'S MORE TO THIS THAN JUST A BIG CREATURE."

"HE'S MORE UNDER-STANDING THAN YOU THINK. THAT'S WHAT THIS CALL IS ABOUT."

"THE BUREAU HAS TWENTY-FOUR HOURS TO STOP THAT THING.

"AFTER THAT, WE HANDLE IT OUR WAY."

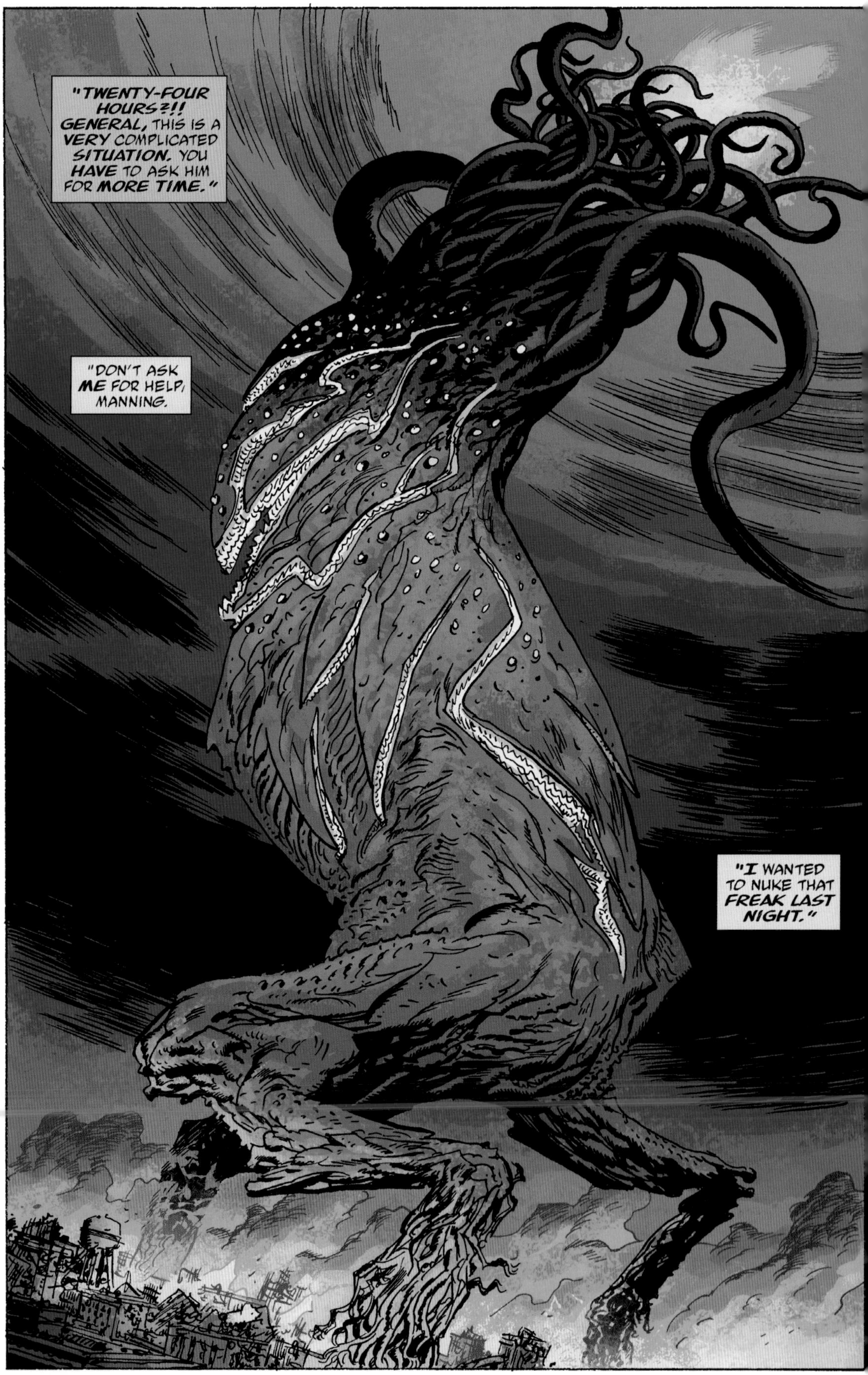
"TWENTY-FOUR HOURS?!! GENERAL, THIS IS A VERY COMPLICATED SITUATION. YOU HAVE TO ASK HIM FOR MORE TIME."
"DON'T ASK ME FOR HELP, MANNING.
"I WANTED TO NUKE THAT FREAK LAST NIGHT."

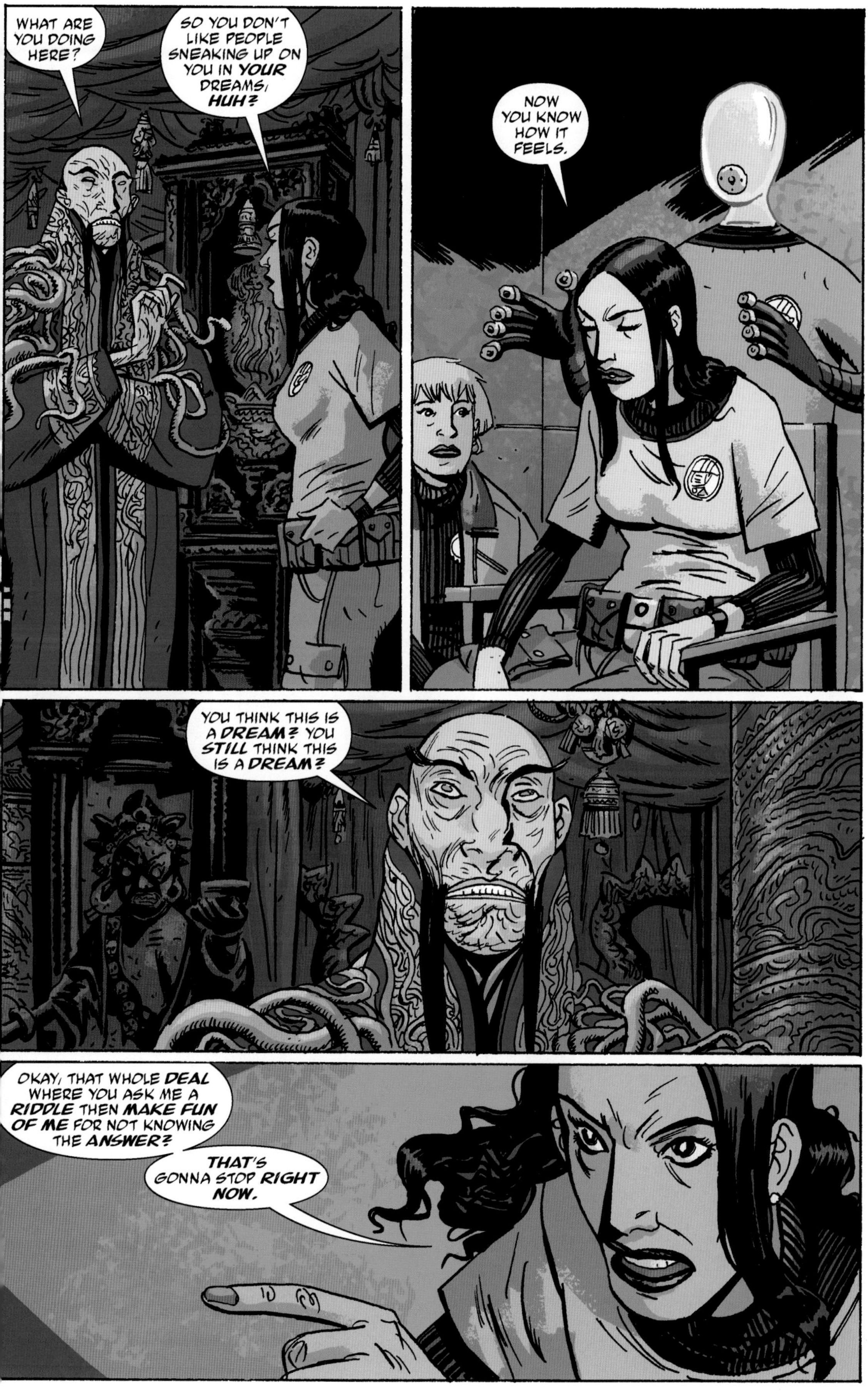

WHAT ARE YOU DOING HERE?
SO YOU DON'T LIKE PEOPLE SNEAKING UP ON YOU IN YOUR DREAMS, HUH?
NOW YOU KNOW HOW IT FEELS.
YOU THINK THIS IS A DREAM? YOU STILL THINK THIS IS A DREAM?
OKAY, THAT WHOLE DEAL WHERE YOU ASK ME A RIDDLE THEN MAKE FUN OF ME FOR NOT KNOWING THE ANSWER?
THAT'S GONNA STOP RIGHT NOW.

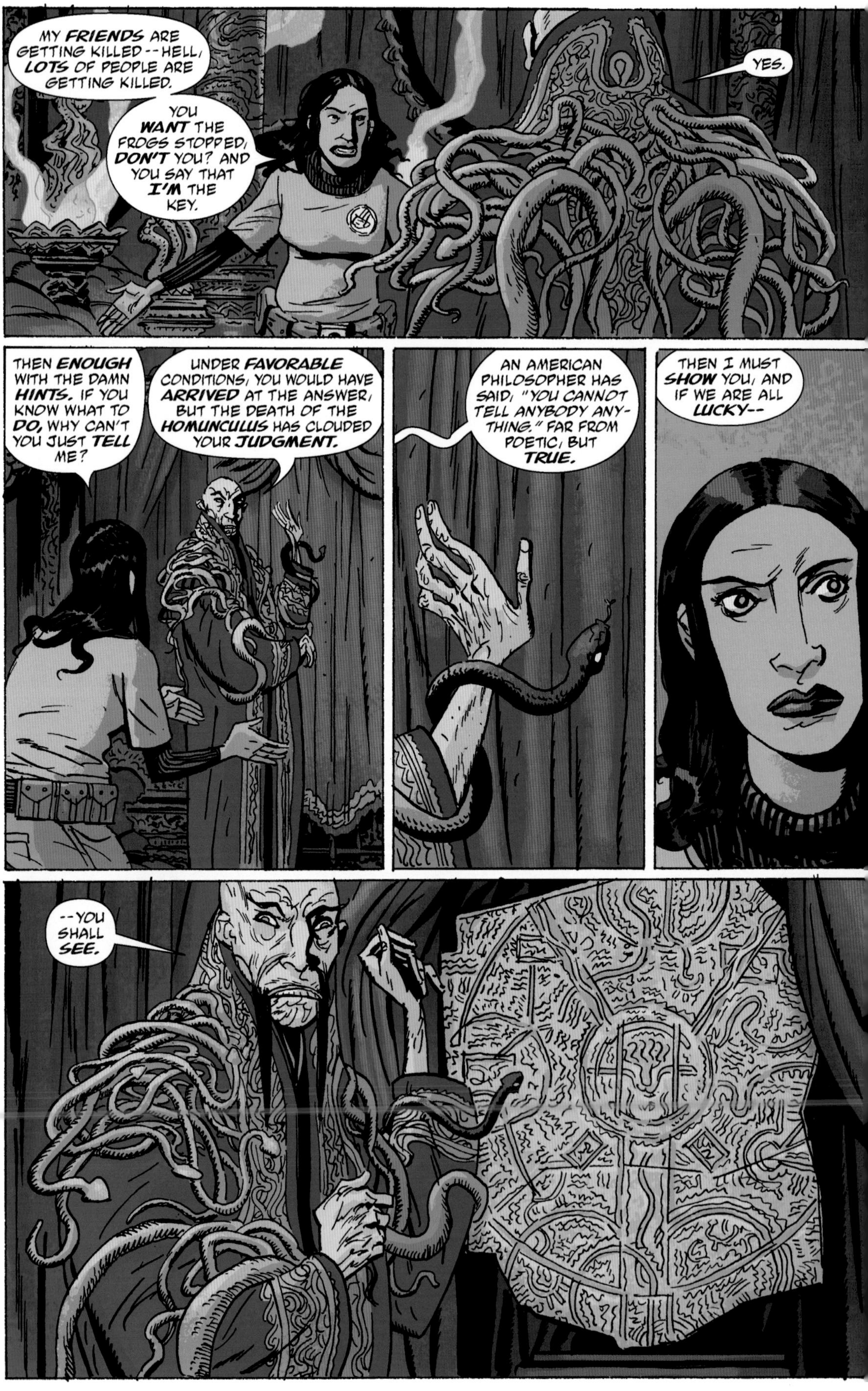

MY FRIENDS ARE GETTING KILLED--HELL, LOTS OF PEOPLE ARE GETTING KILLED.
YOU WANT THE FROGS STOPPED, DON'T YOU? AND YOU SAY THAT I'M THE KEY.
YES.
THEN ENOUGH WITH THE DAMN HINTS. IF YOU KNOW WHAT TO DO, WHY CAN'T YOU JUST TELL ME?
UNDER FAVORABLE CONDITIONS, YOU WOULD HAVE ARRIVED AT THE ANSWER, BUT THE DEATH OF THE HOMUNCULUS HAS CLOUDED YOUR JUDGMENT.
AN AMERICAN PHILOSOPHER HAS SAID, "YOU CANNOT TELL ANYBODY ANYTHING." FAR FROM POETIC, BUT TRUE.
THEN I MUST SHOW YOU, AND IF WE ARE ALL LUCKY--
--YOU SHALL SEE.

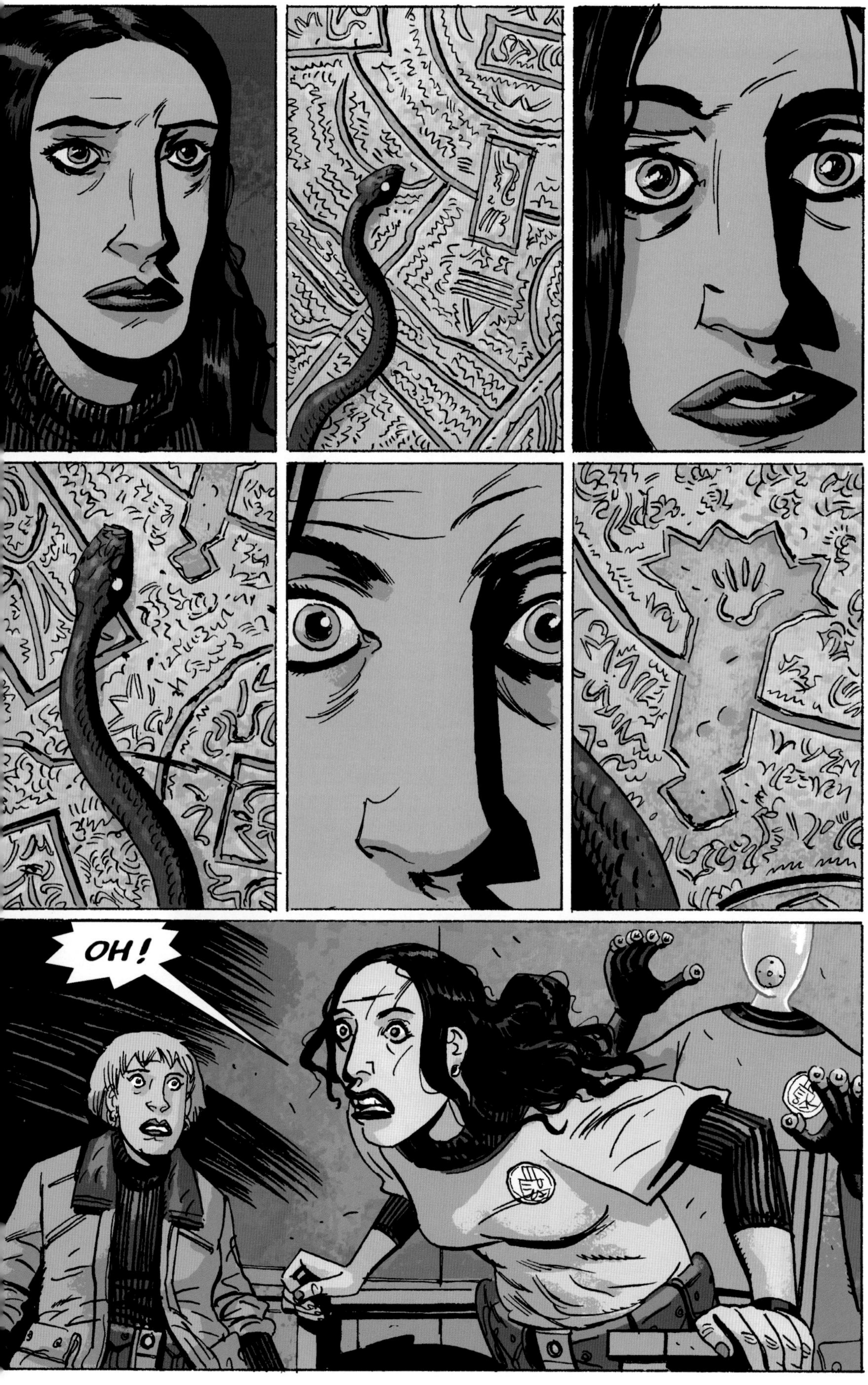
OH!

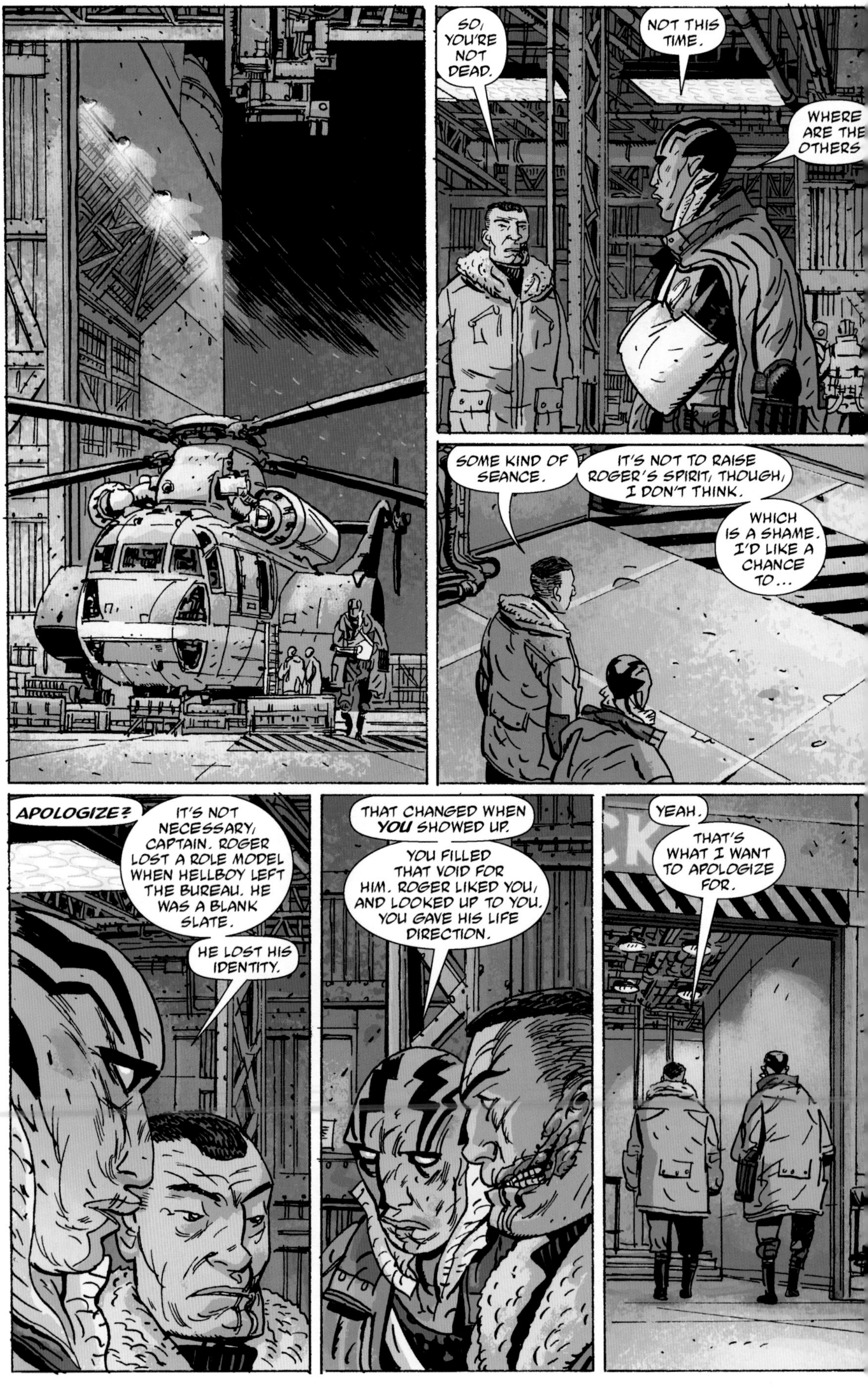

SO, YOU'RE NOT DEAD.
NOT THIS TIME.
WHERE ARE THE OTHERS
SOME KIND OF SEANCE.
IT'S NOT TO RAISE ROGER'S SPIRIT, THOUGH, I DON'T THINK.
WHICH IS A SHAME. I'D LIKE A CHANCE TO...
APOLOGIZE?
IT'S NOT NECESSARY, CAPTAIN. ROGER LOST A ROLE MODEL WHEN HELLBOY LEFT THE BUREAU. HE WAS A BLANK SLATE.
HE LOST HIS IDENTITY.
THAT CHANGED WHEN YOU SHOWED UP.
YOU FILLED THAT VOID FOR HIM. ROGER LIKED YOU, AND LOOKED UP TO YOU. YOU GAVE HIS LIFE DIRECTION.
YEAH.
THAT'S WHAT I WANT TO APOLOGIZE FOR.

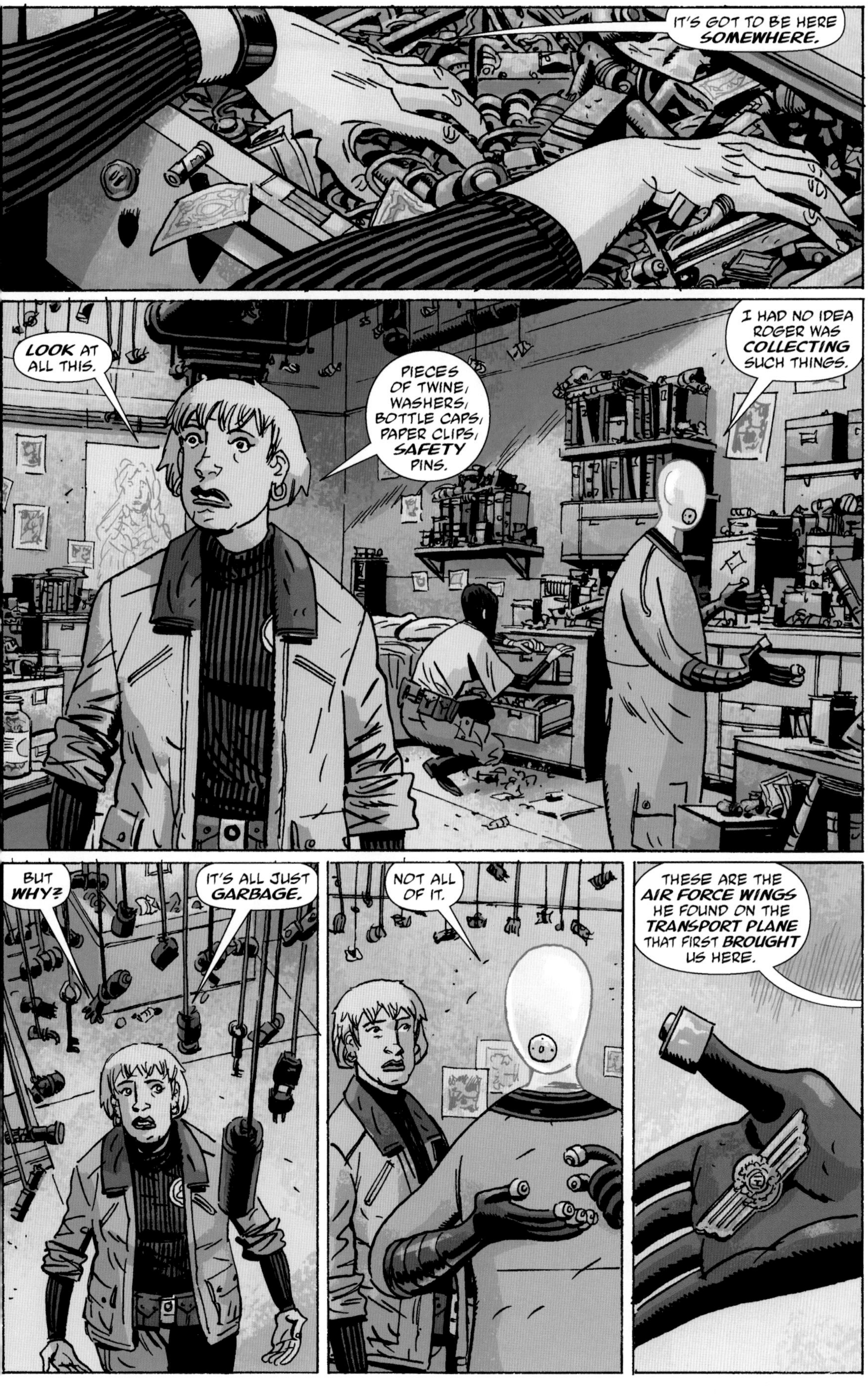
IT'S GOT TO BE HERE SOMEWHERE.
LOOK AT ALL THIS.
PIECES OF TWINE, WASHERS, BOTTLE CAPS, PAPER CLIPS, SAFETY PINS.
I HAD NO IDEA ROGER WAS COLLECTING SUCH THINGS.
BUT WHY?
IT'S ALL JUST GARBAGE.
NOT ALL OF IT.
THESE ARE THE AIR FORCE WINGS HE FOUND ON THE TRANSPORT PLANE THAT FIRST BROUGHT US HERE.

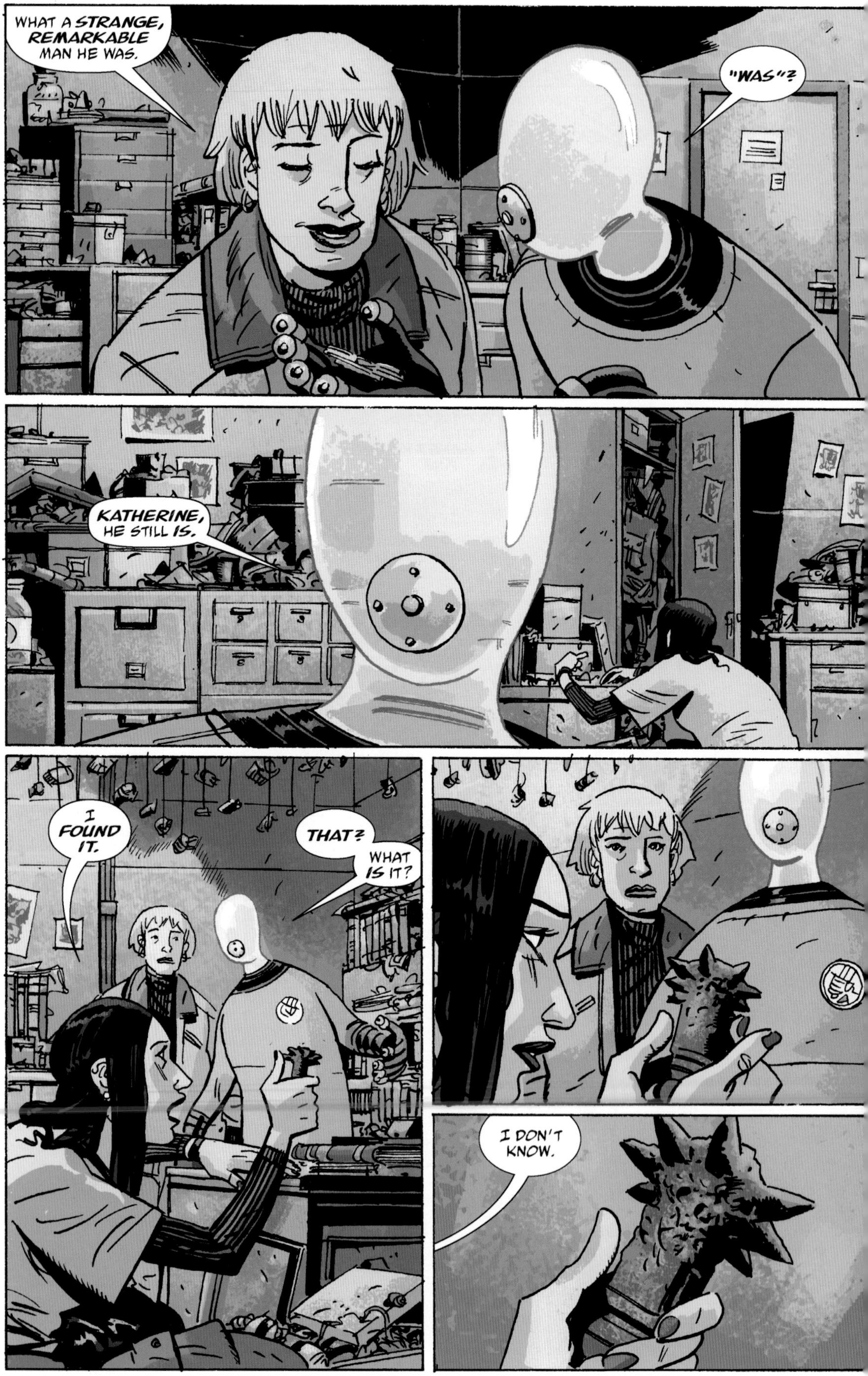
WHAT A STRANGE, REMARKABLE MAN HE WAS.
"WAS"?
KATHERINE, HE STILL IS.
I FOUND IT.
THAT? WHAT IS IT?
I DON'T KNOW.

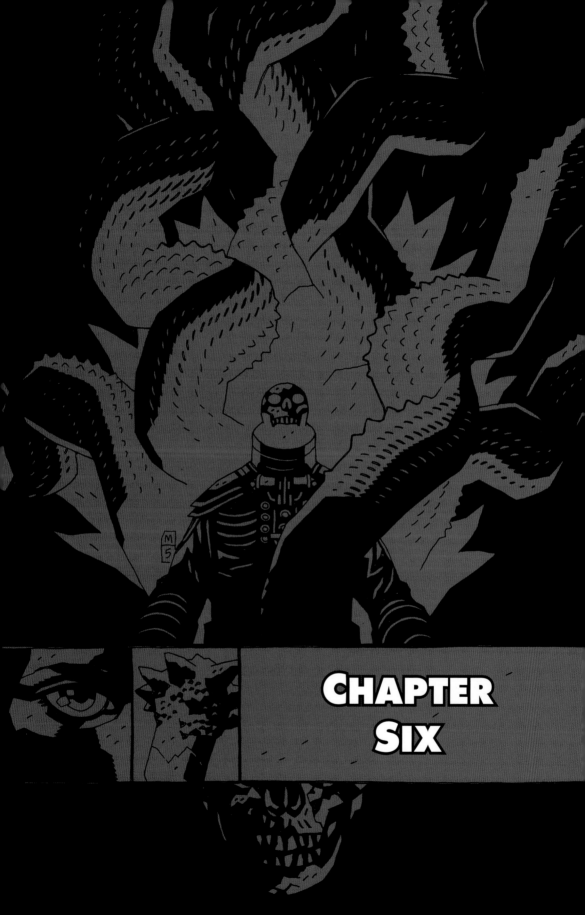

# CHAPTER SIX

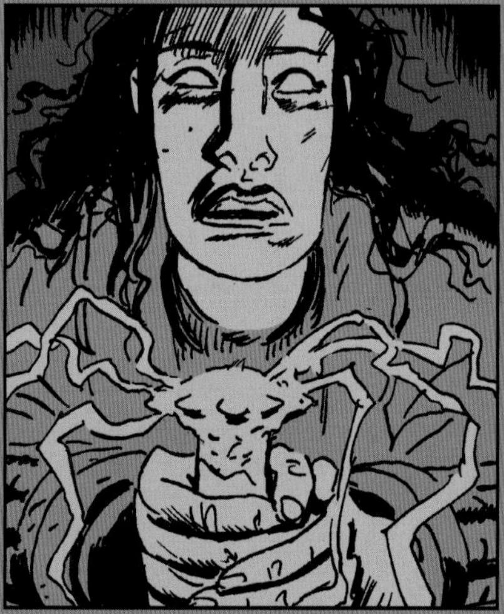

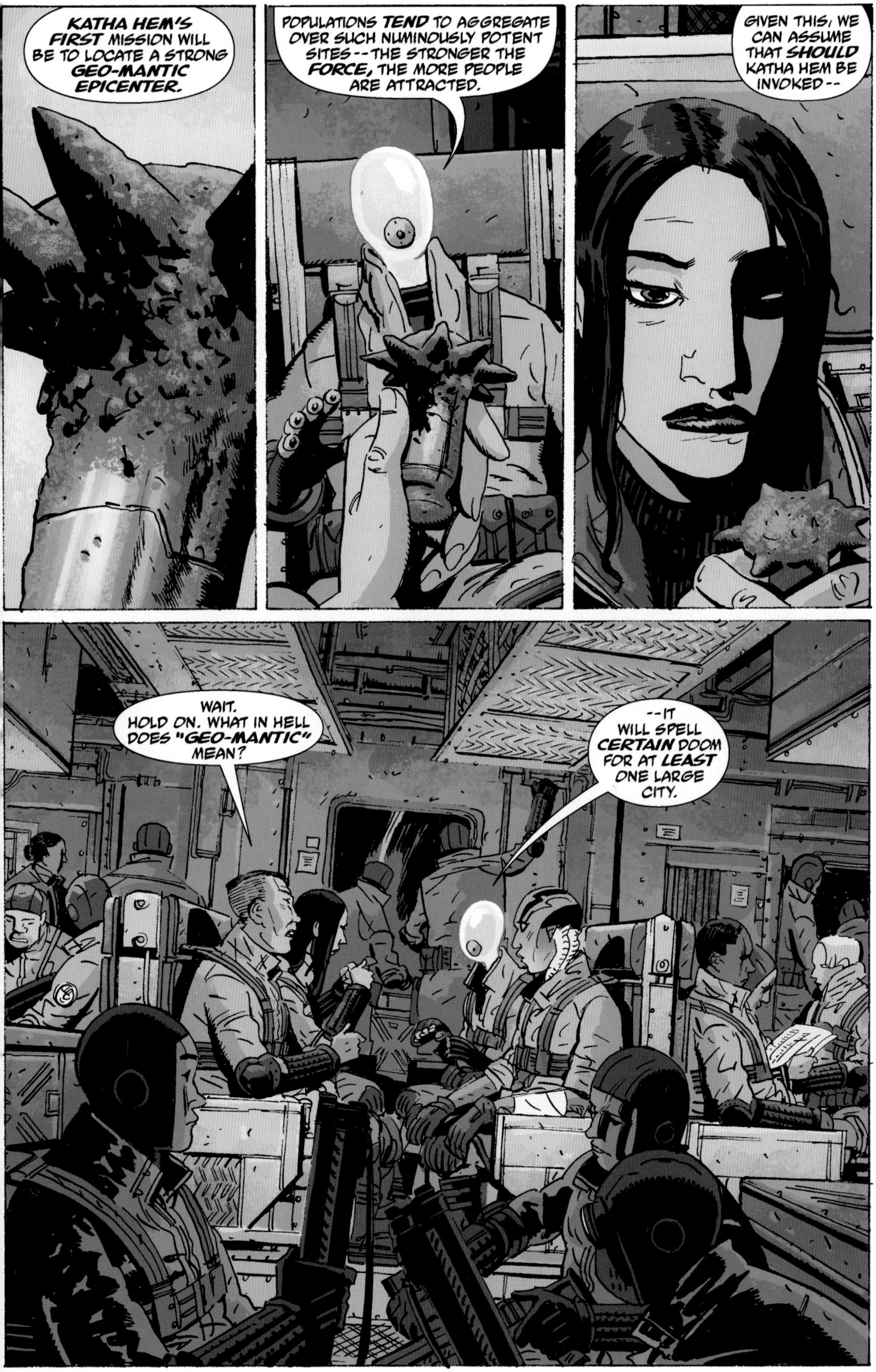
KATHA HEM'S FIRST MISSION WILL BE TO LOCATE A STRONG GEO-MANTIC EPICENTER.
POPULATIONS TEND TO AGGREGATE OVER SUCH NUMINOUSLY POTENT SITES--THE STRONGER THE FORCE, THE MORE PEOPLE ARE ATTRACTED.
GIVEN THIS, WE CAN ASSUME THAT SHOULD KATHA HEM BE INVOKED--
WAIT. HOLD ON. WHAT IN HELL DOES "GEO-MANTIC" MEAN?
--IT WILL SPELL CERTAIN DOOM FOR AT LEAST ONE LARGE CITY.

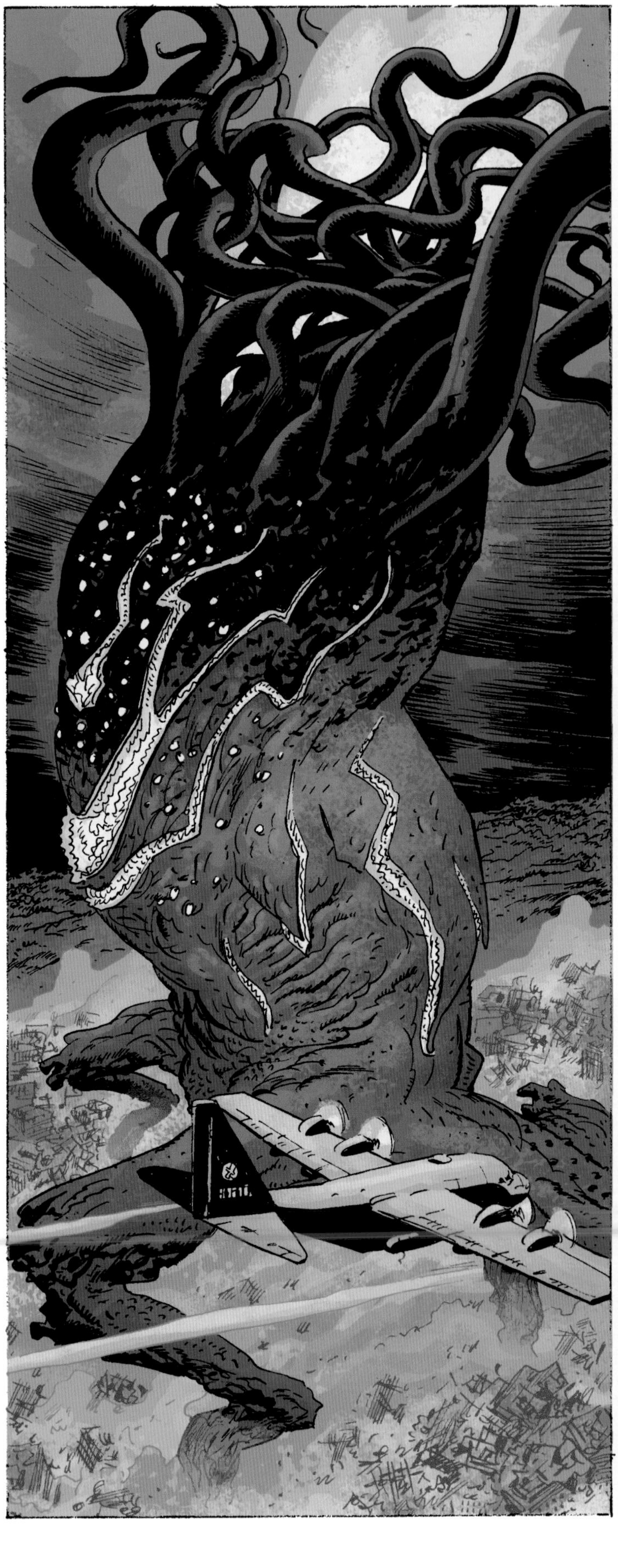

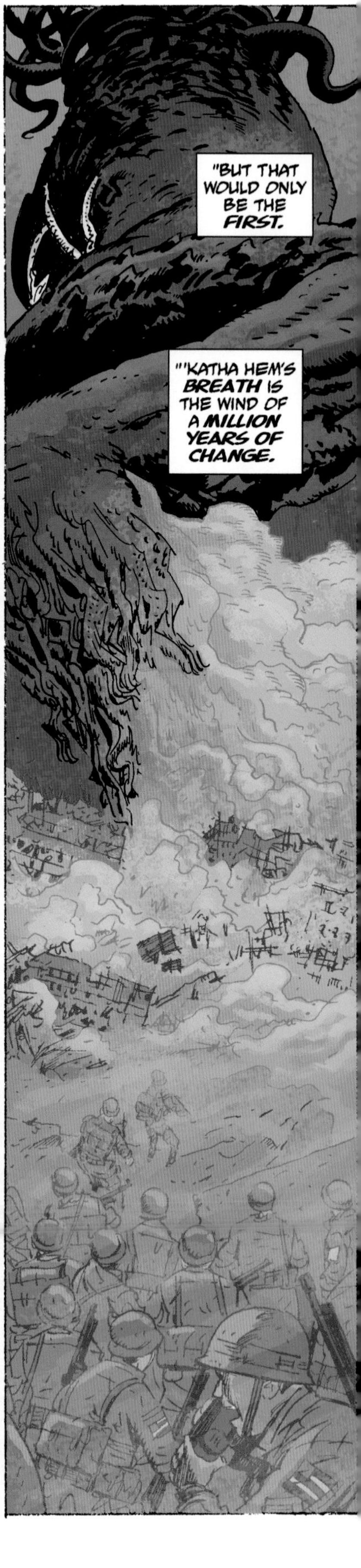
"BUT THAT WOULD ONLY BE THE *FIRST.*
"'KATHA HEM'S *BREATH* IS THE WIND OF A *MILLION YEARS OF CHANGE.*

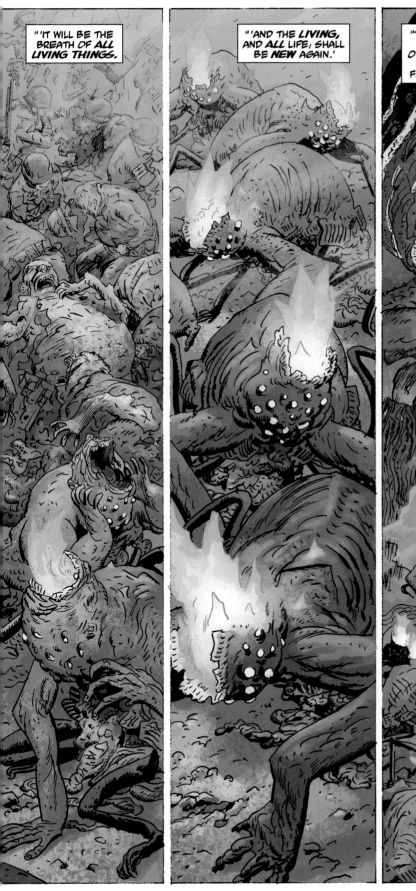

"'IT WILL BE THE BREATH OF *ALL LIVING THINGS*.

"'AND THE *LIVING*, AND *ALL* LIFE, SHALL BE *NEW* AGAIN.'

"THAT IS A *TRANSLATION* OF THE TEXTS, BUT NO ONE SHOULD IMAGINE THAT WE'LL BE *BETTER OFF* FOR ALL THIS *'CHANGE.'*"

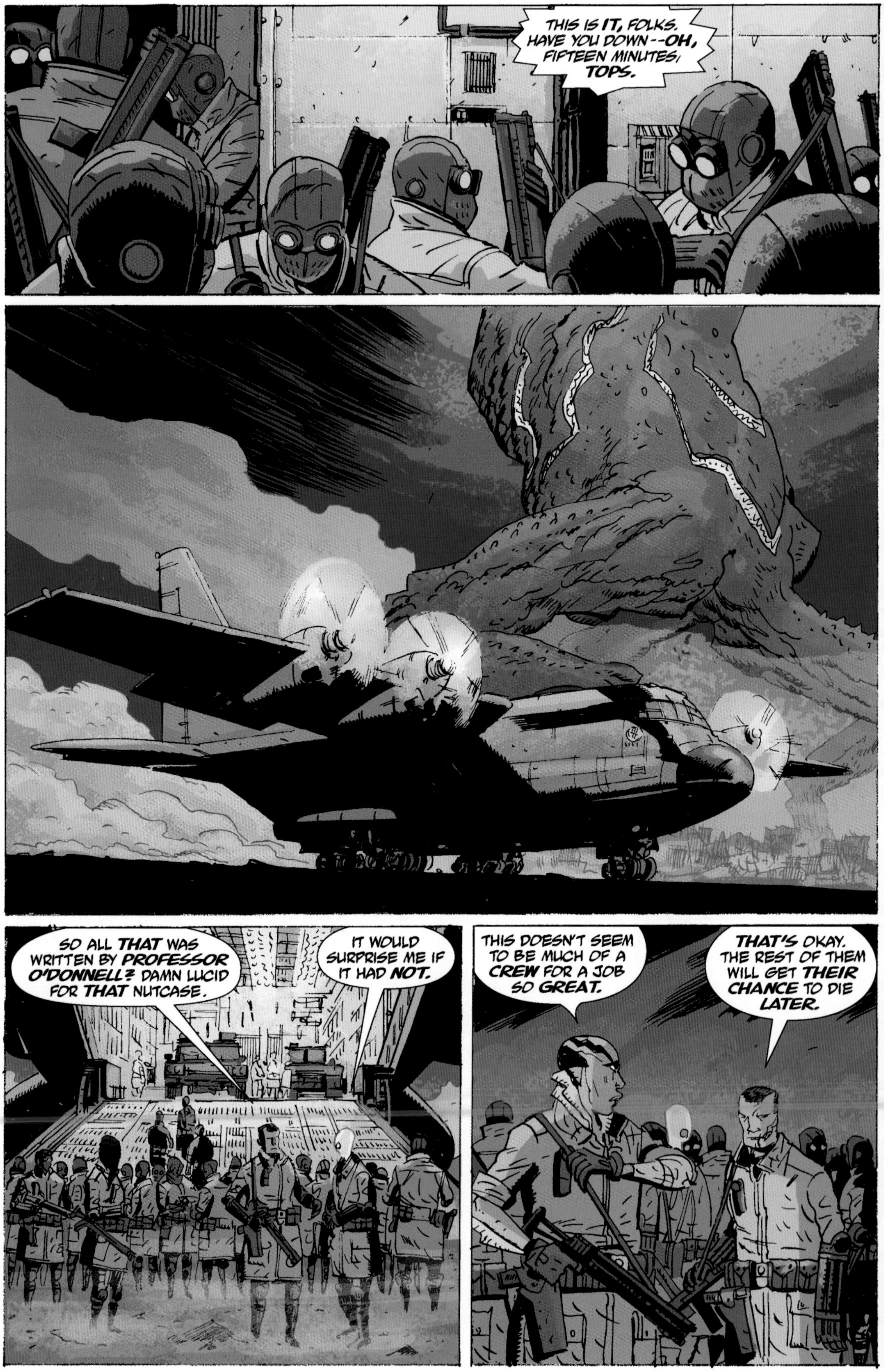
THIS IS IT, FOLKS. HAVE YOU DOWN--OH, FIFTEEN MINUTES, TOPS.
SO ALL THAT WAS WRITTEN BY PROFESSOR O'DONNELL? DAMN LUCID FOR THAT NUTCASE.
IT WOULD SURPRISE ME IF IT HAD NOT.
THIS DOESN'T SEEM TO BE MUCH OF A CREW FOR A JOB SO GREAT.
THAT'S OKAY. THE REST OF THEM WILL GET THEIR CHANCE TO DIE LATER.

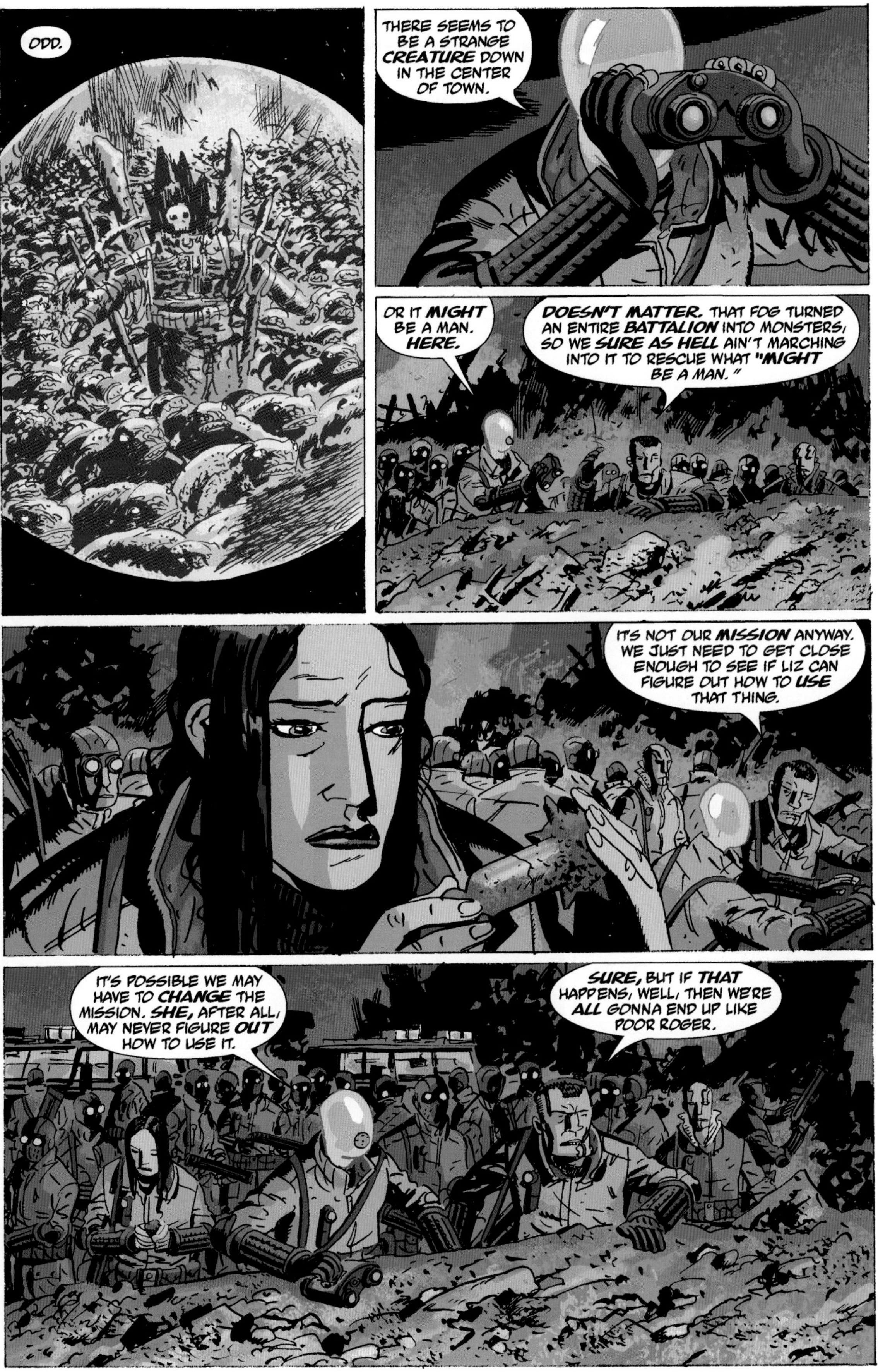
ODD.
THERE SEEMS TO BE A STRANGE CREATURE DOWN IN THE CENTER OF TOWN.
OR IT MIGHT BE A MAN. HERE.
DOESN'T MATTER. THAT FOG TURNED AN ENTIRE BATTALION INTO MONSTERS, SO WE SURE AS HELL AIN'T MARCHING INTO IT TO RESCUE WHAT "MIGHT BE A MAN."
IT'S NOT OUR MISSION ANYWAY. WE JUST NEED TO GET CLOSE ENOUGH TO SEE IF LIZ CAN FIGURE OUT HOW TO USE THAT THING.
IT'S POSSIBLE WE MAY HAVE TO CHANGE THE MISSION. SHE, AFTER ALL, MAY NEVER FIGURE OUT HOW TO USE IT.
SURE, BUT IF THAT HAPPENS, WELL, THEN WE'RE ALL GONNA END UP LIKE POOR ROGER.

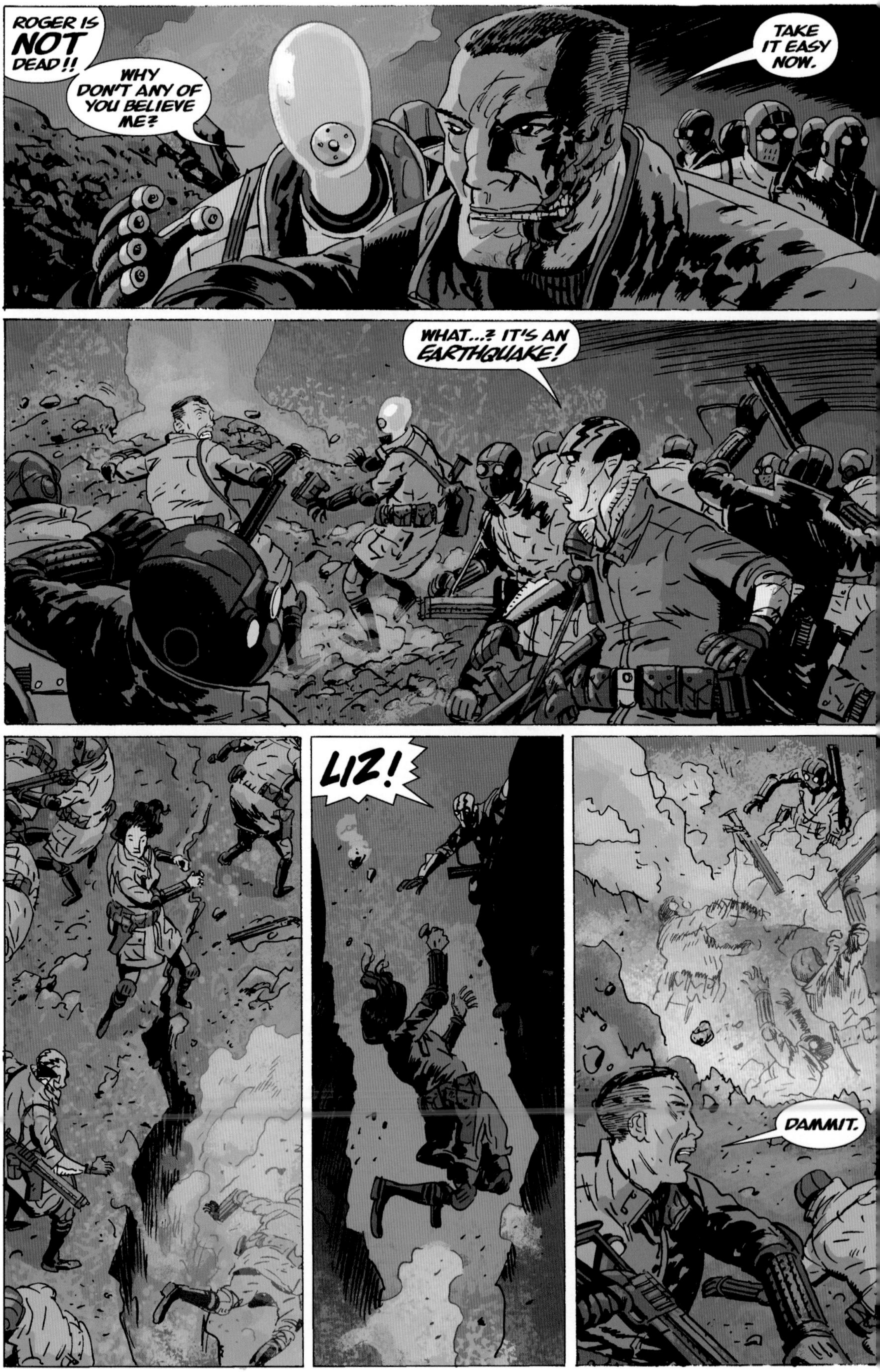
ROGER IS NOT DEAD!!
WHY DON'T ANY OF YOU BELIEVE ME?
TAKE IT EASY NOW.
WHAT...? IT'S AN EARTHQUAKE!
LIZ!
DAMMIT.

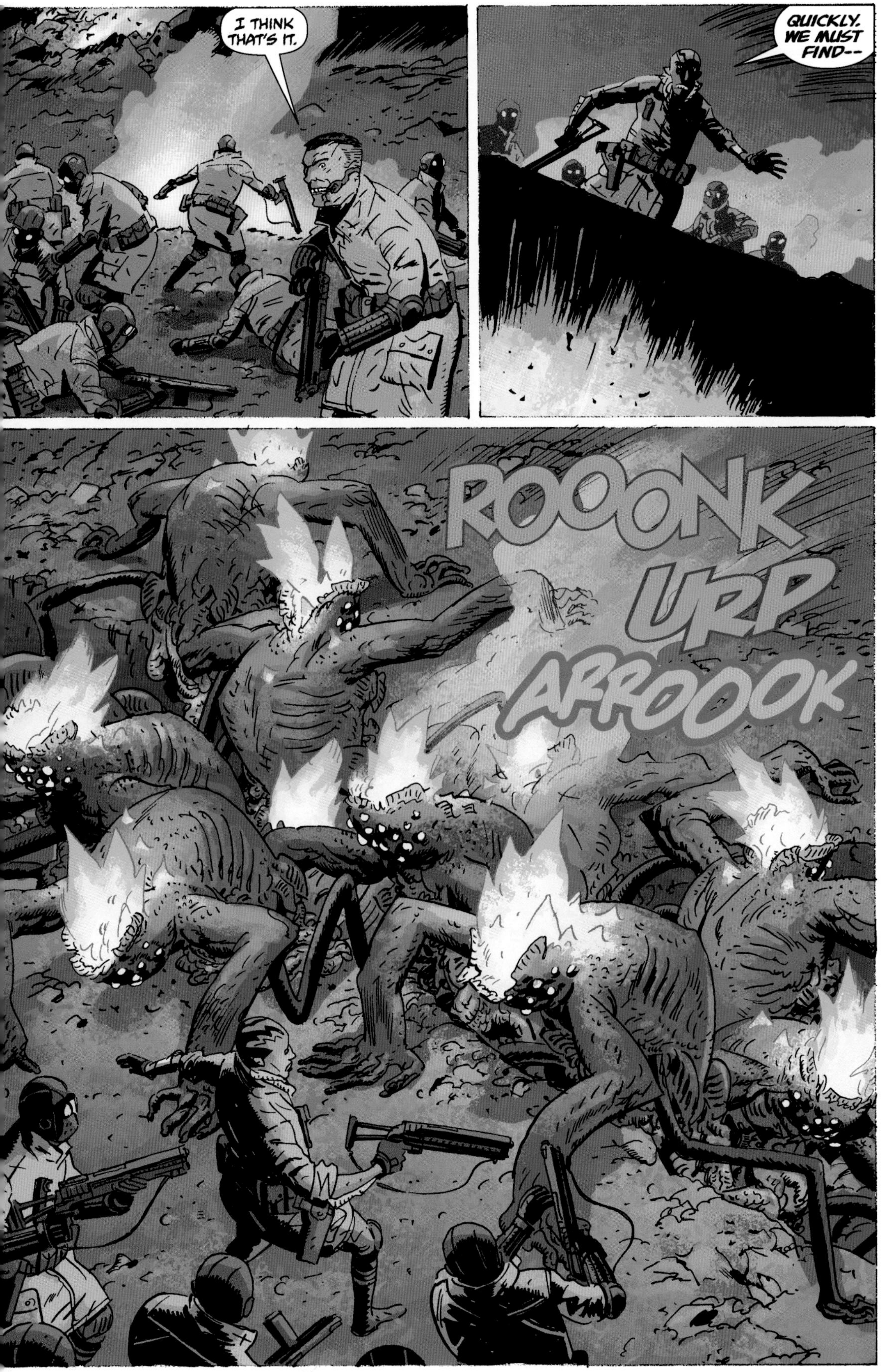

I THINK THAT'S IT.
QUICKLY. WE MUST FIND--
ROOONK
URP
ARROOOK

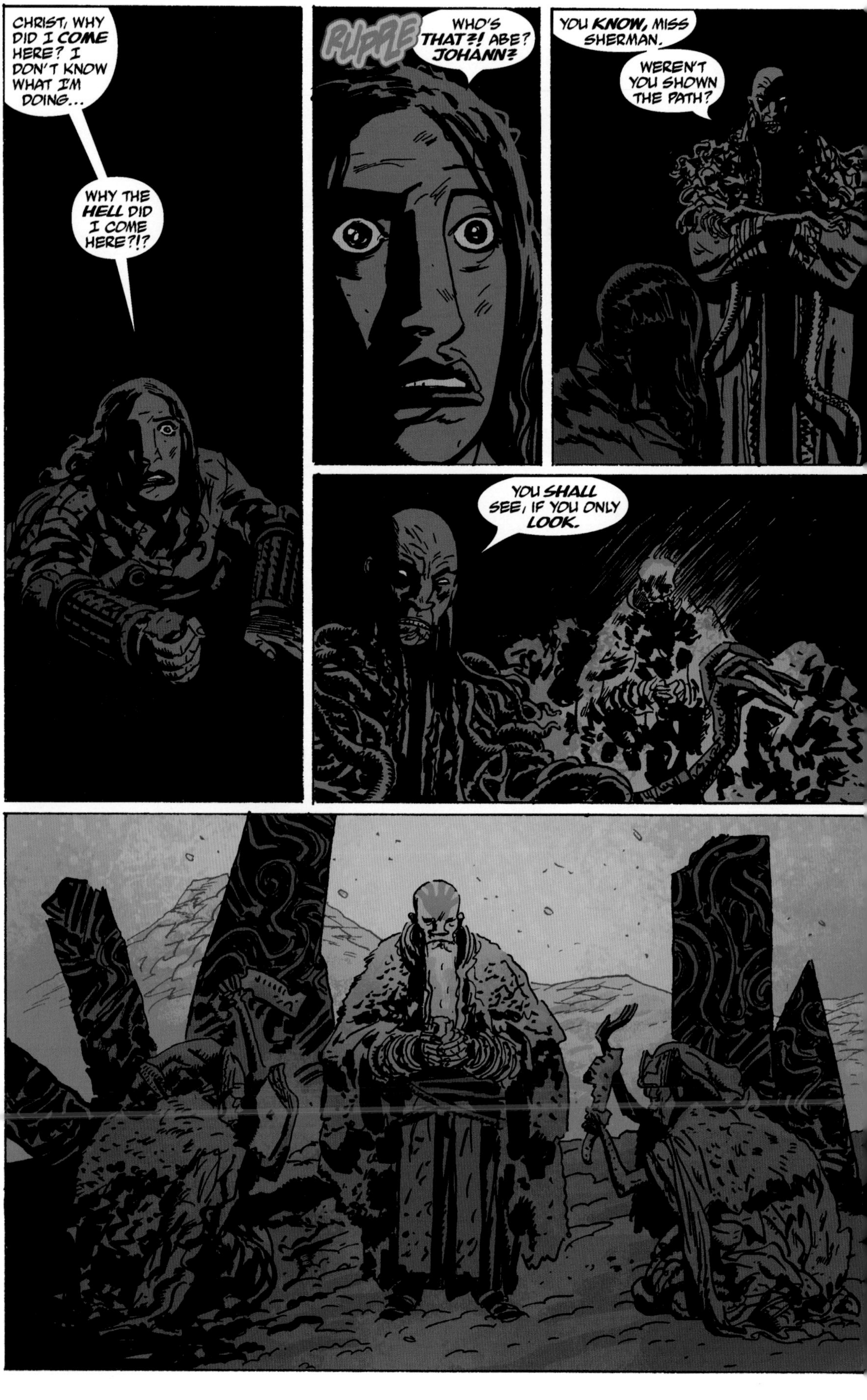

CHRIST, WHY DID I COME HERE? I DON'T KNOW WHAT I'M DOING...
WHY THE HELL DID I COME HERE?!?
RUPPLE
WHO'S THAT?! ABE? JOHANN?
YOU KNOW, MISS SHERMAN.
WEREN'T YOU SHOWN THE PATH?
YOU SHALL SEE, IF YOU ONLY LOOK.

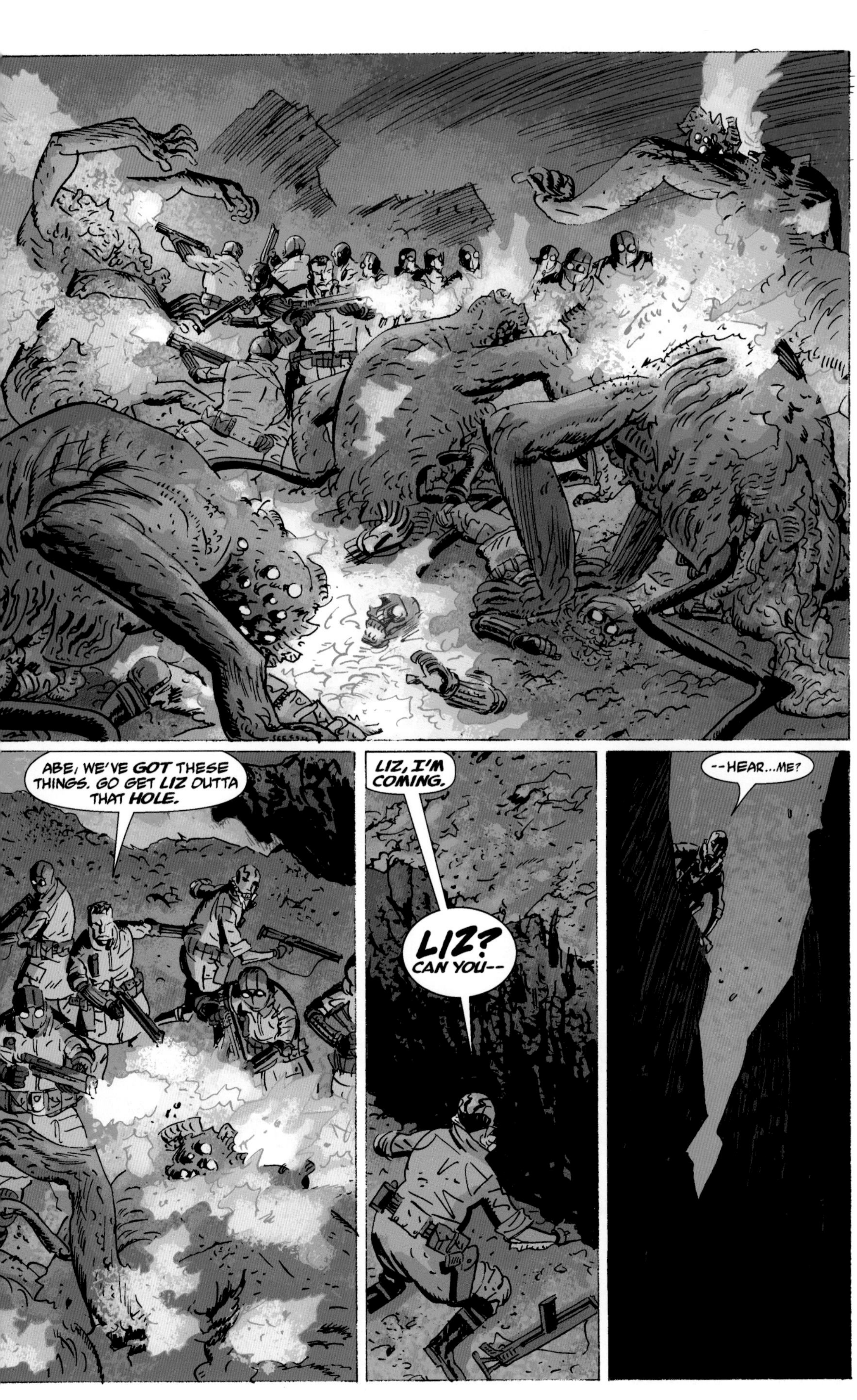

ABE, WE'VE GOT THESE THINGS. GO GET LIZ OUTTA THAT HOLE.
LIZ, I'M COMING.
LIZ? CAN YOU--
--HEAR...ME?

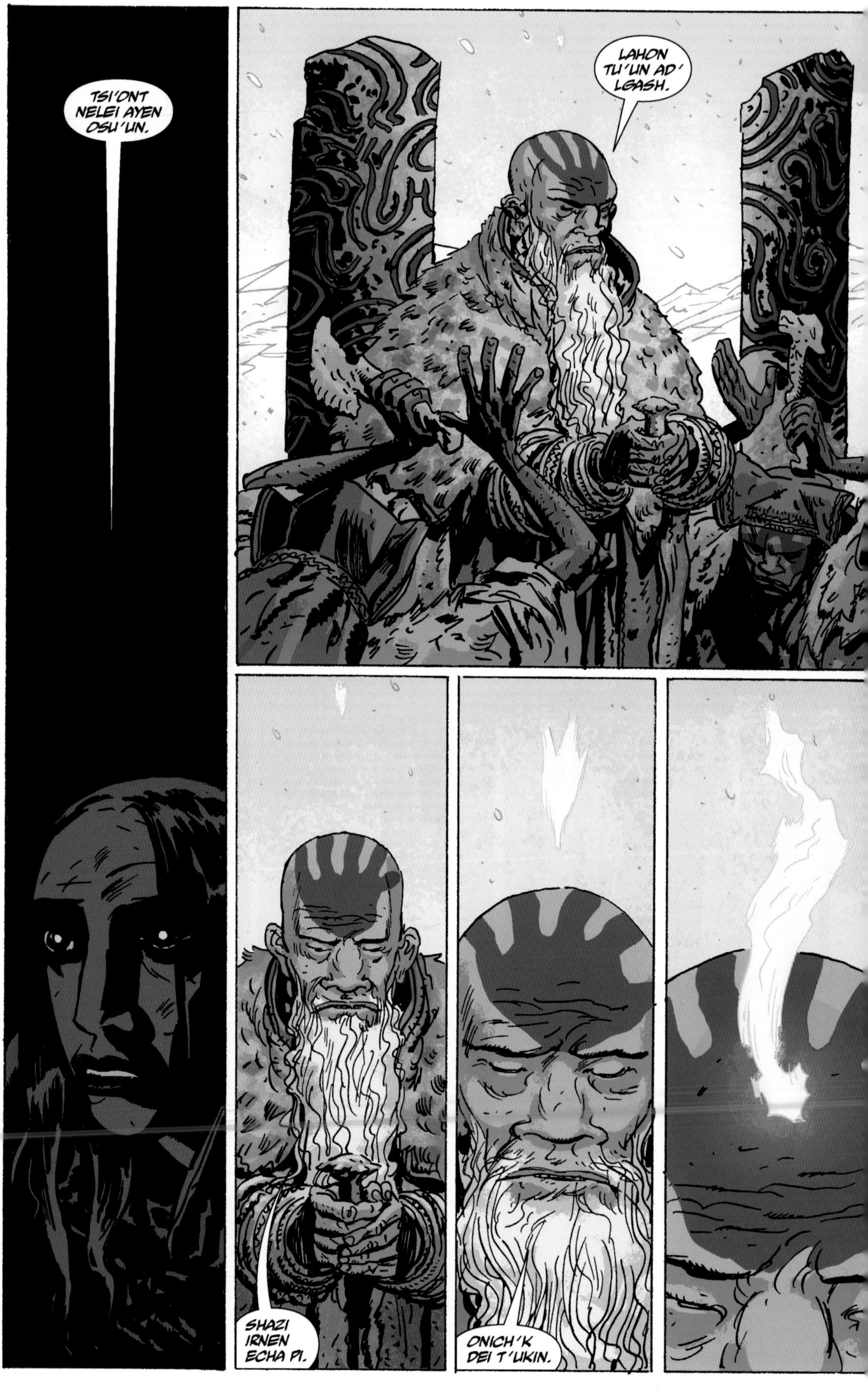
TSI'ONT NELEI AYEN OSU'UN.
LAHON TU'UN AD' LGASH.
SHAZI IRNEN ECHA PI.
ONICH'K DEI T'UKIN.

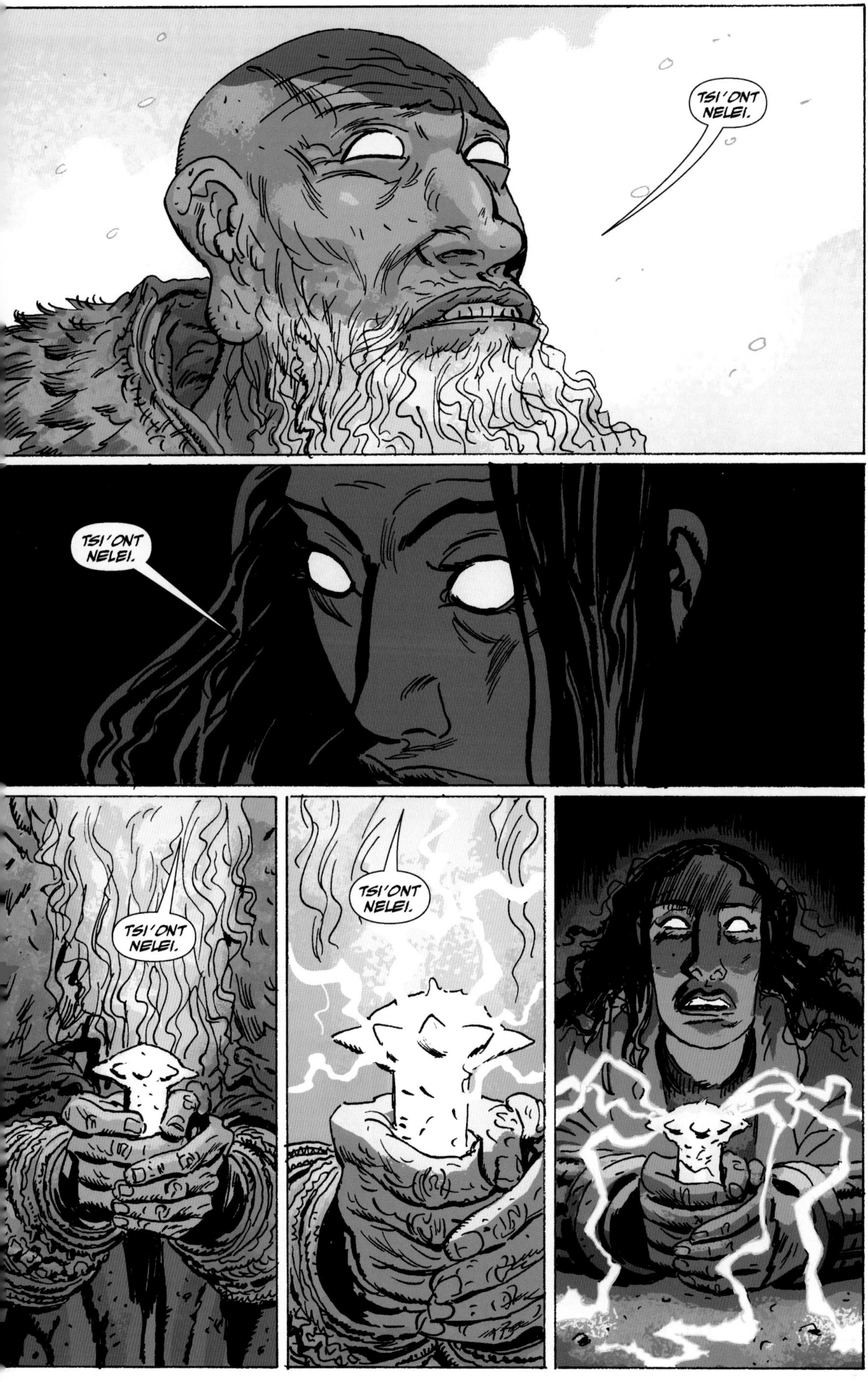
TSI'ONT NELEI.
TSI'ONT NELEI.
TSI'ONT NELEI.
TSI'ONT NELEI.

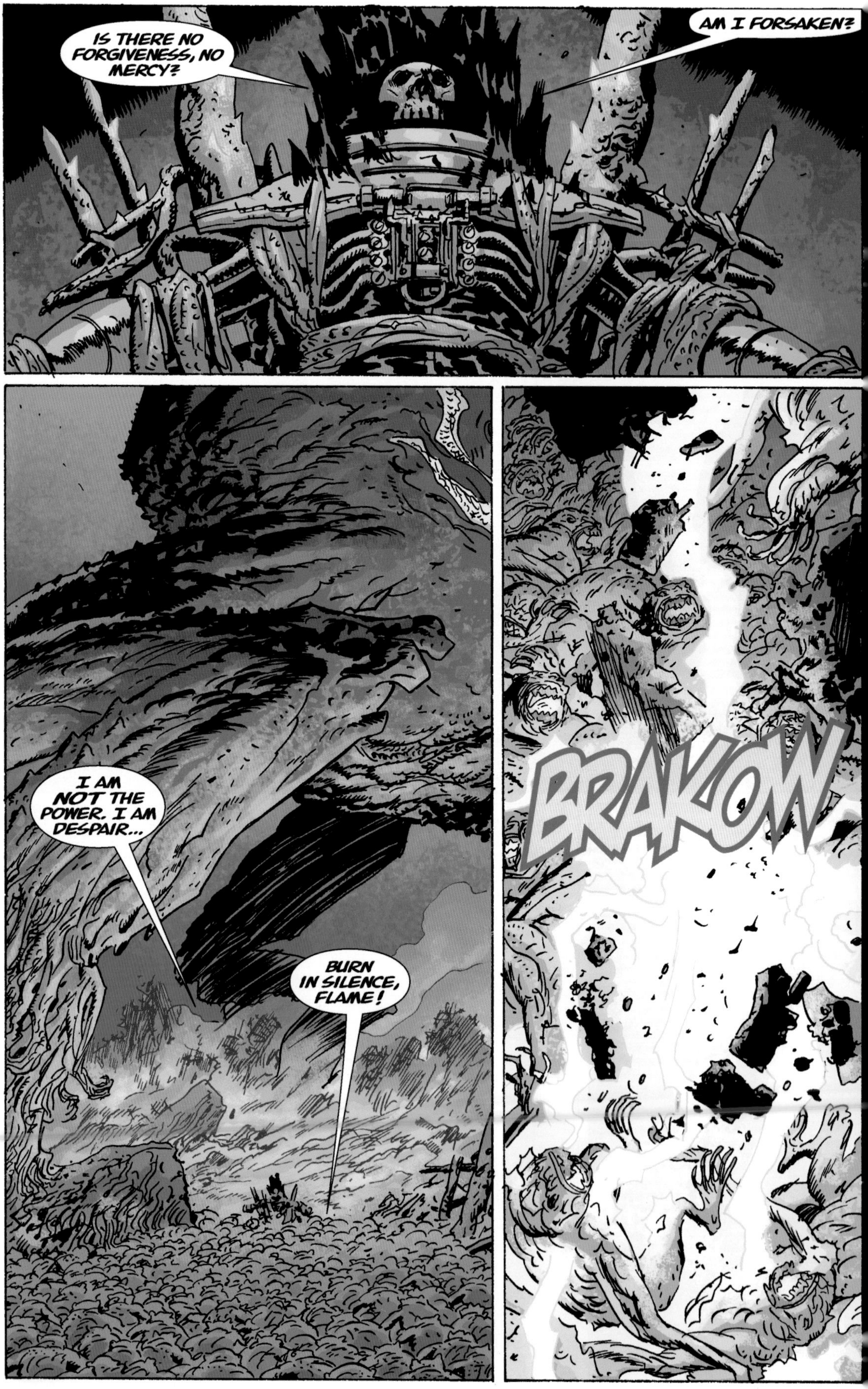
IS THERE NO FORGIVENESS, NO MERCY?
AM I FORSAKEN?
I AM NOT THE POWER. I AM DESPAIR...
BURN IN SILENCE, FLAME!
BRAKOW

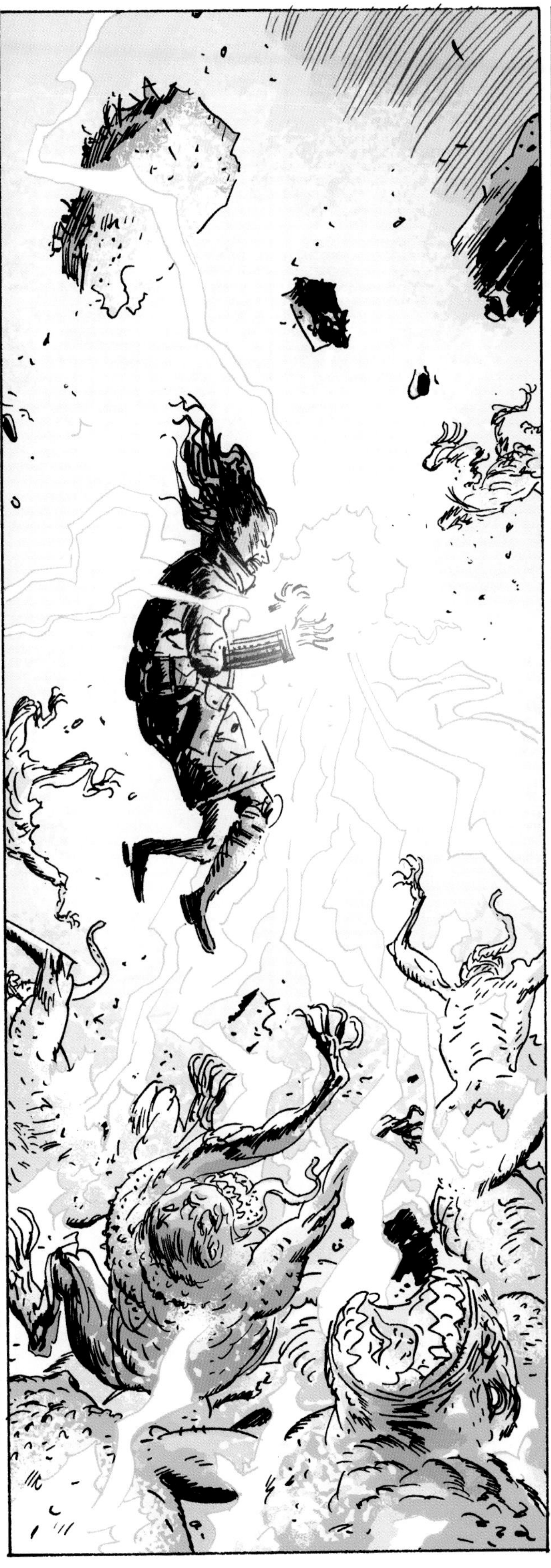

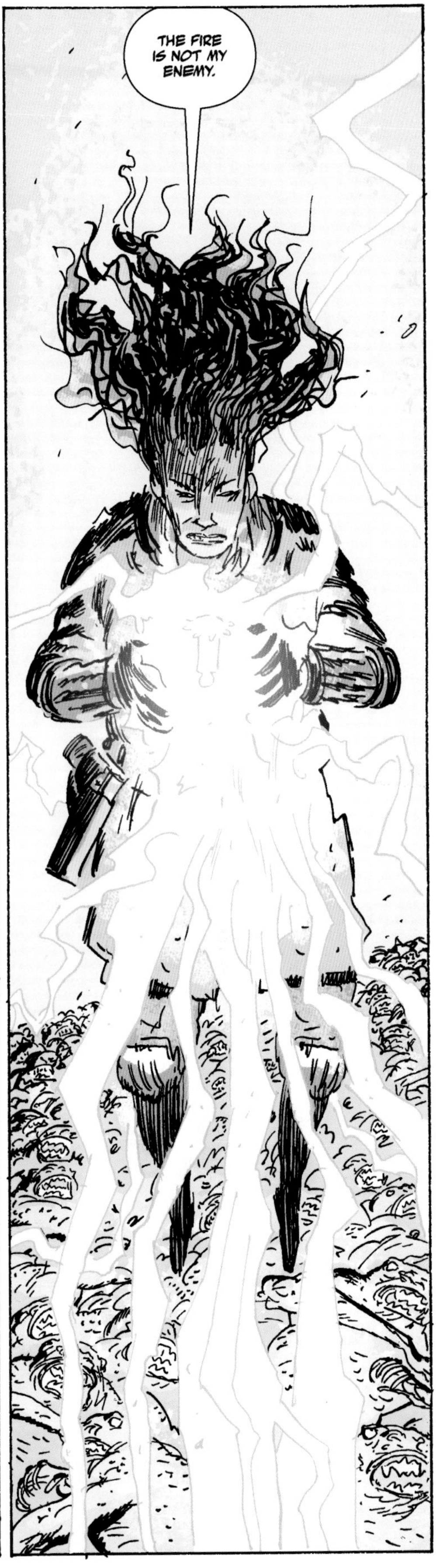
THE FIRE IS NOT MY ENEMY.

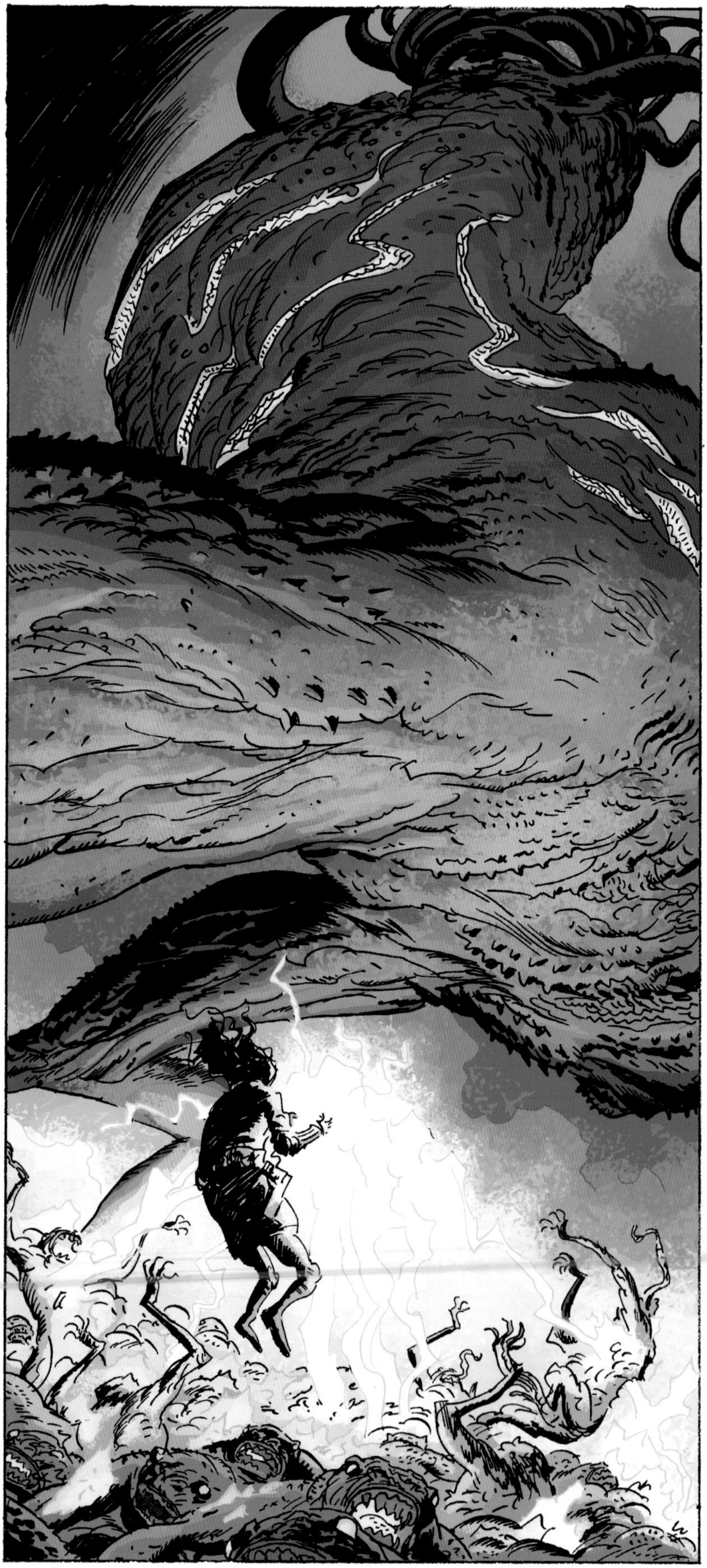

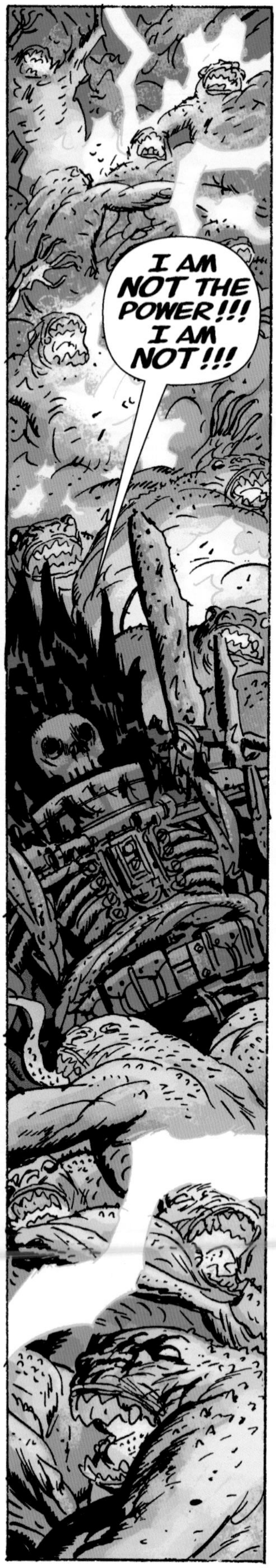
I AM NOT THE POWER!!! I AM NOT!!!

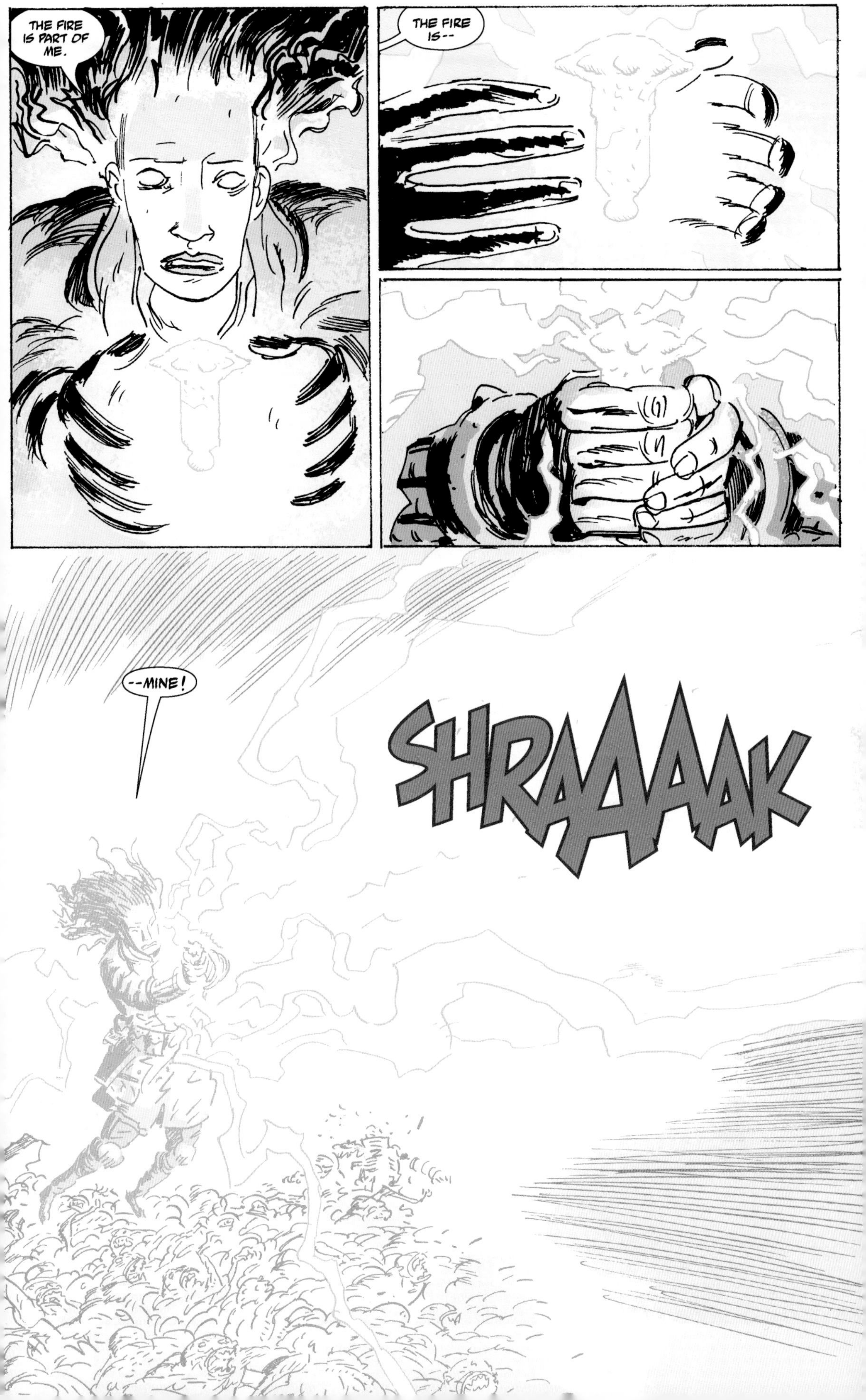
THE FIRE IS PART OF ME.
THE FIRE IS--
--MINE!
SHRAAAAK

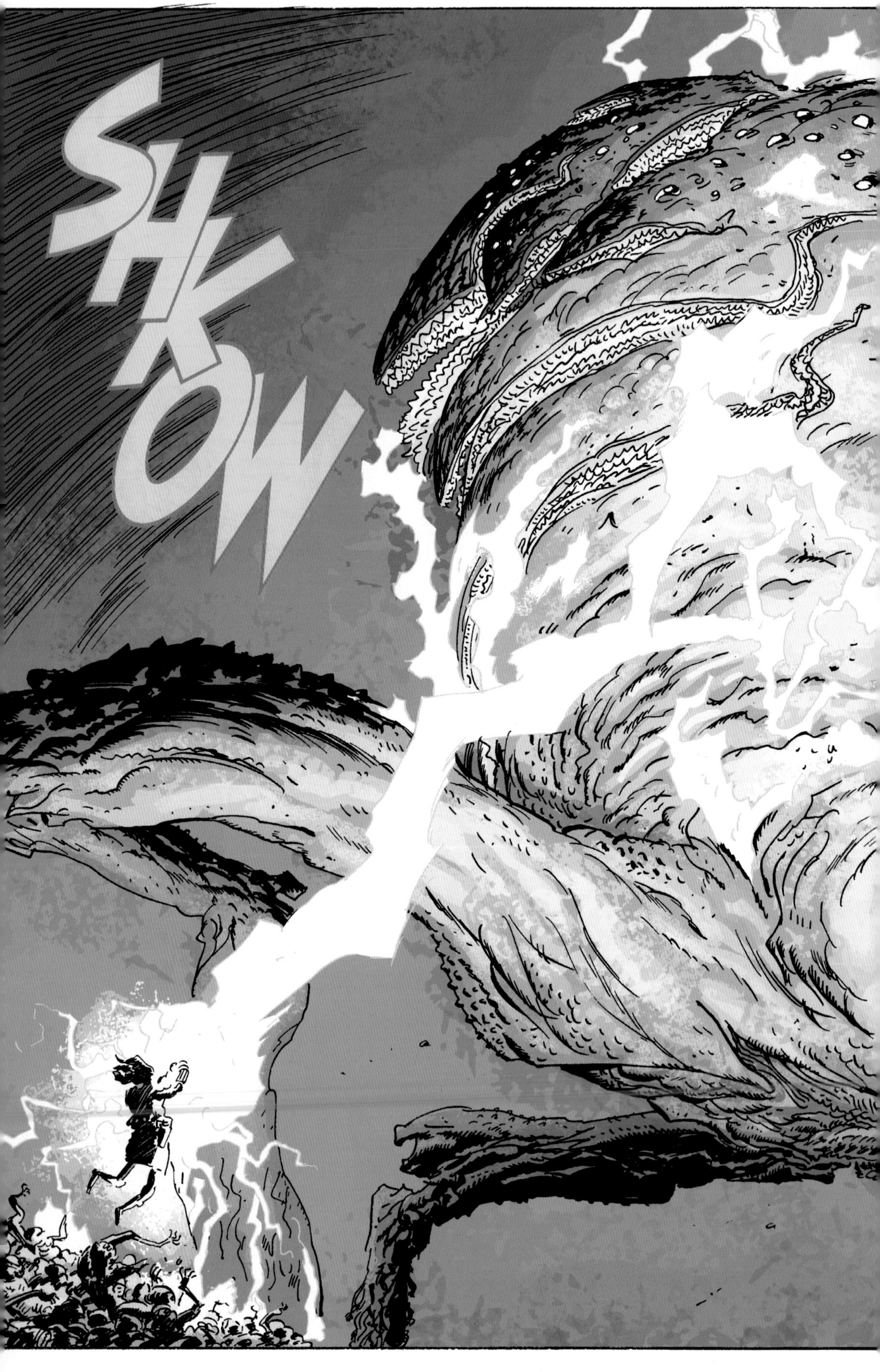
SHKOW

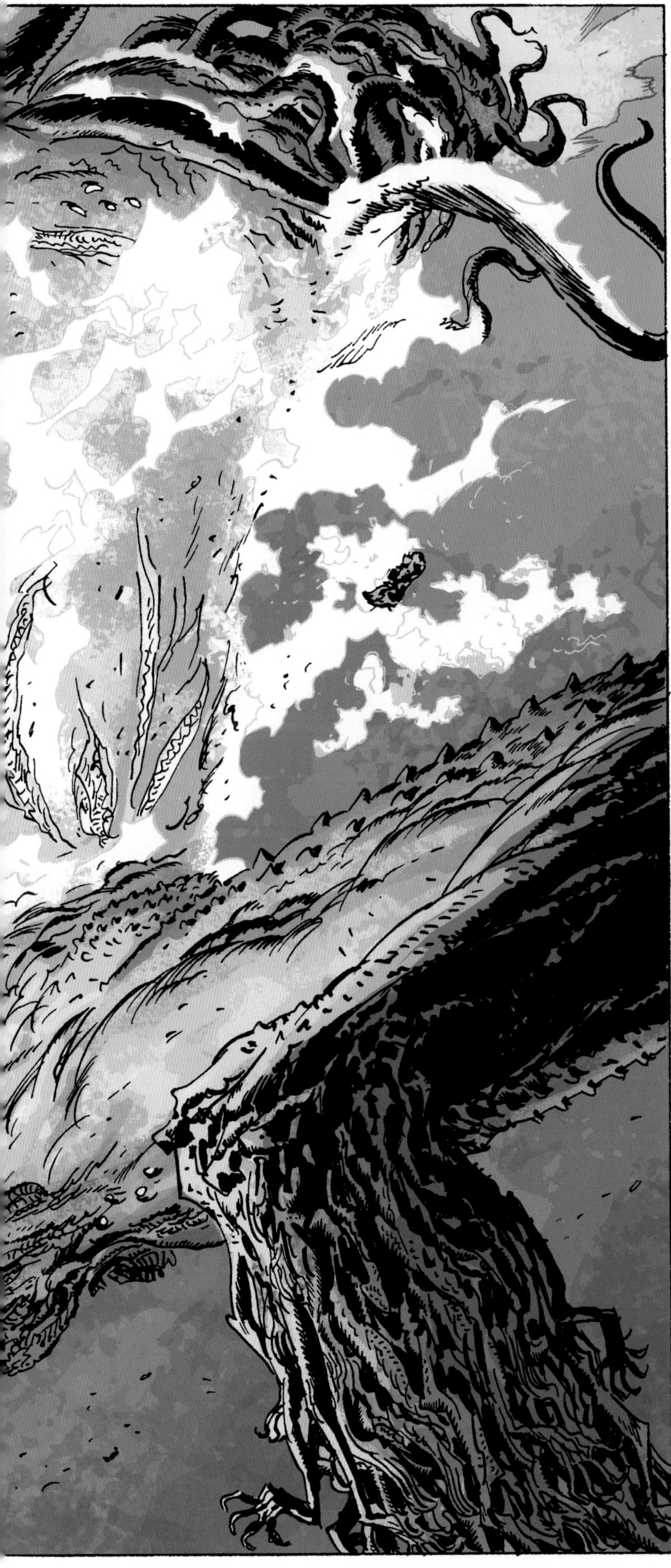

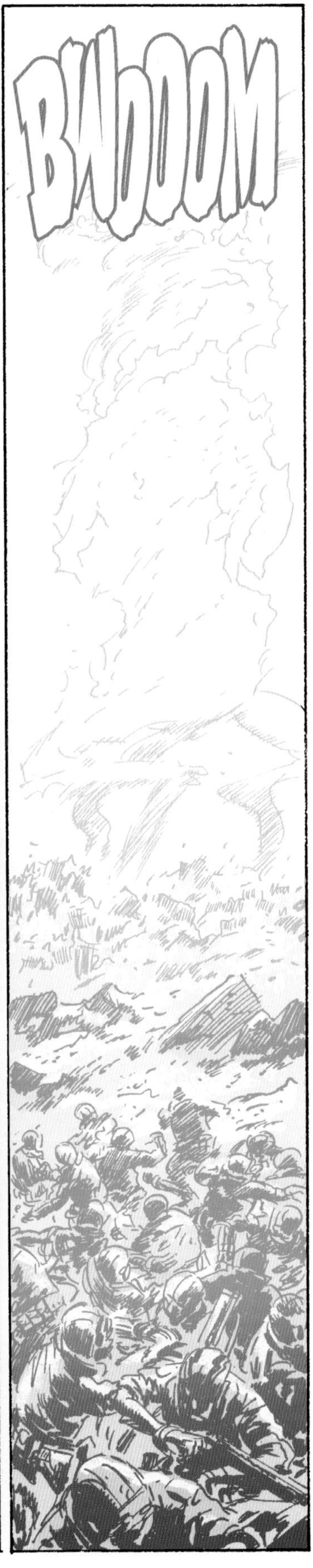
BWOOOM

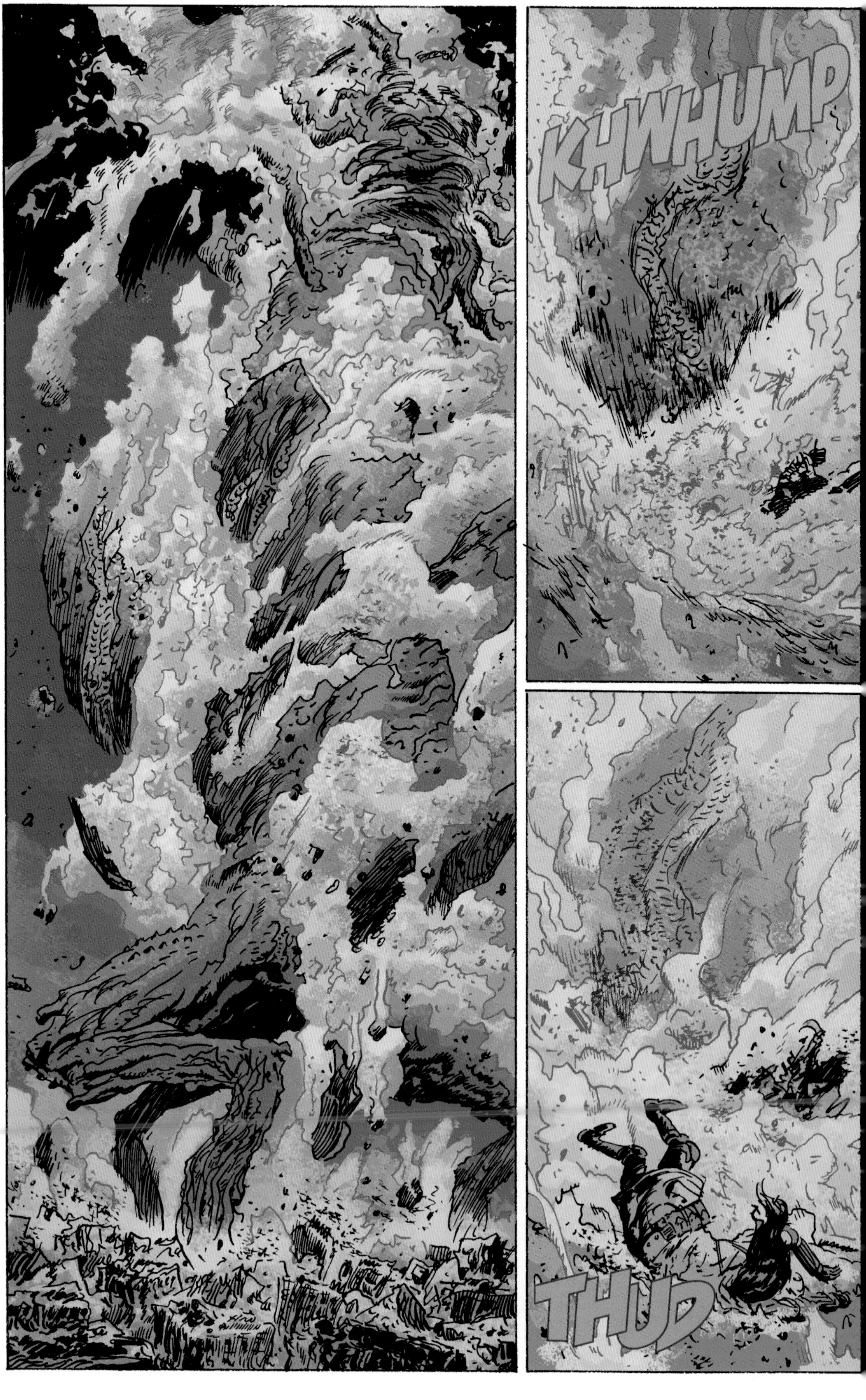
KHWHUMP
THUD

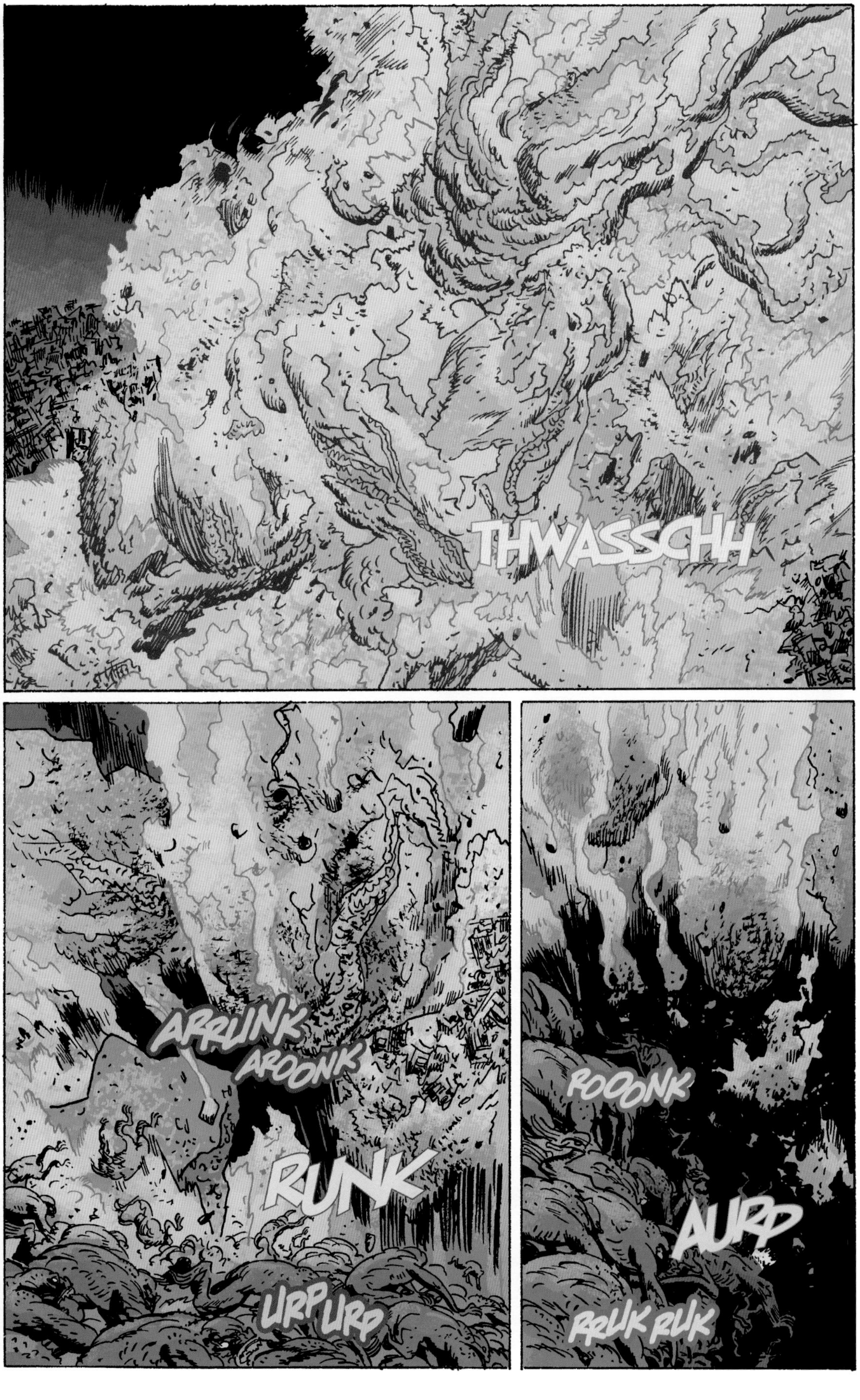
THWASSCHH
ARRUNK
AROONK
RUNK
URP URP
ROOONK
AURP
RRUK RUK

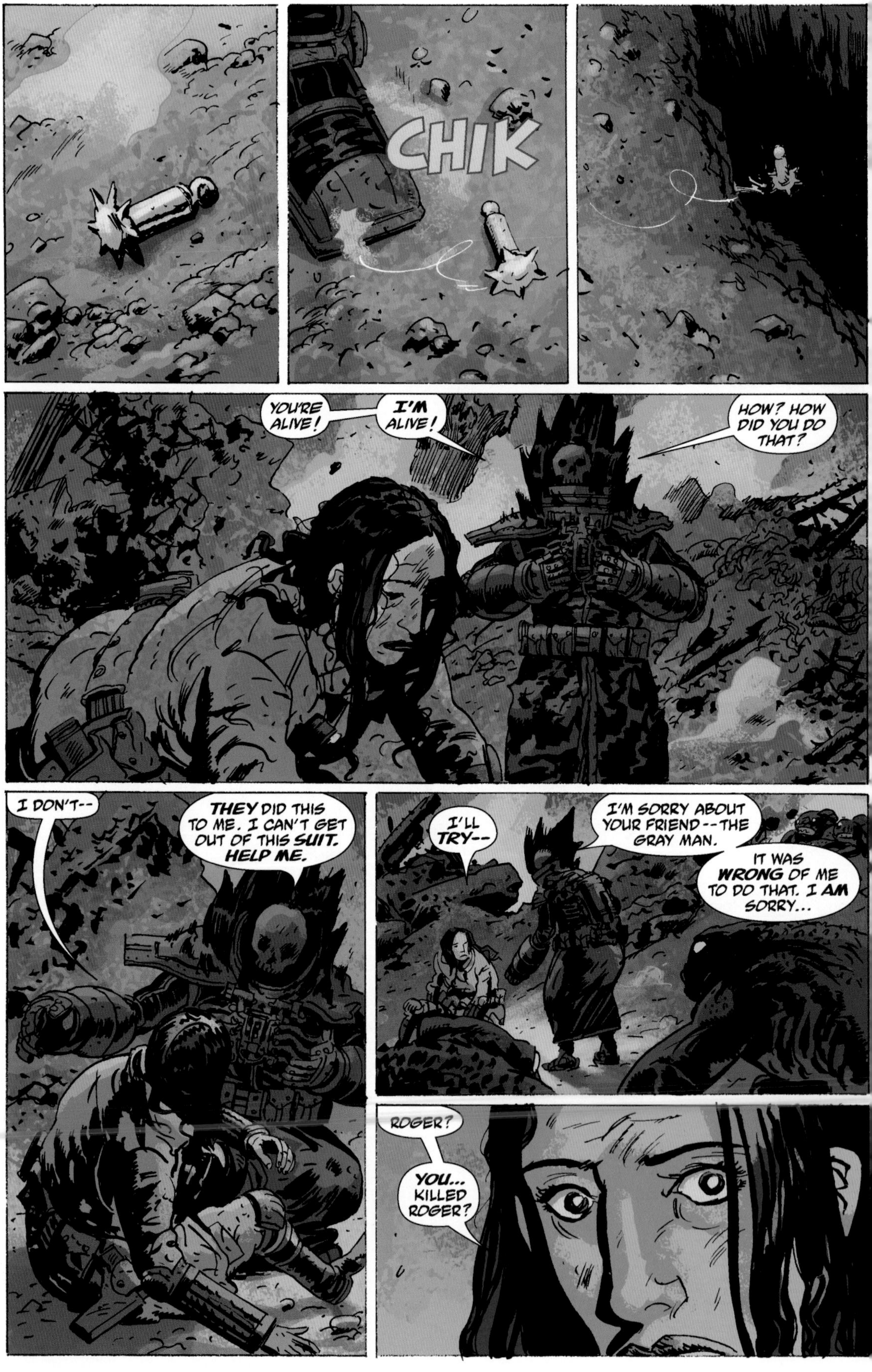
CHIK
YOU'RE ALIVE!
I'M ALIVE!
HOW? HOW DID YOU DO THAT?
I DON'T--
THEY DID THIS TO ME. I CAN'T GET OUT OF THIS SUIT. HELP ME.
I'LL TRY--
I'M SORRY ABOUT YOUR FRIEND--THE GRAY MAN.
IT WAS WRONG OF ME TO DO THAT. I AM SORRY...
ROGER?
YOU... KILLED ROGER?

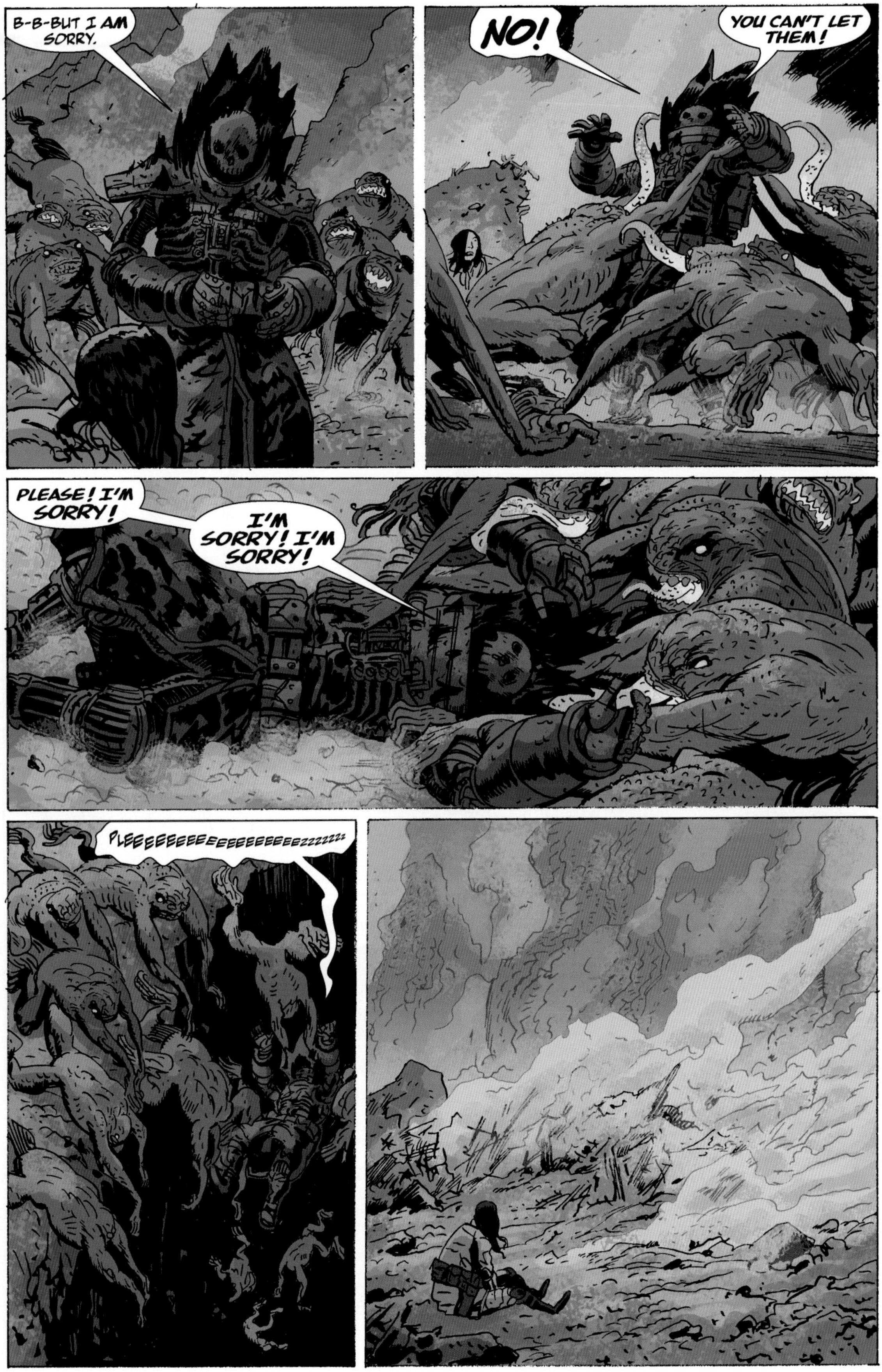
B-B-BUT I AM SORRY.
NO!
YOU CAN'T LET THEM!
PLEASE! I'M SORRY!
I'M SORRY! I'M SORRY!
PLEEEEEEEEEEEEEEEEEEZZZZZZZ

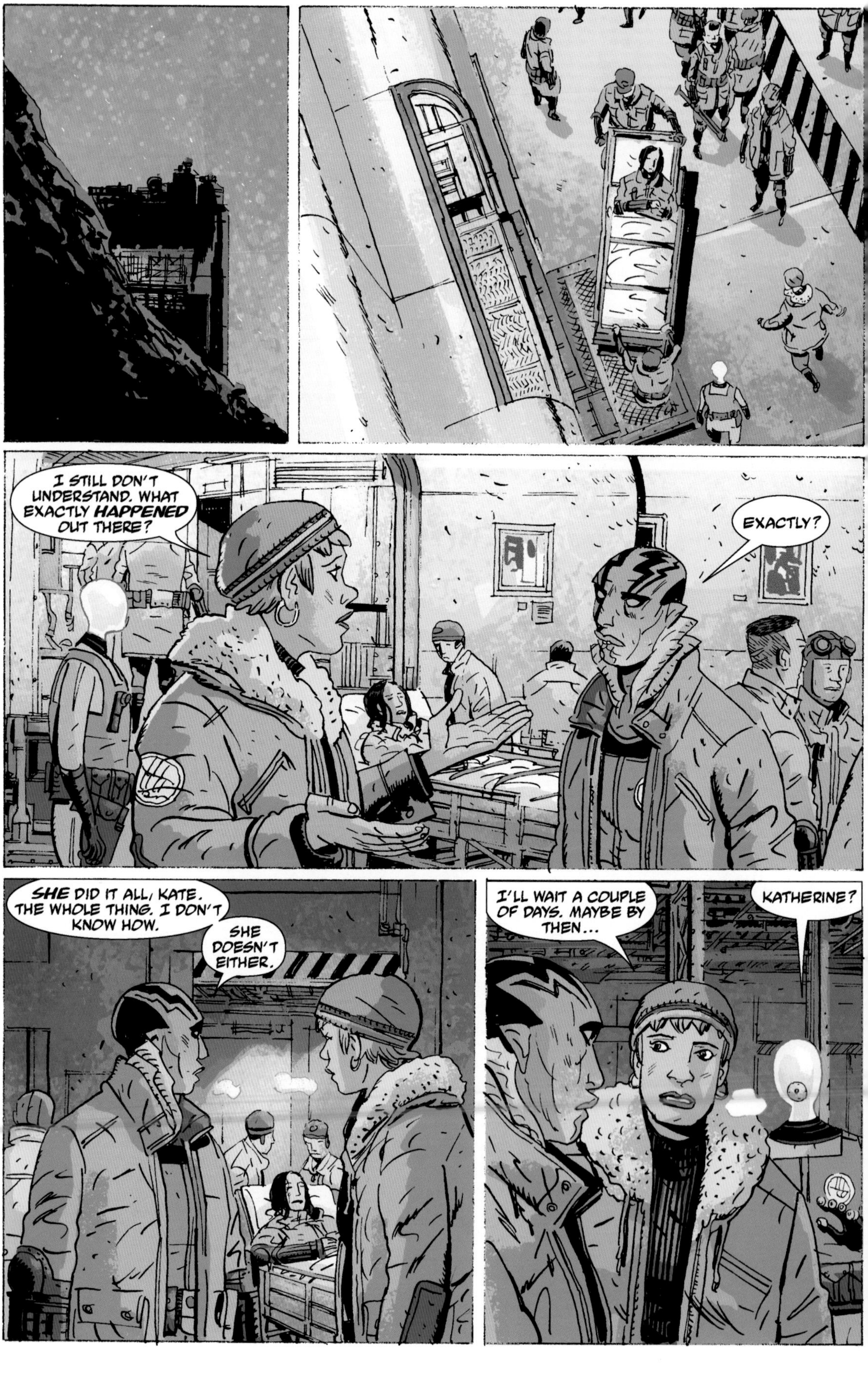
I STILL DON'T UNDERSTAND. WHAT EXACTLY HAPPENED OUT THERE?
EXACTLY?
SHE DID IT ALL, KATE. THE WHOLE THING. I DON'T KNOW HOW.
SHE DOESN'T EITHER.
I'LL WAIT A COUPLE OF DAYS. MAYBE BY THEN...
KATHERINE?

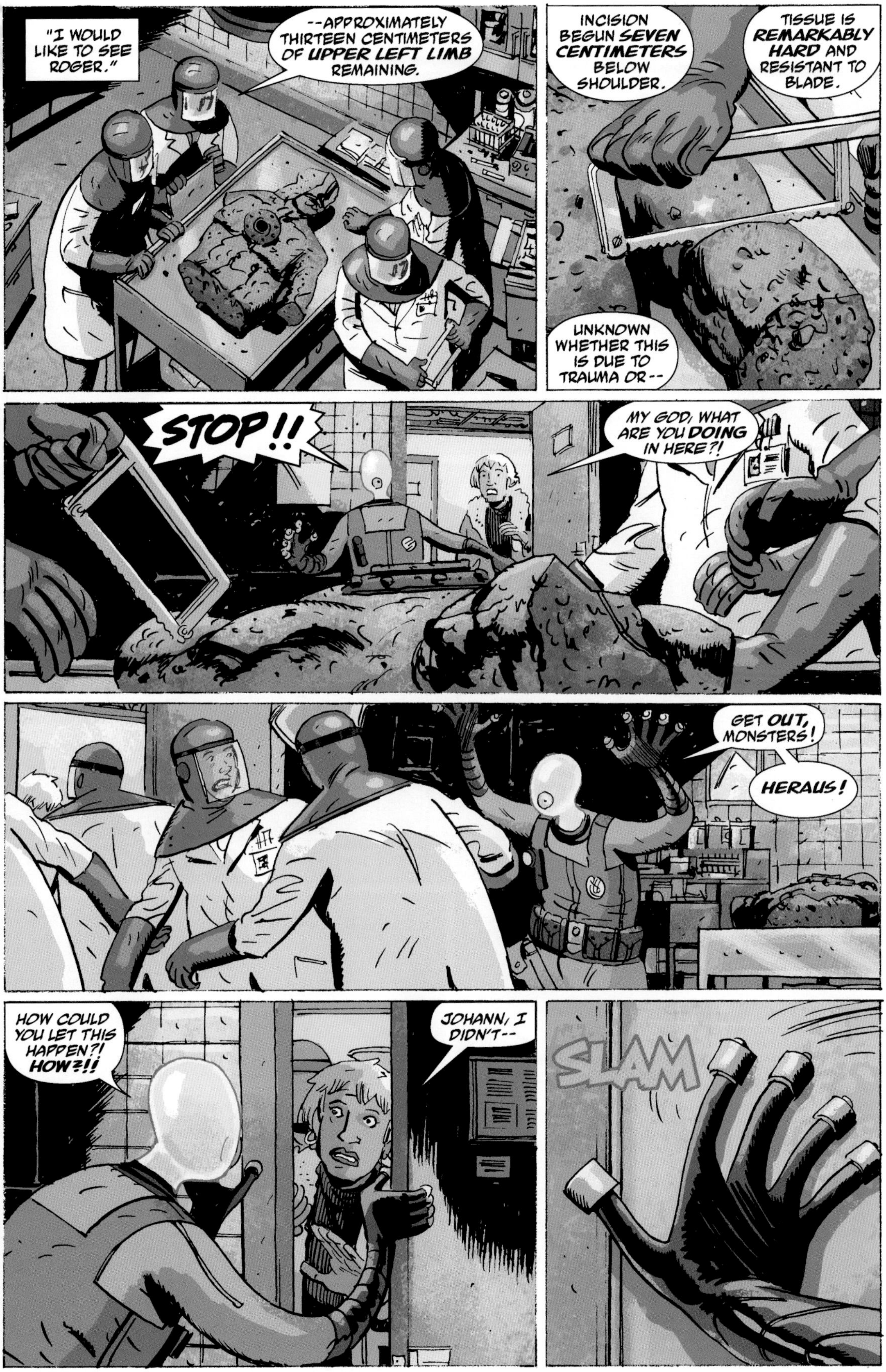
"I WOULD LIKE TO SEE ROGER."
--APPROXIMATELY THIRTEEN CENTIMETERS OF UPPER LEFT LIMB REMAINING.
INCISION BEGUN SEVEN CENTIMETERS BELOW SHOULDER.
TISSUE IS REMARKABLY HARD AND RESISTANT TO BLADE.
UNKNOWN WHETHER THIS IS DUE TO TRAUMA OR--
STOP!!
MY GOD, WHAT ARE YOU DOING IN HERE?!
GET OUT, MONSTERS!
HERAUS!
HOW COULD YOU LET THIS HAPPEN?! HOW?!!
JOHANN, I DIDN'T--
SLAM

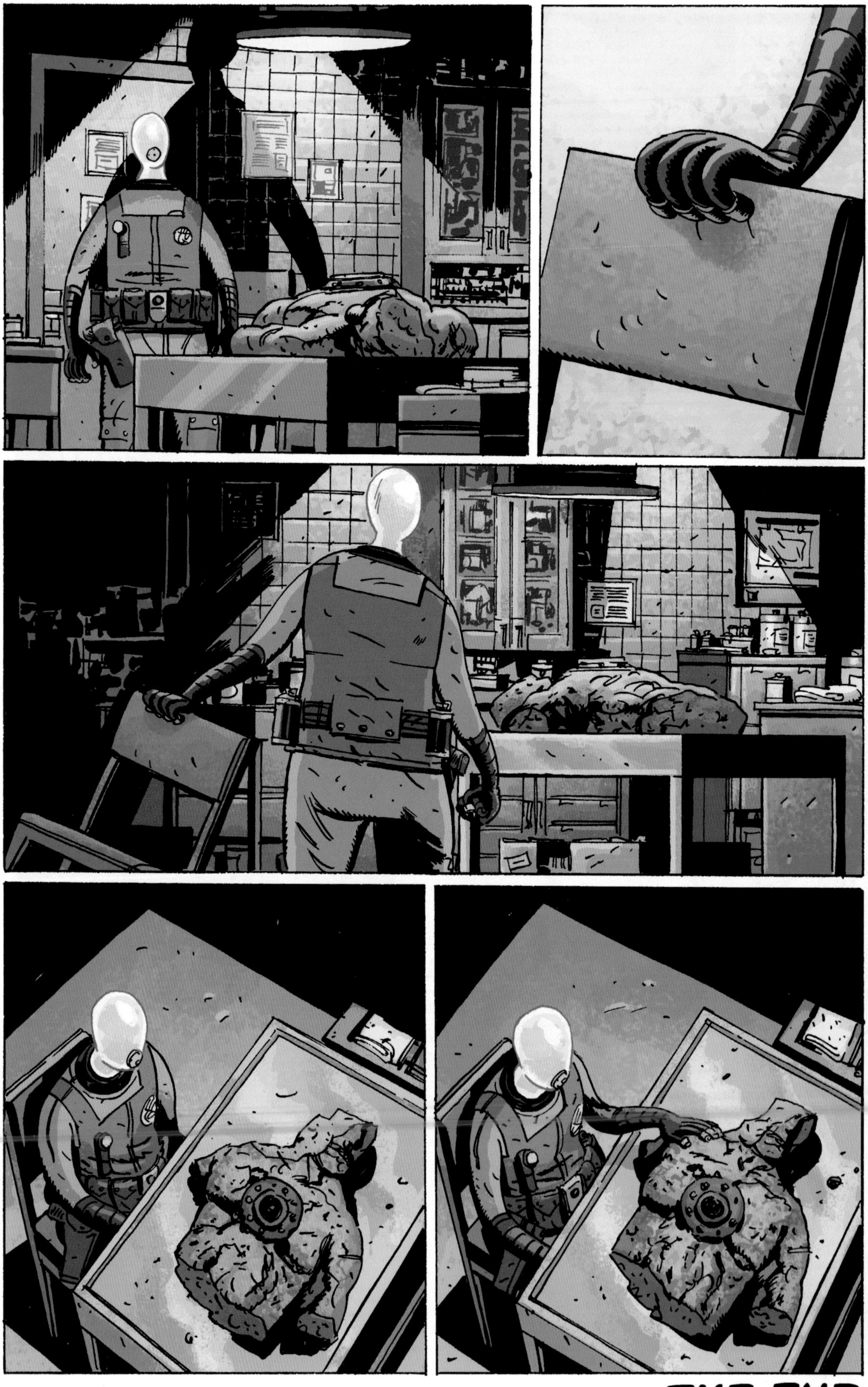

THE END

# Afterword

For me, making up stories is a little like build-ing furniture, but with twelfth-century tools and only the vaguest idea what I'm trying to build. There's a lot of grunting and banging, a lot of hammering on square pegs to get them to fit into round holes. It's fun and I love it, but, usually, it's a lot of work.

I don't remember *The Black Flame* being any work at all.

Shortly after John agreed to co-write *B.P.R.D.* he suggested we create some kind of old-school supervillain. I grew up reading Marvel Comics by Stan Lee and Jack Kirby, so I was all for it. In fact, when I saw Guy's design for the Black Flame (first created to appear briefly in *The Dead*) my first thought was, "That guy's the Red Skull of the Hellboy 'universe.'" Now, what if there was a guy who *wanted* to be the Red Skull, *made* himself into Doctor Doom, and then, slowly, turned into . . . something else? Add to that the escalating frog problem and Liz Sherman's mystery "friend," and there you go. John and I put the whole thing together over a single lunch—no grunting and very little banging. I know it won't always be that easy, but this time it was.

About working with John Arcudi . . .

If there was any kind of formula for how we work together I'd tell it. It's the kind of thing people ask about, but, at least so far, there's not. On *The Dead* it's pretty easy for me to say who did what, and it will be pretty easy

on the new one we're doing, *The Universal Machine*, but on this one the lines are pretty blurry. For example, it was my idea to have the Black Flame walk into that boardroom in his Black Flame suit, but I did it because it seemed to me like such a John Arcudi kind of scene. At the same time, there are several creature moments that feel to me like my stuff, but I knew nothing about them till I saw them on the page. That's good. I do have to say that most of the subtle character stuff is coming from John. The thing with the "Chinaman" and Daimio's "treatments" . . . I'm as much in the dark about that as you are. We will just have to trust him.

My thanks to everyone for everything, and sorry about Roger, but fighting monsters is rough business and sometimes the nicest people get hurt.

Until next time . . .

MIKE MIGNOLA

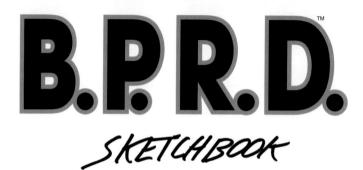

# B.P.R.D.™

## SKETCHBOOK

During work on the *B.P.R.D.: The Dead* storyline, Mike and John had already told me what was in store for the upcoming *Black Flame,* so designs were jumpstarted a little earlier for both the title character and Katha-Hem. The new Black Flame himself pretty much took final form from the beginning: below is the first sketch I did of him after talking to Mike about the idea of a "Dr. Doom"-styled villain in a blast-furnace suit and flaming skull mask. Opposite are a couple drawings of the original Black Flame for Pope's office scene, and more designs refining the details of the power suit, with Mike himself designing the chest plate when he drew the cover to *Black Flame* #3.

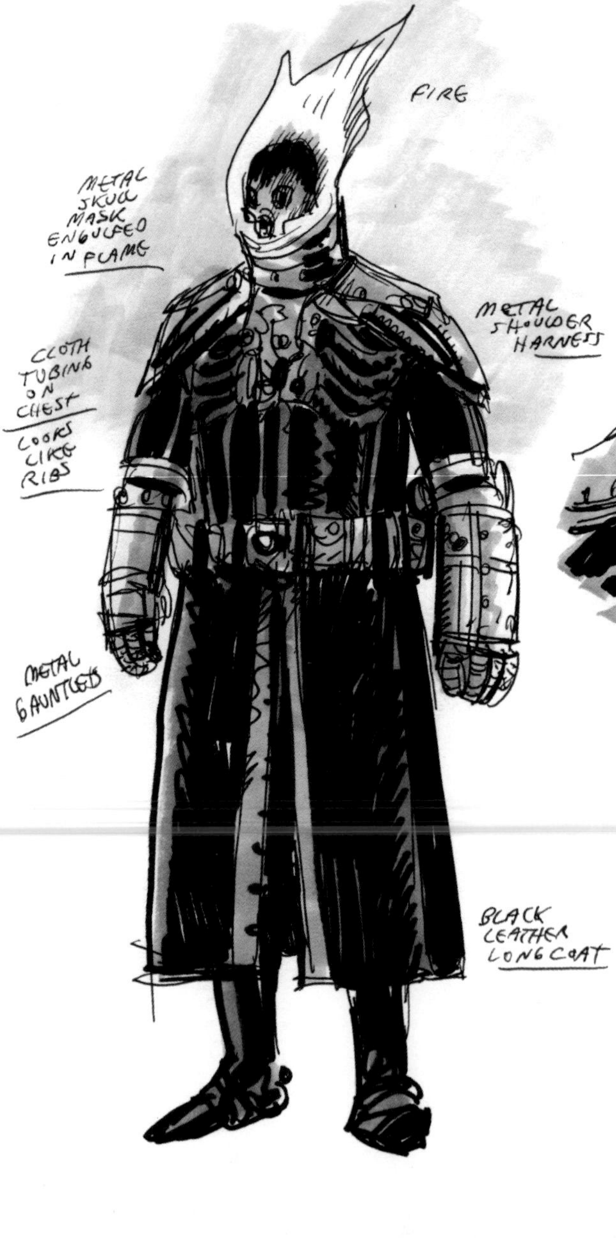
FIRE
METAL SKULL MASK ENGULFED IN FLAME
METAL SHOULDER HARNESS
CLOTH TUBING ON CHEST
LOOKS LIKE RIBS
METAL GAUNTLETS
BLACK LEATHER LONGCOAT

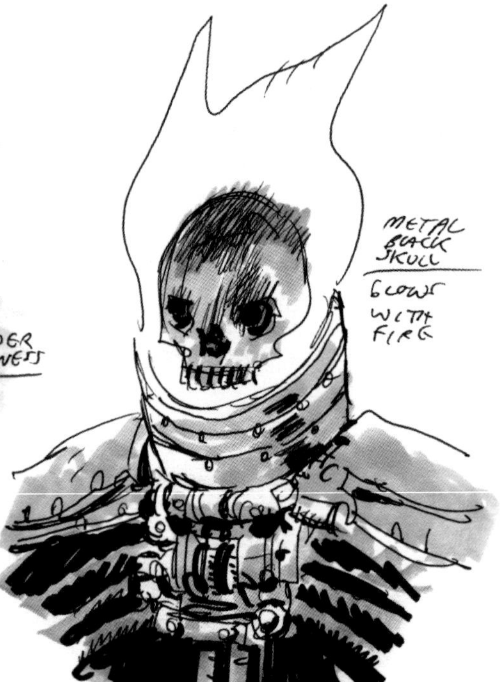
METAL BLACK SKULL
GLOWS WITH FIRE

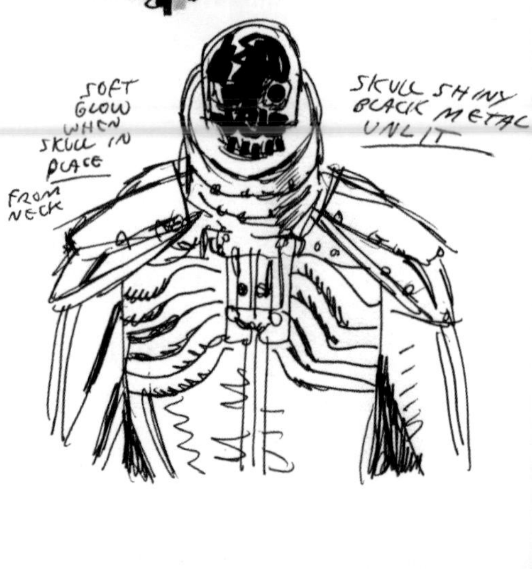
SOFT GLOW WHEN SKULL IN PLACE
FROM NECK
SKULL SHINY BLACK METAL UNLIT

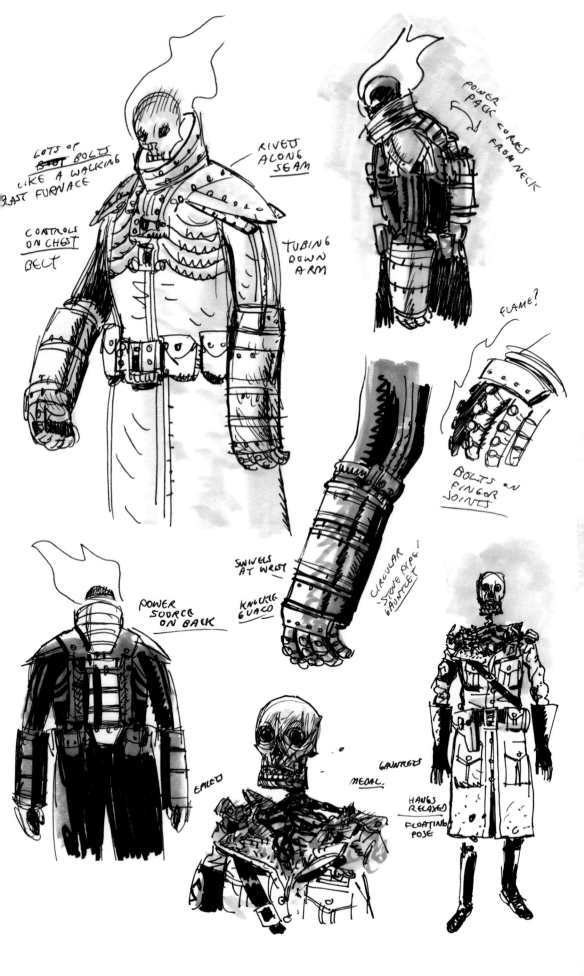

LOTS OF ~~BOLT~~ BOLTS
LIKE A WALKING
BLAST FURNACE

CONTROLS
ON CHEST
BELT

RIVET ALONG SEAM

TUBING DOWN ARM

POWER PACK COMES FROM NECK

FLAME?

BOLTS ON FINGER JOINTS

SWIVELS AT WRIST

KNUCKLE GUARD

CIRCULAR "STOVE PIPE" GAUNTLET

POWER SOURCE ON BACK

EPILETS

MEDAL

GAUNTLET

HANGS RELAXED

FLOATING POSE

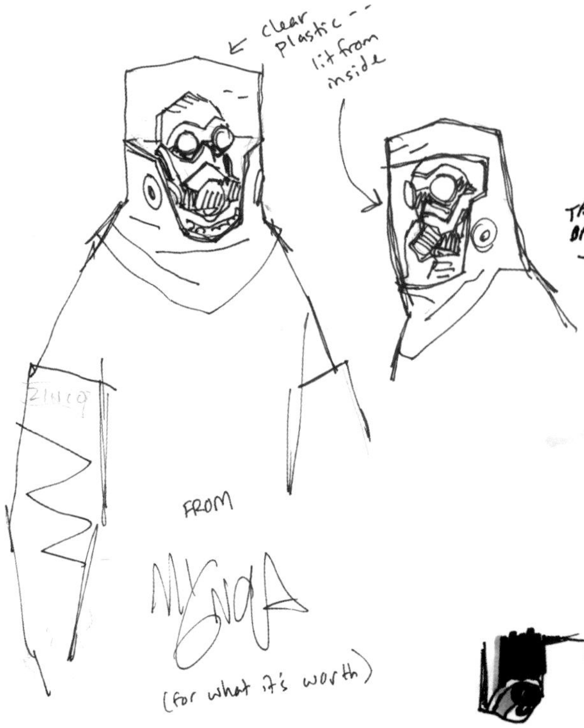
clear plastic -- lit from inside
ZINCO
FROM
(for what it's worth)

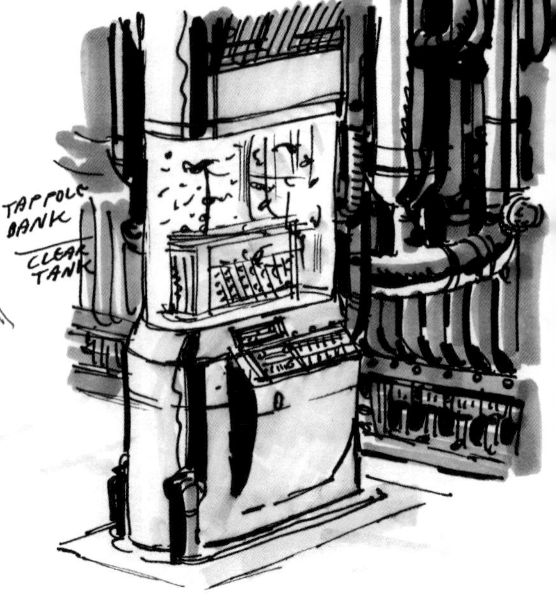
TADPOLE BANK
CLEAR TANK

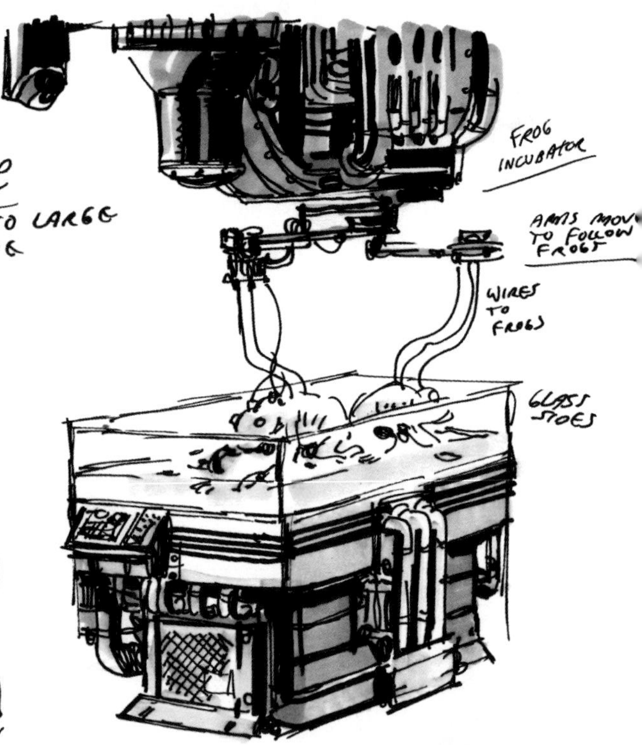
FROG INCUBATOR
ARMS MOV
TO FOLLOW FROGS
WIRES TO FROGS
GLASS SIDES

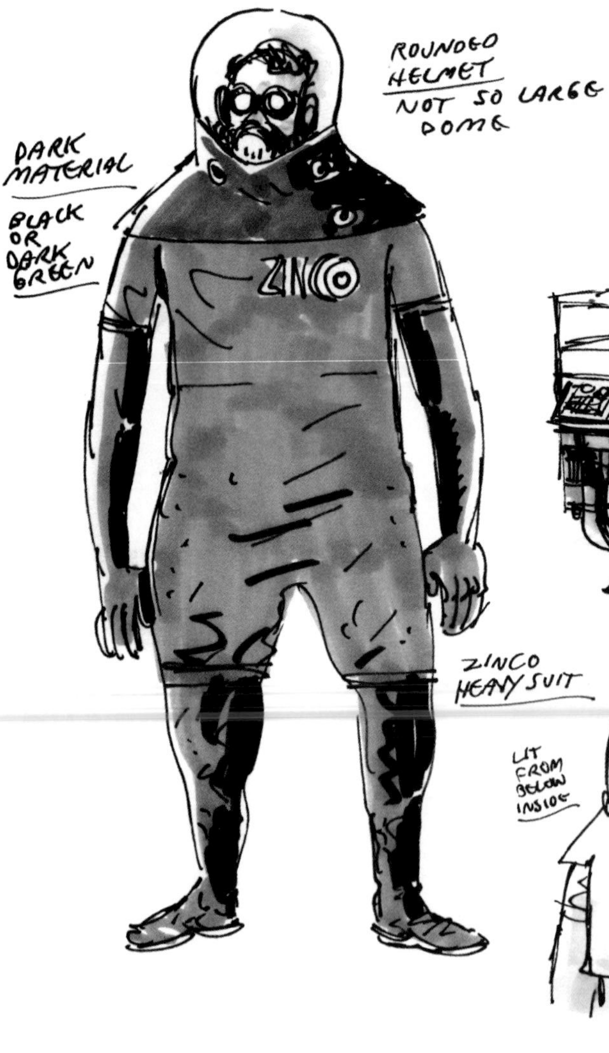
ROUNDED HELMET
NOT SO LARGE DOME
DARK MATERIAL
BLACK OR DARK GREEN
ZINCO

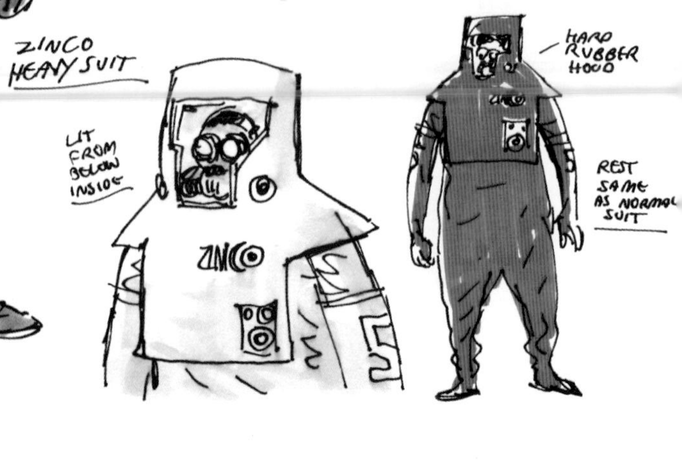
ZINCO HEAVY SUIT
LIT FROM BELOW INSIDE
ZINCO
HARD RUBBER HOOD
REST SAME AS NORMAL SUIT

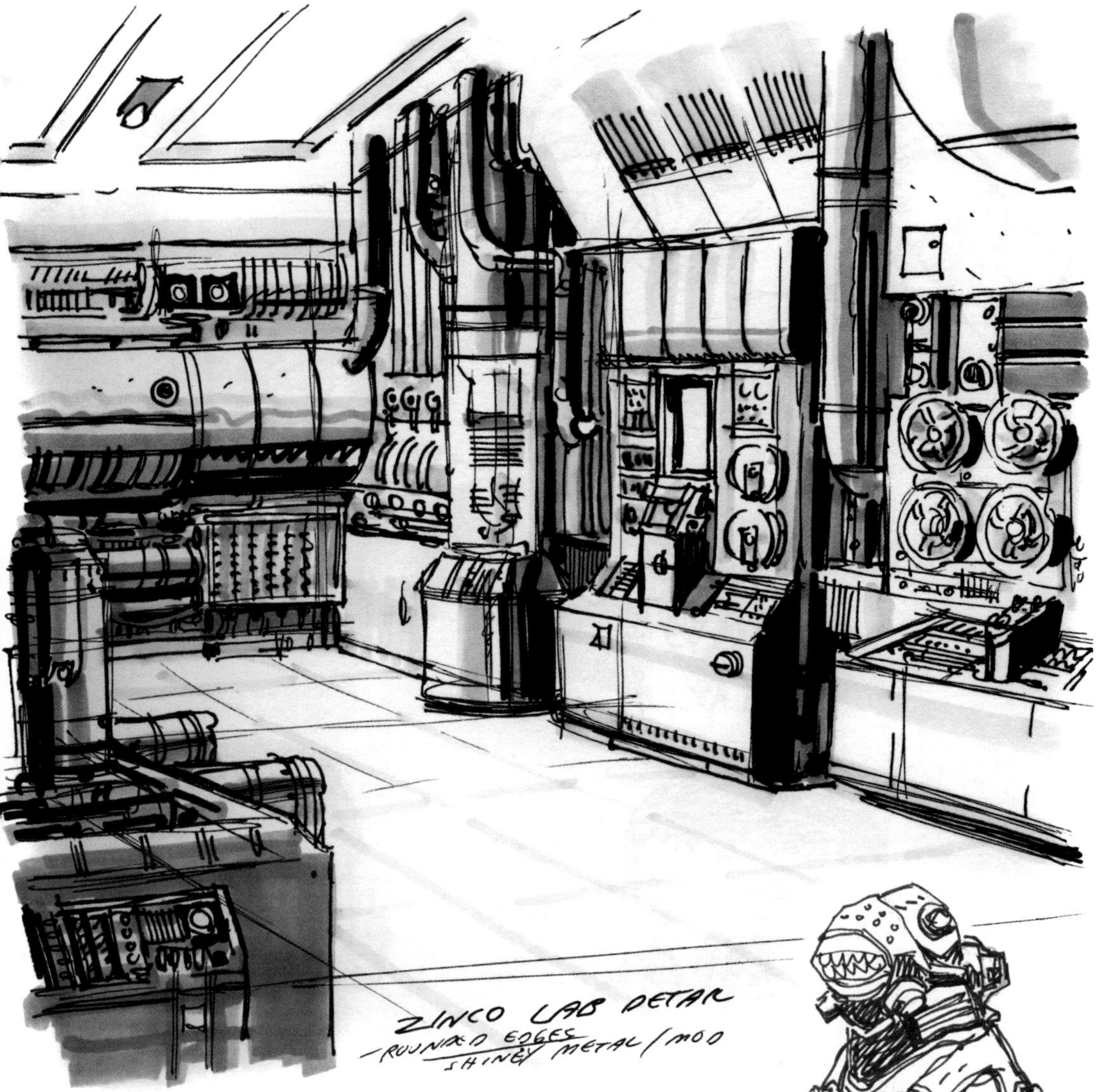
ZINCO LAB DETAIL
-ROUNDED EDGES
SHINEY METAL / MOD

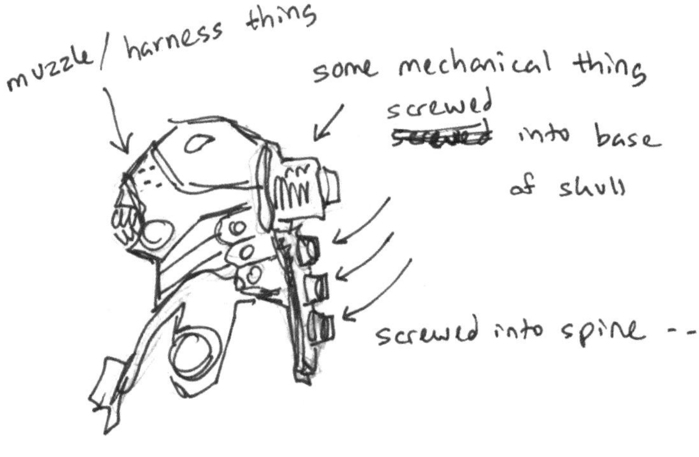
muzzle / harness thing
some mechanical thing
screwed into base
of skull
screwed into spine --

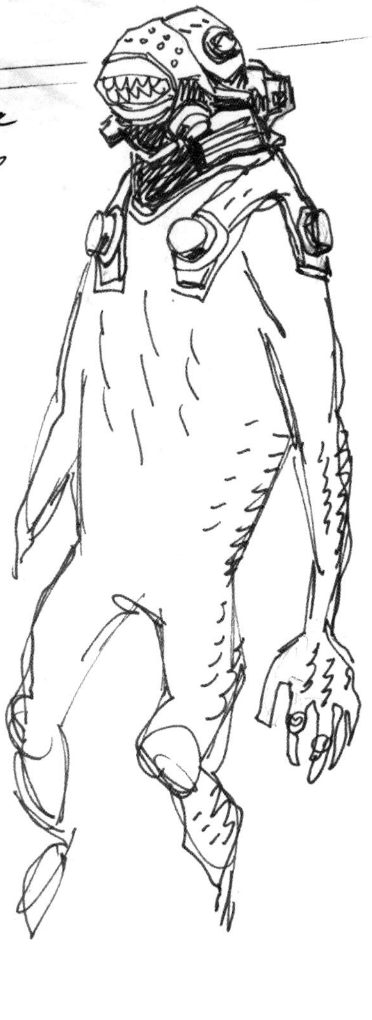

Mike wanted the Zinco lab to be an homage to Jack Kirby, all shiny metal and mod design to set it off from the B.P.R.D. utilitarian look. On this page is an early design done to get the feel of the lab, along with Mike's designs for the frog harness. Opposite top are his Zinco lab suit notes along with my take on his designs and some details for various lab equipment.

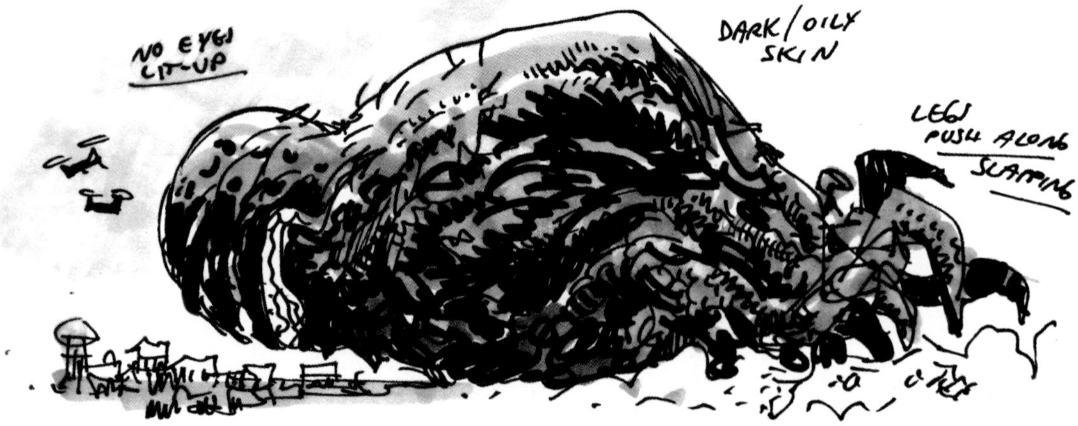
NO EYES LIT-UP
DARK / OILY SKIN
LEGS PUSH ALONG SLAPPING

Above is one of the final sketches to the larvae state of Katha-Hem that was inspired by *Moby Dick* — below is the first take on his adult form that I did during work on *The Dead*. The basic shape would remain the same but the details would change to fit him into the Hellboy universe.

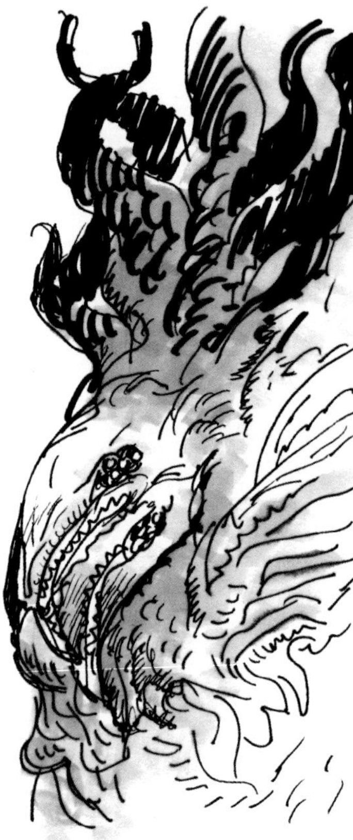

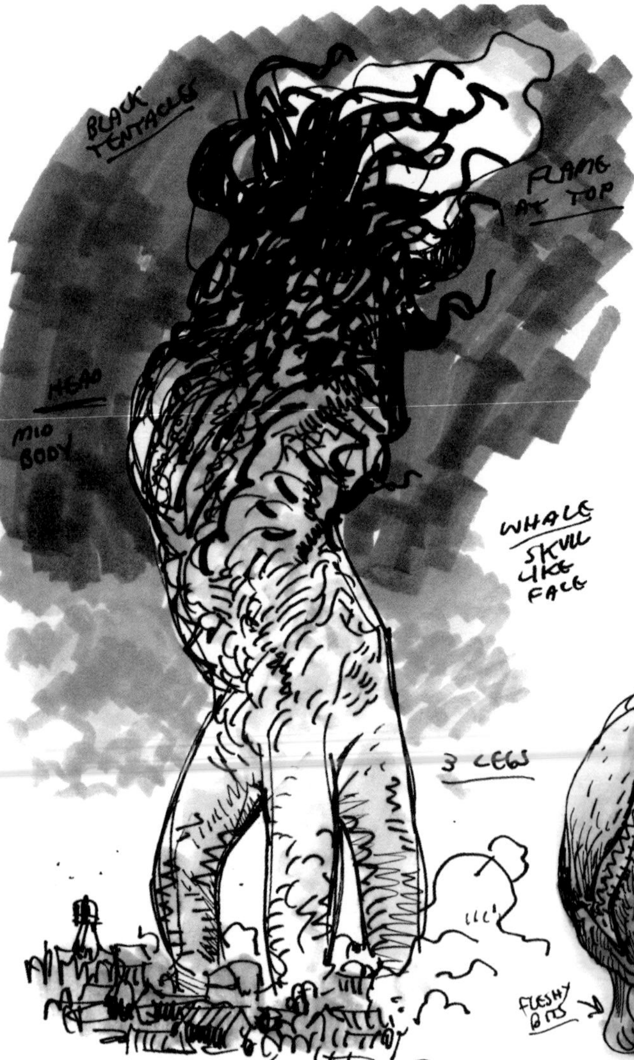
BLACK TENTACLES
FLAME AT TOP
HEAD
MID BODY
WHALE SKULL LIKE FACE
3 LEGS

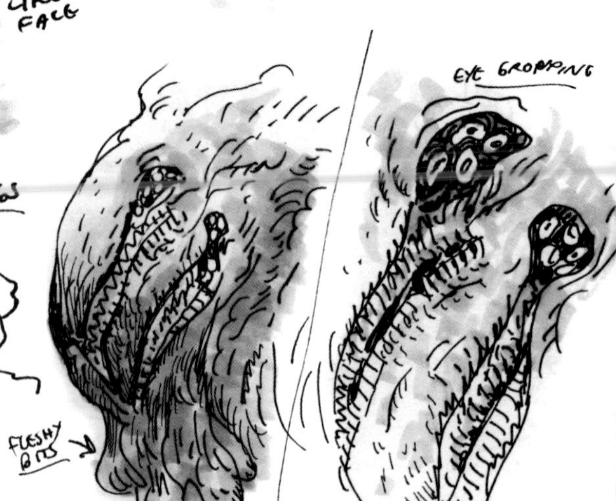
EYE GROUPING
FLESHY BITS

The final take on Katha-Hem was to be more insect-like to tie him into the Ogdru-Hem shown in *Hellboy: The Island*. The whale-like mouth remained from the original design, but the elephant tree-like legs became the insect-like limbs made out of twisted root-like arms.

—Guy Davis
Crab Point, Michigan

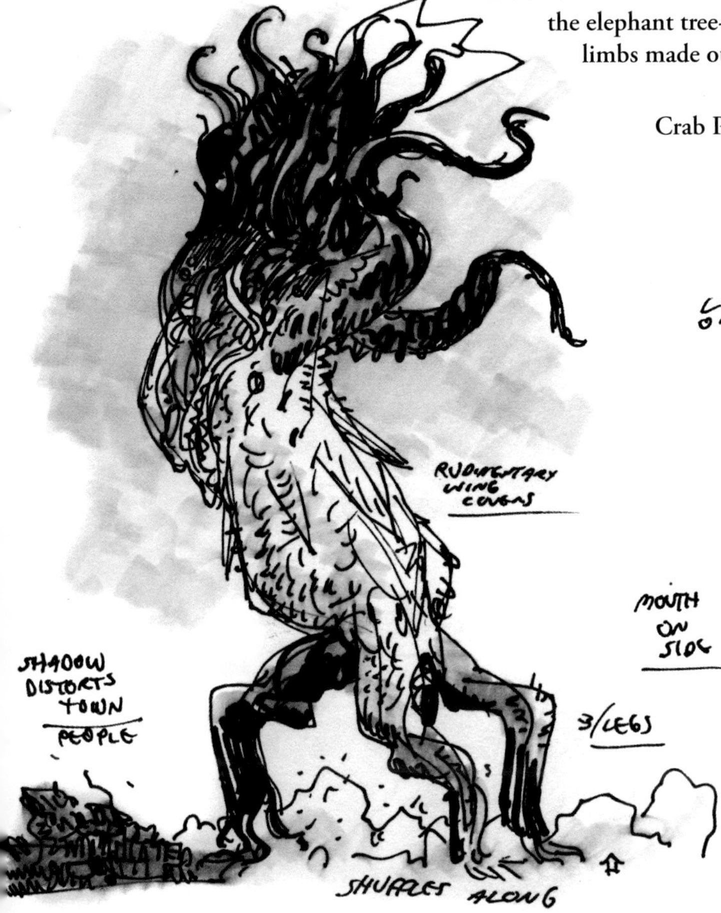
RUDIMENTARY WING COVERS
SHADOW DISTORTS TOWN PEOPLE
3/LEGS
SHUFFLES ALONG

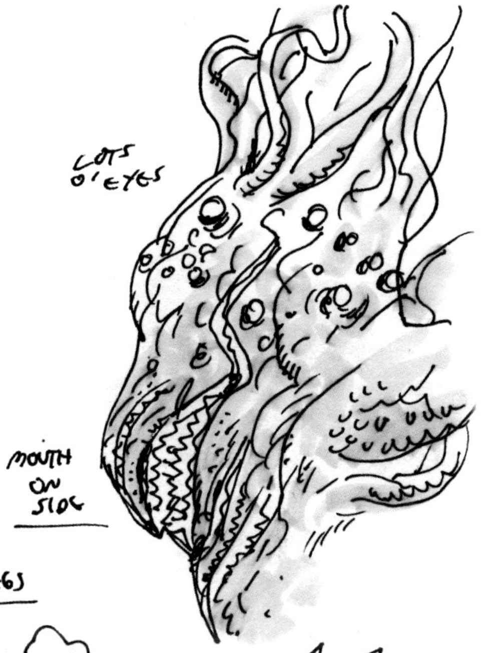
LOTS O'EYES
MOUTH ON SIDE

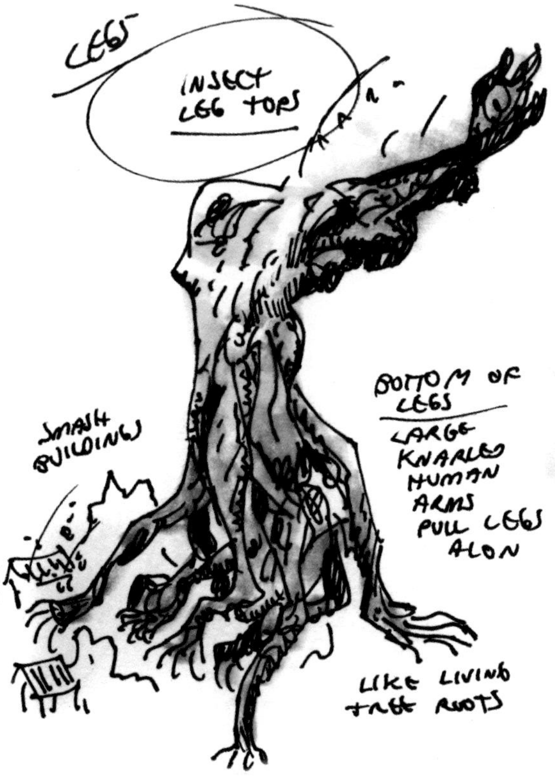
LEGS
INSECT LEG TOPS
BOTTOM OF LEGS
LARGE KNARLED HUMAN ARMS PULL LEGS ALON
SMASH BUILDINGS
LIKE LIVING TREE ROOTS

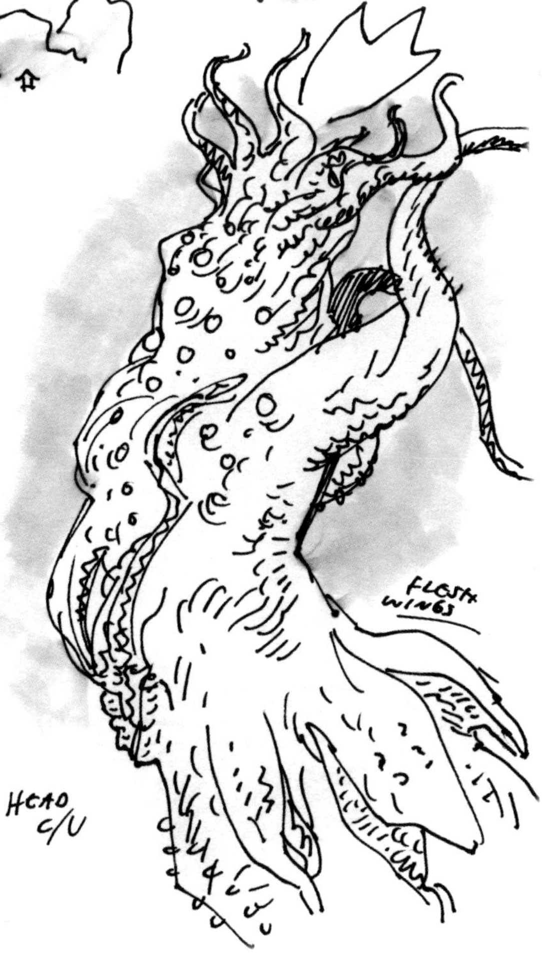
FLESH WINGS
HEAD C/U

# HELLBOY™

## *by* MIKE MIGNOLA

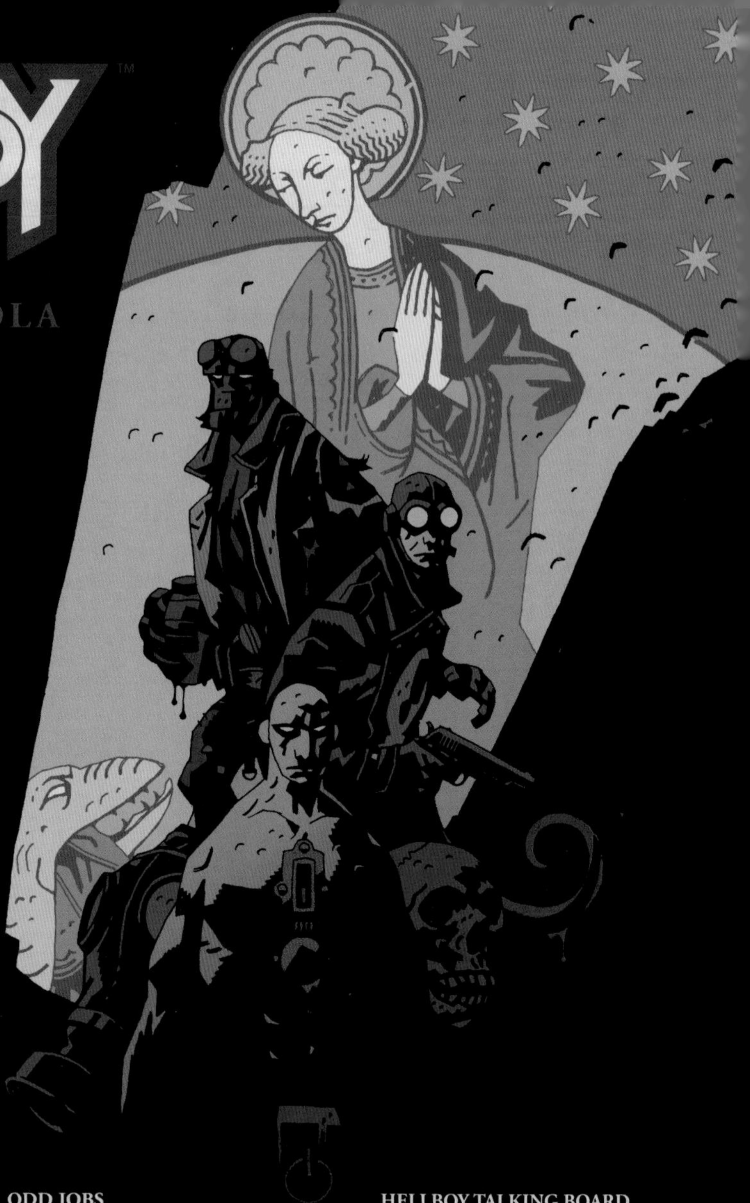

**SEED OF DESTRUCTION**
with John Byrne
ISBN: 1-59307-094-2 $17.95

**WAKE THE DEVIL**
ISBN: 1-59307-095-0 $17.95

**THE CHAINED COFFIN AND OTHERS**
ISBN: 1-59307-091-8 $17.95

**THE RIGHT HAND OF DOOM**
ISBN: 1-59307-093-4 $17.95

**CONQUEROR WORM**
ISBN: 1-59307-092-6 $17.95

**STRANGE PLACES**
ISBN: 1-59307-475-1 $17.95

**THE ART OF HELLBOY**
Softcover
ISBN: 1-59307-089-6 $29.95

**HELLBOY WEIRD TALES**
Volume 1
By John Cassaday, Jason Pearson, Eric Powell, Alex Maleev, Bob Fingerman and others
ISBN: 1-56971-622-6 $17.95
Volume 2
By Cassaday, P. Craig Russell, Jim Starlin, Evan Dorkin and others
ISBN: 1-56971-935-5 $17.95

**B.P.R.D.: HOLLOW EARTH**
By Mignola, Chris Golden, Ryan Sook and others
ISBN: 1-56971-862-8 $17.95

**B.P.R.D.: THE SOUL OF VENICE**
By Mignola, Mike Oeming, Guy Davis, Scott Kolins, Geoff Johns and others
ISBN: 1-59307-132-9 $17.95

**B.P.R.D.: PLAGUE OF FROGS**
By Mignola and Guy Davis
ISBN: 1-59307-288-0 $17.95

**B.P.R.D.: THE DEAD**
By Mignola, John Arcudi and Guy Davis
ISBN: 1-59307-380-1 $17.95

**B.P.R.D.: THE BLACK FLAME**
By Mignola, Arcudi and Davis
ISBN: 1-59307-550-2 $17.95

**ODD JOBS**
Short stories by Mignola, Poppy Z. Brite, Chris Golden and others
Illustrations by Mignola
ISBN: 1-56971-440-1 $14.95

**ODDER JOBS**
Short stories by Frank Darabont, Guillermo del Toro and others
Illustrations by Mignola
ISBN: 1-59307-226-0 $14.95

**HELLBOY BASEBALL CAP**
#17-106 $14.95

**HELLBOY LUNCH BOX (& POSTCARD) 2**
Tin de-bossed full color
#11-836 $14.99

**HELLBOY JOURNAL**
#12-309 $9.99

**HELLBOY ZIPPO LIGHTER**
#17-101 $29.95

**HELLBOY TALKING BOARD**
#10-248 $24.99

**HELLBOY DELUXE TALKING BOARD**
#10-380 $99.99

**HELLBOY COASTER SET**
#13-252 $9.99

TO VIEW HELLBOY BOOKS AND MERCHANDISE VISIT
www.darkhorse.com

To find a comics shop in your area, call 1-888-266-4226
For more information or to order direct:
• On the web: www.darkhorse.com
• E-mail: mailorder@darkhorse.com
• Phone: 1-800-862-0052 or (503) 652-9701
Mon.-Fri. 9 A.M. to 5 P.M. Pacific Time



DARK HORSE COMICS™ darkhorse.com *drawing on your nightmares*

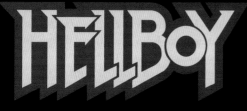